Praise for *Showdown at Rickwood*

"Take your time reading *Showdown at Rickwood*. Skipping a page, or a paragraph, is not an option. It would be like going to the concession stand with the bases loaded in the bottom of the ninth of a tie game— you might miss a crucial moment. And it's that way from Prologue to Epilogue. This book is so entertaining that it reads like a novel that's so good you're sort of sad when you finish."
　　—Wayne Martin, Former Sportswriter, *Birmingham News*

"This is a story you wish would never end. Thank you to the author for making a reader feel like he is on the field and in the stands. Somewhere Pop Boy is smiling and saying, 'Finally someone has recognized what I did.'"
　　—Chuck Stewart, Author and Rickwood Field Historian

"This is a story about a city, a nation, and the lives of individuals whose paths crossed at Rickwood Field. The author masterfully intertwines world events into the history of Rickwood. I applaud the vivid descriptions of the men who journeyed through Birmingham and beyond. It is more than a history to me because it allowed me to peer into the lives of people who made Rickwood Field the legend it is today."
　　—Kelley Gulledge, Professional Baseball Player, 2000-2011

"The account of the Dixie Series game made the pages whirl. What a great moment—a 43-year-old grandfather!"
　　—Jim Palmer, Teacher, Altamont School

"Any baseball fan will agree, this book is fabulous."
　　—Paul Seitz, Pitcher, Birmingham A's, 1960s

"Birmingham baseball is defined by Rickwood Field and the 1931 Dixie Series. Art Black tells these stories again through the lives of the players. So often we see players only by their statistics and what they accomplish on the diamond. Black gives us a more complete story—a story of players who are also men with lives beyond the baseball field."
　　—Clarence Watkins, Author and Member, Friends of Rickwood

SHOWDOWN AT RICKWOOD

SHOWDOWN AT RICKWOOD

Ray Caldwell, Dizzy Dean, and the Early Years of America's Oldest Ball Park 1910-1931

Art Black

Library of Congress Cataloging-in-Publication Data

Black, Art
 Showdown at Rickwood: Ray Caldwell, Dizzy Dean, and the Early Years
  of America's Oldest Ball Park
Inside design by Jerri Beck
Cover design by Beth Conklin

Front Cover: Ray Caldwell *(left)* and Dizzy Dean meet at the 1931 Dixie Series; Rickwood Field entrance as it looked prior to 1928. **Back Cover:** Playing field, Rickwood, 1912.

ISBN: 978-0-9889807-3-0

Blue Rooster Press
1410 Seventeenth Street South
Birmingham, Alabama 35205-6210

Printed in Canada

This book is a story of people and events from a century ago, derived primarily from newspaper accounts. Dialogue was developed from quoted newspaper remarks and from the author's knowledge of events. The author used his best judgment in supplying detail to events while remaining true to the persons involved and the known outcomes.

For all ball players and fans

ABOUT THE BOOK

1931. THE GREAT BULL MARKET has come crashing down and depression has settled over the land.

On a torrid afternoon in Birmingham, Alabama, two minor league teams, the Birmingham Barons and the Houston Buffaloes, are playing Game One of a seven-game series for the baseball championship of the South. The Dixie Series is being waged for the twelfth year between the champions of the Southern Association and the Texas League. Meeting on the diamond this day, Wednesday, September 16, 1931, are an aging pitcher on the downside of his career and a brash up-and-comer half his years. Ray Caldwell, hanging on for dear life in the minor leagues, knows time is running out on his career. His counterpart, Dizzy Dean, knows his baseball future lies ahead. But on this day, forty-three-year-old Ray Caldwell will glorify himself in a dramatic struggle on Rickwood Field.

This book chronicles the 1931 Dixie Series. Incorporated within the narrative are stories of people, places, and events associated with Rickwood Field, a ball park that stands to this day. The book brings to life the people and the times during the period from 1910 to 1931 and revivifies bygone moments of a sport that was integral to American life in the early twentieth century.

Writing a book about minor league baseball of one hundred years ago requires diligence and patience. The principal characters in the drama have long since passed on and, in most cases, so have their children. As people vanish, so does institutional memory. We have the nuts and bolts of years past — team records and player statistics — but little in-depth material. Newspapers of the day, however, contain a wealth of information that is indispensable to a project such as this one. Baseball was the nation's most popular sport in the first half of the twentieth century; therefore, the coverage of baseball and of the Birmingham Barons was generous. Birmingham newspapers of the day covered the Barons as well as they cover college football today.

Other than word of mouth, newspapers were the chief source of news in the first two decades of the century. By the mid-1920s, radio began providing limited reporting of the news. Radio broadcasts of the era, however, were not recorded for posterity. Fortunately, newspapers have survived, thanks to the process of microfilming. The Birmingham Public Library owns microfilmed copies of local newspapers back to the 1870s.

Before writing this book, I intended to research Game One of the Dixie Series, featuring Caldwell and Dean, and include it in a series of short stories about Rickwood Field. The newspaper accounts of Game One made it clear that this was a remarkable game, and I scrolled through the microfilm to learn how the series played out. Games Two, Three, and Four were mundane—little hitting, little scoring—but close contests. The fifth and sixth games turned the tide of battle, and the seventh game in Houston, Texas, decided the championship. In the solitude of the library reading room, I had a spooky feeling these old ball players were speaking to me: "Alright, we're giving you this great story— now see what you can do with it." At that point, I decided to make Game One—Caldwell versus Dean—and the entire seven-game Dixie Series the centerpiece of a full-length book.

SUPPOSE THAT, BY CHANCE, A young boy and an elderly man meet at Rickwood Field on the day of Game One. Suppose that these two characters—real or imaginary—develop a kinship that continues long after the game ends. Further suppose that the boy, now grown, recounts stories for you that he learned from the man. That is the essence of the book you are about to read. The book is about real people, real places, real events, real history from 1910 to 1931. It is of depression and war, recession and prosperity, death and disease; of a flight across the Atlantic; of the fervor of the Hoover Bull Market and the Roaring Twenties; of the closing of an outdated ball park and the opening of a new one; of pennant winners and pennant losers, of high times and hard times, of hopes dashed and dreams fulfilled.

At Rickwood Field, time stands still. The ball players have gone home. The peanut boy must rest. Wind whistles through the grandstand. Frost has settled on the park. A long winter must pass before the crack of the bat is heard again. The grounds are silent—it is a lonesome place.

On your next visit to the 'Wood, I hope you will gaze upon the diamond and reminisce about the personalities and events of which you will read. Replay them in your mind's eye. Imagine, if you will, the happy, laughing throng jamming the park. Listen for the clang of streetcar bells and the honk of automobile horns, for the scuffle of feet and the snatches of gay laughter. Hear the cries of newsboys calling their papers and the clackity-clack of typewriters from the press box.

Listen for the rumble of the train beyond the outfield wall, and smell the puffing engine smoke. Smell the buttered popcorn and the parched peanuts. Picture the spring hats and dresses and the colorful crowd. Picture the ball park of green with a new carpet of grass.

Look across the green to the blue sky beyond. Notice the raked earth of the infield and the red clay of the pitcher's mound. Behold the flag in centerfield waving bonny as ever. Witness the spirited ball players romping about. Imagine big league heroes cutting capers on the infield grass and the town sports cheering them on. As you observe the performance, my hope is that Rickwood Field, for you, will never be the same again.

Read on.

CONTENTS

SHOWDOWN AT
RICKWOOD

Not to know what happened before you were born
is to remain forever a child. — *Cicero*

PROLOGUE

Ray Caldwell, 1931

1

LIGHTNING STRIKES

IF YOU HAD OPENED A newspaper on the morning of September 11, 1919, one story surely would have caught your attention. It told of a pitcher, a no-hit game, and a bolt of lightning. The story went like this:

NEW YORK — Ray Caldwell, the ne'er-do-well of the Yankees of years past, pitched a no-hit game for the Cleveland Indians yesterday against his old team, the Yanks, at the Polo Grounds. No one knows just what has come over Caldwell to transform him into such a pitching wonder, but some people have suspicions.

Eighteen days ago the tall, rangy righthander was hit by lightning at League Park in Cleveland. He was stricken to the ground by the electrical bolt while pitching in the ninth inning with two outs against the Philadelphia Athletics. Thousands of spectators were thrown into a momentary panic by the bolt, which came without warning and made as much noise as the backfiring of a thousand autos or the explosion of a dozen shells from a battery of Big Berthas. Fully half the folks in the stands were affected, and every player felt the electrical current go through his body, their spiked shoes attracting the juice. The catcher threw his metal mask afar so as not to attract the bolts.

Several Cleveland teammates ran to the rescue of Caldwell, who lay stretched out in the pitcher's box. The pitcher rose unassisted, however, and in a minute or so — the effects of the electrical storm having passed — he was able to resume his work. He had but one more man to pitch to. That batter hit a ground ball for the final out just as the clouds broke and the rain came down heavily.

Although Caldwell took the count when the lightning slapped him, he has been a different man since he returned to consciousness. Apparently, a lot of the electricity is still lurking in his system. And now, eighteen days later, Caldwell has hurled a no-hitter. Evidently, the opposing batsmen are afraid to hit his pitches for fear of absorbing the electricity that floored him.

Caldwell has surely put the electricity in his system to good use. What he fooled the Yanks with yesterday was probably a "lightning" ball. He also brought into play a moist ball — a spitball — which he had never thrown when he was with the Yankees. Between the saliva and the electricity, Caldwell had the Yankee bats waving vainly. At times, Ray's voltage was higher than others. When he turned on a whole flock of kilowatts, the ball would burn over the platter and flicker out of reach of the Yankee batsmen. Only twenty-nine men faced Caldwell in the game. Two reached first base, and no one reached second. Caldwell won the no-hitter, 3–0.

IF THE LIGHTNING AND THE no-hit game are all you know of Ray Caldwell, you need to learn more, for his is a most remarkable story.

2
TWELVE YEARS LATER

I MET AN OLD MAN once. The year was 1931 on a fearfully hot day at Rickwood Field.

Game One of the Dixie Series was being contested that day, Wednesday, September 16. The Series was held each year between the winners of the Texas League and the Southern Association to decide the baseball championship of the South. The old man and I, along with twenty thousand other panting, hyperventilating types, witnessed the greatest game in the history of Birmingham baseball that day between the hometown Barons and the visiting Houston Buffaloes.

The game had yet to begin when the old man and I happened upon one another. I was a gander-legged youth dressed in knickerbockers and my best Sunday shoes with a baseball glove on my hand. As I walked the aisle next to the dugout, first base side, I searched for my hero, a pitcher named Ray Caldwell. Then, behind me, I heard a voice — "Oh-ho" — and turned to see a gentleman shuffling down the concrete steps of the grandstand. He was about seventy years old, a little hunched, marking each step with a tap-tap of his silver walking stick.

"Oh-ho. Excuse me." He smiled at me cheerily. "You look like a lad on a mission. Can I be of assistance?"

Immediately I was impressed by this man. All men dressed formally in public back then — dark jacket, white shirt, necktie, and hat. This man, however, was glorious. His hair was a lovely white, his skin clear and bronzed. On his head was a flat straw hat with a bright band. He wore a handkerchief in the breast pocket of his linen suit and a flower on his lapel. His trousers had a crease that would slice a watermelon. Under his arm was the morning newspaper: *Stock*

Averages Touch New Low, the headline. Carefully folded underneath was the afternoon paper: *Selling Causes Cotton Decline.*

Remember, this was 1931. The stock market had crashed two years earlier. We were grappling with a "business depression" — not yet the Great Depression as we know it today. Everyone hoped, nay expected, the depression would end soon.

"Anything I can do for you?" the man asked me.

"I'm looking for Ray Caldwell. I want him to sign my baseball glove."

"Ah, the old ball player. He once pitched in the major leagues, you know."

No, I didn't know that. I raised my hand to shade my eyes from the afternoon sun and gazed about the playing field.

"What might your name be?" he asked.

"Walter. My grandpa's name is Ray. That's why I like Ray Caldwell."

"Did you know Ray Caldwell is a grandfather? Probably about the same age as your grandpa. Forty-three years old, he is. That's pretty old for a ball player."

The man slipped out of his suit coat and draped it across his arm. His white shirt was wet under the arms. His cheeks were flushed and his forehead was covered with moisture. "Quite a spell of hot weather we're having. Ninety-six degrees, what I hear." He drew a cotton handkerchief from a side pocket and dabbed his face.

"That's a dandy shine you've got on your shoes," he said.

"I blacked them this morning. They's Poll-Parrots. They fit me real good."

"Where's your father?"

"He lost his job last week and didn't feel like coming to the game."

The man nodded thoughtfully. "This business depression is rough. Conditions all over are not good. They been hollering about prosperity for a year now: *Just around the corner; already arrived, in fact.* Well, you can count me as one doubtin' Thomas."

I'll be straight with you. Lots of kids would be scared stiff of a grown man, a total stranger, striking up a conversation on matters a kid knows nothing about. But even at my age — eleven — something told me I should listen to this old man. I'm glad I did. Later you'll understand why.

The man sat down in one of the green, slatted box seats next to the playing field. From a gold cigarette case engraved CWS, he removed an Old Gold and tapped one end against the case. He lowered his head and lit the cigarette. He took a long, grateful puff and tossed the match.

"These are lean times, very lean times," he said. "People at the grass roots losing their jobs, struggling to get by — the laborer with his empty pockets and his empty meal barrel. Winter'll be settin' in soon, and there'll be lots of cold, hungry people. They're afraid; we're all afraid. I know a man, never trusted the bank as a safe enough hiding place. Took out all his money — ten thousand iron men, his life savings. Hiding it in his cellar. President Hoover's got to do something. Standing pat's not good enough. I fear conditions'll only get worse." The man rose, his hands clasped behind him. He looked at me hard.

"If you want my opinion, what this country needs is a new direction. The people need to shake things up." He threw his hands out to the side. "We live in the greatest country on Earth, so rich, so powerful, and yet . . . I don't know, my business isn't what it used to be. I sell cotton, white gold in the South, but people aren't buying like they once did. If business doesn't pick up, I don't know what's going to become of us." Then he smiled.

"No sense making a fuss. My name's Charles Stewart. The wife's out for the day — the beauty parlor and the museum, taking in the Italian art exhibit, compliments of that fellow Mussolini."

The man took a card from his breast pocket, scribbled on it with a fountain pen, and handed it to me. "Have your father telephone me. Perhaps I can be of assistance. Where do you live?"

"Near Bush Boulevard. I go to Woodrow Wilson School. I walked here from school. When the man at the gate turned his head, I walked on in."

"You walked to the game by yourself?"

"I've did it before. I don't mind."

"Sneaking into the game, you mean?"

"I mean walking to Rickwood." I looked up at the man. "Say, mister, do you know Ray Caldwell?"

"I've met him."

"Do you think I can get his autograph?"

"Well, he is the starting pitcher today. He'll be out directly to warm up. We'll ask him. He might sign that mitt of yours. Now what do you say we get out of this hot sun, shall we?" We started up the aisle.

"What's he like, Ray Caldwell?" I asked. The old man leaned on his silver cane and called to mind a flashing, black-haired pitcher in his vigorous prime:

"Extraordinary man, this Caldwell. Long years ago he was marked for glory. Could've won the hearts and minds of people all over this land. Could've been one of the greatest ball players who ever lived. Yes, I know Ray Caldwell, and his is a story worth the telling." The man put his hand on my shoulder, and together we climbed the steps to the shade of the grandstand.

As WE WAITED FOR THE game to begin, Charles Stewart told me all he knew of Ray Caldwell — of his being struck by lightning, of his reckless habits, of a baseball career squandered. But I'm getting ahead of my story. There's other things I want to tell you about. As I look back on my life, I owe a lot to Charles Stewart. He was a lovable, red-blooded American who could smoke a cigar and talk baseball. He enjoyed harking back to yesteryear and sharing memories with me. When he got wound up, he was downright interesting to listen to.

The day Charles Stewart introduced himself to me, Birmingham was a thriving industrial center, rich in mineral resources. The metropolitan area by population was the third largest in the South. Everyone was certain that Birmingham's fortune was to be the mightiest city south of the Ohio River. A visitor once remarked:

"Long before I reach Birmingham I hear its roar. Birmingham always reminds me of some great living, throbbing being accomplishing a great task. Then when I arrive up the street, I have the feeling something big is about to happen."

It was a young city, Birmingham of 1931. Sixty years before, there had been no Birmingham. Where tall buildings now stood, waterfowl dipped in marshes and deer came to drink. Where First Avenue now crossed Twentieth Street, young blades shot ducks at a pond. Crows once winged their way, a-cawing, to a cornfield at Park Place and Twentieth Street. But the hills nearby were full of coal and iron and limestone, and pioneers flocked to this land known as Jones Valley. They came to mine the minerals, and almost overnight a wilderness became a city.

Stewart told me that Birmingham of the 1880s was rather a tough burg — "Bad Birmingham." Hard-boiled ironworkers and undesirables from distant corners of the world gathered here. Guns came, and men who knew how to use them. Saloons went up on every corner, with gambling dens in the rear and houses of ill fame above. Popskull liquor was cheap and plentiful. So was violence. A dull night it was when at least one murder did not occur.

Two of the wildest, most unruly sections of the town were Buzzard Roost, on Second Avenue east of Twenty-second Street, and Scratch Ankle on Fourth Avenue below Eighteenth. The Southside, too, had dangerous places: Beer Mash and Pigeon Roost, Scruggs Alley and Tintop Alley, and the most lawless of all, the locale around the old steel mill at Fourteenth Street and First Avenue South — Mule's Ear.

The town grew down the valley, but by degrees it crept up the hillsides, both on the north and on the south. It grew, and grew incredibly, as if by magic. By the turn of the century, the young town was on the way to its first 100,000. In 1910, the population reached 132,000; by 1920, 178,000; and by 1930, 260,000. These were rosy, ambitious days. Great furnaces were built, and Birmingham gave the world iron and steel. Bad Birmingham became the "Magic City."

In the first decade of the twentieth century, Birmingham was barely thirty years old and already the "Magic City." Its broad streets were paved with granite block. Before long, automobiles would share the streets with horses, mules, and streetcars. Above is Second Avenue North between Nineteenth and Twentieth streets; below is Twentieth Street North.

I have always believed that Birmingham occupied one of the most beautiful sites on earth: mountain ranges to the horizon, as far as the eye could see — a blending of hill and dale, mountain and valley. At nightfall from the brow of Red Mountain, thousands of lights twinkled in the valley, and now and then a flash from a giant furnace lighted the heavens, throwing red smoke and flame into the sky. If Birmingham had nothing else, it had a view.

STEWART LOVED BASEBALL, FELT IT to his bones. He savored everything about the game — springtime, sunshine, blue sky, green grass. The white ball and its red stitching. The flash of white uniform. The smell of the bleachers, of dry wood baking in the sun. He loved the sweet music of bat meeting ball and watching that ball, true as a gunshot, skip across the green of the diamond.

Today it's difficult to imagine how central baseball was to life in the early 1900s. It was the biggest spectator sport in America. No other sport, save horse racing and the occasional prize fight, attracted the attention baseball did. College football in the South was a minor sport, a typical crowd being ten-to-twelve thousand. Professional football did not have a significant presence until World War II. Baseball was The National Game, in capital letters, and newspapers covered it year-round. All over this country, people heard the crack of bat against ball. The major league pennant races were compelling, even to the millions who'd never been to a game. Most people didn't know what the big-leaguers looked like — they'd only read about them in newspapers. The minor leagues touched nearly every hamlet and town, and the country was as linked by baseball as it was by its telegraph and railroads.

Professional baseball — the big leagues and the minors — was only part of it. Every town, every village, every factory had a team, its *own nine.* Every town was wrapped up in the honor of the team. The whole community was at fever heat as the visiting nine arrived for the game. It was part baseball exhibition and part social event — the town opened its homes to visitors. Aside from town teams, the youth of the land played on empty lots, on school grounds, and in the streets. Every grammar school, every Sunday school had a team. Men played on teams representing their employers, and the results of the games were written up in the newspaper. My father told me about playing ball when he was a young man. Companies hired men with ball playing skills. The mills, the mines, the factories, railroads, banks, policemen, the post office, the phone company, newspapers — they all had teams, and there were leagues of these teams. They called it "sandlot" baseball, and many ball players playing the sandlot game were discovered by professional scouts.

Stewart told me when he was a boy he would buy a five-cent rubber ball and wind a dime's worth of cotton twine around it to make his own baseball. If he was lucky, he got hold of an old pair of hand gloves and cut out a cover for the ball. Sometimes a league ball came his way but always in a state of disrepair. How he cherished his baseball. Each night he would take it home and nurse it, mend the broken seams, and make it fit for the next day's play.

DURING THE DEPRESSION, AS TIMES worsened, women and men waited in charity lines and foraged through garbage cans for food. People sometimes lost their pride and their hope, but still they played baseball. Back in 1910, *The Birmingham News* said: "Baseball is indisputably the game of the nation. It is the game which has the firmest hold on the people, through all classes, conditions, and sections."

Birmingham was firmly in the grasp of baseball. The ball players were more accessible then than now, and fans knew them personally. Most players lived in boardinghouses about town, and townspeople recognized and spoke to players as they walked the streets of town.

Opening Day was the biggest day of the year for most cities. Opening Day in Birmingham was like the Kentucky Derby to Louisville. "I can hear the sparrows twittering in the grandstand," *News* columnist Judy Brown said as Opening Day 1923 approached. The voices of the thousands disturb not the sparrows in the grandstand, she said — "they're real fans. Baseball season is here, boys and girls, ladies and gentlemen, and life's worth living once more."

The Birmingham Barons and seven other teams competed in the Southern Association. Cities around the league competed fiercely to attract the largest Opening Day attendance, and the winning city received a trophy. For weeks, civic bodies promoted attendance for the game. Cities declared a half-holiday for city hall, the courthouse, and other public employees. Many downtown businesses also gave workers the afternoon off.

"From April to September, nothing was bigger in the cities of the Southern League than the baseball teams that played in them," wrote Benny Marshall of *The Birmingham News.* "The major leagues were a million miles away. . . . The players were swashbuckling citizens whose cheeks always bulged from a cud of Brown Mule or Apple Sun cured. No local hero could figure to walk the block on Second Avenue downtown from Twentieth to Nineteenth without a dozen people pointing him out and a half-dozen stopping to ask him about yesterday's game.

"Kids who were fortunate enough to have a ball player move into their neighborhood in the summer knew the minute he left in the morning, exactly when he came home in the afternoon, and if his wife made him go to the grocery store. Secretly, they wished they could have been his kids."

Early in the century, downtown merchants rewarded ball players for special deeds. In 1904, J. Blach & Co., a department store, awarded a Panama hat to the first Birmingham batter of the season to hit a home run at Rickwood Field and a pair of shoes to the first visiting player to do so. Blach's continued giving prizes for many years. During the 1940s and '50s, they gave every Birmingham player a new suit of clothes every time he hit a home run during the season. A good home run hitter had a closet full of suits, thanks to Blach's.

Much of what you'll read here occurred before I was born. I learned it from Charles Stewart. He told me that before television and radio came along, baseball fans followed their teams by word of mouth. Baseball scores came in over telegraph wire. If you happened by an office, barbershop, or drugstore that owned a ticker machine, you could learn the score inning by inning. Or you might hear a Western Union messenger boy rushing through the street with meager details of the game. You passed the word to your neighbor. Some people paid to attend re-created games called "matinees" in a theater or a vacant room downtown. An announcer received telegraph reports from the site of the game and called every ball, every strike, and every hit to the audience. Often the room was equipped with a large diamond-shaped chart, allowing the announcer to show a player's progress from base to base. It was almost like being at the game.

Every year during the World Series, newspapers across the country erected giant scoreboards outside their offices. Henry Vance, a sportswriter with *The Birmingham News,* called the game through a huge megaphone while standing on a raised platform on Twenty-second Street. As Vance made his calls outside *The News'* office, his colleague, Zipp Newman, recorded on the scoreboard with a piece of chalk each ball and strike, the location on the diamond where the batter hit the ball, and the position of each runner on the bases. Thousands of people watched from streets and sidewalks. Others attended World Series matinees in venues around the city. The moment a World Series game ended, the presses of the daily newspapers printed Extra editions with accounts of the game. Newsboys swarmed downtown streets calling out their freshly printed papers, and carriers rushed papers to subscribers.

Anyone around the game as long as Charles Stewart was is bound to acquire a set of bizarre, if worthless, facts. For instance, Stewart asked me once, "Before radio came along, do you know how people in Birmingham learned that a game had been postponed by bad weather?"

"Do tell," I said. "I'm bustin' with suspense."

In 1922, a siren was placed on top of the First National Bank building downtown. Every ten minutes the siren gave one long blast if a game was to

During the 1910s and '20s, newspapers across the country reported the results of World Series games to throngs gathered outside their offices. Here, two reporters from *The Birmingham News* inform a crowd on Twenty-second Street of the progress of a game, calling out the result of each play and noting on a scoreboard the location where each ball was hit and the position of each base runner.

be played. If the game was rained out, there were two blasts, a pause, and two more blasts.

From Charles Stewart, my father, and my own investigating, I've learned a lot about the history of our national game. Professional baseball in the South dates back to the 1880s. The Southern League was formed in 1885 and remained in business on and off through 1899. There was no league in 1890, '91, or '97. After the 1899 season, the league disbanded. In October 1900, representatives from six cities met at the Morris Hotel in Birmingham to revive the league, beginning in 1901. They decided to call the new league the Southern *Association,* perhaps to distance it from earlier failures.

The Southern Association developed into one of baseball's most stable minor leagues. Six of the charter members — Birmingham, Chattanooga, Little Rock, Memphis, Nashville, and New Orleans — were in the league for fifty years or more. Atlanta entered the league the second year and remained for sixty years.

Mobile joined in 1908 and stayed forty-two years. In casual conversation and in the news media, most fans, reporters, and executives referred to the new league as the Southern League; it rolled off the tongue a little easier than did Southern Association. In this book you'll see the league called by both names, Southern League and Southern Association — they are one and the same.

UNTIL THE 1930S, ALL BASEBALL games were played in the daytime, usually at three or three-thirty. Businessmen and schoolchildren could go to the ball park, watch the game, and get home in time for dinner. Many cities, Birmingham included, did not allow baseball games and other entertainment such as movies on the Sabbath. Fans attending games clamored for rallies by ringing cowbells, honking tin horns, and pounding the seats with soft drink bottles. Drinks were sold in bottles at the ball park, and occasionally bottles became weapons directed at players and umpires. One spring day at Rickwood Field in 1922, a hundred or more pop bottles were hurled toward an umpire's head after he missed a call at first base. The bottles crashed into one another in mid-air, littering the field with glass, but the umpire stood his ground. Policemen rushed into the stands to calm the crowd.

Baseball games were played briskly. Ball parks did not have lights, so games had to be completed before dark. When you watch a game today, you'll see the batter step out of the box after every pitch to take a practice swing or adjust his batting gloves. Sometimes the pitcher will make throw after throw to first base to hold the runner close. Not so back then. In the old days, the umpire kept the action moving: "Come on, fellows, hurry 'er up!" he exhorted the players. Games didn't last three, three-and-a-half hours. Most games were completed in less than two hours, and some were played in an hour and a half. Newspaper reporters and fans complained when games took longer. After the game ended, you'd take the streetcar home or maybe walk downtown, where you'd hear the cries of the newsies: "Sports extra! All the baseball results!" And you could read about the games played that afternoon in the Southern Association and the majors.

Stewart used to tell me about the "dead ball" days of baseball, when teams played for one run at a time, when pitchers were the stars of the game. A team that allowed an opponent to score, say, seven runs in a game was considered a disgrace to the sport. During the dead ball era, roughly 1900 to 1919, most batters didn't swing for home runs; they simply tried to make contact. The batter placed his hands a few inches up the bat handle and poked at the ball with a downward chop, spraying the ball to all parts of the field. Players bunted, stole bases, and scored runs by putting pressure on the fielders rather than hitting the ball long distances. Outfield fences generally were farther back than they are today, and, in most cases, games were won on the bases, not by hitting home runs.

At Rickwood Field in the late 1920s, the rightfield wall stood 334 feet from home plate, a dimension similar to those in stadiums of today. But the centerfield fence was a distant 470 feet and leftfield was 405 away. The only way to hit a home run to left or to center was to hit the ball between the fielders and run the bases before the outfielder could relay the ball home. Whenever someone did hit a home run, spectators generally tossed a few coins on the field, and the ball player eagerly gathered them up after he crossed the plate.

Pitchers were expected to finish every game they started. Harry Coveleski — you'll read about him later — pitched for Birmingham in 1910. He had a win-loss record of 21–10 and completed every game he started except one. During the dead ball days, only three or four balls were used during an entire game, so batters rarely saw a clean baseball. Pitchers scuffed up, roughed up, nicked up, and spit on balls to make them break sharply, and often they worked with loose-covered, softened baseballs. Pitchers and infielders rubbed dirt and tobacco juice and licorice on the ball, and by late afternoon the ball was so black you could hardly see it. Balls hit foul into the stands were returned to the field of play. The ball was replaced only when the stitches began to unravel. The yarn around the ball's cork center was more loosely wound than it is today, and balls often became spongy, even mashed on the side.

In 1919, the style of play began to change. The Reach Company, the manufacturer of major league baseballs, began winding the yarn more tightly, giving the ball greater resilience and more distance. Then along came a slugger named George Herman Ruth, known far and wide as *the Babe*. Ruth used a heavy bat, gripped it at the end of the handle, and swung the full length of his bat with an upward arc. In 1920, Babe Ruth hit fifty-four home runs; no one else had more than nineteen.

Almost overnight, budding Babe Ruths appeared on every major league team. Home runs came thick and fast, and batting averages soared with the new, lively "rabbit ball." In 1928, every starting player and even some of the pitchers in the Birmingham Barons lineup hit better than .300. Those 1928 Barons scored fifteen runs or more in a game nine times. As a team they hit for an average of .331, a minor league record. It could be said that the Roaring Twenties marked the end of the dead ball style of play.

Ball parks of yesteryear were not equipped with electronic amplification. The home plate umpire bellowed out all announcements. Before the game, he faced the crowd and shouted out the starting pitchers and catchers — the so-called battery: "Bair and Munson for Nashville. Tannehill and Pratt for Birmingham." The umpire announced substitute players as they entered the game. He did not announce players when they came to bat. The umpire also made the occasional quirky announcement — "Mr. So-and-So is wanted on the phone" — though such messages generally weren't discernible over the noise of the crowd. Beginning in 1917, the Birmingham Baseball Association enlisted a boy to walk through the stands carrying a large blackboard with the words "Wanted at the Phone" followed by the name of the party. The individual would tip the boy and answer the phone call in the lobby of the grandstand.

The first public address system in the Southern Association was installed in 1928 when newspaperman Henry Vance grabbed the microphone connected to a big amplifier at Rickwood Field. He announced the name of every batter, as well as official scorer rulings on hits and errors. The loudspeaker was placed on the playing field in centerfield.

In the early years of the twentieth century, much of the new talent in the major and minor leagues came from amateur and semi-professional clubs — the factory and mill teams in towns across the country. Complex scouting networks as we know them today did not exist. If a man had a reputation around town as a ball player, a manager might look him over and invite him to try out the following spring. Managers often received tips on players from fans, particularly traveling salesmen.

Here's an example: In August of 1922, the Birmingham Barons were in Atlanta to play five games in three days with only four pitchers available. The Barons manager was Joe Dunn. While strolling the streets the morning the series opened, Dunn ran into a friend who told him of a crackerjack pitcher from nearby Roswell, Georgia, that he could land just by calling him on the telephone. Dunn took the dare, and Johnny Owens, boy wonder, showed up shortly before the game started. As Dunn warmed him up, he could see the kid had a good curveball and natural control, so he offered to let him pitch. Owens started the second game of a doubleheader that day and gave up only one hit in the first four innings. For the entire seven-inning game, he allowed only two runs and displayed unusual poise with runners on base. Owens pitched two more times in relief that season and returned for spring training the following season, but his glory was short-lived; the Barons released him before the season began, and he slipped quietly into obscurity.

FOR AS LONG AS BASEBALL has been played, ball players have made remarkable plays. In August of 1923, the Chicago American Giants played the Birmingham Black Barons in a Negro National League game at Rickwood Field. Floyd Gardner, the Giants rightfielder, was playing deep against the Birmingham batter, George (Mule) Suttles. Suttles crashed a long one, and Gardner ran back to the fence, climbed onto the ledge of the scoreboard and caught the ball with one hand, using a glove much smaller than those of today. *The Birmingham Age-Herald* called it one of the most sensational catches ever witnessed at Rickwood.

In 1931, Birmingham shortstop Shine Cortazzo started "the most spectacular double play ever seen at Rickwood," in the words of *The Birmingham News*. Chattanooga batter Bill Andrus shot a low line drive near second base. Cortazzo leaped, knocked the ball down, and fell to the ground. Lying on his back with his feet pointing toward centerfield, Cortazzo lobbed the ball over his head to the second baseman standing on the bag. The second baseman threw to first for a double play.

Through the years, major league teams made Rickwood Field a stopping point on their way north from spring training. Christy Mathewson of the New York Giants pitched at Rickwood in 1911, '12, and '13. The great Pittsburgh shortstop, Honus Wagner, played at the 'Wood at the end of his career in 1915. Ty Cobb played at Rickwood six times. Rogers Hornsby and the St. Louis Cardinals played Cobb's Detroit Tigers in 1923. Hornsby hit a home run that day that cleared the centerfield fence by ten feet. Old-timers agreed it was one of the longest home runs they'd ever seen.

In 1925, the Washington Senators' Walter Johnson stepped to the mound to pitch in relief against the New York Giants. It was the seventh inning, and nine thousand spectators rose as one, greeting the grand old man of baseball with a gust of applause and a waving of straw hats. Johnson, with a free and easy sidearm delivery, retired the side in order. The Giants and Senators returned in 1927 with an astonishing array: Burleigh Grimes, Stan Coveleski, Bill Terry, Mel Ott, Rogers Hornsby, Goose Goslin, Edd Roush, Sam Rice, Tris Speaker, Fred Lindstrom, and managers Bucky Harris and John McGraw, all future Hall of Famers. Where was Walter Johnson, another Hall of Famer, you ask? He was absent with a broken leg.

Babe Ruth visited Rickwood nine times from 1918 to 1934. Sportswriter Henry Vance claimed he scared the big fellow to death on a visit in 1921. Soon after the New York Yankees hit town, Ruth and team captain Roger Peckinpaugh voiced a desire to see the hills around Birmingham. Vance drove them up Altamont and Cliff roads to marvel at the city in the valley and its mansions, skyscrapers, blast furnaces, steel plants, and giant industries. On the drive back down Red Mountain, the three men came suddenly upon a milk wagon, an automobile, and a streetcar — three abreast — blocking the road. Vance hit the brake, but the car wouldn't stop. He threw the emergency brake to prevent a collision.

"Babe was ready to jump from the car and make a hook slide for the curb," Vance said, "but he stuck with me until the car came to a halt. Later I swelled

Many greats of the game passed through these gates from 1910 to 1927: Ty Cobb, Babe Ruth, Walter Johnson, Rogers Hornsby, and Satchel Paige among them. The entrance to Rickwood was remodeled in 1928.

all up with pride over the thought that I had almost killed a one-hundred-thousand-dollar baseball player."

Later that day between innings of the game, Ruth sat in the far reaches of the outfield, with hundreds of kids chattering and shaking his hand. In four trips to the plate Ruth didn't hit a ball out of the infield. Henry Vance, recalling the heart-stopper on Red Mountain, said, "Maybe Babe was so unnerved over the incident that he didn't like biffing 'em at Rickwood."

All the Negro League greats also played at Rickwood: Satchel Paige, Josh Gibson, Mule Suttles, Buck Leonard, Ted (Double Duty) Radcliffe, Lorenzo (Piper) Davis, and James (Cool Papa) Bell, among others.

RICKWOOD FIELD FIRST SAW THE light of day in 1910. The new ball park was situated on the western edge of town. People arrived at games by horse-drawn buggy, automobile, and streetcar, and on foot. Rickwood had replaced a ramshackle wooden structure named West End Park that some folks called the *Slag Pile*. You'll learn more about these ball parks later. First, I want to recount a little about life in the new century.

In Birmingham before the turn of the century, fashionable homes occupied parts of what is now downtown. By 1910, the residential areas were expanding outward along streetcar lines — east to Avondale, Woodlawn, and East Lake; north to Fountain Heights, North Birmingham, and Norwood; west to West

End, Fairfield, and Ensley; and to the Southside and South Highlands. About this time, the dreaded boll weevil was working its way from Mexico through the southern United States, ravaging King Cotton. By 1910, the weevil had moved out of Mississippi to the Alabama line in Mobile County. Crop losses in Mississippi were heavy, and people were discouraged. By 1913, the boll weevil had appeared in every Alabama county west of Montgomery.

During this time, people complained that newspaper boys were shooting craps and using bad language near *The Age-Herald* building on Sunday mornings. Shooting craps, or "rolling the bones," cost you ten dollars in the courtroom of Judge Hugo Black, who would go on to become a U.S. senator and Supreme Court justice. In 1912, a man was fined five dollars for calling another man a liar. A Greek was fined five dollars for cursing in his native tongue in the presence of a woman. Three people were fined ten dollars each for betting on a pool game on Third Avenue. The proprietor of the Pedigree Hotel was fined twenty-five dollars for running a house of prostitution; the women were fined ten dollars each. Two men were fined fifteen dollars for being drunk.

A frequent sight around town was a man wandering the neighborhoods with a hand organ and a monkey. Wherever he appeared, the monkey man caused a stir. Children gathered from around the neighborhood. Small boys trailed him block to block like the children of Hamelin followed the Pied Piper. As the monkey man began grinding the handle of his organ, the monkey, outfitted in a cap and vest, danced, smoked a pipe, and turned handsprings. After the performance, the monkey held out its cap to collect pennies from excited children.

In the first two decades of the century, the horse and the automobile sparred for dominion of the streets. In 1905, only twelve automobiles were registered in Birmingham. By 1927, there were nearly forty thousand. Streets no longer smelled of animals but of gasoline. It was not uncommon for a horse, frightened by an automobile, to break loose from a hitching post and gallop unattended through the streets. One man in 1910 was not convinced that the automobile deserved a place on the streets:

"After noticing the number of noisy, rattling one-year-old automobiles which are now nearing the scrap pile in Birmingham, I was more than ever convinced that the horse will always be supreme," he said. "For pleasure, the automobile does not compare to the horse. It will soon become a toy, for the gaited horse is always the chief joy of a man who likes spirited action."

In the 1920s, an occasional beast of burden still roamed the street. A mule entered the Dixie Coffee Company on Second Avenue in 1924, drank water from a sink, walked out, and continued down the avenue. A monkey belonging to a shoe shop made a dash for freedom along Fourth Avenue and Twentieth Street. The monkey scrambled up a pole and hopped along a telephone wire with its tail curled around the wire above. Pursued by onlookers, the monkey jumped onto the ledge of a building and leapt onto a car, where it was apprehended.

The streets of town in the first decade of the century were paved with concrete, granite block, creosoted wood blocks, macadam, chert, and other mixtures. Paving with asphalt began in 1911 on Eighteenth Street, though streets outside of town were unpaved. Automobiles rushed along dirt roads, blowing clouds of dust on people and making life miserable in the summer heat. After a rain, automobiles often became stuck in the mud.

Travel from city to city was uncertain. Road conditions varied, and roadways often were unmarked. For trips of a hundred miles or more, nearly everyone traveled by train. It took one man forty-eight hours to travel from Chattanooga to Birmingham by automobile in 1910. He encountered roads of sand, clay, and slag. More than once his car sank in the mud. Farmers, oxen, and mules came to his aid. Finally, while clipping off at a lively pace, the man drove ten miles down a piece of pretty shell road before realizing he was headed to Nashville, not Birmingham.

Thus it was at the turn of the century. Charles Stewart told me many stories through the years, about Rickwood, about old West End Park, about the ball players. One of his expressions was, "I'll tell you how it was then, a long time ago."

"Walter, do you know why I'm telling you these grand old stories?" Stewart once asked me.

I was befuddled. " 'Cause you don't have a son to talk to?"

"Think, Walter. Why have I chosen you? Why have I poured out my heart to you?"

" 'Cause I like Ray Caldwell?"

"Yes. Because you like Ray Caldwell. And . . .?"

I thought hard. " 'Cause I'm keen on baseball?"

"Yes, because you like baseball. That day you and I met, you were down there by the diamond all by yourself. You walked to the game. No one came with you, not your father, not a friend. You, a boy of eleven, came alone. That touched me.

"Every moment I've spent at this ball park has been worth the while. I literally grew up in this man's town. Met my wife here, found and made my friends here — been here since the first pig trail was laid. My father used to drive an ox wagon through Jones Valley, right where Birmingham now stands. In the early days, they gave away property on Twentieth Street for the price of a cow. There were briars and broom sedge where now railroads and furnaces and fine homes stand. I first struck foot on Birmingham soil in 1880. Back then, it was a rambling, shabby mining town. Saturday afternoons the streets were lined with the covered wagons of farmers and mountain people in town purchasing their weekly supplies. The streets were of slag. When we went to church, we dusted our shoes with handkerchiefs before going inside. I remember a fellow townsman, Phil Givhan, riding his horse into the post office on First Avenue to celebrate the election of Grover Cleveland. Birmingham was a wonderful city then, full of optimism and good fellowship. Hardships had been endured and fortunes won and lost. Ah, the good old days. There I go a-sighing again.

"A tough baby was young Birmingham. I've seen it grow from rough and ready conditions, with a saloon on every corner, into a cultured city. And I am glad to have lived so long and to see the world grow and change. Someday, Walter, you'll be an old man like me. You'll be the only one to know what took place on our Rickwood Field. Listen to me," putting his hand on my shoulder, "fifty years from now this ball park will be gone. Gone! They'll tear it down without a thought, just as they did old West End Park. The stories I've been telling you, you must pass on to your children and their children. If you don't, these stories will be lost forever. You see, everyone will have forgotten Ray Caldwell and all the summertime heroes who romped on these grounds. They'll have heard the names, certainly, but they'll not know what drove these ball players — common folk, all. Many a youngster has come up from the brush to play professional ball — at this very park, Rickwood Field. Some were poor, dog poor — rich in character but poor in earthly goods. They all had an idea they'd turn the world upside down. And some did. What caused the few of them to rise to greatness? I'm sharing their tales with you because you must know, and you must tell the world. Now do you understand?"

And so Charles Stewart shared his love of the game with me. I'll pass along to you what he told me. We'll begin in 1910, when a ball park we know today as Rickwood Field was rising out of the ground. The home field of the Birmingham Barons in early 1910 was still West End Park, the Slag Pile. It was during the summer of 1910 that a boy began making noise around the Slag Pile.

THE EARLY YEARS
1910–1914

CHAPTER 1

THE BOY WHO WANTED TO PITCH

ON A GRAY JULY DAY in 1910, a boy in a faded blue cap gazed about the field at West End Park. He was tall and strapping, with a choirboy face and gray eyes, quick and keen as a bird's. Ball players from the Birmingham Barons were scattered about, waiting to play a baseball game. The field was muddy from a hard rain. The game from the day before had been postponed, forcing a doubleheader to be played this day. Two miles away a new baseball park was under construction. In a few weeks, the Barons would begin playing at Rickwood Field, and the present ball yard — West End Park, the Slag Pile — would pass into history.

"Mr. Ellam, are we gonna play today?" asked the boy. The day was hot and misty, though a gleam of sunshine had found its way through a murky sky. Roy Ellam, the Barons shortstop, walked up pleasantly. "I sure hope so. Coveleski's pitching. Doubleheaders are starting to pile up — one today, another tomorrow. We need to play."

"Mr. Ellam, will you ask him today?" Roy Ellam had heard the question before.

"Yeah, but I'm warning you, he's not keen on boys who fancy themselves as ball players."

Faint and far away, streetcar bells clanged and brakes screeched — the sound of a trolley car whirring to a stop. "He'll be around directly," Ellam said. "When he gets here, I'll ask."

Ellam agonized over what to do. Carlton Molesworth, the playing manager of the Barons, an intense, no-nonsense man, was in no mood for small talk. Molesworth stepped off the trolley. Ellam drifted over. "Say, Moley, there's a kid over there wants to see you."

Molesworth surveyed the grounds. "Roy, have the fellows take a few swings, then get 'em off the field. This field's not in any kinda condition for infield work."

"The kid says he's a pitcher, wants to try out for the team."

Molesworth threw a look at Ellam. "I think not."

"He's a sturdy boy, built on a solid frame. It's quite the best thing about him. And you're always looking for pitchers. He might be just the one you're looking for. And he's right here in our backyard."

"Fiddlesticks!" Molesworth lowered his voice and folded his arms. "Let me tell you how it is. Boys get recommended to me all the time, see? You look 'em over and size 'em up. Only one out of a thousand shows anything."

Molesworth once was a young manager, full of zeal, welcoming every Pollyanna who came along, only to be deceived.

"It beats all, how people think they can judge a ball player. I'll give you an example. I'm walking downtown; man calls out to me: 'Molesworth, I know a boy . . .!' Right then, I know I'm in trouble.

"'Molesworth,' he says, 'with a little training he can help your team. He's a phenom. How 'bout giving the kid a trial?'

"The man wants you to look at the kid. He's sweet on the fellow 'cause he's head and shoulders above the boys he plays with. He forgets the class of ball he's seeing. It's all a pipe dream. You give the boy a tryout and he looks like a plain, ordinary Joe. Jeez. A man 'ud be a plumb fool to spend time on a boy like that. Pure folly, that's what it is.

"And, Roy, I recall once you giving me a tip about a hot prospect—shortstop, as I recall. Remember how that one turned out?"

Ellam grinned. "How was I to know he couldn't hit in our league? He had a good pair of hands, though."

"So does a clock."

Molesworth pushed his cap to the back of his head. "F'crissake, Roy, in our league, you've gotta have polish and experience. Besides, we have a doubleheader to play."

Ellam was deflated. "Gee, what harm can it do, Moley? He's a dreamer. Let him throw to a few of the fellows in hitting practice. We'll pepper him with line drives. He'll see it's harder'n it looks and be on his way."

"I'm not in the market for a sandlotter."

"Shucks, Moley. You remember me my first year—a green young gosling, all dewy-eyed and all."

Molesworth nodded. "Green enough for the cows to eat."

"That's right," said Ellam, who was raised in West Conshohocken, Pennsylvania. "Growing up, I didn't know the big city way of doing things. We didn't have electricity or streetcars or anything. I even wrote you a letter asking if I should bring my own uniform. Imagine that, asking if I had to furnish my uniform. I was a bundle of nerves when I came to Birmingham. I bobbled ball after ball, and the fans rode me hard."

Molesworth chuckled. "They still do. But at least you had a year of Class D ball under your belt. Who's the kid play for?"

"He doesn't."

"So he's a schoolboy."

Ellam shook his head. "He sells soda pop at the games."

"A pop boy?" Molesworth cried. "Ha! Ain't you the kidder. You want me to try out a pop boy? Where is he?"

Ellam pointed to the boy. Molesworth looked him up and down. "Yeah, I've seen him around." The boy was six feet tall, long-limbed and square-shouldered, and stood handsomely erect. His shirt sleeves were rolled to the elbows. White socks peeked out beneath his trouser legs. His cap covered a healthy shock of hair, black as jet.

Molesworth was a small man with solemn eyes and a moon-shaped face. He stood five-foot-seven, weighed north of 160, but was one of the fastest men on the team. He trotted over to the boy. "What's yer name, kid?"

"Clarence Ossie Smith, sir, and I can pitch ball."

"I hear you want a tryout." Clarence looked Molesworth in the eye and nodded.

"Do you know this is Class A baseball?" Molesworth glared at him. "You're only a step away from the big leagues. See these men out here? They've been playing professional ball four, five years. Some have already spent time in the big tops. What makes you think you can play for the Birmingham baseball club?"

"I've been playing on the local lots for a few years. I'm in good condition. Everyone says I got a good arm. I got two kinds of curveballs, and I can throw smoke. I've met some of the players on your team, and I'd like to play for you." He paused. "One of these days, I'll be in the big leagues."

"Well, that's fine, that's fine," Molesworth said, studying the boy's face. Just a baby, the manager told himself. Cheeks the color of apples. Not even any peach fuzz on them cheeks. Well, he is good timber. Maybe I can use him.

"How old are you?"

"Just turned eighteen."

"You're too young. Come back next year."

Clarence hung his head. Then, for some reason, Molesworth went soft. "Kid, before you get to the big leagues, you'll have to learn to pitch to my hitters. Be on the field tomorrow for hitting practice. Twelve-thirty. You can shag fly balls.

Clarence Smith grew up in a family of girls on Cotton Avenue in Birmingham. Here he is at home with his seven sisters, parents, and dog in 1908.

No promises, but if your arm's as good as you say, maybe we'll let you throw to some of our hitters."

Clarence ran all the way home. That night he walked the floor. Up and down, up and down, for hours. It is not known how much sleep Clarence got that night — likely very little. He was back at the ball yard early the next day. On the field, the New Orleans Pelicans and their star player, Joe Jackson, were taking batting practice.

Clarence had always loved baseball. Born in Tennessee, he was the third of eight children, the only boy. His father, Bruce, was a carpenter. The family moved to Birmingham when Clarence was ten. About the age of fifteen Clarence began his career as a merchant of the ball yard and became a ball park habitué, a regular. Every afternoon he ran from his home on Cotton Avenue to the Slag Pile to sell Cokes and peanuts, to noodle around and watch the Barons play. He knew the rhythms of the place, and his humble position bought him entrée into the inner circle of the Birmingham Baseball Association.

Clarence marveled at the feats of the stars. Now he'd be working out with the team. No matter that it would only be running down fly balls during practice and picking up stray balls that missed the mitts of careless fielders. All he wanted was an opportunity. And he *would* make the most of this opportunity. Sadly, the gangly boy with jet-black hair and gray eyes had but thirteen years to live.

SOMEONE HOLLERED FROM THE OUTFIELD: "Hey, Pop Boy! I'd take off that there white coat if I was you." It was Molesworth. Clarence ran toward the manager. "Yes, sir! Yes, sir! I wear this when I work in the stands."

"Come here, kid." Molesworth, bat in hand, was hitting fly balls to the far reaches of the park. "Okay, here's what you do. I'll be hitting fungoes to the outfielders, see? You stand with me and take the return throws. No foolishness. Then, when my fellows start their batting practice, you fetch the balls the outfielders don't get to and throw 'em back to the infield. Follow me?"

"Thank you. Thank you. I'll do that, yes, sir."

Roy Ellam, the shortstop, walked up and pulled Clarence out of earshot of the manager. "You certainly have caught Moley's fancy. Let me put you wise to Boss Moley. He can be a little stern sometime, but he's a decent guy—honest as the days are long. The ball players like him, mostly. You will, too, in time."

Ellam was in his second season as shortstop of the Barons. His hair was sandy, almost blond; his face bore a trace of freckles. This "greenhorn," once jeered by the fans for his miscues in the field, had received a trial with the Cincinnati Reds in the final weeks of the season past. The Reds found him to be a sterling performer in the field but an uncertain hitter, so they returned him to the minors. A modest, dignified man, Ellam, through hard work and sunny disposition, was the field leader of the Barons and soon would be appointed team captain.

Across the way, ball players were playing pepper games. One man in particular was making a racket, all smiles, cackling at the top of his voice, flashing about like a hummingbird. It was Earl Fleharty, a jolly sport from somewhere in Kansas.

"Noisy place, ain't it?" Ellam said to Clarence. "It's just Flea, letting off steam. He's the busiest, noisiest guy out here."

Fleharty, a pitcher, twenty-three years old, was a jovial sort. Every day he was batting or pitching or fielding bunts or running about the field, yelling at the top of his voice. You could hear him from the streetcar tracks to the ends of the park. The look of jaunty good humor on Fleharty's face revealed a good-natured, placid, slow-thinking chap. He didn't look much like a pitcher, nor a ball player for that matter. They called him "Flea," though he was portly and vigorous. Fleharty's grin was famous. During his pitching motion, he clenched his teeth and parted his lips into a smile that exposed every molar. He was in his third season with the Barons. His first year, 1908, he was stricken with malaria and missed half the season.

"Flea, shake hands with young Clarence," Ellam said. "Moley's letting him work out with the team."

Pitcher Earl Fleharty displays a menacing look in this picture at West End Park in 1910. "Flea" was one of the noisiest players on the field, his voice heard from the streetcar tracks to the ends of the park. He showed an interest in young Clarence Smith and helped teach him to pitch in 1910.

"Well, well, if it ain't ol' Pop Boy! Put 'er here, ol' top. How's things?" Fleharty stuck out his hand and beamed. "Yeah, I've seen him around in his white coat, totin' his wire basket of peanuts. A big, husky fella he is. He told me he could th'ow the ball. It's good to have another fella to talk to." Fleharty waved his arms excitedly. "We like to make merry around here."

Fleharty razzed the youngster. "Pop Boy, get wise to this: I hear fans complainin' about boys running through the aisles shouting 'Peanuts! Cigars! Chewing gum!' and spilling Cokes on folks. That wuddn't be you, wud it?"

"No, sir, that ain't me. Them's kids doing that. Honest Injun. Cross my heart."

"If you say so. Say, Pop Boy, you going to pitch to us?"

"I hope so. For now, Moley wants me to shag flies."

About then a ball player walked by with a sizable chew of tobacco in his left cheek. "There goes Rowdy Elliott," Fleharty said. "Hey, Rowdy, come say howdy to Pop Boy."

Carlton Molesworth's eyes were round and brown, set in a moon-shaped face. He stood five-seven with a wide girth but was one of the fastest men on the team. Not only was he the Barons manager, he was the team's centerfielder from 1906–1911.

The fans jeered Roy Ellam in his first season with the Barons, 1909. He made bobble after bobble at his shortstop position but was determined to make good. He remained with the Barons for seven seasons. "He always meets people cordially and with marked politeness," said a newspaper reporter in 1912.

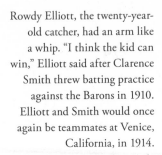

Rowdy Elliott, the twenty-year-old catcher, had an arm like a whip. "I think the kid can win," Elliott said after Clarence Smith threw batting practice against the Barons in 1910. Elliott and Smith would once again be teammates at Venice, California, in 1914.

Rowdy Elliott, a stocky little catcher, just turned twenty, walked by with a businesslike stride. "H'are ya?" He spat out an amber stream and went about his business.

"Pop Boy, you know Rowdy, the kid catcher. Best hind-ketch in the league," Fleharty said. "Tough as a hickory switch. Got a whip tied to that right side. It's absolute suicide for runners to try and steal on him.

"Know what his real name is? Harold. But don't call him that. He styles himself Rowdy. Likes it that way. Got no family. Orphaned at seven, they say. Wouldn't go to no orphanage. Got a job as a newsboy, sellin' papers. I guess it's true—he don't talk about it.

"Pop Boy, you'll not be around a better bunch of fellas. Evenings, we go gadding about with the boys—a picture show, a game of pool. Not a man on this club drinks whiskey. No 'night owls' on this club, no sir. We all foller Moley's rule: Everyone in by eleven-thirty."

" 'Cept you and Rowdy," Roy Ellam said. They all laughed.

"Hey, there's Bob Messenger doing jumping jacks," Fleharty said. "You know him, don't you?"

"Yeah, he's fa-a-ast!" said Clarence.

"I'll say, like a Wisconsin deer. Fastest man in the league, faster'n Jackson even, and that's saying something. He's our rightfielder. A man faster'n him's not been born yet. Blew in here from the Windy City, Chicago. Played for the White Sox. But he ain't no swell-head. Sort of a queer bird, though. I won't bother introducing you. He don't say much. Ain't nothing to do with you — it's just his way.

"You hear about the game at Chattanooga? He hit three infield ground balls and beat out every one of 'em for hits. The catcher let a ball get by, and he scored. From second base!"

From home plate came a loud, ringing sound. Roy Ellam turned to watch the New Orleans Pelicans take pre-game hitting. The batter was centerfielder Joe Jackson, a poorly educated country boy from South Carolina. At present, Jackson was leading the league in hitting at .360, far ahead of second-place Bill McGilvray of the Barons at .324.

"That boy, Jackson, he's a tall, skinny-looking kid," Ellam said, "but he's got a pure, natural swing. Every time he puts his bat on the ball, it's a line drive, a bullet. What a fine base runner, too. He's a born ball player, that fellow."

Joseph Jefferson Jackson would finish the year with the league's highest batting average and advance to the major leagues. He hit .408 for the Cleveland Indians the following season and was on his way to becoming the greatest hitter of his time. Nine years later in 1920, "Shoeless Joe" Jackson was banished forever from organized baseball for helping the Chicago White Sox throw the 1919 World Series. Many, however, declared he was a gullible victim.

CLARENCE FINISHED THE DAY RUNNING down balls in the outfield as the Barons took batting practice. Molesworth couldn't help but notice the fine arm Clarence displayed, firing baseballs from the deepest parts of the field.

"Pop Boy! Be ready tomorrow!" Molesworth commanded in a voice like the snap of a whip. "I need another arm. You'll be in the box tomorrow against my hitters."

Clarence looked at Roy Ellam with eyes round and large. His heart jumped. Oh, golly!

Then Molesworth motioned to Clarence: Come with me. They went under the stands, and Molesworth pulled out a trunk from storage. Inside were remnants of seasons past: old, worn uniforms — shirts, pants, socks, caps. He gave Clarence a mismatched set of rumpled but serviceable pants, tattered shirt, and weathered cap.

Eagerly, Clarence jammed the cap squarely on his head and tried on the scratchy wool pants. Jiminy Chrismus, these trousers must be from 1906, he thought. The legs of the bloomers had long since lost their elastic and hung to his ankles, covering a pair of frayed, blue baseball stockings, but Clarence liked the way the clothing hung on his frame. He looked smart in the new uniform. He threw back his head and straightened his shoulders. He puffed out his chest. "There, now, look at me," he whispered with a broad smile. "Oh, you are a dandy." And he sallied forth in all his glory.

BATTING PRACTICE THE NEXT DAY. Arthur (Lil) Marcan, second baseman, awaited the pitch. "Put it over, kid, if you want to stay on that mound."

Clarence reared back and with a flourish of arms and legs threw his best high hard one. The ball, white and whirling, exploded into the mitt with a report like a rifle. "A little high," Marcan said uneasily, with a peek at the pitcher. Some of the Barons, with tanned faces, were sitting on their heels just off the infield, batting the breeze. "You can't hit 'em when you can't see 'em!" one laughed.

Clarence fired again. The ball had a jump on it. With a compact stroke, Marcan hit a dribbler down the third-base line. Marcan was a clever fielder and a foxy base runner with a head full of baseball brains but not much of a hitter. He was the Barons leadoff man and the first of five straight M's in the batting order: Marcan, Messenger, Molesworth, McBride, and McGilvray.

The ball players blistered the Barons second baseman: "C'mon, Lil! You can do better'n that! The kid's a busher! Hit the ol' apple!"

Many wondered how "Lil" Marcan got his nickname. Some thought it was because of his size. Others said "Lil" was a pet name. Actually, Herman (Germany) Schaefer was responsible. Schaefer was a ball player—a showman and a clown of the diamond from 1900 to 1918. Once, while playing a game in the rain, he wore a raincoat over his uniform. Schaefer was a teammate of a young Marcan on the St. Paul ball club in 1903 when the team stopped for the night on the road. Schaefer registered the players at the hotel. Pen in hand, he wrote the name of a girl in front of each man's last name: Mildred, Lizzie, Agnes, Hortense. In front of Marcan, he put "Lil." The newspapermen found out, and from then on, Arthur Marcan was "Lil."

Marcan spit on his hands and grabbed a handful of dirt. Clarence went into his windup and reached way back for his fast one. The ball had a fancy hop as it flashed across the dish. Marcan hit a flare just over the infield. Disgusted, he tossed his bat and shook his head: "Sonofagun!" Bill McGilvray, the balding first baseman, jumped in. He was Large William—standing six feet tall, big for

Bill McGilvray, "Large William," was six feet tall, large for his day. In 1910, he placed second in the Southern Association in batting behind "Shoeless Joe" Jackson of New Orleans.

his time. A mountain climber, he had been up and down Pikes Peak and Mount Shasta.

Clarence didn't have much of a windup. Most pitchers of the day pumped their arms—once, twice, three times—then brought the ball high above their head, kicked their leg high, and delivered the pitch. Not Clarence. He took the ball in his right hand, looked at it curiously for a moment, then reared back and threw.

Large William reached in his hip pocket for a pouch of Star Navy. He removed a walnut-sized jaw full of scrap, calmly placed it in his cheek, and stepped in to hit. Clarence eyed McGilvray from the pitcher's box, oozing confidence, his faded cap resting on the side of his head. He threw McGilvray a dandy, looping curve that bounced in the dirt. Swing and a miss. "Now you pitchin', Pop Boy!" Earl Fleharty shouted.

McGilvray eyed the ball he had missed and looked at Clarence. A corking good pitch, he thought. On it went. Bob Messenger, the rightfielder, took his turn—Silent Bob from Farmingdale, Maine, a bookkeeper in the off-season, one of the quietest men in baseball. Then came Harry Coveleski, a side-wheeling, lefthanded pitcher, fluent in English, Polish, German, and Italian, and one of five baseball-playing brothers. Clarence threw assorted curves. He threw his fastball with jazzy speed. One by one, the batters banged away, but no one could hit him — at least not well.

For days after, Earl Fleharty showed a sporting interest in the youngster. With a critical eye, Fleharty told him to throw fastballs, slow balls, breaking balls, and changes of speed. "Pop Boy, you gotta understand, the ball's gotta do something at the last instant— hop, slide, sink, or sail. The best pitchers in the world are those speedy fellows who've got a jump on their fastballs. Even if the batter knows they're gonna th'ow a fastball, the ball will jump different each time. And your curve has'ta break sharp, not hang over the plate. It's gotta *snap* across the plate. If it stays flat an' hangs . . . well that ball'll look as big as mother's washtub and, believe you me, the batter'll just kill it. Roughly translated, I'm sayin' you gotta mix—up—your—pitches. Git me?"

"Yes, sir," Clarence said. He was all ears.

Fleharty pointed to his noggin. "What I'm saying is this: Use the ol' noodle, and your arm will do the rest. Th'ow the ball in, out, high, low, fast, slow. Th'ow overhand, three-quarter overhand, sidearm. Take a little off the ball, then add to your fastball. You gotta have brains in your arm as well as your head.

"You have a queer windup, but I wouldn't change that, no how." Fleharty mimicked Clarence's habit of looking at the ball and throwing quickly with barely a windup. "Your motion's different from ever'one else's, and it'll fool hitters. The ball gets on 'em fast, and they're not ready for it."

Then he ordered: "Take hold of this here baseball. Now lemme see how you hold your fastball." Clarence put the first three fingers of his right hand across the seams of the ball.

"Whassat? Chris', that's how you th'ow the ball? With three fingers? You can't control the ball holding it like that, and if you can't get it over the plate, you're a goner. Two fingers! Two fingers across the ball! As we say back in Kansas, 'Put them words of wisdom in your saddlebags and you'll be all the wiser.'"

Clarence listened to every word the man said. "Thank you. Yes, thank you, I'll do that."

The season of 1910 was drawing to a close, and for the first time in four years, the Barons were in a pennant race. A new ball park, Rickwood Field, had been under construction for four months. On August 13, the Barons would play their final game at West End Park. Five days later they moved into Rickwood Field, and Birmingham went baseball mad.

CHAPTER 2

A NEW BALL PARK

ON SUNDAY MORNING, AUGUST 14, 1910, the league standings showed New Orleans, Atlanta, and Birmingham, first–second–third, in a close race. Two weeks prior, star pitcher Harry Coveleski, the Mighty Pole, had pitched a no-hitter. Now, baseball was the leading topic in the home and on the street, among young and old, male and female, black and white. Birmingham was baseball mad.

The Barons had last won the Southern Association championship in 1906. For three years, 1907–08–09, the team had been out of the league race from the drop of the flag. For three years, the team had been shattered and torn by adverse fortune, a beaten club even before it took the field. The club owners had lost money year after year. Fans grumbled about Manager Carlton Molesworth, criticized the performance of the team, griped about the ball park, West End Park—the Slag Pile. In their hearts, fans were convinced they were tied to a hopeless loser. Three straight years near the bottom of the standings will do that to a populace. A winning team was a fancy, a nice thing to read about but never to happen.

The year 1910 broke fresh and fair. The team would soon change owners. A new ball park was promised. Better ball players would be forthcoming. But winter's goodbye still lingered in the air. Fans remembered the gray, cheerless yesterdays—three years of dark and dismal failure. They still doubted; they had to be shown. In the spring of 1910, a few faithful fans journeyed to West End Park to watch the Barons play their customary exhibition games against big league teams. "Well, I know we're overmatched, but I'll see what they have," they said.

The first game was a victory for the Barons. "Freak of nature," said the scoffers. "The game was thrown," said the detractors. Over two weeks against big-leaguers, the Barons won three exhibition games, lost two, and tied one. "Yes, but it was against their backup players," said the doubters. And it was true, the big-leaguers had played their rookies, mostly. Then the New York Giants came to town, playing their regular lineup and throwing two of the best pitchers in the business: Christy Mathewson and Rube Marquard. The Barons lost honorably, 1–0. "H'm, might be something to these fellows," said the optimists. "We said that last year," said the wary. "Wait," said the wise.

THAT SUNDAY AFTERNOON, AUGUST 14, 1910, thousands of people rode streetcars to Rickwood Field. It didn't matter that a game wasn't being played, that not a single player was on the field. The people simply sat in the splendid new grandstand and watched the final stages of construction, as men with hoes—not bats—toiled on the diamond, preparing the new ball park for its opening game, four days away. In New Orleans on this Sunday afternoon, the Barons, gunning for their seventh straight win, were playing the league leaders, the New Orleans Pelicans. Coveleski was pitching.

In 1910—ten years before radio—people kept abreast of events through word on the street and over the grapevine. As scores came in by telegraph wire, inning by inning from New Orleans, Western Union messenger boys dashed hither and yon, bearing the news to eager throngs in barbershops, cigar stores, drugstores, and hotels.

"Birmingham leading New Orleans, 1–0, in the first inning!" cried the messenger boys, and the town shook with applause. Interest was high, and when people with telephones learned the news, they passed it on, friend to friend. Others attended baseball "matinees," with an announcer re-creating the game from telegraph reports. Birmingham's announcer for many years, Melvin (Commodore) Orcutt, was calling today's game at the Virginia Theatre on First Avenue North. Messenger boys rushed breathlessly through the streets, updating those not at the matinee:

"Birmingham, 2–0, third inning!" one screamed.

"Birmingham, two more in the sixth!"

In the seventh inning: "Rowdy Elliott triples, and Ellam scores, 5–0."

"Birmingham, four more in the ninth, 9–0."

And moments later: "Birmingham wins, 9–3! Coveleski beats Hess."

The final result, with meager details, was lettered over mirrors, windows, and walls in stores and offices for those who hadn't heard.

"Birmingham is baseball wild," declared a local newspaper. "The reason is apparent. Birmingham is now playing magnificent ball, is in a position to threaten those just above, and is making a strenuous dash for the pennant. And there is another reason. Birmingham is about to open formally and dedicate its new and magnificent baseball plant."

One morning back in mid-July, a reporter with *The Age-Herald* newspaper visited the three directors of the Birmingham Baseball Association: owner Rick Woodward, President Robert Baugh, and Treasurer W. D. Smith. The reporter, Hugh Roberts, sat down with Woodward and his two lieutenants. "So what shall we call the new field?" Roberts asked. "The sporting writers have not agreed, and it is probable that they could not." Messrs. Woodward, Baugh, and Smith looked at one another but they, too, could not agree on a name.

"Leave it to the fans," suggested Mr. Woodward.

"Yes," agreed Mr. Baugh. "Tell them through *The Age-Herald* to suggest names to the paper and from the list received, a suitable one will be selected."

Done. And two days later the new ball park had a name: Rickwood Field, cleverly uniting the first and last names of owner Rick Woodward. The name *Rickwood* was accepted from nearly two hundred proposals and was the only one that received more than one vote. It was suggested by four different people.

"The name won by popular vote," Roberts wrote. "It is very appropriate, and it sounds well. And it is a compliment to the man who made the park possible, Rick Woodward."

IN THE OPENING OF THIS book, I introduced you to Charles Stewart, the man who befriended me on the first day of the 1931 Dixie Series at Rickwood Field. Stewart loved Rickwood, yet he considered West End Park—the Slag Pile—a dead swell ball park. He attended many games there as a young sport. I can see him now recalling those days, jabbing his cane into the ground and crying: "Oh-ho, what slapdash maneuverings went on at the old Slag Pile! How we jollied one another and razzed the umpire—threw pop bottles at him, hooted him off the field, made him run for his life. It carries a fellow back, those days."

The old West End Park sat right next to Alice Furnace, a pair of pig iron blast furnaces. From the stands, one could almost feel the heat, could almost see the gurgling, glowing metal, could almost hear the sizzling white-hot pig iron, could almost smell the coal smoke, the gases, the fumes. Alice Furnace doesn't exist anymore, but the heat, the noise, the smell Stewart never forgot. He told me:

"Nowadays, whenever I'm a-walking past a mill and the smoky smell gets in my nose, it takes me back to the days of the Slag Pile. We were a city of thirty thousand then. I drove a carriage to the ball games—out dusty First Avenue—and parked on the ball grounds. Sometimes I took the wife, and we'd stop for a picnic along the way. I was just a young man then . . ."

West End Park was a humble, wooden affair. Home to the Barons from 1896 to 1910, it was located on the western edge of Birmingham near the juncture of First Avenue North and Seventh Street, adjacent to the tracks of the Alabama Great Southern Railroad. A mountain of rock-like slag from Alice Furnace was the dominant feature of the site, hence the name Slag Pile.

The Slag Pile had a wooden grandstand behind home plate and bleachers along the first- and third-base lines. In the beginning, the grandstand seated six hundred spectators. Including the bleachers, seating capacity was around two thousand. In 1903, the capacity was expanded to thirty-five hundred. A portion of the grandstand was reserved for ladies and their escorts; smoking was not permitted in that section. Beyond the outfield fence were railroad tracks. An occasional train, pulled by an Alabama Great Southern engine, would pass behind the leftfield fence, travel toward rightfield, and move off into the distance. Sometimes the puffing engine would come to a halt, and the railroad men would glance at the scoreboard, watch the game for a bit, and wave to the players. On the other side of the tracks was a mountain of hardened, gray slag, maybe five hundred feet in length. Viewed from behind home plate, the pile of slag

On Birmingham's western edge, near First Avenue North and Seventh Street, stood West End Park, the "Slag Pile," home of the Barons from 1896–1910.

was immense, extending from rightfield to centerfield to leftfield and beyond—all the way to the Alice Furnace. Though the slag pile was distant from the grandstand, one could usually make out faint figures of spectators watching the game from Mount Slag.

Slag was a byproduct of the iron-making process of the Alice blast furnaces. Through the years, railcar loads of red-hot slag had been poured onto this site, like lava from a volcano. A busy little yard engine would push a carload of molten slag up the hardened slag pile and unload its brilliant, yellow-orange haul. Nighttime, it was a wondrous sight. Liquid fire rolled down the slag heap, flames leapt high, and the black sky turned brilliant red. After cooling and hardening, the slag turned a dull gray.

Hugh Roberts, the *Age-Herald* reporter, called it a "shack of a grandstand," West End Park. By 1910, as Clarence (Pop Boy) Smith was pitching batting practice to the Barons, the wooden stands were rotting and dilapidated. Roberts wrote on the eve of the final contest: "Every fan should go to the game with a hammer for the destruction of the present stand. When the park is deserted not a single plank should be left standing. That pile has stood too long already."

In the distance is Alice Furnace, which produced the mountain of rock-like slag beyond the outfield fence. Spectators often watched games from Mount Slag.

But the dreamer would say this spot was hallowed ground, that West End Park glistened with musty but beautiful memories of the past. Cy Young pitched on these grounds in 1910 at the age of forty-three. Connie Mack managed his Philadelphia Athletics here early in his fifty-year career. The Chicago Cubs of Tinker, Evers, and Chance appeared in 1908, nineteen-year-old Ty Cobb in 1906, Christy Mathewson in 1905. Other immortals, revered by baseball purists, strolled the stage: Jack Chesbro and Wee Willie Keeler of the New York Highlanders, John McGraw, Rube Marquard, and "Iron Man" Joe McGinnity of the New York Giants, Napoleon Lajoie of the Cleveland Indians, Rube Waddell of the Athletics, Mordecai (Three-Finger) Brown of the Cubs. On and on.

WEST END PARK WAS SITUATED on low ground, and after a hard rain, the playing field and environs were covered in water. Those who didn't arrive at the park on horseback or by wagon came by streetcar. From the streetcar stop on First Avenue, patrons approached the grounds over a board walkway three hundred feet in length. In later years there was no boardwalk, and after a rain, mud and water were shoe-top deep. From the open, muddy terrain, customers walked to the park gate through a narrow alleyway, their hats and bonnets bobbing up and down. White patrons purchased tickets from a booth in the alley. Black folks bought theirs some distance away, where they conveniently entered the colored bleachers.

The grandstand at West End Park did not contain built-in seating. Spectators sat on board seats without backs, sweating and howling, eating peanuts, and drinking Celery-Cola, a celery-flavored drink manufactured on Morris Avenue in Birmingham. Those who paid an extra twenty-five cents could get a wooden chair in the grandstand behind home plate. Carriages were parked along the foul line in leftfield, and players scrambled around buggy wheels and horses' legs to field balls hit in that direction.

Overflow crowds were great for boys who hung around the park. The boys rented chairs to spectators, good ones going for half a dollar and those of three legs for a quarter. They peddled soap boxes—for sitting or for standing—to the highest bidder, usually for fifteen cents. When the supply of chairs was exhausted, the boys borrowed chairs from nearby homes and rented them for a profit. When every seat in every stand was occupied, men and boys would jump the railings and romp across the diamond to find standing room, a tide of humanity encircling the field. Police were on hand to preserve order, but they were fans themselves, and as long as there was no violence, they paid little heed to what was done or said.

The crowd rooted vigorously for the home team, and if the umpire made a decision with which fans didn't agree, they let him know it. In fact, it would be fair to say the fans aided the umpire in making decisions, and in those days there was only one umpire.

Here's what happened one day in 1902: A Chattanooga batter, Ike Durrett, hit a ball back to the Birmingham pitcher, who threw to first base to retire the batter. While the out was being made, Bert Myers, who was on second base, raced for home, cutting the corner at third and missing the bag by fifteen feet. The umpire did not see Myers miss third because he was watching the play at first, and Myers scored. The Birmingham catcher argued that Myers' run should not count, and players on both teams joined in the argument. A crowd from the grandstand went onto the field to "give testimony," arguing mightily that the runner did not touch third base. Umpire Joe Burke consulted the official scorer, who stated that the runner missed third. Burke thought and thought about what to do. He made several propositions, none of which pleased either team. Birmingham would accept only that the runner was out; Chattanooga insisted he was safe. For an hour, the umpire tried to effect a compromise. Finally, he called Myers out for failing to touch third base. This pleased the crowd—they cheered and marched back into the stands.

The crowd jumped another umpire in a game that season. Birmingham second baseman Frank Delahanty hit a ball deep into the outfield and ran all the way to third base for what appeared to be a triple. In his haste to round the bases, Delahanty failed to touch first base, and the umpire called him out. Cries of "robbery" and "mob him" rang out as excited men poured onto the field from the bleachers. Policemen and ball players ran out to meet the onrushing throng. After a brief quarrel, the fans retreated to the stands, at which point Delahanty walked to the plate and confessed to the crowd that he had not touched first base and that the umpire was correct in calling him out.

At the turn of the 1900s, baseball was an uncertain enterprise in the South. Every penny counted; a ball club's finances did not permit extras. A team usually consisted of four pitchers, two catchers, four infielders, and three outfielders. The team's equipment consisted of one catcher's mitt, thirteen bats, thirteen uniforms, three bags for the bases, and a handful of baseballs. The Slag Pile had no dugouts; players sat on board benches—one board long enough for thirteen men to crowd upon in the broiling sun with a keg of water spiked with lemon juice. One of the Birmingham players was an enthusiastic rightfielder named Walt Sorber. One day in 1902, an Atlanta batter hit a ball over the fence for a home run, but Sorber didn't give up. He ran through the wooden fence, taking two boards with him, and had the ball back in the hands of the catcher before the batter reached home. The hit, nevertheless, was ruled a home run.

The same year death visited West End Park. A violent rainstorm erupted before .
the start of a game, forcing spectators and ball players under the bleachers. A rush
of wind rocked the bleachers. Moments later another gust hurled the stand to the
ground, reducing it to a mass of timbers. Back of the bleachers flowed a stream
that the rain had swelled to a raging torrent. A newspaper boy, George Swanton,
was thrown into the stream and pinned beneath the water by the timbers. Ball
players and spectators rushed to his rescue but too late. His body was laid upon
the players' bench until his people could be notified.

Club management tried to keep the infield of West End Park in fairly good
condition, but little or no attention was paid the outfield. Every penny the club
took in was needed to meet payroll and other expenses—there was no money in the
treasury to spend on leveling the outfield or mowing grass and weeds, which often
reached the players' knees. Only when play in the high grass became impossible did
the outfield get attention.

One day in 1898, a visiting player hit a ball just out of reach of the Birmingham
shortstop, a red-haired boy from Cincinnati named Edward Gilligan. Grass a few
inches high covered the field back of the basepaths, and Gilligan could not find the
ball. The batsman was circling the bases with great speed, and Gilligan was frantic.
His teammates, seeing him kicking around in the grass, came to his aid. Finally,
Gilligan found the ball lodged in a crawfish hole—hundreds of such holes were
scattered about the field. As Gilligan was digging the ball out of the hole, the runner
was hustling from second base and rounding third. By the time Gilligan could
recover and throw the ball, the runner had made it all the way home. He had made
a home run on a ball hit to the shortstop position.

By 1909, the fans were clamoring for a new park. "It's a barn," they grumbled.
Hoping to keep people happy, management promised a new ball park before the
beginning of the next baseball season.

A FORTUITOUS EVENT OCCURRED FOR the Birmingham Baseball Association when
industrialist A. H. Woodward offered to buy controlling interest of the team
from J. W. McQueen, vice president of Sloss-Sheffield Steel and Iron Company.
Woodward made his offer before the end of the year 1909, then went to Orlando,
Florida, to spend the winter with his family. McQueen debated Woodward's offer
and in January 1910 sent Woodward a telegram accepting his terms.

The name of the Barons new owner was A. H. Woodward, but if you called him
that, no one would know whom you were talking about. Allan Harvey Woodward
was known to friends and acquaintances as "Rick." As a young boy, he had been
extremely interested in the mysteries of the needlecraft "rickrack," so his father
began calling him "Rickrack," the name eventually being shortened to Rick. Rick

Rick Woodward was 33 when he purchased the Barons in January 1910. He immediately made plans to build a new ball park of concrete and steel to replace West End Park. Woodward liked to don a uniform, put a mitt on his hand, and toss a ball with the players before watching the game from the dugout. His father was not sympathetic with Rick's pet hobby at first, but he, too, eventually became a fan.

Woodward, a mining engineer by profession, was vice president of the Woodward Iron Company. He was thirty-three years old and one of the wealthiest men in Birmingham. While in Orlando, Woodward began making plans to build a new ball park, not of wood but of concrete and steel.

The Birmingham News remarked, "The Birmingham Baseball Association, by the change in ownership, has more money behind it than any other association in the Southern League or any other minor league. The franchise is now in the hands of a man with lots of money and a man who will not mind spending money to put in a good team. He is a real sportsman and wants results." Suddenly, as if by magic, baseball spirit had been revived in Birmingham, and old-time fans were talking baseball again.

When the sale of the team was completed, newspapers across the South were anxious for a photograph of the new millionaire owner. No one in town had one. *The News* mailed a letter to Woodward in Orlando requesting a picture. "I haven't a photograph to my name," Woodward answered, "and, anyhow, the fans would rather see a winning ball team than to see my picture in the paper." Woodward arrived back in Birmingham on the last day of February 1910. He immediately went to Pittsburgh to inspect the latest in ball park construction.

In the major leagues, wooden ball parks of earlier days were giving way to massive structures of concrete and steel. In 1909, Connie Mack's Philadelphia Athletics moved into a new home, Shibe Park, which had a covered grandstand and uncovered bleachers down the left- and rightfield foul lines. Later that year, Forbes Field opened in Pittsburgh, also with a covered grandstand. Woodward patterned his proposed ball park after Forbes Field. He also received valuable suggestions from Mack, including how to arrange the seats for the best view of the field and how to configure the diamond to minimize the sun in players' faces.

The Barons new estate, Rickwood Field, would be located on two streetcar lines—the south Ensley and the north Bessemer—and was a twelve-minute ride from the heart of the city. The new grandstand accommodated three thousand spectators—twenty-five hundred in chair seats and five hundred in box seats. The bleachers seated another two thousand for a total capacity of five thousand. Grandstand seating would be in movable "opera chairs," not the uncomfortable, tacky neighborhood chairs of West End Park.

Rick Woodward's father, Joseph, a wealthy capitalist and financier, did not sympathize with his son's pet hobby, baseball. Rick had played on the college baseball team at the Massachusetts Institute of Technology in the late 1890s and, after coming home to Birmingham, played on a team sponsored by the Birmingham Athletic Club. A few years later, he organized what he called "a real crackerjack ball club" for his company, Woodward Iron, in the Birmingham City League. The elder Mr. Woodward felt that baseball had hampered Rick's college studies and would do the same for his business career. His father went to the first game at Rickwood Field, "mostly to jeer," Rick recalled, but eventually became a believer in Rick's enterprise and rarely missed a game.

"It happened this way," said Woodward. "The opening day arrived, and my father decided he'd go and see what I had done and what was happening, so he went out to Rickwood Field. At that time there was no netting in front of the grandstand, and I recall how nervous he was and that [pitchers] Earl Fleharty and Lou Bauer stood, one at the right of him and the other at the left, with mitts on, ready to protect him if a ball came that way." Soon after, the elder Mr. Woodward consulted with his son regarding Rick's investment in the ball park, on which he owed more than $60,000. When Rick told him that he would have to sell bonds bearing seven percent interest to meet the obligation, Mr. Woodward offered to buy the bonds, much to Rick's relief.

Before there could be a Rickwood Field, a final game would be played in the shadow of the Slag Pile. On Saturday, August 13, 1910, Birmingham hosted

Mobile in front of an overflow crowd at West End Park. Down in a box seat in the grandstand, Rick Woodward was pulling on a cigar. Woodward cheered loudly early in the game, as Rowdy Elliott singled to score Clyde McBride, giving Birmingham a 1–0 lead.

In the sixth inning, Carlton Molesworth stood at third base, hands on hips, his breath whistling. The Barons manager and centerfielder had just spanked a triple into the high grass of deep centerfield. Molesworth then watched McBride take a firm toehold in the batter's box, lash his hickory stick, and deliver a single. Molesworth crossed home plate, scoring the final run at West End Park, as the Barons won, 3–0. Hugh Roberts observed that "there were no tears shed when the game was over and the last shout had reverberated from beneath that miserable pile of weatherboarding. Tomorrow the carpenters begin the destruction of the old grandstand. It gives way to progress and enterprise."

Five days later, Rickwood Field, the finest ball park in the southern states, opened its doors.

CHAPTER 3

RICKWOOD FIELD OPENS

ON THE AFTERNOON OF THURSDAY, August 18, 1910, downtown Birmingham was deserted. Merchants large and small had closed their doors. City Hall was closed. Doctors, lawyers, butchers, plumbers, barbers — everybody — all closed for the afternoon. Nearly eleven thousand people abandoned the business district. It was the biggest day in the history of the young city, as men, women, and children of all colors journeyed to Rickwood Field. The Montgomery Climbers provided the opposition. Coveleski would pitch.

At three o'clock, an hour before game time, practically every seat in the magnificent grandstand and bleachers was taken. And these bleachers and grandstand were of concrete and steel, not dilapidated weatherboarding. A pep band kept the crowd spirited, as players of both teams took warmup swings and tosses. The whole of Birmingham had turned out, it seemed. The park was crowded, impossibly crowded. Spectators were on the field looking for places to stand or sit. Already the crowd was larger than that of any day, ever, at old West End Park, yet streetcars brimming with people still arrived.

At three-thirty, it was time to dedicate the park. The formal exercises were simple; there was little pomp or ceremony. Judge William Kavanaugh, president of the Southern Association, spoke of the new ball park as "the finest home of baseball in the Southland and one of the finest in the world." He christened the grounds by pouring champagne on home plate from a silver loving cup. Manager Molesworth was called forward and awarded the loving cup by the Birmingham Baseball Association. The club also presented him with a silver-handled walking cane that he might "use in his old days when he is unable to play baseball." The band roared "Dixie" and bedlam broke loose.

The weather was oppressively warm that August afternoon: ninety degrees, not a cloud in sight, not a breeze stirring. An enterprising advertiser had distributed paper fans to all. With eleven thousand people elbow to elbow, constantly moving and waving fans, the arena looked like breaking waves on a stormy sea. The playing field, covered with new sod, was still rough. Workmen had labored throughout the day with rakes, brooms, wheelbarrows, smoothing and rolling the infield, and continued doing so until the moment the game began. Playing conditions were acceptable—the players would commit no errors this day. Fully four thousand spectators were standing along the foul lines and in the outfield, well back of the outfielders. Spectators on the playing field had sun in their faces, but none left their positions. Packed and jammed into the stands and on the field, the crowd shouted "Play ball!"

The starting pitcher for the Montgomery Climbers was old Bill Duggleby, age thirty-six, not old as a man is old, but old in baseball years. Three years before, Duggleby had been a major-leaguer. Now he was back in the minors, nearing the end of his trail. Birmingham's pitcher was lefthander Harry Coveleski, age twenty-four. An ardent Catholic, Coveleski attended six o'clock Mass every Sunday morning and High Mass if there were no Sunday game.

In 1908, Coveleski had been a central figure in the National League pennant race. He had been called up by the Philadelphia Phillies late in September from a minor league team in Lancaster, Pennsylvania, and was asked to start three ball games against the New York Giants in the season's final days. The Giants were in first place, tied with the Chicago Cubs. In his first start on September 29, Harry Coveleski shut out the Giants, 7–0. Two days later he beat them, 6–2. Two days after that, he defeated the great Christy Mathewson, striking out the final batter in the ninth inning with the tying runner at third base. It was his third win against the Giants in five days, and almost single-handedly Harry Coveleski had prevented the Giants from winning the pennant. Forever after, he would be known as the "Giant Killer."

Back with Philadelphia the following season, 1909, Coveleski lost ten of sixteen games, and the Phillies traded him to Cincinnati. He opened the 1910 season pitching in seven games for Cincinnati with marginal results. In May of that year, Birmingham was in the market for ball players, and new owner Rick Woodward purchased Coveleski from Cincinnati for $1,000. He joined the team one month into the season—three months before the opening game at Rickwood Field.

HARRY COVELESKI WAS BORN HARRY Frank Kowalewski in 1886, in Shamokin, Pennsylvania, one of five sons of Polish immigrants. His father worked as a coal

In 1910, Harry Coveleski had perhaps the greatest season of a Birmingham pitcher, before or since. He pitched eight shutouts and a no-hit game and completed every game he started except one. His record of 21–10 included five losses by scores of 1–0 and another by 2–0. Only twice did opposing teams score more than three runs against him.

miner, and Harry left school at the age of twelve to work in the mines, as did his brothers. In the late 1800s and early 1900s, millions of people from southern and eastern Europe had come to the United States to work in mines and factories and to toil as unskilled laborers. Baseball would be enriched by the sons of these Slavic and Italian émigrés, as it had been by Irish and German immigrants years before. Young Harry was a slate picker and a "donkey boy," driving mules with supplies into and out of the mines. Sitting on a pine board, he worked from seven in the morning until seven at night, six days a week, separating coal from rock and slate. He earned three dollars and seventy-five cents a week, an average of five cents an hour.

In the coal mines of eastern Pennsylvania, life was short, mean, and largely without prospects. There was nothing unusual about a twelve-year-old Polish boy working in the mines for seventy-two hours a week. What is remarkable is that Harry and his brothers ever got out of there. Harry's younger brother, Stanley, a Hall of Fame pitcher, said, "I couldn't play much baseball because I never saw the sunlight. Most of the year I went to work in the dark and came home in the dark. Never knew the sun came up any day but Sunday." When he came home from work, Stanley Coveleski would "put a tin can on a log, or tie it to a tree, and stand maybe forty or fifty feet away and throw stones at it." More than likely, brother Harry did the same thing.

The sons of immigrants who made good in baseball escaped the poverty of the mines and achieved the American dream. Indeed, four of the Coveleski brothers would play pro ball; the fifth brother, Jake, died in the Spanish-American War. After his stirring performance as the Giant Killer in 1908, Harry Coveleski went home to Pennsylvania a local hero and worked the off-season as a laborer in the mine.

Harry fell into professional baseball almost by accident. Pitching for the Bunker Hills, a sandlot team in his hometown of Shamokin, he was spotted by a scout for the St. Louis Cardinals and signed to a contract to play for the Kane, Pennsylvania, club in 1907. The league disbanded before the year was out, and Harry joined an independent team, the Wildwood, New Jersey, Ottens, where his brother, John, played infield. There, Harry drew the attention of the Philadelphia Phillies, who in September 1907 signed him to a contract for $250 a month. A year later he became the Giant Killer.

In the first game at Rickwood Field, the two pitchers, Birmingham's Coveleski and Montgomery's Duggleby, dueled for the first five innings without allowing a run. To open the bottom of the sixth, old Bill Duggleby hit second baseman Lil Marcan with a pitch. A sacrifice bunt failed, and Marcan remained at first base. Next up, Carlton Molesworth crashed a drive into the crowd standing in right centerfield for two bases. Marcan made a desperate play to score from first base but was out at the plate. Clyde McBride then delivered a double down the rightfield foul line to score Molesworth with the first run of the game and the first run ever at Rickwood Field. The crowd had been waiting to explode and did so when Molesworth scored. Thousands of men and women rose to their feet and roared "like an angry lion in its cage." They beat drums, rang bells, and pounded chairs with pop bottles. The vibrations rocked the new stadium. In the space of five days, Molesworth, the team's manager and centerfielder, had scored the final run at West End Park and the first run at Rickwood Field.

Montgomery, however, came back in the top of the seventh, tying the score, 1–1. In the top of the ninth, Montgomery threatened again. Derrill Pratt, who had grown up in nearby Pell City, came to bat with a runner on second base. Pratt hit a long fly ball down the rightfield line, and the crowd held its breath. The Barons rightfielder, Bob Messenger, made a long run and appeared to catch the ball but disappeared into the crowd in foul territory. Messenger later said he caught the ball but stumbled over a spectator sitting on the ground. The umpire ruled that Messenger had dropped the ball. The base runner scored, and Pratt went to second base.

Montgomery now had a 2–1 lead and was threatening for more. The next batter hit a screamer, the ball a streak of white headed for rightfield. First baseman Bill McGilvray leapt high—impossibly so—and speared the ball. The play saved a run and ended the threat. Still, the Barons were down, 2–1, going into the bottom of the ninth. Birmingham players took their seats on the bench, waiting to bat. Players and fans, both, were disheartened by the events of the day, particularly by Messenger's falling into the crowd. One fellow in the stands directly behind the bench complained loudly, hoping Messenger would hear him: "Coveleski would win all his games if the other players would support him." Coveleski turned to Messenger and said, "I know you caught the ball, but if you had only come out sooner everything would have been alright." At that point, the spectators got noisy again. Coveleski and Messenger, after more words between them, jumped to their feet and exchanged blows. Manager Molesworth and others separated them, and almost immediately the two players shook hands. Then the Barons attempted to win the game.

Clyde McBride was the first batter in the bottom of the ninth, and Bill Duggleby hit him with a fastball. McGilvray hit a bouncer to the third baseman, who tried, but failed, to get McBride at second—runners now at first and second. Rowdy Elliott bunted, sending the base runners to second and third, and the crowd was up and yelling wildly. Roy Ellam followed with a perfect bunt on a squeeze play, scoring McBride and tying the game. The next batter followed with another beautiful bunt, and McGilvray dashed home with the winning run.

The grandstand resounded with the shouts of thousands of delighted fans. No one in Birmingham had seen so many people at a ball game before. Some five thousand people were seated in the stands, with a like number on the playing field, a mass of perspiring humanity. Now the great throng was charging for the exits like a mighty army storming the trenches. A daunting sight it must have been. All these people, and each one hoping to be first in line to take the streetcar home.

For Birmingham, it was a crowning day. The crowd had been large, the game had been won, and the team was in a pennant race. Rickwood Field had been fittingly opened.

THE SEASON OF 1910 WAS a marvelous one for Harry Coveleski. When he joined the Barons in mid-May, the team was in seventh place. He won five of his first six starts—in essence, challenging his teammates to "follow me." And indeed, the Barons did. Following Coveleski's lead, they climbed to sixth place, to fifth, to fourth, to third. After opening Rickwood Field, they won sixteen of the next twenty games to move into second place behind New Orleans, and that is where they would finish.

In late summer with his team in the pennant race, Coveleski won eleven straight games. His season record was twenty-one victories and ten defeats. Five losses were by scores of 1–0, another by 2–0. In only two games did he allow the opposing team to score more than three runs. He completed every game he started but one. He pitched eight shutouts. He threw a no-hit game. He threw a second no-hitter for nine innings but lost the game after allowing a hit in the tenth inning. One could argue that never, ever—before or since—has there been a better performance by a Birmingham pitcher in a single season.

BY THE END OF 1910, Manager Carlton Molesworth had turned the ball club in a winning direction. He now had a team in place that would challenge the best teams in the league year after year. Of the bedrock players—Bill McGilvray, Rowdy Elliott, Roy Ellam, Clyde McBride, Lil Marcan, Bob Messenger, and Molesworth himself—all but Elliott remained with the club for most of the next four years. Molesworth retired as a full-time player in 1911 at the age of thirty-five but continued as manager for the next ten years. With his keen judgment of young ball players and owner Rick Woodward's purchases of seasoned players such as Coveleski, the Barons would finish first, second, or third in the league for eight straight seasons. Birmingham baseball fans no longer shuddered at the arrival of each new baseball season. They lost their fear and their weak hearts. For the Birmingham fan, hope was at its full.

Before leaving Birmingham after the season of 1910, Harry Coveleski stopped by Blach's department store to pick up a pair of shoes awarded to the Barons pitcher who won the most games. Then he rejoined Cincinnati for the final three weeks of the season. In his first game back in the major leagues, Coveleski beat Brooklyn, striking out twelve batters. He lost his next two games. The second loss was utterly dreadful, an improbable sixteen runs allowed to the New York Giants. With that, Cincinnati gave up on Coveleski and sold him to one of Birmingham's rivals in the Southern Association, the Chattanooga Lookouts.

The following May, Coveleski returned to Birmingham with his new team. "Gee, this is a great old town," he said, looking about Rickwood Field with a big smile. He confessed he was fonder of Birmingham than any other town in the league. No doubt, Coveleski was glad to be back, though he was now pitching for Chattanooga. The delight was evident in his face. He was happy to see Molesworth—and told him so. He embraced all the Barons with whom he had played the year before. Downtown, little boys hollered at him from the sidewalks, and Coveleski spoke to each one.

"My old hard luck seems to be following me," he sighed. "Occasionally I pitch a good game, and the club can make no runs. When I pitch a rotten game, they make runs but not enough. But things will soon be getting better with the club, I think, and I will then begin to deliver in old-time style."

On Monday afternoon, Coveleski was scheduled to pitch against Birmingham. "I hate to do it, but I am going to beat you," he said, smiling. Later, it began to rain, the rain coming in torrents. When the game was called off, a large number of people were seated about the stands hoping to see Coveleski pitch. He was still a great drawing card in Birmingham. The game was played the next day, and, indeed, Coveleski's "old hard luck" had followed him. He lost in eleven innings, 3–2. The Barons beat Coveleski four straight times that season. Finally, in August, Coveleski entered a game against the Barons as a relief pitcher and defeated his old team. But the next year, 1912, the Barons beat Coveleski three straight times. Coveleski's work for Chattanooga in 1911 and 1912 was mediocre, but his performance in 1913 delivered him to the brink of the major leagues once again: winning twenty-eight and losing nine for Chattanooga and pitching thirty-two complete games. The Detroit Tigers purchased Coveleski's contract for 1914, and he gave the Tigers three masterful seasons, winning twenty-two, twenty-two, and twenty-one games. He pitched more than three hundred innings each season, and with the heavy workload his arm went bad. He made only eleven starts the next year and one start the year after. Then Detroit released him.

Over the next few years Coveleski attempted comebacks in the minor leagues with Little Rock; Altoona, Pennsylvania; Oklahoma City; and McAlester, Oklahoma, but his baseball career was over. In 1922, he worked as a plainclothesman for a Ford Motor plant in Michigan. Two years later he returned to his hometown of Shamokin, Pennsylvania, and in 1926 began work with the police force. In 1930, he opened a café and was fined for serving alcohol in violation of the Prohibition law. To pay the fine, he took a job as a watchman in a silk mill, eventually earning enough money to open a tavern he called "The Giant Killer." In 1950, Harry Coveleski passed away at the age of sixty-four.

CHAPTER 4
POP BOY SIGNS A CONTRACT

MY FRIEND, CHARLES STEWART, LOVED to rattle on about Coveleski, one of the greatest of all Birmingham pitchers. As he talked, Stewart would lift a cigar out of his breast pocket:

"I'm accustomed to cigarettes, but I certainly love the aroma of a good cigar," he would say. "It soothes my nerves." He would study the cigar, roll it between his thumb and forefinger, clip the end with a small pearl-handled knife, and pass it under his nose, close his eyes, and savor it. Then he would light it and puff on that cigar without letting go of it, the smoke coiling above his head with a warm, nutty aroma. He would shake his head slowly and take the cigar from his mouth—"Oh-ho, dee-lightful."

The first time he told me the tale of Clarence (Pop Boy) Smith, Stewart asked me, "Walter, do you believe in fairy tales?"

"You mean like Aladdin and the Magical Lamp?" A trifle breathlessly. He shook his head:

"Not exactly. It's more like wishing and wanting something real bad, and with pluck and a little luck you get what you've been wishing for. Your dream comes true."

And whenever I think about Pop Boy's story, it is like a page from an old fairy story. When you size it up and look at it from beginning to end, it's almost make-believe. True, there are no sleeping princesses, no giants climbing beanstalks, but Pop Boy dreamt of playing professional baseball, and he lived his dream, though he didn't exactly live happily ever after.

Clarence (Pop Boy) Smith
launched his career with
Birmingham by throwing
batting practice to the Barons.
He impressed Manager Carlton
Molesworth, who signed him
to a contract for $90 a month
in 1911. Clarence was farmed
to Anniston and recalled to the
Barons in 1912.

DURING THE WANING DAYS OF the 1910 season, the year Rickwood opened, Clarence Smith became a thoughtful student of the game, and pitcher Earl Fleharty continued as his instructor. Clarence was forever on the field keeping busy. During spare moments before games, Fleharty taught him the principles of pitching. The boy's memory was good, but his attention was better. Not only was he anxious to learn, he wanted to better his instructor. When Manager Carlton Molesworth allowed Clarence to pitch batting practice, the players figured Clarence for a raw youngster. Soon they discovered he had "stuff." His quick-breaking curves and changes of pace had them biting at the ball and popping up weak flies. Molesworth, the watchful leader, noticed that his veteran players couldn't hit Clarence, yet he was sparing in his praise.

"I think young Clarence was quite a find for you," Roy Ellam told Molesworth. "He looks like a jewel of the first order."

Rowdy Elliott, the catcher, spoke up: "I think the kid can win." One by one, the others agreed: That boy is straight goods. He looks like a real pitcher.

Molesworth had already made up his mind about Clarence but had been waiting for the veterans to come around. "There's enough good in that boy for six full-size men," he told the players. "Next year he's gonna be a member of this club, but don't let's say anything just yet. I don't want his chest to swell out."

Molesworth needed ball players, good ones. Prior to 1910, the Barons had finished in the bottom half of the standings nearly every year for the previous ten. Molesworth had taken a liking to Clarence, liked his manner. The boy was a willing worker with loads of desire; a little cocky, maybe, but good pitchers are like that. As the season drew to a close, Molesworth approached Clarence. "You've been getting in some pretty good licks against my hitters," he said, "and I like your style. I wanna ask you—how would you like to play pro ball next season?" Molesworth told Clarence he was thinking of offering him a contract. Clarence thought the great man was kidding but said he was anxious, extremely anxious, to show what he could do. You'll be in fast company, Molesworth warned him.

Molesworth said he was going to his farm in Frederick, Maryland, for the winter. "That's where I grew up. I'll be huntin' and fishin'. I know where all the squirrels and rabbits hang out. I tell you, there's nothing like a good day of huntin' and fishin' and the thrill of riding a spirited horse. I'll be back in Birmingham the first of February or thereabouts. Watch the newspapers—they'll tell you when I've arrived. Come by the office. We'll talk."

Clarence knew that when Molesworth returned, things would begin to stir, and a ball club would soon be in the making.

THE DAYS AND NIGHTS PASSED slowly for Clarence. The sun shone and the rains fell; the winds blew and the frost settled. Christmas came. All Christmas week the streets were crowded with toy merchants and balloon vendors. Newspaper boys yelling their papers were drowned out by leather-lunged vendors yelping toys and fireworks: "Here yah, git yer toys! Ver-ra, ver-ra cheap, lay-dee! Great-a bargain, mis-terr!" On the curbing they hawked tiny Santa Clauses climbing a wire and toy monkeys walking a string. Happy, laughing crowds bearing gifts hurried along sidewalks. In the hurry and bustle, they jostled and bumped each other, but everyone smiled. Dodging and twisting through the throng, children offered wreaths of holly and bunches of mistletoe. Girls in blue bonnets tended Salvation Army kettles, merrily jingling their bells. Children peered into handsome shop windows arrayed with glittering ornaments and wonderful toys. Merchants said trade was good.

On Christmas Eve, a mass of humanity lined every street and avenue. Liquor was on the breath of some, though this was a "dry" town. Christmas trees were everywhere. Messenger boys rushed through the streets with mysterious packages. Every man, woman, and child had a horn or a bell, each trying to blow and ring louder and stronger than his neighbor. At twilight, one could hear voices caroling from house to house. The laughter of young and old persisted into the early hours of Christmas morning, Sunday, and in the afternoon came the constant buzzing and popping of fireworks.

As December turned the corner into the new year, firearms, church bells, factory whistles, and locomotive whistles — hundreds of them — greeted 1911. For two days during the first week of January, the temperature did not rise above twenty-six degrees. But after that, all over the South, days were like spring. On the thirtieth of January in Dallas, Texas, it was eighty-eight degrees. Clarence had the world to himself, and he watched the newspaper every day.

On February 2, the paper proclaimed: "The backbone of winter is broken. So predicts the groundhog, who according to custom, made his first appearance of the season Thursday at noon and waggled his ears. . . . After sniffing at the weather, he looked at the ground and failing to see his shadow, wagged his ears some more and went his merry way."

Clarence turned the page to the sporting section. His eyes fell on the headline at the top: "Molesworth Leaves for Birmingham." In the morning light, his eye ran quickly down the column of the story, inch by inch: "Molesworth is coming. Manager Molesworth will don his business raiment. . . . He'll leave Frederick, Md., his wintering place, today. . . . And baseball is slated for a sharp pick-up hereabouts before the present month has shed its swaddling clothes."

Clarence all but shouted: "He'll be here tomorrow!" And the goose honked high.

The next day came fine and beautiful. Clarence made his way to town, to the headquarters of the Birmingham baseball club. After what seemed like hours, the greatest man on earth came hurrying in. Fearing Molesworth had forgotten him, Clarence offered a meek smile. Molesworth removed his hat.

"Welcome. How d'ye do, young fella? Step into the office." He hung his hat and extended his hand in greeting. "Do sit down, please."

Clarence looked at him with open mouth and worshipful eyes. What a man, he thought.

"I struck town today," Molesworth told him, "and I'll be puttin' up at the hotel until my living arrangements get squared away. Say, but it's mighty good to be back in Birmingham. Darn fine day. Yes, sir, spring's a-coming. Funny lot, we of the baseball clan — we always like to see springtime come around. It's in our bones, I guess." Molesworth laughed heartily. "I know why you're here. You wanna talk contract. I've never failed to keep a promise, ya know. As soon as you and me finish up here, I'll be mailing out contracts to ball players. Some of 'em will write back and demand more money. They'll say they won't sign until they get it. *Holdouts,* I call 'em. Then when practice starts they'll read in the papers about some youngster looking good, and they'll realize we have someone who can take their place. Yep, nothing brings a veteran to camp quicker than a bunch of young colts who mean business. When they see that, they come a-runnin'. Happens every year. Yep, I expect these contracts to come back thick and fast."

Molesworth settled back behind a well-worn rolltop desk. The room had the smell of fresh coffee and stale cigar smoke. Clarence found the aroma of hot coffee comforting. The door creaked. A messenger boy in a Western Union cap poked his head inside the room: "Telegram for Mr. Molesworth."

"Right here, young fella. Can I pay you for your trouble?"

"No, suh, I was coming this way, anyway," the messenger drawled.

Molesworth, handing him a coin, "Here, take this just the same."

"Thanky," the boy said graciously. "How's the team looking?"

"It won't be long now until we get a ball club on the field. Then I'll be better able to tell what sort of team we have." A thin, gray line of smoke curled from a panatela. Molesworth crushed the cigar and tossed it into a brass spittoon.

"You can tell the fans for me that the Birmingham Baseball Association is going to try and give them a corking good team, but it would be foolish to predict a pennant at this time." Molesworth smiled amiably and with that the messenger boy nodded and walked out.

Tearing open the yellow envelope, Molesworth said, "This wire here's from Rowdy Elliott in Hot Springs, Arkansas. Lotsa ball players go there this time of year to train before they report to their teams. Rowdy's playing with the National Leaguers. Says here he wants me to send him a uniform."

Just then the telephone bell jingled. Molesworth was in good humor as he spoke to a Mr. Horace Fogel, long distance:

"We're glad you're coming, yes, indeed." Molesworth was smiling as he spoke into the mouthpiece of the candlestick phone. "I had a delightful winter, thank you, sir. Time hurries by when you have a good pair of bird dogs to follow." Molesworth leaned back in his chair. "The Birmingham Hotel's expecting your team, yes it is." Subconsciously, he rolled an ink bottle between his fingers. "The field? Oh, it's in grand condition!" Molesworth looked at Clarence and winked. "Looking forward to it. Same to you, sir. G'bye."

Molesworth took the receiver from his ear and placed it in the cradle. He swiveled his chair and with a broad smile said, "That was the president of the Philadelphia National League club. They know about our new park, Rickwood, and they'll be training here. Be here the first of March."

Sitting in front of the manager, Clarence was anxious. He looked at the remarkable man opposite. He fidgeted with the bill of his cap, avoiding eye contact. Molesworth sensed the boy's unease and got up.

"How 'bout we get some air in here?" He strolled to the gritty windowsill, parted the thin, white curtains, and threw up the sash. Instantly a fresh breeze rustled through the fly screen, stirring the curtains and allowing morning sunlight to stream in.

"There now. Much better." As Molesworth walked back to his desk, noises of the street came through the open window: the footfalls of pedestrians, laughter, gay voices, the snarl of a motor truck engine, a newspaper boy crying his papers, the hoofbeats of horses pulling a delivery wagon, the sharp clanging of a streetcar.

"Coffee, son?"

Clarence shook his head. Molesworth pressed his fingertips together and looked Clarence in the eye. "So you want to play for the Birmingham baseball club?"

"Yessir. I'm ready to sign."

"Well, let's talk cold turkey. I have a contract here." Molesworth shuffled a sheaf of papers on his desk. He waved a pink sheet of paper—a pause—and picked up his fountain pen. He pursed his lips, brought one end of the pen to his mouth, and pondered a moment. Clarence looked at him hopefully.

On the contract, after the words "To Pay to the Said Party of the Second Part," Molesworth wrote a figure in clear, bold hand:

"Ninety dollars a month. Yep, that's my offer: ninety dollars a month. Whaddya say?"

Clarence was expecting more, though he hoped the great man wouldn't notice. Molesworth read the look on the boy's face. The tobacco smoke in the room was thick enough to set Molesworth to leaning back and talking about the old days.

"Clarence, I want to tell you a story, something I bet you didn't know. A few years ago," Molesworth began, "the mighty Ty Cobb was a gangling country boy from Georgia trying to get a start in baseball. He was just an ordinary boy, nothing special about him—the kind of boy who, after doing something unusual, the neighbors remarked, 'The same spindle-legged kid what used to run around here? I can't imagine it.'"

Molesworth took a fresh panatela from his breast pocket. "Tyrus got his start with a semi-pro outfit in Anniston, just down the road from here. Best as I recall, he was about the same age as you. He was going out into the world for the first time, and a dime looked as big as a dollar to him.

"When he signed his contract with Anniston, know how much it was for?" Molesworth looked Clarence in the eye. "I'll tell you how much; it was the magnificent sum of fifty dollars a month—plus board. Yep, you heard me right. They paid him fifty dollars a month, and he lived with a family there in town. That was, oh, 'bout seven years ago. Well, today he's just about the best ball player on the face of the earth and very likely the highest paid, too. Now what do you think of that?"

"Say, gee," Clarence stammered. "I . . . I guess I oughter sign my contract."

Molesworth told Clarence how Cobb almost became a Birmingham Baron. The summer after Anniston, Ty was playing with Augusta of the Sally League. The year was 1905. Molesworth was playing the outfield for Montgomery, a half-season away from joining the Barons. Harry Vaughn was managing the Birmingham club. Vaughn was born during the Civil War and had been a major league catcher for Cincinnati in the 1890s. In 1905, he was forty-one years old and the Barons first baseman and manager. He stood six-foot-three in his stockings and weighed somewhere around 225 pounds. Everyone called him "Dad." Molesworth took the cigar from his mouth and turned it round and round between his fingers.

"Dad Vaughn's outfield was shot to pieces with injuries," Molesworth explained, "and he was looking for another body. Understand, the Birmingham club had very little money in those days. This was before Mr. Woodward bought the ball club and put his heart and soul and pocketbook in it. Dad Vaughn, with a limited purse and looking for a ball player, called on the major league teams but got no results. None 't all." Every now and then Molesworth paused and smiled thoughtfully through the cigar smoke.

"About that time there came stories out of Augusta of a youngster who was settin' the woods on fire. So Dad says, I might as well go after that boy. He can catch a fly ball, and we need an outfielder. He's nineteen years old, and they say he is a wonder. And he'll come cheap, too."

Clarence nodded politely. Molesworth rose from his desk and walked dramatically to the open window. Clarence wondered, When's he gonna finish? The man might smoke a whole cigar in the time it takes him to finish this tale. Molesworth, gesturing with his cigar, continued:

"And the fans said, 'Ah-hah! The boy, Cobb, is an amateur—a rank amateur—just like the Birmingham Baseball Association. Why don't they spend some real money and get the material we need to pull us out of a hole?'" A chuckle rumbled deep inside Molesworth.

But Dad Vaughn was desperate. Hell, yes, he was. He made the trip to Augusta and saw the young phenom, Ty Cobb. Dad liked the boy's fire and dash and laid his cards on the table. "I would like to buy this fellow Cobb," he told the Augusta club, "if your price is reasonable." The Augusta manager answered:

"You can have him. We'll give him to you for a cool hundred and a pipeful of smoking tobacco."

There was a twinkle of amusement in Molesworth's eye. "I can spin a yarn as good as the next man."

Molesworth returned to his chair, crossed his legs, and continued. "So Dad, believing the deal had been done, got back on the train and came home. Meantime, the Augusta folks said to themselves, come to think of it, the Detroit club has got an option on him. We must find out what they will pay.

"So they communicated with Detroit. Right away Detroit smelled a mouse. They communicated back, offering a sum of money bigger than the Augusta club had ever dreamed of. It was nothing like the price big league clubs pay for minor-leaguers nowadays, but it was several times what Birmingham had offered.

"Detroit wired the Augusta club: 'We are sending the money by express. Send us Cobb.' And of course Ty went up to the Tigers and became a big star. And now you know the story of how Ty Cobb missed by a hair's breadth of playing in this man's town," Molesworth said, smiling. "Oh, by the way, Dad Vaughn, who's now a little further along life's pathway, is presently a barkeep in a saloon outside Cincinnati."

"You don't say," Clarence said.

"Yep, mighty queer story but the absolute truth." Molesworth rolled his cigar over to the corner of his mouth and puffed out a circle of smoke.

"Alright now, where were we before I got off track? Ah, your contract. So it's like this: I'm offering you ninety dollars a month to play for the Birmingham baseball club, fair 'n' square. What do you say? Wanna think about it?"

"No, sir," Clarence said. "I'm all in. I'll sign."

CLARENCE STEPPED FROM MOLESWORTH'S OFFICE and breathed the fresh February air. It was a fine Friday afternoon with a friendly sun, and the city was astir. Birmingham in 1911 was a dynamo. The population of the city and its environs was over two hundred thousand, and growing. It was a rushing, bustling city, with great crowds hurrying in the streets, people boarding streetcars, and traffic rattling and clattering about. Motorcars dashed around street corners at speeds reaching twenty-five miles an hour, cutting through lines of pedestrians and neither slowing nor sounding their horns.

Thirty years before, Birmingham had been a little coal and iron town. Today it was the South's workshop, a great city humming with industry, an iron and steel center with blast furnaces, coke ovens, and foundries . . . machine shops, rail mills, and railroad repair shops . . . cotton mills, gristmills, cottonseed oil mills . . . potteries, brick kilns, carriage and wagon works . . . marble and stone plants and brass and bronze works. Busy Birmingham—a city of broad streets, modern shop windows, and handsome buildings. The streets, full of people and automobiles, were an inspiring sight. Smart shoppers were dressed in chic spring clothes. Sometimes fifty to a hundred people gathered on street corners, yet the broad avenues never felt crowded. In the heart of the city, one could hardly walk three blocks without observing frantic building activity. As one office building was completed, another "skyscraper" was projected to be built. Truly, Birmingham was becoming the "Magic City."

In the march of progress, the business section was always torn up, a chaotic mix of lumber and brick, pleasant smells of sand and lime—big concrete mixers, gaping sewer lines, muddy streets. Hordes of workmen sang lustily as they excavated for a new office building.

"My, what a building boom this town is having," observed a visitor from New York. "How much deeper are they going to dig that hole?"

Carpenters, ironworkers, brickmasons, plasterers, painters, decorators, and laborers were all employed. With coal and iron in brisk demand, it looked as though Birmingham had just tasted a good cocktail. On the south side, hundreds of feet above the business section, visitors took streetcar rides along the graceful, upward sweep of Highland Avenue. Red Mountain rose in the distance. Visitors who thought of Birmingham as a city of steel works and smoke and noise and overalls were surprised to find wooded slopes, elegant homes, and curving streets, gaily harnessed horses and expensive house dogs. They were surprised to find baby carriages attended by nursemaids and well-dressed children happily at play.

Birmingham of 1911 had a reputation among travelers for fine restaurants and all-night cafés. Downtown streets and walkways were lighted brilliantly, with blocks of arcades and gleaming, blinking electric signs. The day of the horse-drawn vehicle was nearing a close. Large motor trucks carried loads of goods. Automobiles were parked along the curbstone in front of tall buildings. As one car moved, another took its place. And these were not scrubby cars but were shiny and streamlined, ranging from big seven-passenger touring cars, polished and gleaming with brass and nickel plating, to thousand-dollar roadsters. Drivers of carriages, delivery wagons, and motorcars were constantly in a snarl—honking and tooting, ignoring the rules of the road. Sometimes half a dozen vehicles traveled abreast and met face-to-face. Chaos reigned. Occasionally a horse, frightened by an automobile, broke free from a hitching post and dashed down a street, dragging a buggy. Or a bull escaped from a stockyard, bellowing down the street, scattering the crowd into nearby doorways.

FROM THE HEADQUARTERS OF THE Birmingham baseball club, Clarence walked with long, rangy strides. The tides of life swirled about. A jingling, horse-drawn milk wagon, its rounds complete, rumbled down the street. An iceman, still at work in the early afternoon, halted his team of horses, walked to the rear step of the wagon, and began sawing on a huge block of ice. An army of youngsters underfoot hounded him for bits of ice. The man whistled merrily as he delivered ice to a café.

From down the street came the beat of heavy horses' shoes. A dray, pulled by a magnificent span of horses, hauled huge rolls of paper to feed the press that would print the day's newspaper. Clarence stopped at the corner of Second Avenue and Nineteenth Street, waiting for a policeman to raise his hand and halt traffic. The officer peered in half a dozen directions at once and swung his club lightly, whistling to himself, "Birmingham is a grand old town." A flock of plump, gray pigeons walked about, pecking at the ground. The air was rich with a ball park smell.

"Peanut! Hey, gotta da hot peanut! Roast-a peanut. Ah!" Pietro, the peanut man from the old country, stocky of build with coal black hair and dark, glowing eyes, had come here to make his fortune. Standing on the street corner, morning 'til night, he sold peanuts from his roaster cart. "Pss-ss! Sh-ss!" whistled the steam valve. With fluttering fingers, Pietro filled bags of peanuts, and in a swift, nimble motion, twisted the corners and sealed them shut. Clarence gave the grinning vendor a nickel for a warm bag of snugly packed peanuts.

"Ah, Italia eez a bee-u-ti-ful country," Pietro sang. "De sky eez so blue. De people dere are so nice-a an' fine, jus' like-a here. Hey, gotta da hot peanut!"

From nearby on South Twentieth Street came the scorch smell of hot irons and the scent of woolens. Lum Mow stood outside his steamy Chinese laundry watching automobiles dash past. Twenty-eight years before, Lum had left his wife and homeland to try his fortune in America. Birmingham was but a village in 1883, but Lum saw a "velly great town" and settled here as the first Chinese resident. Someday he hoped to return to his wife in China, but in 1911 he was a contented businessman who believed in the virtue of "minding your own business."

Three blocks up Twentieth Street in a barbershop, a bootblack shined a man's shoes. His name was Moustapho Faraga, but to his customers he was Jim Thomas. Though not handsome of person or flashy of dress, Jim was likely the classiest bootblack in the country. He, too, came across the water—from Arabia—speaking nine different languages. In his lifetime, he had crossed the Atlantic, the Pacific, and the Indian oceans, the Red Sea, the Black Sea, the Mediterranean Sea, the Persian Gulf, and the Gulf of Aden. He had visited most of the forty-six states and nearly every large city in the world.

Three blocks down Second Avenue, past a fruit stand and a stockyard smell, a booming voice rang out:

"Ten dollars, eleven, twelve. Make it three fives anyway. The shoes on the beast are worth that." It was the monthly auction of horses and mules at the stables of J. Fies and Sons. "Five, five, and seven and a half; make it ten."

Wagons, buggies, and carriages were camped around the place at the edge of the business district. Two old men sat whittling sticks. Inside, hundreds of horses and mules, stamping on the boards of their stalls, were surrounded by stockmen, dealers, traders, farmers, and mountaineers—poor whites and southern blacks, countrywomen in calico dresses, and townsmen in fresh-washed overalls. Buyers had come from the shores of Mobile Bay, from the foothills of the Tennessee mountains; from Meridian, Mississippi, to the west and Columbus, Georgia, to the east. Some had traveled half the night. Many had brought their families and eaten dinner on wagon bodies and under shade trees. Inside the building, the air was heavy with the smell of hay, oats, and animals.

Up and down the runway pranced mules of all colors: gray and bay, roan and sorrel, black and striped. And horses, too: beautiful, glossy, high-bred, broad-rumped steeds, with festooned fetlocks and wavy manes. And short-barreled cart horses, full of life, their tails swishing and swatting flies, their jaws chewing hay. A handsome Shetland pony stood on the block, and the children rubbed its soft nose, tugging at their mamas and daddies, pleading with them to bid for the pony. Many could not spare the money. Finally it sold for a hundred dollars—pony, cart, harness, and all.

Women in flowered cotton dresses and cloth sunbonnets, and young girls with braided hair, walked toward the stables, some with parasols, for it was a bright, sunny day. Clarence would be along shortly. Perhaps he would give one of the solemn old mules an apple or a lump of sugar. That was his intention, as soon as he took care of business. Clarence hurried across Nineteenth Street, walking as though he had someplace to go and meant to get there. He opened the door of the Florence Hotel cigar store. A bell jangled, and he stamped in to the smell of tobacco and magazines and the fresh ink of newsprint. A revolving wooden fan whirred overhead. On the glass top of the cigar counter, newspapers were stacked next to a jar of highly colored penny confections. Inside the counter was a small showcase, lined with kiln-dried cedar, containing expensive, imported cigars. Presently a dark, easygoing man appeared behind the counter.

"I was told I could buy a subscription to *The Age-Herald* here," Clarence said.

"That you can, young man. One month or three?"

"How much?"

"Seventy cents for one month; two dollars for three."

"Two dollars for three months? I can get *The Birmingham News* for two-fifty. For six months!"

The man puffed on a pipe and reached for the noon edition of the paper, fanning its pages. "*The Age-Herald* is bigger and better. They ship it by rail to points all over the South, and up and down the East Coast. Have you seen the deluxe Sunday edition? *The News* doesn't even *have* a Sunday paper."

Clarence looked at the man. "Well, I guess I can afford it. I just signed with the Barons. I got to know what they're saying about me."

"You? A ball player? I don't believe it." The man drew a pair of spectacles from his waistcoat pocket and looked hard at Clarence.

"You're too young. Molesworth signs only the best. *The best*. No amateurs. But you're a big, strapping fella. What's your name, son?"

"Clarence Smith. I live on the west side, Cotton Avenue, near the ball park."

"Sorry, never heard of you." The man stirred the tobacco in his pipe and went on:

"Kid, you seem to have a good head on your shoulders. I have some advice: Squirrel away some of the money you'll be making. Put it in the savings bank down the street, and you'll earn four percent on your deposits. Look after your nickels and dimes, and the dollars'll take care of themselves; that's what I always say, boy."

Clarence gave the man two dollars and walked toward the door. "Maybe I will," he said. "Keep an eye on the newspapers. You'll be reading about me."

CHAPTER 5

POP BOY MEETS THE MAJOR-LEAGUERS

CARLTON MOLESWORTH INVITED CLARENCE TO get a jump on the other players before they arrived for spring training. "What I want to ask you is this," Molesworth said to him. "Come to the ball park. I'll be about the grounds, getting the field in shape before the fellows arrive. I can use your help, and you can work the winter frost out of your arm."

Every day from the newspapers Clarence got the latest dope on the team:

February 6: Manager Molesworth is busy about the local headquarters mailing out contracts to the Barons of 1911.

February 11: Baseball sap is rising and if the warm weather continues, the fans will soon begin to blossom. Manager Molesworth is here, busy making arrangements for the opening games and the spring training of the Birmingham squad.

And this: Molesworth has signed a local boy, Clarence Smith, who will try for the position of pitcher. Smith is a big husky fellow with a nice assortment of curves and terrific speed. The manager has had him under his eye for some time and while he may not be ripe for the Southern League, it is the opinion that he has the makings of a good man in him.

February 19: McGilvray and Ellam have returned their contracts. "Am eager for the fray," writes McGilvray, who has been working as a clerk in the treasurer's office in Denver, Colorado. . . . Rowdy Elliott and Clyde McBride are in Hot Springs, Arkansas, and Molesworth has sent them uniforms. They will play in the exhibition games at Hot Springs and will be ready for work when the team reports March 8.

February 24: Teams composed of major league ball players engaged in the first exhibition game of the year yesterday at Hot Springs, when the All-Americans defeated the All-Nationals. Elliott was the catcher for the Nationals.

March 1: It may happen that Rowdy Elliott and Clyde McBride will be numbered with the temporary holdouts. Neither has returned his contract. But little attention is being paid this delay, however. Both men, the management believes, will come ambling in within the next few days. Both are valuable men and both are popular with the local fans.

March 2: The Philadelphia Nationals arrived last night and are quartered at the Birmingham Hotel. Horace S. Fogel, president of the club, headed the party. Director Schwartz, Manager Dooin, Trainer Dee, and various newspapermen were also along. The Phillies will remain in Birmingham until March 20. They will have the use of Rickwood for practice work, and during their stay many match games will be played against the Barons. The weather, which has been so pleasant, was fretful throughout yesterday.

March 3: The day broke fair for the Phillies yesterday, and at 10 o'clock they rode out to Rickwood Field. The gates, which had grown a trifle rusty in the cold of the winter, were flung wide, and merrily the visitors trooped through. The sun had chased the dew from the young grass. The diamond, just a trifle damp from the rain of Wednesday, stood out bold and clear to the vision. The baseball writers of Philadelphia unlimbered their cameras, and began firing, taking photographs of the park, the grandstand, and the players. After practice the entire bunch chased each other about the field. After which the bath and rubdown followed. . . . It is really the awakening of baseball in Birmingham. And the fans are glad.

March 7: Earl Fleharty, pitcher; Clyde McBride, outfielder; Rowdy Elliott, catcher; William McGilvray, first baseman. The above were registered in Birmingham yesterday. Fleharty, Elliott, and McBride got into uniforms yesterday afternoon and with Manager Molesworth went through the first workout. They batted the ball, chunked a little, and ran about a bit. Fleharty is pretty heavy apparently, but he dropped right into a swinging trot around the park yesterday during the practice time of the Phillies, and he looks very much like the man who pitched here last season.

March 8: Baseball activities hereabouts are beginning to take on the southerly hum that will awaken fans who have slept soundly through the arrival and early workouts of the Phillies. Things will thicken at Rickwood this afternoon, and by tomorrow the field will teem with frisky Barons and Phillies. Manager Molesworth will be a little surprised if more than two or three Barons are missing when the last train comes in tonight.

Molesworth cautioned Clarence — told him how to act around the big league Phillies so they wouldn't laugh and call him a raw rookie, a "busher." But Clarence was too raw, too green, to be a professional ball player. No sooner did he put on his uniform than he went straight to the Phillies bench like an eager schoolboy to announce he was better than any of the pitchers the Phillies had. Molesworth pulled him back. Clarence bristled, certain Molesworth was hiding him from the big-leaguers so they wouldn't know how good he was. Days later Clarence pitched his first game for the Barons. It was only one inning, and it was an exhibition game, but it was against the major league Phillies. Earl Fleharty pitched the first three innings. Another pitcher followed. Then Clarence trooped to the mound for the ninth. A loud fan in the bleachers, someone with a foghorn voice, got busy:

"Come on, Kid Smith! Go it, Kid! You da one!" His cries resounded across the grandstand.

Clarence took his place on the mound, his cap perched jauntily on his head. He could hear the man sing out. People stirred in their seats and looked at the rooter. He was large and red-necked, with a face like a frostbitten apple. He wore a brown suit with a scarlet necktie and a derby hat pulled low. He puffed happily at a fat, imported cigar. A trail of blue-gray smoke circled his countenance. In the pitcher's box, Clarence was tight as a coiled spring. He stood for a moment and surveyed the business. He rolled the ball in the palm of his hand and gave a tug to the bill of his cap. He pulled on the sleeve of his shirt. He held the ball in front of his face and looked at it intently. Had he lost his nerve? No, not he. Suddenly he fired the ball, and the batter lined a base hit.

"It's awright, Kid!" the rooter thundered, his face red with excitement and his eyes popping with anxiety. The stub of his cigar trembled in his mouth.

"Give us a good 'un now. We countin' on you. Oh, pleeze!" Clarence allowed another hit, and there were two men aboard.

"Get busy, Kid. I hear the Phillies. They're talking about a green rookie, a busher, sayin' they gonna knock you outta da box. See here, you Phillies, this here kid's the gen-u-i-i-ne article. He'll be playing in the major league one day. Yes, he will. And don't you f'get it!"

The rooter, perspiring, unbuttoned his coat, as his lips nervously rolled the soggy end of the cigar. Rising to his feet, he tilted a bottle of pop to his lips. He raised his derby skyward in honor of Clarence, the old soda vendor. Everybody sat up and took notice. They tooted tin horns, rang cowbells, and banged tin pans. The red-faced rooter shifted the cigar from one side of his mouth to the other:

"Let 'em have it, Kid. Give 'em one of your choicest. Steam it in." The next batter grounded out, weakly. One away. The rooter tilted back in his seat and put his thumbs underneath his suspenders.

"That's the stuff! Give us some more!" He sang the words. "Play ball, boys. Double play. Help the kid out." The rooter was on his feet again, rolling up his sleeves, chanting:

"Now you pitchin', Pop Boy! You the big cheese, Kid! Don't you know? We do! Come on, let's get these chumps! Awright, batter up, Phillies."

Pop Boy glanced at the crowd with a confident smile. He wiped his forehead with his sleeve and toed the rubber with his right foot. He nuzzled the ball to his chest and nodded at the catcher. Throwing his arms above his head, he twisted his body, kicked his foot high, and lunged forward, putting everything he had into it. The ball whistled toward the plate. The batter swung and sent a grounder to second baseman Lil Marcan, who scooped it and threw to shortstop Roy Ellam, who threw to first baseman Bill McGilvray. Double play. The bleacher fans rose as one, and the rooter collapsed into his seat, energy spent. The Phillies didn't score.

Six days later, Clarence pitched again in relief against the Phillies — this time, six innings. He surrendered five runs but impressed everyone as a "comer." Little did he know he was headed for despair.

MARCH 25 BROKE COLD AND dreary. Spring was knocking at the door, and Birmingham was gloriously alive with peach and plum blossoms. Though the peaches might not be as fine as those in Georgia, the blossoms were just as pink. The Detroit Tigers were in town to play the Barons. These Tigers had been American League champions three of the past four years. Their centerfielder, Ty Cobb, was twenty-four years old and already the winner of four batting titles. The Georgia Peach was the biggest star in the American League, and the best paid. Now, in 1911, he was about to begin his seventh year. It was to be his greatest season in baseball.

The Tigers won the game that day, 11–3. Clarence pitched the seventh and eighth innings, facing Cobb twice. The first time, with the bases loaded, Cobb grounded out to second base. The next inning, after the Tigers again filled the bases, Cobb walked to the plate. At six-foot-one, Ty Cobb stood a few inches taller than the average man. His eyes were intense, piercing, steel blue. He liked to swing three bats to limber up and then cast two aside before stepping into the box.

Clarence peered in at Cobb. The big league star peered back. Cobb batted from the left side, holding his hands inches apart, well up the bat handle, ready to choke up or swing freely. Instead of planting his feet flat and firmly in the box, he stood on his toes, feet close together. On his toes he could quickly shift his body to suit the pitch. When he didn't intend to swing hard, he didn't set himself. The object was to get on base and run hard — to turn singles into doubles and doubles into triples.

Ready now, Clarence wound and threw the first pitch to Cobb. *Ball.* Cobb took a quick practice swing with his ash bat. Clarence reared back and threw again — Cobb watched it go by. *Ball two.* Cobb stepped out of the box to rub dirt on his hands, showing his backside to Clarence. Quickly, Cobb stepped back in. As Clarence threw his third pitch, Cobb shuffled the position of his feet. *Ball three.* With three balls and no strikes, Cobb, big league star, knew what the bush-leaguer would throw next: a fastball. Clarence took a deep breath. His muscles twitched. He clenched the baseball with three fingers and a thumb. He swung his arm back and let fly.

Cobb took a vicious chop, and bat met ball with a special *CR-R-A-A-CK!* At the flash of the bat, the ball rose high and deep into rightfield, a terrific drive all the way to the fence. The crowd roared. The three base runners took off. Cobb ran hard to first base and made the turn, cutting the inside corner of the bag. Streaking for second, he glanced back at the rightfielder gathering the ball near the fence. Legs churning, Cobb touched second base and turned sharply, kicking up dust. Running full speed for third, he hurled his body at the bag, hooking his left toe on the corner of the base in a fadeaway slide — a roaring three-bagger, clearing the bases of all three runners. Clarence, in two innings of pitching, had allowed seven runs. By now, Molesworth had decided Clarence wasn't ready for the Southern League. A week before the season opened he told Clarence:

"You have speed, a curve, a good changeup, and big ambition, but you're too young for the Southern League. I'm sending you to Anniston for the season. It's a Class D club, but a fella's gotta start somewhere."

Molesworth looked into Clarence's blank face, searching for words. The manager had peered into many such faces and knew how to send a boy on his way. For some, it was a final farewell. Others, like Clarence, were sold to a lower-level minor league club, with a chance to return to Birmingham the next season.

"Son, life certainly hands it to you sometimes." Molesworth put a hand on the boy's shoulder. He assured him that a rift of blue and a glorious sun were in sight.

"You've got lots of promise, and there's no doubt you'll make a good pitcher. I'm telling you the straight, honest truth: You'll be back next spring and you'll play for me next year — if you take care of yourself. Some of the older heads will try and get you to go out with them, to have a few drinks, and joyride with light women. Now listen to me — I've been in the game a long time, and I'm sure of what I say: Turn a deaf ear to those people. If you follow my advice, you'll be back with the Barons, and eventually you'll go up to the big leagues."

Clarence stood rigid, his face solemn as an owl's. The blood rose hot in his cheeks, and he blinked tears from his eyes. "Be sure to write your ma and pa," Molesworth said. "You were raised right, and you come from good people. May luck be with you."

Clarence felt pretty rotten. He skulked home, a failure. Nobody believed in him. Boy, did he sulk. He was awake all the black night, the wind singing in the chimney. A fine fix you're in, Clarence Smith, he said to himself. Molesworth's words rasped on his ears: *Gotta start somewhere. Sending you to Anniston. You'll be back. Be sure to write.* Clarence strode the floor, back and forth, his hopes to be famous crushed. I wisht I was dead, he thought. *Too young. Class D. Gotta start somewhere . . . gotta start somewhere.* Then an idea came to him: He would throw out his arm and end his career. Yes, that's what he'd do.

Morning dawned. The restless night was over, and Clarence walked gravely to the ball park. Two college teams, Birmingham College and Sewanee, would be playing that afternoon. The college boys were on the field early, practicing hitting and fielding. Clarence volunteered to pitch, and all morning he threw to the players. He put all his might, every ounce, behind each throw, for two, three, four hours. Scars of battle were on his baseball pants. It was enough to ruin an ordinary arm, but it failed to injure his.

The next day, a Tuesday, he took stock of his lot and decided to leave for Anniston. The league opened its season the second week of May. Clarence won his first game, and his second. Within a month, he had six wins; twice he pitched twelve innings. The summer days dragged by. All the teams in the league played with twelve men on their rosters. Clarence pitched both games of doubleheaders six times, and people began calling him "Doubleheader Smith." That season he

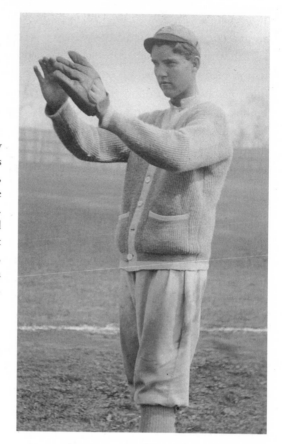

Most pitchers of the early 1900s pumped their arms once, twice, or three times, then brought the ball above their heads and threw. Clarence Smith took the ball in his right hand, looked at it for a moment, reared back, and threw with hardly a windup at all.

appeared in more games than any other pitcher in the league, winning twenty-two and losing sixteen. The Anniston Models won the pennant in a close finish with Gadsden.

A little earlier we talked about Clarence Smith's story being like a fairy tale come to life. Clarence had signed a professional contract with the Birmingham Barons but failed to make the team. Even though he made a good record with Anniston and helped win the pennant, many people thought Clarence to be no better than a Class D pitcher, that he should remain with Anniston, that he was no more than a pop boy. Some fairy tale, right? But Molesworth had not given up on Clarence. On the last day Birmingham was allowed to reclaim him, owner Rick Woodward telephoned the Anniston club to announce the Barons were buying him back. The decision cost the Barons one hundred dollars, the amount Anniston had paid Birmingham.

The fairy tale was just beginning.

W*HEN* C*LARENCE REPORTED TO THE* Barons the following spring of 1912, he was still an unrefined pitcher. He hadn't mastered an overhand curve and still threw his fastball with three fingers. Earl Fleharty was no longer with the club — he'd been sent to Nashville. There was a new pitcher on the staff, Ray Boyd, who had won thirty games in the minors the previous year and before that had pitched a few innings in the major leagues. Boyd helped Clarence with his fastball. Molesworth, once a pitcher himself, worked with Clarence on his curveball and his pitching delivery. The spring of 1912, ten pitchers were bidding for five positions on the team. Day by day, Clarence became a better pitcher, gaining confidence. Boyd told him:

"Kid, you've developed a helluva curve, an' you can throw the ball through a knothole, but you're gonna have to learn to change speeds on that fastball. You do that, and I think you can win some ball games."

The Chicago Cubs came through Birmingham two weeks after training camp opened. Clarence pitched six innings, and the Cubs never threatened to score. The newspapers began regarding the strapping nineteen-year-old with wonder. "Young Smith is phenomenal," the papers said. One morning Clarence walked into the clubhouse at Rickwood Field, his spikes clattering against the gritty floor. A solitary gas heater in the middle of the room cut through the chill of the spring morning. Players were dressing, coming and going, leaving for the field, playing cards. Someone had started a game of checkers. Ray Boyd was sitting under a dim electric light with his head in a newspaper. Twenty-five years old and in his fifth year of pro ball, Boyd had pitched briefly for the St. Louis Browns and the Cincinnati Reds. His repertoire included a drop ball and a spitball, a fastball and a curve. As Clarence walked in, Boyd flaunted the newspaper:

"Can you beat it? Hey, Pop Boy, have you seen this noospaper? You're a phenom, it says. They like your paces. Look a-here." The other ball players stopped in their tracks, as Boyd began reading loudly, drawing out the words:

"'Young Smith has shown more real stuff than any other flinger on the Baron staff. He has speed, curves, and phenomenal control. He is fast mastering the art of pitching, too. His youth and ambition might be the causes of his excellent work.'"

Boyd bowed deeply to Clarence. Laughter bubbled up from every part of the room. Clarence modestly laughed it off. Slowly, emphatically, Boyd continued reading:

"'At the present time he looks more capable than any youngster who has broken into the Southern League ranks in many springs!'"

"Funny thing," Boyd sighed, "I won thirty games at Ottumwa last year, an' they ain't said nothing that good about me." And he let out a snort of laughter.

ONE DAY THAT SPRING OF 1912 at Rickwood, Clarence had a chance to watch a master at work — the great Giants pitcher Christy Mathewson. The New York Giants were the powerhouse of the National League. That day, however, Mathewson was less than masterful in a game against the Barons, pitching five innings and giving up five runs. Boyd, the Barons starter, was hit hard in three innings, and the Giants won, 13–5.

Two days later, on April 1, the Detroit Tigers were back at Rickwood. Ty Cobb, baseball's mightiest, had won another batting title in 1911, hitting .420. During the off-season, he had performed as the leading man, a football star, in a play called "The College Widow." The show toured the country, and at Birmingham's Jefferson Theater, the audience demanded a curtain call. On the field, Cobb was belligerent and menacing, a feared competitor who could upset a whole ball club with his play. He was one of the game's greatest players, yet he had few friends, even among teammates. In exhibition games, where nearly all players loaf because nothing is at stake, Cobb always gave his best.

"Some of those people came a long way to see you," he would say. "They have probably never seen you before, and they may never see you again. The impression they carry off with them is the picture they get of you in that game, and if you want to make good on everything they have been reading about you and everything they think you are, you've got to go at top speed to keep them from being disappointed."

In the game against the Barons, Cobb tapped a ball a foot in front of the plate for an out, grounded to the pitcher for another out, and struck out. But in the sixth, he singled and stole second. The next batter, Sam Crawford, hit a fly ball to right that Bob Messenger caught for an out. Cobb tagged at second and took off like a wildcat, spikes churning and dust swirling. Messenger threw the ball to the shortstop. Cobb stopped at third, then dashed suddenly for home. The shortstop fired the ball to the catcher, but the throw was high. The umpire tossed his mask, and the crowd rose. Cobb slid. The catcher lunged. Cobb swerved wide, kicked out his left leg, and hooked the corner of the plate in a whirling cloud of dust. The umpire swept his arms wide, palms down. "S-A-A-F-E !!" And the park rang with a storm of applause. The Tigers won, 4–0. The following day, the two teams played again. On the other side of the world, a crowd gathered near Belfast, Ireland, to witness the greatest ship in the world begin its sea trials. In eight days, the *RMS Titanic* would leave on its maiden journey across the Atlantic Ocean.

MOLESWORTH HANDED CLARENCE THE BALL and told him: Go pitch against those Tigers. Give it a whirl. The Tigers remembered the Pop Boy from the year before. We'll pound him all over the lot, they told themselves. As Clarence's warmup pitches crackled into the catcher's mitt, the plate umpire, mask in hand, turned to the grandstand and bellowed out the batteries:

"Dubuc and Stanage for Detroit. Smith and Ryan for Birmingham. Play ball!"

The first batter for Detroit grounded out. Clarence pitched to the next man, a righthanded batter named Baldy Louden. Clarence threw a fastball, and Louden hit it a lick over the outfielder's head. The ball rolled to the distant leftfield fence, and Louden circled the bases for a home run. Detroit led, 1–0. The Tigers scored two more runs in the top of the third, 3–0. After that, it was all Birmingham. The rooter, his round face beaded with sweat, puffed nervously on a cigar as a thin boy with freckles wandered by peddling ice cream cones.

In the bottom of the third, the Barons loaded the bases. Bill McGilvray rattled the scoreboard in right for a double, sending all three runners home and tying the score. The rooter howled with a voice like a thunder cloud's. The Barons were swift, sure, and snappy in their work, scoring three more runs in the fourth and one in the sixth for a 7–3 lead. Clarence held the Tigers in the hollow of his hand, pitching the entire game and throwing his best stuff. The fastball worked well, and the curve fooled batters. His control was wonderful — he showed steadiness and nerve under fire. He gave the Tigers nine hits, well-scattered, and the runners on base didn't trouble him. Cobb reached base twice on base hits. Both were dainty pop flies falling just beyond the infielders. At bat, Clarence matched Cobb, hitting two clean singles. The Barons won, 7–3.

Clarence left the field like a peacock with its tail feathers spread. Outside the park, youngsters gathered in excited groups: dirty-faced, romping barefoot boys, street urchins, and newsboys on their routes.

"There he is!" they cried. "Say, Pop Boy! Oh, Pop Boy!" They rushed to the dashing hero with a sea of outstretched arms. Little shavers in knee pants. Tousled-headed boys in patched pants and play-worn overalls — they thrust grimy bits of paper in his face and tugged at his sleeve.

"Mr. Pop Boy, will you sign this . . . please? Oh, please."

"Alright, guys. Wait your turn. I'll sign 'em all. Give me some room, alright?" The round, wide eyes of the children with their rosebud mouths watched his every move. One of the bigger boys, real serious-like, spoke up:

"We like the way you put down the great Cobb today."

Pop Boy could smile. He was a member of this brood once. During his barefoot days at the turn of the century, he had admired the Piano Mover, Frank Smith. As a boy, Clarence had pulled on Smith's coattails and hounded him for a signature. Frank Smith won eighteen games for the Barons of 1903 and went straight to the White Sox, pitching two no-hitters and winning 139 games during his big league career. Between baseball seasons, he toiled as a furniture mover for his father in Pittsburgh, once claiming he could carry a baby grand up four flights of stairs.

Clarence moved among the crowd of children. "On with you, you scamps and scalawags," he scolded the waifs playfully. "Move on." And the boys skittered like mice.

"Don't let it go to your head," Molesworth warned. "Just when you think you're the cock o' the walk . . . "

THE BARONS OPENED THE SOUTHERN League season with a loss to Montgomery, 4–1. It was April 11, 1912, and the magnificent *Titanic* was crossing the North Atlantic from Southampton, England, to New York City. Two days later Clarence pitched and lost a game against Montgomery. He also lost his nerve and his control that day. He lasted but four and a third innings, as Montgomery's twenty-one-year-old outfielder, Casey Stengel, singled four times and walked in five trips to the plate. Barely twenty-four hours later, *Titanic* was running near top speed across the dark waters of the Atlantic, 1,150 miles due east of New York. The Barons, playing in Mobile, had just lost another ball game. Before midnight, in the piercing cold, *Titanic* struck a floating mountain of ice. Silence. The sea was smooth as a lake. The great iron heart of the ship ceased to function; the engines stopped. The unsinkable *Titanic* reeled, rocked, and struggled. The greatest ship in the world slid beneath the surface to her grave. For weeks, the newspapers talked of the *Titanic:* of those who were rescued and those who were not, of survivors' tales and of Captain Smith, of Congressional inquiries and who was at fault.

The Barons, too, were sinking. They had expected to be a pennant contender in 1912, but on April 21 their record was 3–7, and they were next to last in the standings. The town, the team, and the papers were in near panic. Team owner Rick Woodward dispatched Manager Molesworth to Cincinnati to look for players. Major league teams would soon be trimming their rosters, and Birmingham was ready to deal. In early May, the Cincinnati Reds agreed to sell the Barons a third baseman, Rafael Almeida, and a pitcher, Bill Prough. By the time the two arrived, the Barons had turned their season around. They were in second place and soon would be in first. Almeida became one of the team's best hitters and Prough a star pitcher.

Clarence began the season slowly, losing two of his first three games. People wondered if he were ready for the Southern Association. The doubters still viewed him as the pop boy in the stands, not Pop Boy Smith, professional ball player. Big-time ball players came from far-off places, they thought, from Cincinnati, Kansas, or Ottumwa, not from the west side of Birmingham. Hugh Roberts, sports editor of *The Age-Herald,* wrote of Smith:

"Because we have known the youngster all his life, we had an impression that he was not strong enough. It is human nature to sigh for the cleverness of strangers when it often happens that we have more clever boys at home. . . . Very often, therefore, you draw a lemon from Maine when you have a real ripe peach in Birmingham." The journalist warned: "Look out for Smith."

The spring of 1912 ripened into summer. Molesworth stuck by Clarence, using him mainly in relief — in games when the Barons were behind. On May 12, Clarence's pitching record was three wins and two losses when a *Birmingham Age-Herald* reporter, Bill Ax, made a startling prediction:

"Smith — you may bank your reputation on this — will be in the big *shew* in 1914! He's a comer beyond all question."

On May 17, Ray Boyd pitched the Barons into first place, and other teams began playing catch-up. In early June, the Barons led Chattanooga by five and a half games. On July 4, they were eight and a half ahead of Memphis. Two weeks later, they led second-place Chattanooga by ten. By the end of July, Mobile had moved into second place, seven games back. By the middle of June, Clarence had started seven ball games and relieved in six. His pitching record was three wins and three losses. Molesworth began using him exclusively as a starter — no more relief. He won six games in a row, lost a game, then won three more. Major league scouts took note. Molesworth called Clarence "one of the most promising young pitchers that I ever saw," and said, "there is no doubt in my mind but that he will go higher. I believe that we will be able to sell him for a neat sum to the majors this season. Although the kid has much to learn, he has a good memory and is not hard to teach."

On August 8, 1912, the Chicago White Sox purchased Clarence and centerfielder Jimmy Johnston from the Barons for $2,000 each. Both players would complete the season with the Barons and report to the White Sox in 1913. Clarence Smith finished the season with sixteen wins and eight losses. He was only twenty years old, and his team was sweeping to the Dixie flag.

CHAPTER 6

A PENNANT IN THE BALANCE

CLARENCE SMITH HAD A WINDOW seat in a speeding train. It was August 27, 1912, and night out. A big white moon shone. Clusters of stars hung like lamps in the sky. All one could see were the darkness of the land, the shapes of trees, and lonesome farmhouses set back from the tracks. The land was full of drowsy country noises — bullfrogs bawling, owls hooting, crickets singing, cattle lowing.

It was intensely quiet inside the grinding railroad car. A small electric fan whirred busily above the aisle. People spoke in whispers. Outside, the mournful whistle of the train wailed above the whining of the wheels. Lights of small town railway stations swept past. People walked along dusty roads that resembled little rivers. Gas lamps glimmered in the gloom of night. Here and there a dim candlelight flickered in a distant window. The train rumbled on, past town squares and business centers, past main streets lined with frame houses.

The Birmingham Barons were aboard that train, traveling northeast, New Orleans to Birmingham. They would arrive home early in the morning to begin a four-game series with the Mobile Sea Gulls. Two hours earlier, the Barons had lost a game to the New Orleans Pelicans, the winning run for the Pels crossing the plate in the bottom of the ninth. The inglorious defeat had crushed the players' spirits. By sundown, they were on their way home, relieved to be free of the city.

For two weeks, Mobile had been crowding the Barons at the top of the standings. The Gulls had won their last nine games and stood only three games behind the Barons. The strain of the pennant race was engraved on the face of every man on that train. Only fifteen games to play and a pennant was on the line. Tomorrow the Barons and Gulls would begin the most important series of the year.

The mighty locomotive rushed across Mississippi, its whistle splitting the night. Now and then, the train slowed through a sleeping town or steamed into a station behind the sound of its engine bell. Manager Molesworth moved down the aisle, hands thrust in his trouser pockets, his round, pudgy features bearing a six-cylinder frown. Lord, I'm tired, he thought. In the pale light of the day coach, a boy headed his way with a bundle under his arm, calling out the evening newspaper. Pointing to the front page, he cried:

"Pack of wolves attacks railway man! This morning! Prospect, Alabama! Freight train arrives and saves his life!"

Molesworth muttered to himself, "There's wolves after him and Gulls after me. Goes to show, the good Lord'll let you know when there's someone worse off than you." A smile flickered at the corners of his mouth.

"Afternoon paper, sir?" Molesworth reached into his trouser pocket and gave the newsie a nickel. "Mr. Molesworth, sir, if it means anything to ya, I think your boys'll win the flag."

"Thank you, young fella. I hope you're right." Molesworth settled wearily into a seat next to Clarence. As he unfolded the newspaper to the front page, his eye fell on the story halfway down:

> The arrival of a freight train at Prospect, Ala., early Thursday morning saved the station agent from a horrible death by a pack of wolves. Wednesday night while calmly resting on the station platform, the agent was startled by gleaming balls of fire that seemed to flash from out of the ground. Dark, slinking, sinuous forms moved silently around him. The railroad man retreated to his two-by-four office. He shut and barred the windows and doors. The wolves surrounded the little box station. They got under the platform. They stood up before the windows, threateningly. They grew bolder, and one big beast attempted to jump through a grated window. The agent killed him with a shotgun. The pack devoured the body. Presently, another wolf tried the stunt. Again the agent let loose the gun. A few minutes later the rumbling of a freight train scared the wolves away. After telling his story to the engineer, the agent boarded the freight, refusing to stay at the station.

Molesworth dropped the paper. Who writes this nonsense? he wondered, shaking the paper until it crackled in his hands. He folded the paper and shut his eyes. Clarence looked at him out the corner of his eye:

"You look a bit fagged, Moley."

Molesworth nodded gravely. "Don't I know it?" In a few moments, he began pulling himself together. "Son, we'll be running into a red-hot club tomorrow, Mobile. They won again today."

Molesworth glanced out the window. "How do you feel — your arm, I mean?"

Clarence shrugged. "Feels good. Fine as silk."

"You got a young arm, by golly."

Molesworth knitted his brow. "I was just thinking. You were a striking figure when I first laid eyes on you — a long-legged, awkward kid, running over with nerve and ambition. Right from the beginning you told me you wanted to be a big-leaguer. Remember?" Molesworth's fretful look turned into a smile. "I had to send you to Anniston that first year, and you kicked hard about it. I'm older than you. I've been at this for a right smart while, and to my way of thinking, you weren't ready for this league. We needed to polish off yer rough edges."

Clarence nodded. "I was plenty blue about it."

"Funny, ain't it? You could've given up and jumped down a rabbit hole, but, no, you did the proper thing. You made tracks to Anniston without a complaint and won, what, twenty-two ball games? That's mighty fine work in any man's league. Now you're a young man, just starting to make your fortune, and the big league scouts have discovered you. My, what a fellow you've become. All of twenty years old and about to go to Chicago and play against the best ball players in the great cities of this country. You'll be out in a big wonderful world. Your dreams, they shore came true, didn't they?"

Molesworth broke off and his mind harkened back. "When I was a youngster, I had no way of knowing I'd play professional ball. It was a simpler time. They didn't have all the minor league clubs of today. There wasn't a lot of scouting. Most of the ball players came from semi-pro clubs around their hometown. If a man made a big reputation in his hometown, word might get back to a big league club, and he was given a trial. If he was fortunate, he stuck with the club. When I was fifteen, sixteen years old, I traveled among towns with the Pawnee Bill Wild West show as an acrobat. We had three men in the act, and I was the middle man. That was back in 1892."

"The year I was born," Clarence said, surprised.

"Golly, what an old man I am. How old do you suppose I am, Clarence? You don't know, do you? Thirty-six, that's what I am."

Clarence wagged his head. "You can still play outfield with the best of 'em, Moley."

"I still got a little speed, eh? Anyway, we were talking about Pawnee Bill. His real name is Gordon Lillie. He's friends with Buffalo Bill, and through him I got to know Buffalo Bill. Would you believe that the last time Buffalo Bill was in Birmingham, he looked me up and gave me fifty passes to his Wild West show? He shore did.

"After that, I went home to Maryland and started playing baseball. I was eighteen, a pitcher, playing amateur ball around Frederick. We played a number of semi-pro teams, and I had the good fortune to win thirty-two straight games. As I said, there wasn't any scouting going on in those days, but the Washington National League club heard about me and decided to give me a trial. That was August of '95.

"Well, gosh ding my buttons," Molesworth said, raising his voice above the rumble of the train. "Here I was, a little fellow, all five-foot-five, 170 pounds. The morning I walked in on the Washington manager and told him who I was, he says to me: 'Huh! I thought you was a big man. They told me you was six feet tall.' That's how he put it: 'They told me you was six feet tall.' Well, I might have been six feet broad on occasion, but I was never that long in my life, but I tried to make the best of it. 'Well,' I said, 'I'm here, and if you don't like me, it won't cost you nothing but my railroad fare.' So he decided to give me a trial. They kept me three months, and I pitched in a few big league games, but they felt like I needed more seasoning, so they shipped me to the minors. I never did get back to the big tops.

"I gave you some advice once, and that was to lead a clean life. Remember me telling you that, my boy? I said to mind your p's and q's and not listen to the old heads who'll want you to take a few drinks. Believe me, the players who do that will always be in the bush leagues. When I broke in with Washington, my third night there, some of the rules-breakers invited me to join them on a hell-raising party. I thanked them, sarcastically, then I turned and left — went home and hopped in the hay. The boss of the club heard about this and it made a hit with him. Years later he told me this had done more to keep me on the club than any stuff I'd done as a pitcher. They don't want men who carouse at night. They want men who take baseball seriously. You haven't lived long enough to gain wisdom that comes with age. In this hard-boiled world, you have to fight tooth and nail for all you get, so I'm telling you: Take care of yourself and save your money. And never be a roughneck — on or off the field."

Finally, Molesworth told Clarence, beware the fan. "When you're going good, he'll try to make an idol out of you. He'll introduce you to women you should not know. He'll insist on buying you liquor. Turn him down cold. He's the same man who'll lavish money on you when you're going good, and when you're not, he'll sit in the grandstand and beg the team to release you."

Both men turned their heads to the window. A minute passed. Neither spoke; neither stirred. The only sound came from the rocking of the train.

"I hear Mobile's going to throw Demaree against us tomorrow," Molesworth said.

Al Demaree was the best pitcher in the league. Nearly twenty-eight years old, he had been in professional baseball five years. He had a sidearm motion and a wide, sweeping curve that had held eleven opponents scoreless on the season. Demaree lived the off-season in Chicago, using his right arm to sketch pen and ink drawings for a newspaper. John McGraw's Giants had recently paid Mobile the fabulous sum of $10,000 for Demaree, and he would be theirs at the close of the season.

Molesworth placed a hand on Clarence's knee. "Son, you've given us a lot of good innings. I started you off slow the first of the year because there were more experienced men ahead of you. I know you didn't like it, but you were just a youngster and I had to break you in. Some folks didn't think you were good enough to make it in this league, I reckon. Not me. I thought you were one of the best young pitchers I'd ever seen, and I told the newspapers so. It took a while for you to get going, but you took fire and pitched wonderful ball. Son, you've been my best pitcher down the stretch. I've been doing some hard thinking, and I want you in the box tomorrow. You've beaten Demaree once this year, and you can do it again. There'll be a big, noisy crowd. It'll be rough sledding, but you can do it."

Clarence looked over at Molesworth, and for the first time their eyes met: "Say no more, Moley. I'm all ready."

The manager pulled out his watch: half past nine. He rose, swaying lightly with the motion of the car. With unusual kindness, he gripped the shoulder of his young pitcher. "Time I turned in," he said, stretching his legs. "I must go. G'night. See you in the morning." And with that, Molesworth headed down the darkened aisle in the direction of his sleeping berth.

LATER THAT EVENING WORD SPREAD through the car that Lil Marcan, the second baseman, had called a meeting — players only. One by one, they all gathered in the smoking compartment and sat on upholstered leather seats. Marcan was standing on a stool in pajamas and slippers. Thirty-one years old, Marcan hailed from Brooklyn. He'd been around baseball long enough to be esteemed by others. He never would be a major-leaguer, yet people who knew about such things regarded him as one of the finest baseball generals to ever stroll a Southern diamond.

"Awright, everyone listen up!" Marcan shouted. "I s'pose everyone knows Mobile won today. They're right on our tail. They're one tough bunch, and we'll have our hands full. Let me tell you how it is: We been leading this race from the jump. Everyone's a little down right now. We shoulda won that game today; we lost it, 2–1. We're the best team in the league; we all know it. If we can lick these guys the next two games, I think we'll take the pennant. What I'm asking is this: Everyone train hard. Get to bed on time. No monkey business. You know Moley's rule: in bed by eleven-thirty."

From the back of the room, someone glared at Marcan: "You accusin' anyone, Lil?"

"I ain't 'cusin' no one of nuthin'. All's I'm saying is maybe some fellas got a little careless in their training in N'Orleans."

The scene got a little intense. Then someone else spoke: "Men, Lil's right." It was Roy Ellam, the shortstop and de facto team captain. Molesworth had left Ellam in charge of the team last April while the manager was in Cincinnati looking for players.

"See here, Lil's been in baseball eleven years," Ellam went on. "He was playing with St. Paul when they won two pennants. The rest of us hadn't won nothing. This Mobile club is a cocky bunch right now, and they'll put up a game fight. We've got to bear down if we're gonna win this thing."

Ellam looked into the face of each man in the room. "We need to show more pepper on the field, me included. We need to play with nerve. We need to play like we're behind every time we come to bat and every time we're in the field. Do I have each man's support?"

The players nodded. Not a soul stirred. Then one nudged another, and a chorus of men in harmony began a refrain:

> See that ragtime couple over there,
>> Watch them throw their shoulders in the air,
> Snap their fingers —
>> Honey, I declare,
> It's a bear, it's a bear, it's a bear.
>> There!
> Everybody's doin' it,
>> Doin' it, doin' it,
> Everybody's doin' it,
>> Doin' it, doin' it.

It was one of the ragtime dance tunes the country was crazy about, an Irving Berlin tune. A storm of laughter filled the room. The men clapped and hooted; the mood lightened. The singers were four Barons who had entertained the team on long train rides all season. The leader of the quartet was pitcher Bill Foxen. Fred Dilger, the catcher, was bass, Jimmy Johnston, centerfielder, baritone, and Large Bill McGilvray, first baseman, tenor. They had fun with "Everybody's Doin' It Now," "I

Wonder Who's Kissing Her Now," "Love Me and the World Is Mine," "Who Are You with Tonight?" and a Renaissance choral piece, Allegri's "Miserere."

AUGUST 28, 1912, A WEDNESDAY, at Rickwood Field — a perfectly still afternoon, not a breath stirring the flags around the grandstand. The Mobile Sea Gulls, winners of their last nine games, blew into town gingered up to take first place in the standings. Jaunty and full of fight, they walked into the park as if they owned it. Al Demaree looked like Fifth Avenue, New York, faultlessly tailored in gray business suit and blue-gray necktie.

Fans pushed into the park with spunk and spirit, for it was the first meaningful game of the summer. Their passion had waned in June as the Barons moved far ahead in the standings. Now that the race had tightened, they were all in, and before the game began they had filled every seat. As usual, many of the spectators were black, sitting in the colored bleachers down the leftfield line. They were some of the rockin'est, roarin'est rooters in town. Spectators, black and white, overflowed the bleachers and lined the edges of the field. Their mingled voices pulsed with energy.

It was a pearl of a ball game — the best of the season. The two pitchers, young Clarence Smith and the older Al Demaree, worked with furrowed brows. Molesworth directed from his cane-bottom chair beside the dugout. Every play and every move counted, and the fans stayed until the end. Back and forth the game went: a run for Birmingham, a run for Mobile, a run for Birmingham, a run for Mobile. The teams battled for every inch of ground.

The Barons scored in the bottom of the first, Lil Marcan getting hold of one of Demaree's sidearm shoots for a screaming double to right centerfield. He scored on an infield out. Mobile tied the score in the top of the second: 1–1. During the inning, Clarence Smith arrived at a three-ball, two-strike count on shortstop Dee Walsh. The batter fouled off the next eleven pitches. On pitch number seventeen, Clarence struck out Walsh.

In the bottom of the second, Birmingham retook the lead. McGilvray doubled, and Ellam drove him home: 2–1, Birmingham. In the top of the third, Mobile got the run back: 2–2. In the fourth, Mobile scored again: 3–2. In the bottom of the fourth Birmingham scored: 3–3. Birmingham forged ahead in the sixth, 4–3, and scored again in the eighth: 5–3.

The hour was late when Mobile came to bat in the top of the ninth. The two pitchers, Smith and Demaree, were still in the game. It had been a taxing contest, stubbornly fought, inning by inning. With one out in the ninth and Birmingham leading, 5–3, two runners reached base for Mobile. The sun was setting all yellow and red, and shades of night circled Rickwood. The fans sensed a decisive moment. "Them's the tying runners on!" they hollered. "You the works, Pop Boy. Go get 'em!" In the half-light, Clarence coaxed a feeble pop-up to the first baseman for the second out. The last batter would be a pinch-hitter for Demaree, and Clarence struck him out. The game was over.

The Barons won again the next day — and again the next, in ten innings. On day four of the series, they won once more, coming from four runs down. They had defeated Mobile four straight games, and the pennant was theirs.

In 1913, Rudolph Valentino left Italy for America. He was eighteen years old, not yet the Great Lover. In January of 1913, Clarence (Pop Boy) Smith departed Birmingham for Cuba to pitch three weeks of winter ball for the Havana Reds. On a day in early February, he found himself the biggest man in Cuba, pitching sixteen innings and winning the game with his own base hit in the sixteenth inning, 2–1. The fans of Havana carried him from the field and showered him with gifts. Before the month was out, Clarence had returned to Birmingham on the way to joining the Chicago White Sox. At the age of twenty, Clarence Smith was a major-leaguer.

The first game of the Birmingham–Mobile series, August 28, 1912, was a pearl of a ball game. Here, Mobile takes its only lead of the game, as Joe Dunn singles to center to score Dee Walsh in the fourth inning. Clarence Smith is on the mound for the Barons. Note the wooden fence and the scoreboard in rightfield. Home runs seldom cleared the distant leftfield fence. Balls occasionally were hit over the shorter rightfield fence.

The Chicago White Sox of 1913 were a middle-of-the-pack performer. After winning the World Series of 1906, they had finished no higher than third nor lower than sixth in the American League. They would not win another championship until 1917. To remain vigorous, a pitcher's arm needs constant activity, but in 1913 with Chicago, Clarence was given little opportunity to showcase himself, pitching an inning here, an inning there, nothing more. Three pitchers — Reb Russell, Jim Scott, and Eddie Cicotte — started most of the team's games. The pitching staff also included a future Hall of Famer, Ed Walsh. Walsh was thirty-two years old and had lost the cunning and power from his mighty right arm.

By the first of July, the White Sox had decided they no longer needed Clarence and offered him to the Atlanta Crackers. Before the trade could be completed, Clarence pitched four innings against the Detroit Tigers, allowing only one hit. The White Sox called off the deal. Three weeks later he received another chance, pitching four innings against the Washington Senators and not allowing a hit. Chicago fans wondered why he had not been pitching more. By the end of the season, however, he had appeared in only fifteen games for a total of thirty-two innings.

IN EARLY 1914, EUROPE WAS restless. European powers harbored territorial ambitions and competed for colonies. For a decade, Germany, Britain, Russia, and France had been building great armies and navies. Nationalism was sweeping the continent, tensions were widespread, and there was talk of war. Back in the States, the White Sox embarked for spring training on the West Coast. The old saloon keeper and former Barons manager, Harry (Dad) Vaughn, meanwhile, had been in poor health for a year. As the White Sox headed west, Dad Vaughn, the man who had hoped to sign Ty Cobb, died of pneumonia at his residence in Cincinnati.

The White Sox journeyed for six days and nights across the country in a train with all the comforts of modern travel—sleeping cars, observation car, buffet, bath, barbershop, writing desks, and library. A bulletin board displayed news and stock reports. Ordinary sleeping cars of the day used gaslight; the White Sox Special had electricity.

Arriving in California, the White Sox split their squad in half. The first team trained in the northern part of the state near San Francisco, the second team in Los Angeles. After two weeks the teams switched sites. The White Sox played their practice games against Class AA Pacific Coast League teams—San Francisco, Los Angeles, Sacramento, Oakland, Venice—and college teams. Clarence Smith, in his second year with the Sox, was a member of the second team. Ed Walsh, the pitcher with the lame arm, played leftfield. Most of the other players on the second team were rookies who had little chance of becoming big-leaguers. The second team was so bad and lost so many games that fans and newspapers called them the "Goofs."

In a practice game against Los Angeles, Clarence pitched the first four innings, simply going through the motions. Ed Walsh told him to try his best while he was out there. "Oh, go in and pitch yourself," Clarence shot back. The team's coach, Billy Sullivan, suspended Clarence ten days for "sassing" back. Two days later Sullivan lifted the ban because he needed a pitcher.

On March 29, the White Sox were two days away from returning to Chicago. The Goofs were playing a game in San Francisco, and Clarence was being pestered by a party of fans in the "booze cage," a section of bleachers enclosed by chicken wire. Irritated, he snapped back: "I should worry! We'll be back in the United States next week." As it turned out, Clarence would not be going back to the "United States." The next day, the Sox sold him to the Coast League Venice Tigers. He would remain in California with the "foreigners."

Venice was a beach resort town, only nine years old, fourteen miles from Los Angeles. With a population of ten thousand, it was the smallest city in the country with an AA team. The Venice Tigers were a member of the Pacific Coast League, regarded by many as virtually a third major league because of its player talent and high salaries. Two old friends from Birmingham were members of the Venice team—the little catcher named Rowdy and the noisy Kansan who taught Clarence to pitch, Earl Fleharty. After two seasons in Birmingham, Rowdy Elliott had spent a year with Nashville. He was now playing his second season for Venice. Fleharty had pitched the past two seasons for Nashville. The three of them now were teammates again. Small world.

For Clarence, the season of 1914 was fitful. He didn't pitch until the eighth game of the season, when he allowed four runs in four innings of relief. Two weeks passed before he pitched again. The season was a month and a half old before he pitched as a starter. During June and July, he hardly pitched at all. When he did pitch, it was to relieve a teammate whose game was hopelessly lost. Clarence was an easy target for newspaper writers and fans. Because of his "back in the United States" remark during spring training, the reporters began calling him "U.S. Smith."

Venice was in and out of first place the first half of the season. On June 27, the Tigers were playing in San Francisco, while across the Atlantic Ocean war clouds were gathering. Venice fell behind, 8–0, in the second inning. Into the game came Clarence in another hopeless cause. He was met by considerable gabble from San Francisco Seals players and fans. The first two batters against

In the middle of June 1912, Clarence Smith had a pitching record of 3–3, then won six consecutive games. During the streak, Manager Carlton Molesworth called him "one of the most promising young pitchers I ever saw. There is no doubt in my mind but that he will go higher." The Chicago White Sox purchased him in early August 1912. His record for Birmingham in 1912 was 16–8. He was 20 years old.

him hit a double and a triple. The Seals poured it on, scoring six more runs in the four innings he pitched. The San Francisco fans had a merry time jeering and cheering "U.S. Smith." All he could do was grin back. Venice lost, 15–1.

The next day, Franz Ferdinand, archduke of Austria, was shot dead in Sarajevo, Bosnia. As bulletins came in over the wires, ball players, indeed most Americans, wondered: Sarajevo—where is that? The Balkans—what are they? What does it all mean?

Chains of alliances existed among the great European nations. Austria-Hungary believed the country of Serbia had played a role in the murder of the archduke. A month later, at the end of July, Austria-Hungary invaded Serbia. Russia, bound by treaty, sided with Serbia. With striking suddenness, the nations of Europe declared war on one another. Developments came tapping in over the wires daily: Germany, allied with Austria-Hungary, declared war on Russia and invaded Russia's ally, France; Britain and Japan declared war on Germany; Austria-Hungary declared war on Russia; and France declared war on Austria-Hungary. The whirl of events occurred in the first three weeks of August 1914, and a limited war between Austria-Hungary and Serbia escalated. Over the next year, other nations became involved, and the European war became the first global war. It would be known as the Great War and "the war to end all wars."

CLARENCE PITCHED ONLY SEVEN TIMES for Venice during the final three months of 1914, allowing twenty-nine runs in nineteen innings. In a game on September 4, his teammate, Babe Borton, fired a bat toward the bench after making an out.

The bat landed near Clarence and kicked stray gravel into his face. The two players scuffled, and Clarence came out with a bloody nose, Borton with a black eye. Clarence pitched three more times that season—three innings, four innings, and four innings, giving up four runs, six runs, and four runs. His career with Venice was over.

Clarence spent most of the next four seasons, 1915 to 1918, on familiar ground: in the Southern Association, not with Birmingham but with New Orleans. In 1915, he won twenty games; in 1916, twenty-three. In those two seasons he beat his old team, the Barons, five times. In 1915, he pitched a twelve-inning game against Atlanta, giving up only two hits. In 1916, he pitched a seven-inning, no-hit game against Little Rock.

At the end of the 1916 Southern League season, New Orleans sold Clarence to the Cleveland Indians, where a wonderful thing happened. In his first game with the Indians, he pitched two innings of relief against the Philadelphia Athletics and won the game with a base hit in the ninth inning. But that was not the wonderful thing. The wonderful thing came six days later when Clarence made his first pitching start for the Indians. It was a meaningless game, really—a late September game between the league's sixth- and seventh-place teams at League Park in Cleveland. For Clarence, however, it was a sweet moment, pitching against Walter Johnson of the Washington Senators.

Johnson as a ball player truly stood above the rest. He was admired all over America for his modesty, humility, and dignity—a man so humble, so revered in the nation's capital that fans felt unworthy of even loosening the latchets of his shoes. On this day, Clarence and Walter Johnson pitched on even terms for nine innings—strike for strike, run for run. Clarence left the game after nine innings, the score tied, 2–2. In the thirteenth inning, his teammates scored a run to beat Walter Johnson, 3–2.

In his next start, Clarence pitched opposite the man soon to become baseball's most famous player. Babe Ruth was in his second full season in the major leagues—a full-time pitcher, one of the best. Ruth, pitching for the Boston Red Sox, was still four years away from joining the New York Yankees. Clarence pitched the first five innings this day, giving up two runs and five hits. He lost the game to Ruth and the Red Sox, 2–0.

The Cleveland Indians kept Clarence on their roster for the first three weeks of the 1917 season, then sent him back to New Orleans, where he won fifteen games. America entered the World War in 1917. Young men began signing up for the armed forces, and baseball's minor leagues found it hard to fill their rosters. A "work or fight" ruling went into effect on July 1, 1918, requiring ball players to work in an essential wartime industry or risk being drafted into military service.

The Southern Association responded by canceling the second half of the season, and Clarence signed with Salt Lake City of the Pacific Coast League. He made two appearances, both dreadful. In the first, he pitched six innings, allowing eight runs and twelve hits. Five days later on July 12, he pitched a game against the Vernon Tigers. In the third inning, a Vernon batter hit a foul ball down the leftfield line. Umpire Ralph Frary tossed a substitute ball to Clarence, a customary practice to keep the game moving. Someone retrieved the foul ball, however, and threw it to Clarence. Clarence preferred to use the original ball—the foul ball—instead of the umpire's substitute ball. The umpire directed Clarence to surrender the foul ball and use the substitute. Clarence refused. The umpire insisted that Clarence surrender the foul ball and use the new one. Indignant, Clarence threw the ball in the direction of Umpire Frary. Frary ordered Clarence out of the game. Clarence apologized, but Frary stood his ground. Enraged that he had been thrown out of the game, Clarence threw the second ball squarely into Frary's face at close range.

The president of the Salt Lake club, H. W. Lane, fined Clarence $250 and suspended him for the rest of the season. "It was a shocking display of temper," Lane said, "and no man can work on this ball club who has no better control of himself than Smith showed tonight." The suspension was moot, as earlier in the day the Pacific Coast League announced it would end the season two days later out of respect for the war. That night Smith telephoned *The Salt Lake Tribune* newspaper and asked that an apology be printed on his behalf. "I am extremely sorry for my act," he said. "I was beside myself with anger, and I didn't know what I was doing. I have always played clean ball, and this is the first time anything like this ever happened to me. It was a trick unworthy of any ball player, and I want to ask you to make this public apology on my behalf."

The Pacific Coast League ended its season for patriotic and economic reasons, as had the Southern Association. Attendance had dwindled due to the war, and league clubs were suffering heavy losses. Fans taunted the players over the work or fight ruling: "Stop playing baseball! Why don't you go to work?"

The war ended four months later in November 1918, and baseball was back in business. Clarence landed in Fort Worth, a Class B team in the Texas League. Here, his life took a turn. He reported to the Fort Worth Panthers in April 1919 but days later he was sick in bed. On April 26, the team announced that Clarence had tuberculosis, the deadliest, cruelest disease known to man; there was no cure. At the time, tuberculosis was the leading cause of death in the U.S. Approximately 150,000 Americans died of TB in 1919.

Tuberculosis typically attacks the lungs and moves through the air from person to person through coughing and sneezing. Some individuals develop TB within weeks of becoming infected; others do not become sick until years later. It is impossible, therefore, to know when — or where — Clarence contracted the disease. Today, TB is treated with antibiotics, but in the early 1900s, patients went to sanatoriums for treatment. There, they lay in beds on big open porches, receiving rest, fresh air, sunshine, and nutritious food.

On May 12, 1919, Clarence left Fort Worth for St. Joseph's Sanatorium in the mountains of Asheville, North Carolina. Before Clarence left Fort Worth, the Detroit and Cleveland American League baseball clubs sent him a check for $200. On the way to Asheville, Clarence stopped in Birmingham, where *The Age-Herald* newspaper acknowledged his plight on May 18: "Pop Boy Smith, now in Birmingham, is in a very serious condition both physically and financially, and the ex-Baron pitcher must depend on his friends to help him defray his expenses at Asheville, where he goes to regain his health."

The following day the newspaper again pleaded for aid: "He is badly in need of funds and owing to his condition is unable to work. The players over the league have subscribed liberally to a fund to help care for him, and it is thought that maybe some of the fans in Birmingham, where he got his start, would be willing to lend a helping hand to this ex-Baron who is now in distress. He needs it, boys."

In late June, *The Age-Herald* received a letter from Clarence stating he had nothing to do all day in Asheville but read about the games of the Southern Association. He also confided his fear that he would never play baseball again. On July 4, the Birmingham Barons and New Orleans Pelicans played a doubleheader at Rickwood Field. During the game, pitchers from both teams took off their caps and walked through the stands with an appeal for donations in his behalf.

Days later, the people of Birmingham received a thank-you letter, published in the newspaper:

> To the Birmingham Baseball Fans:
> Please accept my sincere thanks for the generous Fourth of July gift of $529.88 which I received from you through W. D. Smith, president of the Birmingham Baseball Association. It helps a fellow's feelings a lot to know that he is not forgotten by his old friends and boosters just because misfortune has made him step down out of the spotlight for a while. Believe me, I am in the big game now, fighting the battle against ill health. But so long as I have the old Rickwood fans rooting and pulling for me as strongly as you proved to be doing on the Fourth, I assure you that I'll do my best and not weaken, and with such support I feel sure I'll wind up in the final ninth inning with the score on my side.
> Very Sincerely Yours,
> Clarence (Pop Boy) Smith

Clarence remained at the sanatorium until October of 1919. He was twenty-seven years old and had recovered well enough to land a baseball job for 1920 in Gorman, Texas, not as a player but as manager of the team. The Gorman ball club was a member of the West Texas League, a Class D league, the lowest level of professional ball. Still, it was steady work, and here, as everywhere else, they called him Pop Boy. Later that season the Gorman franchise moved to another Texas town, Sweetwater. Clarence returned to Sweetwater the following season, 1921, and was reunited with his old friend from Birmingham and Venice, Earl Fleharty, now a pitcher for Sweetwater. The Sweetwater Swatters finished second in the league. Clarence managed Sweetwater again in 1922, but the league disbanded after the season. He found another job managing the Clovis, New Mexico, Cubs in 1923. The team finished third in the league.

For years, tuberculosis had been weakening Clarence's body, breaking down his resistance. During his days in Texas, his condition seemed stable: not worse but no better. In early 1924, Clarence was thirty-one years old, negotiating a return to the big leagues as a scout. On Saturday, the sixteenth of February, at two o'clock in the morning, he awoke with a sudden fit of coughing and a hemorrhage. Then he was gone.

BIRMINGHAM FANS WOULD REMEMBER YOUNG Clarence Smith as a slip of a kid selling peanuts and Cokes at the West End ball park, would remember him laying the foundation of his baseball career on the corner lots of the town. In 1910, he became young Pop Boy Smith, practicing at the ball park before and after the crowd had left for the day, receiving instruction from Manager Carlton Molesworth. He tried out for the team in 1911, was found wanting, and was shipped to Anniston. But Clarence was the apt pupil, the willing worker, the natural ball player. He made the team in 1912, won respect, and from the grandstand came the cries: "Now you pitchin', Pop Boy!" The next year he was pitching in the major leagues. At every stop, he bore the name Pop Boy. Odd, isn't it, how a man is given a nickname and never loses it?

Then came the war, then Fort Worth. Doctors discovered in him the germ of tuberculosis, and he was doomed. Instead of brooding and calling it quits, he continued in the game. When he died, they brought him back from Texas, to the town where he attained fame—to Birmingham. They laid him to rest in Elmwood Cemetery and, after life's fitful fever, he sleeps well.

THE WAR YEARS
1915–1918

CHAPTER 7

BURLEIGH GRIMES OF CLEAR LAKE

WHEN I MET CHARLES STEWART for the first time, I was eleven years old. At that age, I didn't know what I wanted to do with my life, but when Stewart began filling me with his baseball talk, I started getting ideas. He and I had a conversation about it once. It went like this:

"I was thinking I could be a famous newspaperman when I grow up," I said to him. "You know, write stories about ball players an' all. That's something I could do, don't you think so? You've done tol' me a lot, an' I could use it all in my stories."

"You sound like a wise young man," he said. "Oh-ho, become a newspaperman — yes, I think that would be a good thing for you to do. I certainly do. You'll start out as a copy boy, buzzing around the newspaper office, running the reporters' typed stories to the deskman for editing. If you prove to have a good head on your shoulders, you'll become a cub reporter, then a regular reporter. You must study hard and read everything you can get your hands on. You must read and read some more. Learn every subject under the sun — that's real important in being a good newspaperman. The more you know, the more you can write about, and everyone, all of them — the newspapermen, the readers — they'll think you're the cream off the top of the bottle. Once you get printer's ink in your blood, there'll be no stopping you. Yes, I believe you'll be a crackerjack newspaperman. I wish I'd thought a' that when I was your age."

I said, "Well, you gotta tell me more so I can write about it when I grow up. Do you remember any other stories?"

"Walter," he said to me, "I was thinking about a trip I took many years ago, along about 1915. The war in Europe was on, and in two years America would join the conflict. The Barons went to Orlando, Florida, that year for spring training. Usually the team did their spring training at Rickwood, but that year they went to Florida for the warm weather, to get in condition quicker, to get a jump on the other teams in the league.

"I'd been a fan of the Barons for a few years," he said, "and I became acquainted with the young sports editor of *The Birmingham News,* Henry Vance. Henry had been assigned to travel to Orlando to write about spring training. He asked me if I'd go along and assist—get comments from ball players, things like that." Stewart lowered his voice, and a big grin crinkled over his face: "I think the real reason he wanted me around was to carry his typewriter.

"Well, Henry kept that typewriter in a big black leather case. When we arrived in Orlando, I carried the case into the lobby of the hotel. You should've heard the bellboy. Oh-ho! When he found out the only thing in that big case was a typewriter, he said, 'Boss, I thought sho' you all had some booze in that big case.'"

When Stewart got to talking, you just sat and listened, so I smiled and kept my trap shut. On he went:

"Orlando is a pretty little town, but as it turned out, that spring of 1915 was one of the coldest they'd ever seen. It was hard for the team to get its work done. We could've accomplished about as much on the training field in Birmingham as we did in Florida. There weren't many teams training in Florida then. Birmingham was the first Class A minor league team ever to train there. Among the major-leaguers, you had the Cubs in Tampa, the Athletics in Jacksonville, the Phillies in St. Pete, the Dodgers in Daytona Beach. Louisville, a Double A team, was down there, and the Barons played games against them. We played the Dodgers on a cold day in Daytona; all the players wore sweaters. The Dodger players were real nice—even gave some of their bats to our players.

"Carlton Molesworth was still our field manager. A good manager he was—they'll tell you that from Medicine Hat to Timbuktu, experts will. He was a conscientious cuss—good habits, a good judge of young ball players, good at keeping the morale of his players at high ebb. Molesworth managed the Barons fourteen years. He and the owner, Rick Woodward, had great respect for each other, and Moley never worked under a contract. He and the management had a handshake agreement that he could come back every year for as long as he wished.

"Anyhow, I'd like to tell you about our trip to Florida. That spring I saw the best young pitcher who ever played for the Barons. His name was Burleigh Grimes."

"That's a funny name," I said.

"Maybe so, but he's probably the best pitcher in the major leagues today. Back then some of us called him 'Bertie.'"

I couldn't help but giggle. "I wouldn't want anyone calling me that."

Stewart pretended not to hear me. He continued:

"Burleigh had signed to play with the Barons in 1914, but he came up with a sore arm and got off to a poor start. They sent him to Richmond that year, where he would have a better chance to play. The next year he came back to Birmingham and made a good record. The year after that, 1916, was even better, and off to the majors he went.

"I'll never forget that spring training of 1915," Stewart said. "For those boys — a lively set of fellows, twenty, twenty-one years old — it was the trip of a lifetime."

Daybreak, Thursday, February 25, 1915; Clear Lake, Wisconsin

A heavy brown horse pulling a farm wagon clip-clopped across a frozen lake. At the lake's edge, the morning light was a blaze of orange in the night sky. Stars cluttered the heavens. Nearby, a smoky oil lamp flickered in a farmhouse window. In the town of Clear Lake, Wisconsin, electric lights glittered on Main Street. As morning broke, streaks of light rose in the sky. High on the wagon seat, a man and two companions were bundled against the cold, speaking not a word. They wore heavy mackinaws, wool pants, long woolen underwear, and stocking caps pulled over their ears. A coarse Wisconsin wind whipped about. Swirling, falling snow cut into their faces. The wagon bumped along.

The horse stepped onto dry land and set out through a snowy forest. The driver flicked the reins on the rump of the horse. Breathing hard, nostrils flaring, the horse tossed its head and huffed the final quarter-mile into town, wagon tracks trailing in the snow. At the train depot, the driver tugged on the reins of the bridle — Whoa, there — and the old mare stopped. Someone brought out fresh water, and the weary animal dropped its head into a tin drink tub. The morning light was a reddish gleam. Hot, hissing steam gushed from a waiting train. The yardman walked over, swinging a lantern. Down from the wagon seat sprang Burleigh Grimes, suitcase in hand. The old horse nickered and shook its head vigorously. Burleigh put his hand on the bridle and gave the animal a pat. The horse flicked its ears, head high and proud. Burleigh said good-bye to wife Ruth and brother Shurleigh and walked inside. A glint of morning sunlight fell across the floor.

"Close the door!" someone bellowed.

Clear Lake depot reeked of coal smoke and damp, wool clothing. Farmers in bib overalls milled around a big-bellied iron stove, whipping their arms and stamping their boots. Waiting to ship their goods, they spoke of prevailing prices while shaking the cold from their bones. Salesmen from the Twin Cities—Minneapolis and St. Paul—arrived on the morning train and walked across the station platform. A local man with a long, gray beard noticed Burleigh and shook his hand.

"How does it feel to be goin' away?"

Another man, puffing at his pipe, spoke: "So long, boy. Be sure and write."

Burleigh nodded and smiled. No time for small talk. Outside on the steam-filled platform, a whistle blew. The train was in the station, steam up, firebox glowing red. "Allll aboooaarrd!" A bell rang—time to go. A long journey lay ahead: from northwest Wisconsin south through Illinois, Kentucky, Tennessee, and Alabama; across Georgia; down to Florida—fifteen hundred miles—to Orlando, where the Birmingham Barons were gathering for spring training. This would be Burleigh Grimes' first full year with Birmingham, his fourth year in professional ball. Twenty-one years old, a pitcher, he was determined to make this his final season in minor league ball. His ambition was to play in the major leagues.

Burleigh Grimes, a wholesome boy with sandy-brown hair, grew up on a farm along the bank of Clear Lake. In the wintertime when the lake froze, he walked across it on the way to school. All the children of Clear Lake, in fact, walked to school—a distance of two miles or more, for some. Clear Lake was a town of five hundred residents near the Minnesota border, where people worked with their backs. It was a land of lakes, streams, and dairy farms. Herds of milk cows grazed in pastures of grass and clover. Throughout Polk County, crops of many kinds did well. Wheat, corn, oats, rye, barley, peas, and beets filled farmers' bins in autumn. Land was cheap; thousands of acres could be purchased for twenty to fifty dollars an acre. It was dairy country, with three dozen cheese factories and butter-making creameries. Farmers from miles around brought produce, cream, and livestock to Clear Lake to ship by rail.

Every home and every building in Clear Lake was heated by wood fires and lighted by smoky kerosene lamps. Meals were prepared on wood-burning cookstoves. Bread, cakes, cookies, and pies were baked at home. Butter was churned at home until a small creamery came to Clear Lake, providing farmers with a ready market for their milk and cream. Sometimes wagons and buggies lined up in front of the creamery, waiting for milk to be weighed. Electric power had come to Clear Lake the previous summer, and the town replaced its old gasoline streetlamps with electric lights. The first moving picture theater opened. On Saturday night, about the time Burleigh Grimes was due in Orlando, the Rex Theatre featured a three-reel action thriller, "The Midnight Strike," for ten cents.

To the north and east of Clear Lake stood dense groves of white pine. Trees grew so tall, so thick, the sun didn't shine, and sometimes it looked like twilight in the middle of the day. Many farmers spent the dreary winter months deep in the forest in low-roofed logging camps, cutting timber in places like Prairie Farm, Reeve, Graytown, and Rice Lake. Burleigh Grimes' father and uncles did that, as did Burleigh.

The children of Clear Lake learned their verses, their spelling, and their diction from books called *McGuffey's Readers* and practiced their sums on a slate. The schoolhouse had four rooms, two downstairs, two up, with a wood-burning stove in the middle of each room. There were no electric lights or plumbing. Those who sat near the stove were always too warm; those farther away, too cold. Sometimes the children's hands and feet were so cold it was hard to read and write. Students put their dinner pails on the floor in the back of the room. Hats and wraps hung from hooks on the wall. Each room had a tin pail with drinking water, and everyone drank from the same dipper. When water or firewood was needed, the teacher sent two boys to fetch it. In the spring and fall, children came to school barefoot; in the winter, boys and girls wore long, home-knit woolen stockings. When the weather was cold or stormy or the snow too deep, some couldn't get to school. If some were ill or if parents made them stay home to work, it was alright with the teacher. The children came to school as they could.

Burleigh Grimes led a vigorous life. He quit school after the eighth grade and took a job cutting timber from four-thirty in the morning until nine at night for a dollar a day. When he earned a raise to thirty-six dollars a month, he thought it a fortune. During summers, he played on Clear Lake's town baseball teams. The youth team was called the Red Jackets and the adult team, coached by his father, Nick, was the Yellow Jackets. Nick Grimes had been an amateur ball player in the 1890s. One day a pitcher threw him a curveball, and Nick quit the game then and there. "When they get so they can start a-curvin' that thing," he said, "I'm through."

In the spring of 1912, Burleigh Arland Grimes was eighteen years old. His father gave him fifteen dollars, and Burleigh went to Eau Claire, Wisconsin, a Class D team sixty miles from home, to become a professional baseball player. Burleigh asked Russell Bailey, the manager, if he could work out with the team and pay his own expenses. The manager agreed. After three weeks, the team was going to cut him from the squad, so Burleigh said, "Mr. Bailey, I paid my own expenses. You ought to at least give me a shot." The manager relented, but he still didn't give Burleigh a contract.

The team played a game in Rochester, Minnesota, and Burleigh was ordered to take up tickets at the gate. In the first inning, one of the players ran over and told

Burleigh Grimes played town ball for the Clear Lake Yellow Jackets from 1908 to 1911. Burleigh is on the left in this photograph, 14 years old, in 1908. In 1912, he signed a professional contract with Class D Eau Claire, Wisconsin. The league disbanded a few months later.

Burleigh the manager wanted him. When he got to the field, Manager Bailey told him to warm up. Then with the bases loaded and nobody out, Burleigh went into the game. First pitch: base hit. Two runners scored, but they were the only runs he allowed. He finished the game, and when it was over, the catcher came out to shake Burleigh's hand.

"Kid, he's going to offer you sixty dollars. Get eighty out of him." The manager took Burleigh into the clubhouse. "I'm signing you up," he said. "Sixty a month."

"I think I ought to get eighty," Burleigh replied.

"Somebody told you to say that," Bailey said. "Alright, I'll give you eighty." And that was Burleigh Grimes' first contract. The next year he advanced to the Class A Chattanooga Lookouts of the Southern Association. Then it was on to Birmingham, briefly, then Richmond, and, for the 1915 season, back to Birmingham. Folks around Clear Lake were proud of their native son. The way they figured, he already had gone as far as anyone from the town ever had, or probably ever would. But those folks didn't know Burleigh Grimes. He was out to prove he was no minor-leaguer.

Burleigh was not a big man, but he was a sturdy five-ten, 175 pounds. A competitor? Never was there a ball player as fierce as he. Conditioned? One had to be in condition to endure the life of a Wisconsin logger. When teammates told how they stayed in shape in the off-season by hunting and fishing in fields and streams down south, Burleigh smiled. You never worked so hard as when you've tramped through wooded country on snowshoes during a cruel Wisconsin winter.

Even after he began playing ball, he returned in the off-seasons to work the logging camps with husky, two-fisted lumberjacks. Logging days began at first light and lasted until dark. Men cut timber in groups of two—one on each end of a crosscut saw. When the day was done, they walked back to a big supper and a hard bunk in a log sleeping camp, with a big black stove and a roaring wood fire. Come spring, when melting snows filled streams and rivers to overflowing, the loggers departed except the chosen few who "drove" the logs to the mills to be sawed into lumber. Burleigh hauled timber by sleigh, either to the rail line or to the riverbank, where it could float downstream when the ice broke in the spring. It was hard, dangerous work, and he did it from October to February, until time for baseball again.

Burleigh's path to Birmingham was forged by a mishap in a logging camp, and it was only good fortune that he escaped with his life. It happened near Rice Lake in late January 1914, after his season with Chattanooga. His team of horses was pulling a load of logs, seven tiers high, down a steep grade in the snow. The sled hit a stump, and chains holding the logs broke. He didn't have time to jump clear of the load, and the tumbling logs pinned him to the ground. One of the horses was killed. It took several lumberjacks to free him.

"If one or two of the logs had shifted a particle, I would have been crushed," he said. As it was, a log had rolled across his left arm. The arm was mangled but, thankfully, the left arm was not his pitching arm. The Chattanooga ball club, wary of his condition, sold him to Birmingham for $400. A month later, in March 1914, he reported to Birmingham with his left arm in a cast. During spring training, he hurt his pitching arm and never got into condition. Early in the season, he lost two games and was shipped to Richmond, a lower-level minor league team. Burleigh could still hear the words of Barons Manager Carlton Molesworth when he was demoted in 1914:

"Grimes has a world of stuff, but he has much to learn in the pitching line. He should make us a winning pitcher next year." Well, next year was now, and Burleigh intended to be one of the pitchers on Molesworth's staff.

Burleigh's main pitch was a spitball—a legal pitch then, illegal now. Pitchers had thrown spitballs since the turn of the century, when they discovered that moisture between the fingers and ball minimized friction and reduced the ball's spin. The ball approached the plate looking like a fastball, then moved sideways or down. Most often, the moisture applied to the ball was saliva—thus the term "spitball"—but pitchers needed something to generate saliva. Burleigh and a few others chewed slippery elm, the fiber from the inner bark of the North American elm tree. To deceive the batter, a spitball pitcher often feigned throwing the spitter, then threw a different pitch, such as a fastball or curve. Before going into his windup, Burleigh would bring his gloved hand and pitching hand together in front of his face and either wet his fingers or pretend to. Then he would deliver the pitch. The batter didn't know if it would be a spitball or not.

IN SPRINGTIME WHEN THE TALL grass rustles, young ball players emerge to catch trains to their training stations. As Burleigh Grimes set off for Orlando in February 1915, Europe was awash in destruction, with guns thundering over the land. In August of 1914, war had broken out in Europe, nudging America into an economic depression. U.S. foreign trade declined; industries began closing; coal and steel production fell; mines were shutting down; banks were losing deposits and foreclosing mortgages. Automobile sales dropped. The stock market closed for four months. Business operations were at a standstill, and people by the tens of thousands were out of work. For many Americans, it was the hardest of hard times.

> In over thirty years of working experience, I have never seen the like, when a man who is willing, anxious, and capable of doing work satisfactorily, cannot even get a chance, tho' he may look his eyes out of his head for such a happy opportunity. Because the work is not there.
> — *An unemployed man in Washington State, December 1914*

Before long, the embattled nations of Europe would turn to America for food and manufactured goods: automobiles, wagons, harnesses, clothing, shoes. Orders from abroad stimulated the economy, and jobs came back. Furnaces, mills, and factories enjoyed steady business, and by the fall of 1915, prosperity began to emerge.

A lean year was expected for baseball in 1915. Attendance at moving picture theaters and vaudeville houses had slumped. During the season of 1914, teams of the Southern Association had been allowed to carry sixteen players and spend a maximum of $4,000 a month on salaries. In 1915, the limits were reduced to fifteen players and $3,200. Clubs such as Birmingham could afford to spend more, but player and salary limits helped maintain competitive balance in the

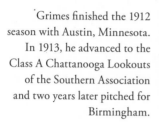

Grimes finished the 1912 season with Austin, Minnesota. In 1913, he advanced to the Class A Chattanooga Lookouts of the Southern Association and two years later pitched for Birmingham.

league. To meet the new salary limits, Birmingham had to reduce the salaries of three players for 1915.

It had been a hard winter for ball players. In off-seasons past, players found jobs to earn extra income. But in the fall of 1914, jobs were scarce. Most could not find work. Now with the coming of spring 1915, ball players were in good spirits. Soon they would be drawing a regular paycheck to play baseball. For Burleigh Grimes, the worries of the world seemed far away.

Birmingham, like all Class A minor league teams, invited a squad of veterans, recruits, and amateurs to spring training. Those who had played Class A or top-level Class AA baseball were referred to as *veterans*. Players with experience in the low-level minor leagues — Classes B, C, or D — were called *recruits*. Players from city leagues and town baseball teams, the so-called sandlots of baseball, were known as *amateurs*. Amateurs and recruits were the rookies of the team. Very few amateurs were good enough to make a Class A team such as Birmingham. Burleigh Grimes would have been classified an amateur when he played for the Clear Lake town team. He became a professional when he signed with Class D Eau Claire. When he reported to higher level Chattanooga and Birmingham, he was considered a recruit.

IF A BALL PLAYER DID not measure up, either in spring training or during the season, he was released. When a player's discharge was imminent, the sporting press wrote of it almost gleefully. The manager, a reporter would state, was "sharpening his ax," or preparing to get out the "paring knife" or the "pruning scissors." The player was about to feel "the cold blade of the woodsman's ax." The description could even be French Revolution-like: "The ax fell in the Baron camp," a newspaper once stated, "and the heads of nine rookies fell in the basket, while Molesworth, chief executioner, wielded the blade." When the ax did fall, most players were able to catch on with another team, but some would never be heard from again. A young player who showed promise but wasn't quite ready for Class A ball usually was sent to a low-level minor league team "with strings attached," meaning that the original team retained the rights to him and could recall him at any time. Such was the case with Burleigh Grimes—Birmingham farmed him to Richmond in 1914 but brought him back in 1915. And so, in February 1915, it was off to Orlando for Burleigh Grimes and the Birmingham Barons.

CHAPTER 8
SPRING TRAINING IN ORLANDO

FEW BASEBALL TEAMS TRAINED IN Florida in the early 1900s. Most major league teams trained in Georgia, Texas, Arkansas, or one of the other Southern states. The Barons almost always held their spring training at Rickwood Field. Some years the New York Giants, Chicago Cubs, or Philadelphia Phillies trained alongside the Barons in Birmingham, but in 1915, owner Rick Woodward decided that the warmer climate of Orlando would enable the Barons to get into playing condition more quickly, giving them an advantage over their opponents. So in 1915 the Barons trained in Florida, as did five other teams: the Chicago Cubs, Philadelphia Athletics, Philadelphia Phillies, Brooklyn Dodgers, and the minor league Louisville Colonels.

Tuesday, February 23, 1915; en route to Orlando, somewhere in northern Virginia
Carlton Molesworth, the boss of the Barons, left his home in Frederick, Maryland, for the train trip south to Orlando. Molesworth had spent January in Birmingham tending to baseball business: corresponding with teams who wanted to sell players, discussing player salaries with team President Bob Baugh, mailing contracts to players, and deciding whether players who were unhappy with their contracts should be released. After his business in Birmingham was completed in early February, he returned to Maryland before departing for Orlando. Molesworth had turned thirty-nine the week before and was in his seventh full season as manager. During his tenure, the Barons had been league champions twice, only once finishing below third place.

Molesworth was an earnest, sober man; he did not drink and rarely used profanity. The first thing one noticed about Molesworth was his eyes — round

Carlton Molesworth, a lefthanded, .300 hitter during his long career in the minor leagues, admitted he could hit only pitches that were thrown at the level of the letters on his uniform. To get the pitch he wanted, he leaned forward until his head was over home plate, enticing the pitcher to throw at his head. As the pitcher released the ball, Molesworth straightened up and "murdered" it.

and brown in a moon-shaped face. Short in stature at five-foot-seven, with a wide girth, Molesworth owned a physique that was inviting to mock: "Chubby Moley," they called him. Occasionally, a bold soul referred to him as "Gladys"—no one knows why; perhaps it was for his girlish figure.

For sixteen seasons, Molesworth had been a good minor league player, a centerfielder with foot speed who batted over .300 almost every year. His playing career with the Barons began in 1906, and he became playing manager in 1908. He retired from active play following the 1911 season. He had slowed up a bit, and his throwing arm was gone. The Barons in 1914 had fielded a pretty fair ball club. The league race was tight entering the dreary days of August, four clubs still in the running. "We could win the pennant," Molesworth said, "if we had one .300 hitter to stick in there."

In those days, such a hitter was not easy to acquire, but a few days later a .300 hitter did appear in the Barons lineup. It was none other than Molesworth himself. He had changed his status from bench manager to playing manager and inserted himself in the lineup to provide the punch his club sorely needed. In his first game, on July 29, Molesworth went two for three. He was thirty-eight years old, playing centerfield. His body had become round, and instead of bending over to field ground balls, he had a habit of stopping them with his foot. In the final weeks of the 1914 season, Molesworth hit the ball with startling regularity, even stole a few bases. The day Molesworth entered the lineup, Birmingham was in third place, four games behind the leader. Three weeks later the Barons were in first. The added punch from Molesworth had enabled the Barons to pull steadily away from the rival clubs, and when the season closed they were comparatively easy winners. Molesworth swore he wasn't a natural hitter, that he had any number of hitting weaknesses, but along the way he found he could hit any pitcher who would serve him a ball between his belt and his shoulders, along about where the letters were sewn on his uniform.

"If a pitcher doesn't throw that ball somewhere around my letters," he used to say, "I'm helpless. I'll kill any pitching up around there, but that's the only place I can hit 'em." So he figured out a way to make them pitch to his letters. Molesworth knew there was no pitcher alive who could resist the insult of an opposing batsman sticking his head out over the plate. So he would stoop across the plate and lower his head to the level of his letters.

"There never was a pitcher," he said, "who doesn't foam at the mouth every time a batsman puts his head smack over the plate. They'll every one of them say, 'I'll make that fellow get that dome of his away from there or I'll smash it in two,' and accordingly he aims a fastball straight at your skull. That's why I could always hit. At the plate I would assume a crouch with my head directly over the platter. I knew they would throw at it. When the pitch came along, all I had to do was straighten up. The ball would be in the groove, right at my letters. All I had to do was murder it."

Molesworth began his baseball career as a righthanded pitcher, but along about 1898 he ruined that right arm foolishly showing off. He had just turned twenty-two and was playing outfield in the New York State League.

"It was in the spring," Molesworth recounted, "and the weather don't heat up much in New York state in the early spring. I cut one loose from deep right to the plate and somebody says, 'My, that kid's gotta arm.'

"'Pshaw, you ain't seen no arm yet,' I replied, and I immediately cut my cold right arm loose with some long distance throws. I backed against the fence in deep center, and I pegged 'em on a line right into the stands.

"The next day went off lovely. I didn't have to make a single throw. The day following, however, I tried to cut a runner off at the plate, and something snapped. All the coaxing, all the liniment, and all the rubbing in the world failed to affect the arm. I had ruined my greatest ball playing asset, just through a bit

Early in his career,
Carlton Molesworth was
a righthanded pitcher.
He injured his right arm
"showing off" but learned to
throw with his left arm and
was a fine centerfielder for
the rest of his career. Here
is Molesworth at West End
Park about 1909.

of foolhardiness in trying to show myself off before a bunch of people who were patting me on the back." Resourceful, if not desperate, Molesworth developed his other arm and became a lefthanded thrower the rest of his career—fifteen more years.

Molesworth would arrive in Orlando two days ahead of his players. Every player had been mailed transportation money and was responsible for arriving on time. Molesworth liked the makeup of the 1915 squad, especially the four returning pitchers. More than thirty players would compete for fifteen places on the team. Molesworth would look 'em over and size 'em up before swinging the ax.

Competition for the five pitching spots would be keen. Most of the pitchers from the 1914 championship team returned, among them Omar Hardgrove and Dick Robertson. Hardgrove, at thirty, was the eldest Baron, in his fourth year with the team. He had spent the winter in Monmouth, Illinois, and went to Kansas City for a week before boarding a train to Orlando. His wife planned to join him in Birmingham when the team returned from spring training. Dick

Robertson had played winter ball for the Tortorich Sweets in New Orleans, then stopped over in Birmingham for two weeks before heading to Orlando.

Others headed to Orlando included Roy Ellam, blond-haired shortstop. He had piddled about his home in Conshohocken, Pennsylvania, without a job over the winter. Now in his seventh season with the Barons, he was the brainy team captain, a hard worker and not a grouch. In the early days, the fans were forever on Ellam's neck. He bobbled balls afield and bobbled again. The gods of the bleachers jeered, but they couldn't shake his nerve.

"Shotgun" Jack Wallace came from a family of lawyers. He expected to compete as the starting catcher but would not report with the other players. He was content to hunt rabbits and birds around Winnfield, Louisiana, a while longer. Tod Sloan, an outfielder recently acquired from the St. Louis Browns, had spent the winter with his parents in Madisonville, Tennessee. Charlie Carroll, an infielder in his fourth year, had hunted and fished around Durham, North Carolina. Outfielder Jimmy Magee, who had played for Utica, New York, last year, spent the off-season in Pennsylvania. Cecil Coombs, a utility infielder, had played in Bay City, Michigan, and remained there over the winter to manage a bowling alley.

Clyde McBride, an outfielder in his sixth year with the Barons, had remained in Birmingham over the winter. He would always remember a March day in 1911 when he hit safely five times against the New York Giants at Rickwood Field. Three of his hits—one a home run—were off the renowned Christy Mathewson. Charlie (Red) Stewart, an outfielder, was one of three Barons who had to take a cut in pay, and he was not happy. During the off-season, he had made almost as much money working for Edison Electric in Chicago as he did playing baseball, and it was thought he might decide not to come south. Pitcher Dave Roth also received a cut in pay but would report on time from Baltimore. Roth was the only player to bring a wife to Orlando. This time last year he was in the camp of the Chicago White Sox with arm trouble and did not pitch at all until the Barons picked him up in July. The year before, 1913, he had won twenty-two games for the minor league Baltimore Orioles, the same year that a kid named Babe Ruth was pitching for a reform school across town. Tall, lanky Arthur Johnson spent the winter months as a switchman in the railroad yards of Madison, Wisconsin. He had been a pleasant surprise for the Barons last year, winning eighteen games in his first year with the team. He was the only player to get a pay raise and was delighted to be headed to Orlando.

MY FRIEND, CHARLES STEWART, ALSO traveled to Orlando that spring of 1915. Baseball man that he was, he kept a diary of the trip. When I was a young man, he gave me that diary, and I was amazed at the humor and detail in it. I've selected the most entertaining passages for you to read.

Thursday night, February 25, 1915; Union Station, Jacksonville, Florida

Seven rookie ball players were at the Jacksonville, Florida, depot waiting to board the nine-twenty train to Orlando. In their hands were shiny, imitation-leather suitcases. The group included App McDuffie and Al Fields of Birmingham, John Cantley of Ensley, Alabama, and Danny Clark of Meridian, Mississippi.

Cantley pitched for Opelika in the Class D Georgia-Alabama League last year, winning twenty-two games. In one special game, he hit three bases-loaded home runs. McDuffie and Fields are amateurs, their first time with a professional club. Fields, a callow youth, does not have a contract. The Barons have offered him a tryout, but he must pay his own train fare and lodging in Orlando. McDuffie pitched for an outfit in the Birmingham City League last year. He is a big, husky fellow with an appetite that will make him even larger, as long as the necessary grub is provided. Danny Clark, a twenty-one-year-old second baseman, has played two seasons in the low minors. He looks rather hefty, leading an observer to believe that he eats three meals a day and slips into the pantry in between.

On the trip south, the rookies were as happy as larks and held a songfest every fifteen minutes. McDuffie displayed a good soprano voice, while Clark sang tenor. Manager Molesworth, "Chubby Moley," arrived in Orlando tonight looking well fed.

Friday, February 26; Orlando, Florida

The team is bunking at the Empire Hotel on West Central Avenue, a complete and modern hostelry. The players have given Orlando their stamp of approval and have decided to enjoy every minute. All seem lively and happy to be here. What's this? Danny Clark had been in town for an hour when he was seen beating it to a picture show with a lovely dame at his side.

Orlando is a splendid little town with a population of eight thousand, plus another two thousand tourists. This is not a little two-by-four town away from civilization. There are fine automobiles and roads. There are golf courses everywhere and all-night drugstores and restaurants. The town is so clean and well-lighted that you hesitate to throw a cigarette "duck" on the street. There are four picture shows, one of which surpasses anything in Birmingham, and another theater on top of a five-story department store, the "roof garden" of the town. The orchestra at one of the picture shows performs in full dress. Before

Managers of the early 1900s often stood in the third-base coach's box while their team was at bat. Carlton Molesworth, however, managed the Barons from a cane-bottom chair next to the dugout. Here are two views of Molesworth: in uniform and in street clothes. Note the bag of balls and gloves at his feet.

arriving, the players were advised to pack Sunday suits and tan shoes in their grips, as dances are held nightly until twelve-thirty at the town's leading hotel.

Can you beat it? The streets and country roads of Orlando are paved with brick—brick made in Birmingham. The people of Orlando think nothing of taking fifty- or seventy-five-mile hops in their motorcars. Autos here are as thick as flies, fine automobiles in all colors: Hudsons, Maxwells, Cadillacs, Buicks, Chevrolets, and plain, black Model T Fords.

It seems that most of the population are oldsters waiting out their lives. Our sporting blood was stirred as we watched the town sharks pitch horseshoes beneath moss-draped trees. We came upon a vacant lot where ten old fellows indulged in this strenuous pastime, representing almost as many states of the union. Poor old fellows, they would tire at this game, drop out, and their place would be taken by another from the gallery. And when they left the game and donned their coats, they were warned by the crowd not to sit in the shade, that it might be too cool. So they hunted the sunshine and basked in a temperature of seventy-two degrees.

A mile from our hotel is the baseball diamond, Exposition Park, located at the fairgrounds, six blocks from the center of town. The diamond has been carved inside a horse racing track. There is a nice clubhouse for the players, with individual lockers and shower baths, hot and cold. The stands are near home plate and seat eighteen hundred. Many fans will park near the stands and watch games from their cars.

Saturday, February 27

During the off-season, a ball player usually latches onto a good job and earns enough money to keep Jack Frost away. The past winter has been difficult. With the economic depression, money was scarce. About the time the ball season shut down last year, big corporations and little firms started laying off their men, and when players returned to their hometowns, they found many hometown boys unemployed. The players sat idle and gossiped in village drugstores.

A player who did not lay aside a little coin of the realm suffered a hard winter, and as a rule, a ball tosser does not lay much aside. Ball players are the freest spenders on the globe. In the summer, it's easy come, easy go. When the team hits town and a drugstore man has a punch board with prizes offered, the boys stick to the board 'til the last number is gone. That's the way they let loose the coin. Those who did that last summer spent the winter regretting it. It has been a hard winter on the ball players, and they are hailing the coming of spring with joy. It means that revenue will soon start flowing into their pocketbooks.

Sunday, February 28

The moment Bertie Grimes arrived in Orlando, he told newspapermen he did not like being called a rookie, that he was going to be a regular, and he would go up to the majors at the end of the season. Because he is known as a humorist, his statements were taken as jests. Manager Molesworth is partial to Grimes and believes he will be his fifth man. Bertie wasn't ready for Class A ball in Birmingham last year. He came up with a sore arm and never got into condition. He lost his first two games and was shipped to Richmond. But he went about his work full of song and life, and even when the tide of battle turned against him, he wore a pleasant smile. At Richmond, Grimes' sore whip regained its cunning, and two weeks later he twirled a two-hit contest. When he wasn't pitching, he played outfield and led the Virginia League in hitting with an average of .331.

In all cities, you find inconsistent Sunday laws, and Orlando is no exception. Here's an example: On Sundays, the soda founts are not allowed to dispense a drink where fizz water is part of the contents. Yet you can gulp down malted milks and such to your heart's content. No ice cream can be sold on Sundays unless accompanied by cake, and when we had occasion to be served, the boy was in doubt as to whether or not the law forced the customer to eat the cake. To be on the safe side, we ate the two small wafers for which we paid an extra nickel.

Monday morning, March 1; Exposition Park, Orlando

Rise and shine! The bats have been sorted and the gloves oiled up. The first shot was fired in spring training when Manager Molesworth hiked his boys to the ball park. Each day the team will walk to the park for the morning workout, hike back to the hotel for lunch, and then walk back for the afternoon workout. The first thing on the program was the choosing of lockers and then a scramble for uniforms. The boys all seemed anxious to get on the grounds and toss the ol' apple around. There is not a small man in the bunch. They look to be a formidable collection and show a lot of snap and ginger. Their limbs, which were bound up by the frost of winter, have returned to their normal state of usefulness.

There will be practice games—regulars against rookies—almost every day. A bit of work must yet be done on the grounds before they are in shape, and the boys are all lending a hand. Three players have yet to report: catcher Jack Wallace, outfielder Red Stewart, and third baseman Eddie McDonald. Stewart has a year-round job in Chicago if he wants it. He was one of three players to get a cut in pay and is not a bit happy about it, though he has written favorably about coming south.

Molesworth is a good-natured chap but doesn't put up with any clowning or burlesque. The chubby one addressed the players before the first practice: "Boys, it is in your best interest to get in good condition if you want to play for the Birmingham baseball club. The workouts that I have planned must be kept up each and every day. You must work hard so that you will do the club owners and yourselves justice. Regarding your conduct in Orlando, I will only say this: There are a lot of big-money people in this town that came south for the winter. These people expect you to be civilized. There will be no pillow-throwing and no roughhousing in the hotel. That's bush league stuff. If you gentlemen do not know how to behave, I do not want you on my team. You fellows must remember that you are Class A ball players—at least for now.

"As for your nightlife, I wish to say now that every one of you must be in the hotel by eleven-thirty every night. There have been poker games lately, and I have no objection to that, providing the game breaks up at eleven-thirty. If it does not, I will break it up, and there will be no more poker games the rest of the season. That's all, boys. Now let's work hard!"

Tuesday, March 2; Exposition Park

The boys are keeping busy. Each practice begins with pepper games. After that, there is hitting practice, a session at the throwing game, a little base running, and a run around the half-mile racetrack. Finally it's time to hit the showers and walk back to the hotel. Manager Molesworth announced that a sliding pit will be constructed, and the boys must devote a period every day to practice the art of hooksliding. The diamond is now in fine shape, and it is safe to say the Barons training camp will be equal to that of any big league club.

Dave Roth, a veteran pitcher, has much work to do before he gets in pitching trim. He is larger than ever, if that is possible. Twenty pounds overweight and looks like a mountain! Did he have too many oysters in Baltimore over the winter? Dave smokes a big ol' pipe. He chucks the pipe when in uniform, of course, but otherwise it is stuck right there in his countenance, going full blast. Mrs. Roth is chaperoning Dave in Orlando. Dave means business, and Moley feels like he will be one of his best this year.

Wednesday, March 3; Exposition Park

Bertie Grimes was cutting 'em loose with a good deal of steam today, and his arm seemed to have a free and easy swing to it. He spent the winter on his farm in Wisconsin, rolling logs and clearing new ground. He said he kept in the best of shape throughout the winter, and his arm has never felt better. "I couldn't get off to a good start last year," he admitted. "I think maybe the injury to my arm had me worried and made me lose confidence. After I got to Richmond, I had no trouble, and I got by with a good season."

Cecil Coombs, an infielder, has a perpetual smile on his face. He has two baseball bats that he nursed and petted all winter. He seasoned them by the stove, and oiled them with linseed oil every day. Last year at Bay City, Michigan, Coombs played every position on the field except catcher. Long, lanky Arthur Johnson is not a finished pitcher by any means, but he proved to be one of the best in the league last year. Arthur pastimed this winter as a member of the dinner-pail class, working in the railroad yards in his hometown of Madison, Wisconsin. As proof of his manual labor, he has corns the size of silver dollars on the palms of his hands. But the big Swede came south with a roll of greenbacks and is now carrying in his jeans a checkbook on an Orlando banking institution. Not many ball players can boast of a bankroll this early in the year. Arthur worried like crazy when his trunk was delayed on the trip down. All his love letters were in that trunk! If the fans want some real sport at Rickwood this summer, they should call on Arthur to give his imitation of moving picture comedian Charlie Chaplin and his famous stride.

Several millionaires are spending a few bones here this winter. They come out to the park every morning and afternoon to look the boys over. They are tickled to death at the prospect of having a month of baseball. They say they wouldn't mind staying here year-round if the baseball boys were here through the summer. The Tampa newspapers had more about the Barons today than they did about the Chicago Cubs, and the Cubs are training right there in Tampa. The Orlando Commercial Club is promoting the opening game here on March 10 against the Philadelphia Phillies. Every citizen of prominence has been given a yellow badge to wear with the inscription *Boost the Barons*.

Thursday, March 4; Streets of Orlando

Cars flock up and down the streets of Orlando. Most of the cars bear pennants on the sides with the hometowns of their owners. Statistics show that there is an automobile for every man, woman, and child in Orlando. Get wise to this! Instead of numbering the houses in Orlando, they name them, and they attach amusing phrases to the front stoops. Across the front of one house on Orange Avenue is the inscription *It Suits Me*. The house next door says *Chicago Cottage*. Another one: *We Like It*.

A number of the boys invaded a fruit packinghouse this evening, and when they walked away they had tangerines and oranges in every pocket. Some of the fellows went to the extreme of cutting the lining in their coats and packing them all the way through. Most every Baron now boasts a grip full of tangerines and oranges. Boss Rick Woodward is yachting up the coast. Moley expects him in Orlando within a few days, at which time he will don a uniform and romp with the boys in the daily pepper games.

Friday, March 5; Empire Hotel

The boys jumped into strenuous training too quickly, and now a bunch of them have sore limbs. Moley cautioned the boys, but they were so anxious to get going that they cut loose the first few days, and many of them are now so sore they walk as stiff as a peg-legged man. Moley says some of the boys are in such a bad fix he will be forced to cut down on the training to give their muscles a chance to rest. Every man has a quart-size bottle of witch hazel in his locker for rubbing out the kinks.

Many of the boys are amusing themselves at night by playing billiards, while others are engaged in the usual spring training ritual of poker. Some stroll downtown on the lookout for an automobile ride. But all are hitting their beds on time and taking good care of themselves. Big App McDuffie, the Birmingham youngster, is the ladies' man of the outfit. Al Fields, a rookie from Birmingham, said McDuffie is "a bear with the Janes." Fields alleges that McDuffie says he can do more with a woman than a monkey can with a peanut. McDuffie says he is going to carry some grapefruit from Florida back to America. Danny

Clark persisted in telling the big boy that Florida was a state in the union, but McDuffie said, "Florida ain't no state at all, 'cause didn't I learn in geography that it was a peninsula?"

One of the holdouts, catcher "Shotgun" Jack Wallace, reported today. He said if the hunting season had not closed, he might never have reported. Six people in his hometown of Winnfield, Louisiana, dropped dead the past week, which is a lot of people for a small country town. Wallace is congratulating himself on getting away. Tomorrow the team will begin staging practice games each afternoon between the rookies and regulars.

Saturday, March 6; Empire Hotel

Bertie Grimes makes friends easily and knows how to keep from walking to the ball park and back. He has a knack of sliding into a car at just the right moment, at which point the owner must willingly give him a lift. Yale (Tod) Sloan, the fleet outfielder acquired from the St. Louis Browns, is a great fellow with the children. He plays games with them for hours at a time. It may be a ploy to meet the ladies; we don't know.

The ball players are a jolly set, some real cutups. The other day at the dining table, one asked for biscuits. Someone stuck his finger down the middle of one and passed it over. Another stuck a biscuit on one end of a fork and a corn muffin on the other, and pushed the fork up and down as if it were a dumbbell.

Orlando has attracted so much wealth that all its citizens own automobiles. The Barons are very popular, and people often invite them on automobile trips. The ball players have become so accustomed to being driven around in expensive cars that none of them will stoop to be seen with a girl who merely owns a Ford.

Sunday, March 7

The players got the day off. A number of them motored to Winter Park and took their initial workouts as golfers. Some of us went fishing with Manager Molesworth and pitcher Dave Roth at Lake Apopka, fifteen miles away, and bagged fifty pounds of bass, bluegill, and catfish. Fish will be on the menu in the dining room tomorrow night.

Florida rattlesnakes have been talked about so much around the United States that tourists visiting Orlando think the woods are full of them. Eddie Hemingway, a good-natured cuss, found an old rubber hosepipe on the golf links and threw it among a bunch of ball players. Eddie yelled "snake!" and some of the Barons who have been walking stiff-legged with charley horses and such ran one hundred yards in ten flat.

Al Fields, the amateur pitcher from Birmingham, doesn't believe he is getting a fair shot from Manager Molesworth. "I wouldn't sign up with Moley now for anything in the world, for he does not appreciate me," Fields said. "I've got more stuff than Hardgrove, Johnson, and the rest of 'em, but Moley simply don't encourage me or give me a chance. But that's alright — I bet I'll make him sorry, 'cause I'm gonna leave here and get on with some other Southern League club. And mark my words, every time I meet Birmingham, I'll trim 'em to death. Then as I walk by the Barons bench, maybe I won't even speak. Just watch me."

Monday, March 8; Exposition Park

Manager Molesworth swung the ax today, and it fell on the head of pitcher Fields. The big boy was so confident of winning a berth that he was paying his own expenses in Orlando. Fields can throw hard but he's as green as a fall shipment of gourds, and he has not learned how to pitch. Now he is gone. The Barons will storm Daytona Beach in a few days to play the Brooklyn Dodgers. We hear the road to Daytona is a fine turnpike with many sections of brick paving. The boys are making big plans for the trip. They have their cameras ready and will snap pictures of the scenery along the way.

It's beginning to get like real baseball now. The stiffness is gone from the limbs, and the boys are as frisky as young colts. From now until the time the Barons come home to Birmingham, they will be a busy bunch of ball players. Moley has not allowed any loafing. The skylarkers who looked upon the trip to Orlando as one grand picnic and who have never been in professional ball before now realize that training is hard work. Moley has laid down the law to them on the training rules and about keeping good hours, and he will not stand for any foolishness. Each man seems to realize that if he does not deliver the goods and pay strict attention to business, Moley has another man who is just as good, or almost as good. Thirty-one players reported to Orlando. By early May, Molesworth must be down to the Southern Association limit of fifteen players. With the release of Fields, there are now twelve pitchers in camp. Moley plans to carry nine pitchers back to Birmingham, but four of them will be dropped soon after, and he will probably open the season with five pitchers.

Tuesday, March 9; Empire Hotel

Tod Sloan is the best-looking man on the team, and Moley is afraid the girls will kidnap his star player when the Barons arrive in Birmingham. But for some strange reason this good-looking young athlete cares not for the wiles and smiles of the females of Orlando. McDuffie, the rookie pitcher, had snared two girls in conversation when Sloan entered the hotel parlor. The girls said to McDuffie: "Introduce Mr. Sloan to us, please, Mr. McDuffie. He looks so dark, handsome, and . . . mysterious." After the introductions, Sloan politely, but firmly, insisted on leaving. In the office downstairs, he confided to fellow outfielder Jimmy Magee that girls give him a pain in the back of the neck. "Honest, Mac," said Sloan, "girls make me tired. And that one I just met is all swelled up. She's got a Ford and is laboring under the delusion that she's got an automobile. Oh, these girls . . .", and Sloan walked away in disgust, muttering to himself.

Wednesday, March 10; Exposition Park

Bertie Grimes pitched four innings against the Philadelphia Phillies rookies today. John Cantley, the recruit pitcher from Ensley, relieved Grimes and showed more stuff than any hurler yet. Grimes looks fifty percent better than last spring, and he should battle for a place on the pitching staff. He seems to have a world of stuff on the ball. If he can get control of his pitches . . .

Thursday, March 11; Exposition Park

There was a grueling session of hooksliding this morning and a lively practice game in the afternoon. The boys were just about ready to knock off for the day when Manager Molesworth cheerfully announced there would be five more minutes of infield work. Third baseman Eddie Hemingway, the humorist of the team, said sarcastically, "Only five minutes of infield, Moley? Why not ten minutes?" Molesworth was selecting a fungo bat and without looking up, he snapped: "Alright, ten minutes then." "Oh, make it fifteen," Hemingway said. "Fine business," Moley said. "I like your ambition. We'll make the infield practice fifteen minutes and then run around the park twice."

Hemingway was just about to ask Moley for twenty minutes when "Shotgun" Jack Wallace jumped on him. "Shut up, you durn fool. If you keep that up, old Moley will work us to death. Who do you think you're kidding, anyhow?" "I guess I was kidding myself," said Hemingway, as he pondered fifteen more minutes of infield practice, followed by a two-mile run. Molesworth insisted on his pound of flesh. He sent whistling liners down the third-base line at Hemingway for fifteen minutes and then made the whole team run around the park twice. Hemingway's humor did not draw much laughter from the ball players tonight.

Friday, March 12

The Barons' spring trip to Florida is a wonderful advertising opportunity for the city of Birmingham. The winter tourists who attend the practice games every afternoon are surprised by the large number of players. "But I never knew Birmingham was in the National or American League," they say.

"Birmingham is not in the major leagues," replies an onlooker. "It is in the Southern League, and last season the club won the pennant."

"Southern League? Don't believe I have ever heard of it."

"Well, it is a fast baseball league alright, for these Barons certainly can play some ball."

"And Birmingham," mused the tourist, "Birmingham must be some city to support a team so royally that it can afford to come to Orlando for spring training. And bringing more players than the big leagues carry."

The tourist will inquire about Birmingham. After being told it is the most progressive city in the South, he will promise to stop in the Magic City on his trip north. That's the kind of publicity the Barons are mustering for Birmingham.

Monday, March 15; Daytona Beach

Saturday the team rented four seven-passenger touring cars for the trip to Daytona-by-the-Sea to play the Dodgers. The seventy-five-mile junket took five hours. At times it looked as though some of the boys wouldn't make it. Punctures, blowouts, and obstinate generators held up the trip every half-hour or so. The games were canceled on Saturday and Sunday because of rain and cold weather. Monday the Dodgers beat the Barons, 6–0. The Dodgers are all a swell bunch of fellows, not a bit chesty about being big-leaguers. They mixed and mingled with the Barons. First baseman Jake Daubert and one or two others gave the Barons a few of their bats, and the Barons pitched them in the bat bag to take home.

The trip back to Orlando was without incident. The scenery between Daytona and Orlando, for the most part, is beautiful, though some stretches are unsightly. There are majestic palm trees, prosperous lettuce and celery farms, orange groves, and lakes. On other stretches, buzzards stare at you from their perches along the roadside, and the swamplands brim with rattlesnakes.

Tuesday, March 16; Back in Orlando

Today was a day of rest. So far, five players have been released from the team; twenty-six are still fighting for positions. Red Stewart, who had a good job in Chicago, has reported to the team. Orlando has proven to be a delightful place to train. Unlike many training camps, it is not isolated, yet the youngsters do not have the snares of a big city to tempt them. The Barons have made a favorable impression, and the Board of Trade of this pretty city adopted a resolution today to host a banquet for the team. The banquet will take place next week on Baron Day, when the players will be driven around the city in automobiles and shown a good time. Orlandoans seek to outdo one another in their hospitality to the players. The people here are familiar with the record of this dashing group of ball players. They know that in the past five seasons, Carlton Molesworth has won two pennants and has never finished below third.

Ever since their arrival in Orlando, the Barons have comported themselves agreeably. Practical jokes and boyish rowdyism are not a part of this outfit. The Barons leave the hotel neatly dressed for the ball grounds, and upon their return sit about the lobby or attend the moving picture theaters if there are no other social engagements in the evening. There is no standing about on street corners and pulling Class D stuff by staring and welling at every person who passes by. The Barons travel and behave like a big league club. The fans of Orlando appreciate having the champions in their midst. The dignity of the Barons has won them over.

Wednesday, March 17; Exposition Park

Pitcher Omar Hardgrove, the old man of the team, is training diligently every morning and afternoon and is in grand shape. The old boy is shaming the youngsters with his cavorting on the grounds. "Hardy" will run a couple of miles, play pepper ball with anyone who is willing, and run another couple of miles. Then he will alternate pitching to the batters and to the recruit catchers. The old fox won twenty games last year, and his arduous training is being emulated by the other veterans—Clyde McBride, Roy Ellam, and Charlie Carroll. This quartet of veterans understands that baseball is serious business, and they are preparing themselves to be fit when the starting bell rings. In Orlando, it is the veterans who are in the pink of condition, ready to jump into the game at a moment's notice.

Thursday, March 18; Exposition Park

John Cantley pitched five innings, gave up three hits, and hit a home run against Rollins College today. Moley likes Cantley. He has shown better form than any of the other hurlers. If he doesn't make the team, Moley is confident he will do so next year. App McDuffie, the amateur pitcher from Birmingham, will not pitch for the Barons this season. Yesterday he was optioned to Jacksonville, Florida, of the Sally League. He remains the Barons' property, and Moley may bring him back next year.

Friday, March 19

Bertie Grimes can throw his spitball and make it break three different ways: down, in, or out. George Hale, the first-string catcher, says that Grimes has the best spitball he has ever seen and the most difficult to handle. He claims Bertie's spitter breaks four ways—in or out like a curveball, up like an upshoot, or down as a drop. There's one thing in favor of Grimes, and this will help him if he ever gets a real chance to show in the major leagues: He lives clean . . . doesn't drink, smoke, or chew . . . never touched a cigarette in his life.

Saturday, March 20; Exposition Park

The club has been in Orlando for three weeks. We hear that Birmingham received three inches of snow yesterday, the latest snowfall in the city's history.

In the Florida winter resorts, one meets many who are not familiar with baseball. In today's game against Louisville, a Mr. McIntyre, bank president from Chicago, was sitting in the rear of the press box with several ladies. Pat Dougherty, a recruit pitcher from the Canadian League, couldn't throw strikes, and finally Manager Molesworth yanked him from the game. As the perspiring athlete left the field, Mr. McIntyre turned to Mrs. Dave Roth, wife of the Barons pitcher, and said, "Mrs. Roth, when a pitcher is taken out that way, doesn't it offend him? Does it not hurt his feelings?" Mrs. Roth smiled and allowed her handsome husband to reply. "No," Dave said. "He is tickled to death. At least I would be."

Mrs. Roth is the most popular member of the Barons' party. One reason for her popularity is that she can sing and play the piano. One evening she strolled into the deserted hotel parlor and began playing. She ran her fingers nimbly along the keyboard, and before long all the Barons were hanging around the piano. Mrs. Roth sang "When You're a Long, Long Way from Home," and the boys joined in. They were lonesome, and Mrs. Roth sang with such fervor that the more sentimental ones actually began to cry. To lift their spirits, Mrs. Roth began singing "It's a Long Way to Tipperary," the British Army marching song of the European war:

> *It's a long way to Tipperary,*
> *It's a long way to go.*
> *It's a long way to Tipperary,*
> *To the sweetest girl I know.*
> *Good-bye, Piccadilly!*
> *Farewell, Leicester Square!*
> *It's a long, long way to Tipperary,*
> *But my heart's right there!*

During the song, Carlton Molesworth stole into the room, and everyone joined in, even Chubby Carlton. It was a jolly evening.

Monday, March 22; Lakeland, Florida

The continued cold weather has been a serious drawback to good work. Playing in mackinaws and old, heavy sweaters, the Barons tied the Louisville

Colonels, 6–6, in a forty-mile-an-hour gale. It was so cold even the pitchers worked with sweaters on. Despite the cold, raw wind, John Cantley pitched the entire nine innings. Moley thinks Cantley is a prospect and will take him to Birmingham, though he may be sent to a lower league before the season begins.

The Lakeland ball park has no turf on the infield, and the outfield is made of squishy, mushy sand. Lakeland is a hustling little city and appears to be growing every day. The business thoroughfares are all paved, and the town has a "white way" rivaling that of Birmingham.

The citizens of Orlando say this has been the coldest spring they can remember, yet the Barons have been able to get their workouts in almost every day. The same could not be said if they had trained in Birmingham.

Rick Woodward's father owns a beautiful country estate a mile outside Orlando. Rick spent a few days in Orlando with the ball club and worked out every day. Rick has as much speed as ever in the pepper games, and he romped about like a colt. He was forced to quit the camp yesterday and go to Pittsburgh on business. Moley will carry twenty-two players back to Birmingham. Then he will trim the roster before the opening game in New Orleans on April 13.

Wednesday, March 24; Exposition Park

The Barons threw a defeat into the Havana Reds, a Cuban team that has been tearing apart the big league clubs training here in Florida. Bertie Grimes occupied the mound for seven innings. His spitter broke swift and wide; he allowed Havana only four scattered singles, and the Barons won, 3–2. Moley says the only thing that will keep Grimes from winning a spot on the staff is his carelessness with men on bases.

Thursday, March 25; Empire Hotel

Today there was sadness in the ranks of our fine little hostelry, for it was our last full day in Orlando. At the evening meal, crepe was hanging on the dining room door, and black ribbon bows were fastened to the back of each chair at the table. The Barons have been a hit at the Empire Hotel, and the chef has fed them off the fat of the land. The man who runs the hotel, J. B. Magruder, carried the boys out to his orange groves on several occasions and always had a bushel of fruit on tap at the hotel. Rochester, the waiter in the dining room, has decided to go home to his folks in New York state. The Barons have invited him to ride in their private railcar for part of the journey home.

In taking the team to Orlando, the Birmingham Baseball Association killed two birds with one stone. The management made sure the boys were conditioned for the grind of the coming season but also granted them one grand picnic as a sideline. Many hours were spent at the fishing grounds and in the orange groves.

Many strolls were taken around the beautiful lakes. The members of the country club issued every Baron a card granting him golf and tennis privileges.

Friday afternoon, March 26; 1:00 p.m.; Orlando Railroad Depot

Last night the Barons were guests of honor at a delightful banquet at the San Juan Hotel, sponsored by seventy-five of the leading businessmen of Orlando. Afterward the players packed up for the trip home. The people of Orlando turned out at the station to bid the Barons a fond farewell. A large, streaming banner was attached to the side of the private railcar. Agent W. D. White of the Atlantic Coast Line secured a large box of oranges and presented it to the team. Then, with loud cheering from the populace, the Barons vamoosed from the garden spot of Florida, promising to return next spring.

There will be a stopover in Jacksonville for a few hours, and then the car will be hitched to the tail end of the Seminole Limited, headed for Columbus, Georgia. The Barons will play a game against Columbus tomorrow afternoon. Then they will retire to their private car and sleep on the sidetrack until morning, when the Seminole Limited will begin the trek to Birmingham. The team will arrive under the massive dome of the Terminal Station at twelve-fifteen Sunday afternoon.

Saturday, March 27; Columbus, Georgia

Rochester, the hotel waiter, rode with the Barons to Jacksonville. Before they parted company, every player dug down in his jeans for a few coins. It left many of the players stark broke and the rest of them badly bent, but it made a nice little present for Rochester. It goes to show that ball players have hearts. Ball players do not get a salary for the training season, and most of them had undergone a hard winter financially. After rambling around Florida for a month, most have little money left. Rochester, a jovial sort, had made wisecracks to the guys throughout their stay in Orlando, but when it came time to part, tears came to his eyes. He accepted the gift and said, "Boys, it's awful hard to be left by yourself when you've been waiting on a bunch of ball players for a month. I'm gonna go to Orlando again next spring in case you folks train down there, even if I have to walk all the way from Rochester, New York."

CHAPTER 9

BACK TO BIRMINGHAM

THE SEMINOLE LIMITED ARRIVED IN Birmingham from Columbus, Georgia, shortly after noon on Sunday, March 28. The Barons stepped onto the platform of the Terminal Station and immediately began hunting boardinghouses and getting acquainted with soft drink joints.

Sunday afternoon, March 28; 12:30 p.m.

Inquiries from the Barons as to the best places to eat and sleep flew thick and fast. It was the first time many of them had seen Birmingham, and all were impressed from the moment they saw the great rotunda of the Terminal Station. They were calling the town "ace high," even before reaching the downtown business district, where the skyscraper acreage is the largest in the South. If anybody happens to notice anxious-looking young men tramping through the residential streets of Birmingham with battered suitcases, it is probably ball players looking for a home.

The Barons come from all parts of the United States, and they say the girls of Birmingham are the most beautiful and the most stylish dressers in the entire country. Come, girls, to the Birmingham Arms building on Third Avenue, headquarters of the Birmingham baseball club, and pick a mate from among the Barons.

Monday evening, March 29; Jefferson Theater, Birmingham

Tonight was Barons Night at the Jefferson Theater. Members of the squad—twenty-two strong with Manager Molesworth and Secretary Robert Tyson—were guests for the evening for the performance of the operetta "Lady Luxury." The show, "direct from the Casino Theatre in New York," contained a number of song hits, notably "Longing for You," "Dream On, My Princess," and "Kiss Me Once More." The performers were tipped off that the Barons were in the audience and responded with several whimsical gibes at the expense of the young athletes. All in all, the boys were given a good time.

Friday afternoon, April 2; Rickwood Field

The Barons played the Chicago Cubs today, and Bertie Grimes showed a nice line of samples. The Cubs broke their backs trying to hit his spitter, striking out nine times, but rapped him for eleven hits and three home runs to beat Bertie and the Barons, 7–4. Grimes looks good enough to make the squad. He was in mid-season form and could have won the game with better support.

Sunday, April 4

Many have their hard-luck stories, but big App McDuffie, the Birmingham boy, seems to have fallen into the greatest jinx of all. McDuffie made such a good impression in Orlando that Moley said if he had not been overstocked with pitchers, he would have kept Mack as his fifth man. Instead, Moley found him a berth at Jacksonville and sent him there. The first day, Dave Gaston, the manager, called on Mack to pitch against the major league Philadelphia Athletics. Three men were on base at the time. Mack did not have a chance to warm up, and the batter poled one out against him, good for four runs. Mack settled down and did not allow another runner to score. A day or so later the Jax manager released him, and Moley found a spot for McDuffie at Columbus, Georgia. A few days later Mack was pitching for a scrapped-up aggregation of amateurs against the Columbus regulars and beat the regulars, 5–0, but Manager Jim Fox released him. Mack was surprised to death but packed his belongings and beat it to Birmingham. "I don't know why they canned me," McDuffie said, "unless it was because I didn't join in the clubhouse crap games at Columbus. The manager and the whole team spent about half their time shooting craps and gambling. I tried to be a good fellow, but I don't gamble, so I guess they decided I wasn't one of their kind and shipped me out."

"This is the hard-luck story of all time," said sportswriter Henry Vance. "Here is a great big young fellow with a good spitball, a good delivery, a deceptive curve, and a grand slow ball, and nobody wants him? Nobody will give him a fair chance? Can it be that a grand pitching arm like this will lie here in Birmingham and decay for want of work? Who wants a good pitcher? Let him speak up. This McDuffie is no bloomer, and the club that gets him will never regret it."

Tuesday, April 6

John Cantley needs another year of seasoning in a lower league. Moley sold him today to Evansville, Indiana, a Class B club, but Birmingham still retains rights to him. Moley is certain Cantley will be one of his pitchers next year if the majors don't get him first. Moley said, "The boy is young, has the stuff, and the head to go with it, and he is a clean liver. He looks on baseball as a business, not a frolic, and he has a great future before him."

Wednesday, April 7; Rickwood Field

The Pittsburgh Pirates pounded Bertie Grimes for twelve hits and seven bases on balls. Playing second base for the Pirates was an elderly gentleman named Honus Wagner. Honus is forty-one years old. Before Ty Cobb came along, Honus was the biggest drawing card in the game. He is a most ungainly chap—weather-beaten and powerful. The first thing you notice about him are his legs; he is bowlegged and awkward-looking. Next you notice his hands; they are huge. But the man can hit a baseball. He stands in the far corner of the batter's box and moves up quickly to meet the ball. Against the Barons, he had two base hits and ate up the ball in the field with his big ol' hands. He cut off several would-be hits with his darting work.

Friday, April 9

"I'll take him!" Lamar Jeffers, president of the Anniston club, learned of App McDuffie's plight, so he sat down and mailed the big boy a contract. McDuffie is now with Anniston of the Class D Georgia-Alabama League.

Saturday, April 10

The Barons are down to eighteen players, and these Moley will carry until the middle of May, when he will apply the final slash of the ax and cut his squad to fifteen men, whom he will carry for the rest of the season. Burleigh Grimes has made the club. He will pitch in New Orleans on April 18. The practice games are over, and the opening game of the season is three days away. The fans long for the dawning of the real season of swat.

Sunday, April 18

Burleigh Grimes gave up two scratch singles in his first start of the 1915 season against New Orleans. Both were hard ground balls that shortstop Roy Ellam knocked down but couldn't make a play on. A month later, Grimes came down with the mumps and was out for two weeks.

Thursday, August 5

John Cantley, the pitcher that Manager Molesworth farmed out to Evansville, is leading his team to the Central League pennant. The newspaper writers of Evansville, Indiana, call him "Rebel Cantley, the Alabama flinger." Evansville was in third place in the league standings on July 1. The next day Cantley pitched a four-hitter, and the Evas moved into second. He won six times during the month of July, and the Evas took over first place, August 1. On August 5, Cantley pitched a shutout, giving him two wins in the first week of August. For the season, opponents have mustered, on average, only six hits and two runs a game against him. Now, Molesworth is counting on the boy from Ensley to be one of his pitchers for next season.

Tuesday, August 31

The Barons recalled John Cantley on August 14 and ordered him to report to Birmingham in two weeks. The same day, Cantley beat Fort Wayne, 4–2, in Evansville for his twentieth victory. After the game, the two teams — Evansville and Fort Wayne — boarded a train to play a doubleheader in Fort Wayne the next day. Three days later, John Cantley was sick in bed. When Evansville clinched the pennant on August 23, he was under a doctor's care. He missed the team's final games, but the team expects him to be up and about soon.

The Barons, too, are in a pennant race. On August 30, they were four games behind New Orleans with four weeks to play. That day Burleigh Grimes was pitching against Nashville at Rickwood Field. Dolly Stark, the Nashville shortstop, hit a slow roller down the first base line, and Grimes fielded the ball. The ball and the two men converged at the same time. Grimes ran in front of Stark and tagged him out. Stark retaliated by lunging at Grimes and spiking him. Grimes, from foul territory, whirled and threw the ball toward the infield, striking Stark in the head. Stark rushed at Grimes. Grimes threw down his glove and took a vicious swing at Stark, hitting him firmly on the jaw. Grimes was suspended, leaving the Barons with only four pitchers for the next ten games.

Monday morning, September 6, Labor Day

A doubleheader against Mobile is scheduled for Rickwood Field — one game in the morning and another in the afternoon. But the Barons are in no mood to play. The news was flashed into the clubhouse this morning: *John Liam Cantley is dead.* Malaria. The clubhouse is quiet. Heads are bent low and hearts sore. The players had known John for only five weeks in Orlando, but he had been a friend to all. John died last night at his roominghouse in Evansville with his mother at his bedside. He was twenty-four years old.

John took ill three weeks ago when the team was in Fort Wayne. He was a favorite of the Evansville players, and they took turns sitting up with him at night. His father went up from Ensley last week, but when his son took a turn for the better, his father returned home. That was Friday, September 3. By Sunday morning when his mother arrived, John was delirious, but they believe he recognized her. He succumbed at seven-forty-five that night. Mrs. Cantley was inconsolable over the loss of her son.

What if John Cantley had never gone to Evansville? the Barons wondered. Would he still be alive? Would he be helping them win the Southern Association pennant? The Barons played the doubleheader after learning of John's death, but hearts were heavy. They lost the first game and won the second. That evening in Evansville, Indiana, friends of John Cantley gathered for a simple service at his roominghouse on Main Street. Among the pallbearers were Mayor Benjamin Bosse, club President Harry Stahlhefer, and team Manager Charles Knoll. At nine-twenty p.m., John's body was placed aboard a train for Ensley. His mother returned home with the body.

THE BARONS WERE UNABLE TO overtake New Orleans for the 1915 pennant. During the season, Burleigh Grimes won seventeen games, lost thirteen, and struck out the second-most batters in the league. He pitched into extra innings three times: two games of fourteen innings and one of ten. All were tie games called by darkness. In one of the extra-inning games, he came within two outs of a no-hitter. Not a bad record considering he lost almost a month to the mumps and the suspension, but not good enough to make the major leagues. He would be back with Birmingham in 1916.

"Grimes has a great future before him," wrote Henry Vance in *The Birmingham News*. "He is still just a kid with an ideal build for a major league pitcher. He lacks but one thing, and that is the art of saving himself. He is what the ball tossers call a strong-arm pitcher. As soon as he learns to use a good slow ball without men on base to conserve his strength, he will be a finished product. His old right arm is made of iron, but even iron will weaken if taxed. Burleigh puts as much stuff on the ball without men on as he does when the bases are clogged. Just as soon as he learns to let up a bit, take things easy, and pitch with his brain now and then, he will be ripe for the majors."

Burleigh did not return to the lumber camps of Wisconsin after the 1915 season. He stayed in Birmingham to work as a foreman at the big steel works of the Tennessee Coal, Iron, and Railroad Company, testing steel rail as it came off the line. Some of the rail was sent to the allied countries of Europe, the war now in its second year.

In 1916, the Southern Association lowered team salary limits from $3,200 to $2,800 a month and the roster size from fifteen players to fourteen. For the first three months of the new season, Burleigh Grimes was an ordinary pitcher: winning a game, losing a game; winning two games, losing two games. His career, however, was about to take a turn.

Life in America in 1916 was better than ever. Big cities were rising where forests and prairies once stood. People were moving from farms to cities to enrich their lives. Birmingham grew from 3,100 residents in 1880 to 133,000 in 1910 to more than 150,000 by 1916. Automobiles, telephones, electricity, indoor plumbing, and medical advances had made life easier. Mass production had lowered the prices of consumer goods. Americans were savoring more leisure time and greater prosperity.

Though life was better in a material way, infectious diseases flourished in the big cities. People struggled against epidemics of influenza, pneumonia, tuberculosis, malaria, typhoid fever, and diphtheria. During the summer of 1916, Birmingham experienced an outbreak of typhoid, a disease transmitted through contaminated food or water, often due to poor hygiene. In the early 1900s, Birmingham had averaged twenty cases of typhoid a month. In June 1916, however, there were one hundred and sixteen cases, and the following month, four hundred. A city the size of Birmingham normally experienced two deaths a month from typhoid; in July 1916 there were thirty-five deaths.

The city responded with a program of free vaccinations at City Hall. City Commissioner John Hornady as public servant became the first person vaccinated. In front of a small gathering, the chief health officer, Dr. Cecil Gaston, inserted a needle into Hornady's arm. "You see, it is absolutely painless," Dr. Gaston told the audience. "Thank you, Mr. Hornady, it's all over."

The commissioner was relieved: "I didn't even feel it."

"You will tomorrow," a little girl crowed, and everyone laughed. Within six weeks, twenty-five thousand citizens were vaccinated with a series of three shots. The outbreak was traced to contaminated ice cream, and by the end of August, the crisis was over.

A few days after Commissioner Hornady was vaccinated, Burleigh Grimes embarked on a mission to the major leagues. Beginning on July 16, in six straight games he allowed a *total* of five runs and eighteen hits, an average of three hits and less than one run a game:

> *July 16* at Mobile: allowed three hits, two runs, in eight innings.

> *July 20* at Rickwood Field: allowed two hits, two runs, in a complete game against New Orleans, losing, 2–1.

> *July 25* at Atlanta: held the Crackers hitless until the eighth; allowed two infield hits, winning, 3–0.

> *July 28*, an hour before the game, Burleigh's wife was injured in an automobile accident, but he took the mound at Rickwood and allowed Mobile four hits; at bat he drove in a run with a sacrifice fly and won, 6–0. Quietly, the Barons and Pittsburgh Pirates began discussing a trade.

August 3 at Rickwood: pitched his third straight shutout, giving up four hits to Chattanooga; tripled, scored a run, and beat his old teammate Arthur Johnson. Chattanooga Manager Kid Elberfeld said of Burleigh: "He's the best pitcher in the league. He can go to any club in the National League and start out a winner. I've batted against him, and I know. Any major league club that gets him should consider themselves lucky. That's no bull, either."

August 7 at Rickwood: forced Little Rock players to pop up the ball and hit easy grounders, but rain halted play in the eighth with the score 1–1; allowed three hits.

BURLEIGH GRIMES BELIEVED HE WAS being overlooked in the minor leagues and had resolved to quit baseball if he failed to receive a promotion at the end of the season. "If I can't make more money playing ball than the Southern League has to offer, I can do something else," he said. But during Burleigh's fabulous six-game stretch, the Barons and Pirates were close to a deal. By the middle of August, the agreement was done. Birmingham received eight players in exchange for Grimes. One was pitcher Carmen Hill, who in his first year with Birmingham in 1917, would win twenty-six games. Ten years later, Hill would win twenty-two games for the Pirates and pitch in the 1927 World Series against the New York Yankees "Murderers' Row."

Burleigh Grimes was allowed to finish the 1916 season with the Barons. He won ten of his last twelve games and pitched for the last time on Friday, September 8, at Rickwood Field. After retiring the final batter, Burleigh walked off the field to an enthusiastic ovation. He doffed his cap and bowed his head. The next day, Saturday, Burleigh left Birmingham on a long train ride to Chicago to meet his new team, the Pittsburgh Pirates. The following day he pitched four innings of relief to beat the Cubs. Four days later he started a game against the league-leading Brooklyn Dodgers. The game was scoreless until Brooklyn scored two runs in the sixth inning. The Pirates tied it in the seventh. It was still 2–2 when the Dodgers scored the winning run with two outs in the ninth inning.

ON TO THE POLO GROUNDS in New York, where Burleigh faced the Giants, winners of twelve straight games. The game was scoreless until the fifth when the Giants hit a home run. The Pirates tied it in the eighth, 1–1. In the ninth inning, it began to rain, and the game was called with the score 1–1. The Giants continued winning — fourteen more ball games, a total of twenty-six in a row, a record. And halfway through the streak Burleigh had almost beaten them in the 1–1 tie.

Burleigh won his next game against Philadelphia, 8–3, finishing the season with two wins and three losses. He had been a big-leaguer only three weeks, but one thing he knew for sure: He was in the major leagues to stay. He was so confident, in fact, that he balked at the money the Pirates offered him for next season. And he returned to Birmingham to work the winter in the steel mill. By mid-February, with spring training two weeks away, Burleigh and the Pirates had yet to settle on terms. It was the first of many contract disputes he would face during his career. The Pirates enlisted Barons Manager Carlton Molesworth to negotiate with Burleigh. Molesworth called Burleigh into his office at Rickwood Field and convinced him to sign.

When he left for training camp at Columbus, Georgia, Burleigh said, "I'm going to be a regular with the Pirates this season. You may bank on that. I did pretty good when I joined the club last season, but being there in the spring will give me a better chance to show 'em what I have. Naturally I was a bit nervous when I broke in up there, but now that I have had experience in the majors and have seen that big league batters have trouble with some of my offerings, the old confidence has returned. I figure by the number of men sent to the Barons in exchange for me that the Pirates think pretty well of me, and with all these things in my favor, I naturally have confidence of sticking."

CHAPTER 10

BURLEIGH GRIMES, BIG-LEAGUER

HIS STEEL SPIKES GRITTED HARD against the pitching rubber. Chewing on slippery elm, Burleigh Grimes peered at the catcher for the sign. He tugged at his cap and glanced at the base runner. He hid his face with his glove. Behind the glove, two fingers of his right hand went to his mouth. Spitball? The batter wasn't sure. Grimes curled his lips in a snarl, glaring at the batter, his eyes blazing with hate. The batter dug in. The pitcher dipped into his motion. With a high kick and a lunge, he delivered the pitch: a high fastball near the chin. Down went Frankie Frisch of the St. Louis Cardinals. Burleigh Grimes threw three more pitches, each one aimed at the batter. The last one spun Frisch around, and he went down. "It was one of the few times in baseball that I was really scared," Frisch said, "and Burleigh just stood there and laughed at me."

As a major-leaguer, Burleigh Grimes was a fearsome figure: his cap a half-size too small, pulled tightly on his head; his whiskered face dark and sinister; his teeth yellowed from slippery elm. He did all his pitching with a two-day growth of whiskers. He didn't shave the day he pitched, or the day before. Hitters said he was the meanest thing they ever saw, and they called him Ol' Stubblebeard. Burleigh Grimes didn't wear the two-day stubble to look mean. The towels in the dugout were covered with resin that ball players used for gripping their bats. When Grimes wiped his face with a towel, the resin burned his skin. So did the juice from slippery elm. His whiskers protected him.

Burleigh Grimes hated hitters; he walked with a swagger that annoyed them. Batters dared not dig in against him. He threw his fastball up and in, pushing them off the plate. "Be ready," batters would say. "On any pitch, he might spin your cap around." And if he didn't knock you down, he had you set up for the

Burleigh Grimes, playing for the Barons in 1916, wrote his ticket to the major leagues during a six-game span in July and August in which he allowed an average of three hits and less than one run a game. During the streak, Birmingham and the Pittsburgh Pirates began negotiating a trade.

spitball, low and away. To help his spitball, Burleigh chewed slippery elm, the bark from the elm tree. In springtime, the bark loosened up, and he sliced it right off the tree. He chewed the fiber to produce saliva, and he put the saliva on his fingers. The ball would break like hell—away from righthanders, in on lefties, or straight down. The spitball wasn't necessarily his best pitch, but it was a constant threat. He wanted hitters thinking about it, always. When they looked for it, he'd throw something else, usually a fastball. But you get a reputation as a spitballer and what can you do about it?

"To me, the spitball is like a revolver to a policeman," Burleigh would say. "He may not need it, but he always has it within easy reach. How much I used it depended on how good my fastball was that day. If your fastball was no good, then you were a spitball pitcher."

Off the field Burleigh could be genial, but on the field his fury burned white-hot. He was surly, he was feared, he was disliked. He fought with everyone: opposing players, teammates, umpires, managers. To avoid speaking to Burleigh, his manager sometimes told the clubhouse boy to notify Burleigh when it was his time to pitch. Burleigh Grimes was fierce and driven. Some would call him combative; Burleigh said he had a passion to win. There were pitchers with

Birmingham received eight players from the Pittsburgh Pirates in exchange for Burleigh Grimes. His dreadful rookie season with the Pirates in 1917 included a fight with his manager and a pitching record of 3–16. He was traded to the Brooklyn Dodgers before the next season began.

greater natural talent, but never was there a more determined pitcher than Burleigh Grimes. He feared no batter. With men on base and a dangerous hitter at bat, he pulled his belt tighter and bore down harder. He carried his share of the load and more. Teammates rallied to that kind of pitcher.

For ten years, Burleigh threw at Frankie Frisch every time they met. It annoyed him that Frisch could handle his sinking spitter, so Burleigh threw at him. Frisch could move fast, and Burleigh had a hard time hitting him. One day Frisch bunted down the first-base line and accidentally spiked Burleigh as they raced to the bag, nearly severing a tendon in Burleigh's ankle. The next day Frisch approached him. "Burleigh, I never meant to do that to you." But the next time Frisch came to bat, Burleigh hit him with a pitch. On the way down to first base, Frisch screamed, "Jesus Christ, Burleigh, I apologized!"

Burleigh yelled back: "Yeah, but you didn't smile!"

Year after year, Burleigh pitched in turn and out, and toiled for more innings and more games than anyone. Today he would pitch his turn; tomorrow he might finish for someone else. Burleigh's style typified an era when baseball's rural and working class ball players played with grit and gumption. He explained:

"When I was a teenager, I decided the best I could make back home was thirty-five dollars a week driving horses in a lumber camp. Baseball was my answer....There was only one man standing between me and more money, and that was the guy with the bat. I knew I'd always have to fight that man with the bat as if he were trying to rob me in a dark alley."

Burleigh took part in one of baseball's most famous fights in 1917, his first full year in the majors. It happened during a Saturday night hop to Cincinnati for a Sunday game. Burleigh was playing for the Pittsburgh Pirates, a last-place ball club, and he was having an especially bad year. He had lost eleven in a row and had been passed over by the manager in his last start. At one end of the train, a group of Pirates players were grousing in the washroom when Manager Hugo Bezdek walked in. The other players piped down, but Burleigh, sitting on a windowsill, kept complaining.

"You're getting paid every two weeks, aren't you?" responded Bezdek.

"Well, so are you," Burleigh said.

The exchange of words became bitter and personal. Bezdek, a former college football player, punched Burleigh on the chin. It was a blow that would have flattened most athletes but not Burleigh. He came back fighting. There wasn't much room for swinging, so the two men tussled on the floor like bears. Bezdek got his fingers in the corners of Burleigh's mouth and began tightening the screws. Burleigh almost bit off Bezdek's finger. Both men bled profusely, and the players separated them. The Pirates road secretary asked the manager, "Shall I put him off at the next station?"

"No," Bezdek said. "If he shows the right spirit, I'll pitch him tomorrow."

Burleigh's shirt was tattered and bloody, and when he arrived in Cincinnati, he was wearing his housecoat. But true to his word, Bezdek pitched Burleigh the next day.

Burleigh's season of 1917—his first with the Pirates—was dreadful. His final mark: three wins, sixteen losses. To make matters worse, Carmen Hill, whom the Pirates had traded to Birmingham for Burleigh, won twenty-six for the Barons.

Burleigh's frightful 1917 season began with an exhibition game at Rickwood Field. That day, April 7, he pitched four innings and gave up eight runs to the Birmingham Barons, but the headline in the morning paper dealt with a more urgent matter: "President Formally Brings Country to War." After three years as a neutral power, the United States joined hands with England, France, and Russia in the Great War. At the request of President Woodrow Wilson, Congress had declared war on Germany.

CHAPTER 11

THE GREAT WAR

My friend, Charles Stewart, did not fight in the war, but for someone who wasn't in Europe, he sure knew a lot about the war. He told me how we—our country—crossed an ocean to help end a nightmare that would grip the race of man for four years. He was honored to know many of the men who fought—"our best blood, the young and the strong," he called them. The war was necessary, President Wilson had said, to make the world safe for democracy. It was the century's first great conflagration, and as Stewart would say, "dare I hope, our last." In the beginning, it was known as the European War. When America joined the fighting, it became the Great War. Today we know it as World War I.

An assassin's bullet in Bosnia set off the war in 1914. Within weeks, the leading nations of Europe were drawn in. It was the most frightful war the world had ever seen, lasting four years and costing 15 million lives. The armies fought from trenches across Belgium and northeastern France in an armed frontier called the Western Front. Conditions were miserable: mud, rain, snow, cold, and long marches with heavy packs. Inside the trenches, soldiers endured exposure, frostbite, rats, lice, flies, disease, dead bodies, and artillery shells. The trenches flooded when it rained. Sometimes soldiers didn't wash or change clothes for days at a time. It was trench warfare—fighting with rifles, bayonets, machine guns, mortars, and poison gas. The Western Front hardly moved in nearly four years of fierce combat.

The war had raged nearly three years when America's young men heard the bugle in April 1917. As the year went along, baseball teams began finding fewer players to fill their rosters. When the season began, there were twenty-one minor leagues across the country, but nine would not complete their seasons. Not until the following season, however, did the situation become dire for baseball. The Southern Association was one of nine minor leagues in the country to begin play in 1918, but only one league would finish the season—and it wasn't the Southern Association.

Stewart once told me, "Out at Rickwood we opened the season of 1918 with the same strapping players, the same cheering throng, the same soft drink boys. But things weren't the same that year. We saw empty seats, game after game. The fans rooted for the home team but without enthusiasm. If the umpire made a bum decision, the crowd didn't protest. And why was this? It was the war. When we watched those muscled ball players running around the diamond and thought of our boys in the trenches of Europe, well, it just didn't seem right."

The government issued a "work or fight" order. By July 1, 1918, men aged twenty-one to thirty were required to work in an essential wartime industry, such as shipbuilding or steelmaking, or risk being called to the front lines of Europe. The ball players did not respond to the country's call in large numbers. Those who continued to play baseball were subject to the military draft—they could be here today, gone tomorrow. Many ball players sought jobs in shipbuilding plants to avoid service, and this did not create a favorable impression. Fandom lost interest, and attendance throughout baseball was far below normal. Major league teams played to audiences of two thousand spectators and fewer. Baseball was in an unsettled state.

Twelve thousand boys from Birmingham were in the service. "Our flesh and blood was on the fields of France," Stewart said, "but we had no clear idea what the fighting was about. Then news began arriving that our boys—boys we had known and seen every day—were among those killed or wounded or missing. We were haunted by the thought of our young soldiers lying dead or wounded on the battlefield, by the thought that many of our young boys would never come back."

The "work or fight" deadline was looming when the directors of the Southern Association met in Birmingham on June 10, 1918. The directors knew that on July 1 all men not engaged in a necessary wartime occupation would risk being called to work or fight. Baseball was not considered a necessary occupation. Therefore, all ball players soon would be working in a "necessary" occupation or would become eligible for the military draft. In any event, operating a baseball team would become more difficult after July 1. The Southern Association directors on June 10 issued a resolution stating that the public was more concerned about our army in France than about baseball. Furthermore, they said, it would be both patriotic and economical to cease operations for the period of the war. They said the baseball campaign would be laid to rest on June 28.

"It was bad not to have ball," Stewart said, "but what was the use in mourning? Interest in baseball had faded. The last time I was at the park there was only a corporal's guard on hand, and no one seemed to have enthusiasm enough to root for the home team. We said then it was time to quit, to end the season out of respect for the soldiers. If the ball players weren't eligible to fight, couldn't they at least be involved in some way to help the war along?"

STEWART TOLD ME OF ALABAMA'S very own fighting force, the 167th Infantry Regiment of Alabama's National Guard. The regiment fought in France as part of the 42nd (Rainbow) Division under Brigadier General Douglas MacArthur. The Alabamians bore much of the hard fighting. They excelled in patrolling the dangerous "no-man's-land" and in raiding German trenches. The French called the Alabamians "les tigres" — the tigers. A soldier from Washington, D.C., said of the Alabamians, "I do not know if they would make good parlor pets or proper chaperones for young ladies at the movies, but they sure are wonderful fighters."

The Alabama 167th reached France near the end of 1917 and went to the front lines in February 1918, the low point of the war for the Allies. Up to this time, every major Allied offensive on the battlefront had failed. In July 1918, the Germans attempted to take Paris, launching the Champagne-Marne offensive. The Alabamians helped bear the brunt of the assault. In a fierce and bloody stand, they held their positions, and the Germans were repelled. Paris was saved. The battle marked the turn in the fighting, and the war would end less than four months later.

Charles Stewart told of a man who was engaged in the practice of medicine, a physician, thirty-five years old. "His name was Mortimer Jordan," Stewart said, "and he was known by hundreds of men and women of every class and station. He was a fine man, true as steel, born on the site of the Tutwiler Hotel. His family for generations had been distinguished citizens of Alabama. Mort Jordan was with the 167th in the German assault on Paris. The Alabamians were engaged in a hard fight near Souain, France. A young private of Captain Jordan's company was wounded and fell in no-man's-land. Mort Jordan didn't ask for a volunteer to go through the blood-soaked battlefield to drag the wounded private out. He did it himself. He took the soldier to a place of shelter, but the poor boy died in his arms. Mort Jordan was decorated with a Distinguished Service Cross for his action."

Days later, on the afternoon of July 28, near the Ourcq River, another battle was fought, this one fiercer than before. German artillery rained a terrific barrage — a veritable hell of machine gun fire, poison gas, and high explosives.

The Germans made a furious assault on Mort Jordan's position. Brave comrades fell, dying, dead. On came the German tide, man after man, column after column. From their trench, bayonets fixed, leapt the Alabamians to meet the enemy. Their cheers rang out as German artillery hurled its shells. It was vicious fighting, hand-to-hand, with cold steel, rifle butts, fists—the most savage combat Americans had engaged in. The enemy offered desperate resistance, launching terrific counterattacks, but the Alabamians pushed them back across the Ourcq River, and the Germans withdrew. The initiative had been passed into Allied hands and was never lost.

During the battle, Mort Jordan was determined to protect his comrades, so he moved his first aid station to the danger zone. In the fright of battle, he was hit with shrapnel and fell. Believing his wounds not severe, he insisted others be treated first. He worked, directed, and fought for four full hours before giving in. Pieces of shrapnel were embedded in his back, and fragments of his uniform pressed into his flesh. His uniform was contaminated with poisonous gases of the war zone, and the poisons likely induced gangrene. Mortimer Jordan died five days later at the field hospital in Coulommiers, France.

Then came Mortimer Jordan's letters home, arriving after his death. His letters were "picked out on the faithful Corona, held on my knees, while I am perched on the side of my bunk in a lovely dugout…dirty, ragged, unkempt, weary—but still happy and well content." He spoke of life in France and the bravery of his comrades against the Boche, the soldiers' nom de guerre for Germans:

July 13

The war goes merrily on, but for those who are in it there is not much to see. The picture is too big—drawn on such a grand scale that one must stand afar off in order to get the proper perspective. You folks at home can see much more of the picture than we can. For us there is nothing but a jumble of marching and digging and going here and there as ordered. My impression of the war is a sort of mixture (like a cubist picture) of guns and gas alarms and endless muddy trenches, and interminable dusty roads and a great multitude of men and horses.

. . . Our days are marked by the villages we have occupied. They are all alike. There is always a single, long, winding street, lined on both sides by red-roofed, stone houses. The street is either deep with mud or dust, depending on the weather. There are always flocks of chickens and ducks wandering about. . . . Half of each house is designed for the horses and cattle. . . . The men rejoice in billets in the lofts above the quarters of the "stock." With a good supply of straw for mattresses, what better home could a soldier ask than this?

. . . If the weather be cold, motherly old women will make room at their firesides for our soldiers. And everywhere, no matter what the weather, will be the children, scurrying out to meet the column, diving here and there through the ranks and shouting out a welcoming "good-by," and (I regret to state) swearing strange oaths in good, old-fashioned American; for bad words are the first American ones the French children learn.

. . . As one approaches the front, he is struck with one fact above all others: That is, that in this war, there are none who are immune. Women and children fall just as readily beneath gas and shells as the soldiers. I have grown accustomed to most of the awful things done in this war, but I cannot get used to the sight of children wearing gas masks. Yet, in villages near the front, they carry them around as a matter of course.

July 17

I have a hunch that before the year is out I will see "my girl and my chillun" and all the folks again. That is, unless the most flagrant injustice is done. . . . They must send somebody to the new divisions, and who would be better qualified than us grizzled old veterans who have been through the fire? But I am not building my hopes too high, for no one can ever tell what will be done. If I do not get home until the end of the year, it will be no more than I expected to be the case when I left you last year.

July 20

Just a line to let you know that I am still alive and well. The papers have probably told you about the big Boche drive, and how it was stopped. It was a terrible effort, but the French and Americans blocked it and in turn smashed the Boche. Our division and regiment behaved gloriously. . . . The French say they never saw the equal of our men for sheer nerve and deviltry. Their only criticism was that they are too terrible. They kill the Boches with rifles, bayonets, gun butts, knives, and with their fists. The most wonderful thing is the way they endure a 10-days' shelling in open trenches without budging an inch.

A memorial at the Veterans Administration Medical Center in Birmingham honors the memory of Mortimer Jordan and the Alabama 167th Regiment of the 42nd Rainbow Division. It is located near the corner of Eighth Avenue South and Nineteenth Street.

I have heard so many shells (the air is fairly full of them) and been through so many narrow scrapes that it would take a week to tell half of it.

July 21
. . . I am very happy in the knowledge that I can "stand the gaff," for I was always afraid that when the time came I might "turn yellow." No one can ever know what he would do until the time comes. I expect to cable you every now and then in order to let you know that I am still safe. Of course my writing will be very irregular for a while.

July 23
. . . Tell the kids to be good and behave, for they will have a hard old daddy coming home some day.

Five days after his final letter, Mort Jordan fell in the Champagne-Marne offensive. But the tide of battle had turned, and the Armistice that ended the war would be signed four months later.

AS THE GREAT WAR WOUND down, a new illness was spreading around the world: Spanish influenza. It ravaged first the German army, then spread to France and England. From Europe it was carried on ocean liners and troop transports to America, and by mid-September 1918, had spread over the East Coast. The influenza swept south. In Birmingham during the month of October, there were ten thousand cases and four hundred deaths. The disease developed into pneumonia and other complications quickly. Absolute quarantine was the only way to combat it. Places of public assembly — schools, churches, theaters — were closed for nearly four weeks. City and county authorities were overwhelmed, requiring neighbor to minister to neighbor. People often were discovered dying or dead. In one house, a woman was extremely ill. In bed with her were the bodies of two dead babies, and around the bed were four small children.

It was a situation that required utmost patience and cooperation by the public, said Dr. J. D. Dowling, the city's health officer. "We urge people to remain at home as much as possible and avoid the ordinary contact of the streetcars and stores. Dress comfortably and keep windows open day and night. Those whose duties require them to be in contact with others indoors should, by all means, wear gauze masks."

In November 1918, 233 people died in Birmingham; in December, 376. Thereafter the epidemic waned. Spanish flu killed twenty-one million people in Europe, Asia, and America, more than the war killed. In the United States, half a million people died. The government and the people ignored the crisis to an extent. There was a war to fight, and this was just another hardship to face.

ON NOVEMBER 11, 1918, SHORTLY before two o'clock in the morning, the populace was roused from sleep with a simple statement from the State Department: "The Armistice has been signed." The war was over. Hostilities would cease at eleven a.m., Paris time. The news was delivered through a *Birmingham News Extra* edition appearing on the streets at two-fourteen that morning. Sirens screamed, whistles blew, and bells chimed across the city — hundreds of them — and the celebration began. Newspaper boys were on the streets: *Extra! Extra! Germany surrenders! War is over! Extra! Extra!* All over town, men and women sprang from bed. The shouts of newsboys on the South Highlands awakened people before the newspapers arrived. Many residents were outside on a cold Monday morning in boots and overcoats when a truck rushed up with papers, still damp from the press. Other boys ran through hotel corridors, rousing guests with their cries.

As the day wore on, thousands of people joined the celebration, and what a racket they made! — a din of clanging bells, exploding fireworks, and bursts of gunfire. At noon, streets were jammed and blocked. Streetcar schedules were altered; vehicles detoured for blocks; pedestrians elbowed their way along walkways. At eleven-thirty, city schools closed for a holiday. Businesses closed from two o'clock until four for a parade.

"It was a matter of O be joyful—and we all were," Stewart remembered. "Someone said this day made him think of Christmas, only a hundred percent more so. Someone else said it was like the Fourth of July, only there never had been a Fourth as great as this day. An ordeal that had haunted us for four years was over."

Alabama troops sailed the high seas for home in April of 1919. Arriving in New York, they left for Alabama by train and were honored by parades in cities and towns across the state. Birmingham held the biggest parade anyone had ever seen. It was stirring to watch the men, in full battle gear, march down Nineteenth Street and up Twentieth. Cheers turned into ovations heard for blocks around. Most of the men had gold chevrons on their sleeves denoting wounds in battle. Many had two or three or four such badges of honor. Some wore medals for high courage on their breasts.

The people cheered a daring aviator as he swooped back and forth over the troops, just above the rooftops, in his airplane. At Fourth Avenue, Boy Scouts placed a double rope across Twentieth Street to stem the humanity that hoped to grasp the hands of their heroes. As the line of march went past, men, women, and children broke through the ropes. "Well, I cannot blame them much," said a police officer attempting to stop the rush. When the troops reached Twentieth Street and Park Place, everyone observed a minute of silence for those who never came home, and all joined in singing "America the Beautiful."

THE SHINING MOMENT IN BIRMINGHAM during the war-shortened baseball season of 1918 was provided by a young pitcher named Charles Franklin Glazner, whom everyone called "Whitey." He was a local boy from Avondale with a thatch of hair so white that people called him the "cotton-topped Avondale Blossom." Whitey Glazner, twenty-four years old, was going nowhere in professional ball. He had played four years of Class D, the lowest level of pro ball. In 1917, he had pitched for a semi-pro team in town, the Ensley Indians of the TCI League. However, Carlton Molesworth, the Barons manager, saw something he liked in the boy. Maybe it was his wicked sidearm delivery, maybe his spirit. Whatever, Moley signed him to a contract.

On a cold, blustery day in April 1918, Babe Ruth came to town. This was before Ruth had become a champion home run hitter, before he had become a New York Yankee. Ruth was twenty-three years old and a member of the Boston Red Sox. My friend, Charles Stewart, remembered the day well:

On May 10, 1919, Birmingham held the biggest parade anyone had ever seen. Cheers turned into ovations heard for blocks, as crowds lined streets and rooftops to welcome home the Alabama 167th Infantry Regiment. The Alabamians fought in France as part of the 42nd (Rainbow) Division under Douglas MacArthur and bore much of the hard fighting during the summer of 1918. Here, the men march in full battle gear up North Twentieth Street past Second Avenue.

"We were playing the Red Sox in one of our customary spring exhibition games. It was a cold day, not one for baseball. There were only five hundred spectators. A stiff, northerly wind blew in the faces of the ball players all game long, a wind you could feel in the marrow of your bones. The athletes played the game wearing sweaters and coats.

"In the final inning with the bases full, Babe Ruth came to bat. Whitey Glazner was in the box. The Boston team knew they were facing a raw rookie and began hooting: 'Look out for a home run!' On the very first pitch, Ruth hit a long ball over the fence . . . foul. You should a' heard those ball players holler. I'm sure Whitey was quaking in his boots, but guess what? Ol' Cotton-Top threw a second strike—Pop!—past Ruth. Then he windmilled his right arm over his head, whizzed another one over the plate, and Babe almost broke his back trying to connect—strike three, struck him out. I still have the newspaper from that game, and I love looking at it on occasion. The headline from that paper reads

'Whitey Glazner Strikes Out Babe Ruth with Bases Full in Last Inning.' I wonder if Whitey has that newspaper today."

Whitey Glazner was all set to be the sensation of the league that year. In his very first game pitching for Birmingham, he struck out thirteen batters but lost, 3–2. He had four tough losses and three wins in the early going. Then in May his name was called in the draft. "All they have to do is let me know where to go and furnish a little railroad fare to get there, and you bet I'll grab the first train," he said. "None of this shipbuilding business just to dodge the draft for me."

In late May, Whitey Glazner entrained for Camp Sevier in Greenville, South Carolina, to join other drafted soldiers, mainly from North Carolina, South Carolina, and Florida, in the Eighty-first (Wildcat) Division. Whitey was assigned to the 321st Infantry Regiment of the Wildcat Division. The 321st organized a baseball team to compete against other regiments in the States and overseas, and the team did not lose a single game. Corporal Whitey Glazner was the team's star pitcher.

The Wildcat Division came late to the fight, arriving in France in August of 1918. With less than two months remaining in the war, Whitey and his comrades were sent to the St. Dié sector of France's Vosges Mountains region. They were part of the French Seventh Army and held what was considered a quiet front, although they faced German trench raids and artillery bombardments. A week before the Armistice, the Wildcat moved to the front lines near Verdun. On the morning of November 9, they attacked German lines, encountering heavy machine gun and artillery fire.

On the night of November 10, there were rumors that an armistice might be signed the next day. At daybreak, November 11, the 321st Regiment went "over the top" from the trenches for the first time. The advance was slow, through heavy fog and shell and machine gun fire. The 321st attacked the main German trench line north of Bois de Manheulles. Some of the soldiers entered German trenches; many were either killed or pinned down under enemy fire. At eleven o'clock they were in the act of taking the main German trench line when the firing abruptly stopped. The Armistice had ended the hostilities.

Over the next fifteen days, Whitey's Wildcat Division marched one hundred miles with full packs, along muddy roads and often in the rain, to five secluded villages in rural France. Here, they would spend the winter and spring of 1919 awaiting their return to native soil. With more than two million American soldiers abroad, it would take months to bring them home. Some remained in Germany as part of the Army of Occupation. It was June 9, 1919, before Whitey's division sailed for home.

AT MIDNIGHT OF FRIDAY, JUNE 27, 1919, the train bearing Whitey Glazner and some of his army mates pulled up to the great iron gates of Birmingham's Terminal Station. People gathered 'round with questions:

"Say, Whitey, tell us about the battle the last night at the front."

"Did you kill any Germans?"

"Are you gonna play for the Barons this year?"

Whitey couldn't stop smiling as he shook hands with friends and told them how good it was to be back home after thirteen months in the army. "I wouldn't take a million dollars for my experiences, and say, Bo, I wouldn't give you half a copper for the whole of France." Whitey spoke of the gallant charge on the German trench line the morning of November 11—of high-powered shells bursting around him, the French seventy-five-millimeter artillery guns blasting away, and his buddies going down, never to rise again. Whitey endured shell shock and spent weeks in a hospital in France after temporarily losing his hearing.

"I thought I was a goner several times," he admitted, "and when shells fell among the three of us, killing the other two men, I couldn't even hear one of the big seventy-fives make a report. However, I was given treatments in the hospital, and now I can hear a pin fall five blocks away."

On July 15, Whitey was back pitching for the Barons, facing the Atlanta Crackers at Rickwood Field. After a year in the army, after a near nervous breakdown from shell shock, and barely two weeks after returning home, Whitey Glazner would endure an eighteen-inning pitching duel. It was a grueling, midsummer contest lasting three and a half hours. The opposing pitcher, Dan Boone, left after the ninth inning—halfway through the game. Atlanta scored five runs in the second inning, the result of errors by the Barons, but did not score again for the next sixteen innings. Birmingham squared the game in the eighth, 5–5. From the ninth inning until the eighteenth—nine straight innings—Whitey Glazner retired every batter he faced but one.

As he took the mound for the eighteenth inning, Whitey told Manager Carlton Molesworth he never felt better in his life. "I kept a close watch on Glazner throughout the game," Molesworth said. "He remarked to me several times during the game that his arm never felt better. He was pitching with great ease in the eighteenth—in fact, as easy as in any other inning of the game."

Whitey retired the first batter in the eighteenth inning, then allowed a base hit. The next batter lined out to the leftfielder for the second out. The next batter walked. Even with runners on first and second base, no one doubted Whitey would retire the final batter. Then suddenly his arm played out. Whitey delivered a changeup to his final Atlanta batter. After releasing the pitch, he began rubbing his right arm. He walked toward catcher John Peters and tried to raise his arm. Peters pulled on it, but the arm was dead, completely lame. Whitey walked slowly to the bench, arm limp at his side. A relief pitcher came in to finish the inning. The first batter singled to leftfield to score the winning run for Atlanta. Whitey had lost the game.

Whitey went to a chiropractor for treatment on his arm. There was talk he might not pitch again that season. The nature of the injury never was publicly disclosed. It could have been nerve damage or a pulled ligament. Nevertheless, his pitching arm was badly strained. Within a few days, Whitey said his arm was fine. Three weeks later, he returned to the mound and won a game. He finished the season without further trouble.

The following year and the year after, 1920 and 1921, Whitey Glazner reached the pinnacle of his baseball career. He won twenty-four games for the Barons in 1920. In one memorable game at Rickwood Field late in the season, he and Dazzy Vance dueled one another into extra innings. Vance, a future major league Hall of Famer, pitched for New Orleans, the second-place team in the league, against third-place Birmingham. Neither team scored for the first ten innings. Time after time, the Barons had chances to score—once with the bases loaded—but Vance would tighten up and retire the side. During the game, three Barons and one Pelican were thrown out at the plate. New Orleans scored the first run in the top of the eleventh. Birmingham tied it in the bottom half, 1–1, but moments later Glazner missed a chance to win the game when he grounded out with a runner on third. New Orleans scored a run in the thirteenth inning on a squeeze play to win the game. The game was one in a thousand, daresay the best exhibition of the national sport on any diamond in any league—north, south, east, or west. It was classy ball, no getting around it.

Four days later Glazner won his twenty-fourth game, beating Atlanta at Rickwood. The next season, 1921, he pitched for the Pittsburgh Pirates, winning fourteen games and losing five—tying for the best winning percentage in the National League. Whitey's big league career was brief, only three more years, with more losses than wins. At the age of thirty-one, he returned to the minor leagues to pitch his final seven seasons of ball.

FROM THE EARLIEST YEARS OF the 1900s, black and white ball players across the city had played on semi-professional industrial teams segregated by race. White youths participated in an organized league of amateurs and semi-pro players—the City League—as far back as 1902. Black ball players did not have a semi-pro league until around 1925 but played the game in large numbers just the same. These industrial leagues, for blacks and whites, were the highest level of amateur baseball in the South.

Semi-pro white ball players playing on company teams were the employees of various industries—mills, mines, banks, and so forth. The American Cast Iron Pipe Company—ACIPCO—fielded a white team and a black team. In the early years of the century, three strong black teams played in Birmingham: Acipco, Edgewater, and Ensley. Ensley and Acipco were rivals of long standing. Evidence has been lost to history, but the Edgewater team likely was composed of laborers from coal mines, and the Ensley ball players probably represented the Tennessee Coal, Iron, and Railroad Company (TCI). In 1919, the Big Three black industrial teams, Ensley, Edgewater, and Acipco, began playing some of their games at Rickwood Field. Occasionally, the Big Three would come together and form an "all-star" team to play a powerful out-of-state team.

The celebrated Chicago American Giants played the all-stars at Rickwood in September 1919. The Giants were at the pinnacle of black baseball during the teens, traveling the country—north to Canada, west to California, south to Cuba—taking on all comers, black and white. The Giants' Andrew (Rube) Foster, once a pitcher beyond compare but no longer active, was the team's manager. In 1920, Foster was instrumental in forming the Negro National League, the first successful professional black baseball league.

In 1919, John Peters, the white Barons catcher, said, "I have seen the Chicago Giants play every season, and take it from me, they can beat about half of the teams in the Southern League. Why, they even give the major league clubs a close battle. Rube Foster, the star pitcher of the team, is one of the best pitchers I ever saw. He has everything."

The general public began to notice and appreciate Birmingham's black semi-pro ball players in 1919. Many white fans declared there was more sport, more spirit, more spunk at black games than at games played by the professional white Barons. White fans attended black games in such large numbers—a thousand or more—that a section of seating in the grandstand was reserved for them. Often, black ball games outdrew the white Barons in attendance. "The park has been taxed to capacity almost every time Negro games have been booked this season," stated a local newspaper.

On Labor Day 1919, the Ensley team—Black Barons, they called themselves—played a doubleheader against the Montgomery Grey Sox. Near the entrance of Rickwood Field were barbecue stands, fruit wagons, and hucksters crying their wares. People packed and jammed every seat, and a mob stood in the outfield. The crowd was twelve thousand, Rickwood's largest up to that time—larger, even, than the day Rickwood opened its doors in 1910.

Mills and mines supplied ball players to white and black industrial leagues in the first half of the century. Birmingham's black Industrial League became a feeder to the Negro Leagues and later contributed the first group of black players to the white major leagues. This picture, featuring Acipco and Stockham Valve players, is from around 1942.

A second professional black league was formed in 1920: the Negro Southern League, of which Birmingham was a member. Also in the league were the cities of Atlanta, Jacksonville, Knoxville, Montgomery, Nashville, New Orleans, and Pensacola. Many players from Birmingham's black industrial teams would populate the roster of the first Birmingham Black Barons of the Negro Southern League. The Black Barons later joined the Negro National League. Industrial teams—black and white—continued to flourish for years in Birmingham. The coal mines and steel mills continued developing outstanding ball players, and Birmingham's black Industrial League became a feeding system to the Negro Leagues and later contributed the first wave of black players to major league baseball.

THE YEAR 1919 WAS DECIDEDLY an off year. Gradually, the soldiers returned from war. One by one, ball players drifted back. The world was recovering its balance after the chaos of war. Europe was weary, its economies exhausted, with widespread suffering; hundreds of thousands were dying of starvation and disease. Everywhere there was unrest and turmoil—labor strikes, inflation, race riots. Yet America beheld a tidal wave of prosperity. In 1919, America was the richest nation in the world, with the most powerful economy. More people owned automobiles than ever before and drove them a distance to watch the ball players of the Southern Association. The season of 1919, financially, was one of the most successful for the league, ever. For the first time in years, no club bordered on bankruptcy.

By the turn of 1920, life had returned to normal. Young men were back. From the earliest days of spring came the sound, the crack, of bat meeting ball. Every town, every factory, every mill had a ball club. Multitudes went to ball games again with a clear conscience. War was not on anybody's mind.

"The baseball bug certainly has Alabama in its grip," remarked the engineer of a passenger train in the spring of 1920. From his big locomotive, speeding through village and town, he observed boys on the hillside, in the back lot, and along streets playing ball. The hillbillies, the country boys, were the first to begin playing this spring, he said. "Every lad four years old and up along my run has a ball and a bat, and rural diamonds are springing up like mushrooms overnight."

Yes, the soldiers were back, boys were playing ball again, and everyone was in high spirits. The Roaring Twenties were not far behind.

CHAPTER 12

RAY'S STORY

WHEN I THINK OF IT now, that day in 1931 when I met Charles Stewart, I think of Ray Caldwell. Though I had called Ray my hero, little did I understand him. I didn't know his background, or his travels, or that in 1931 he was on the final journey of his baseball life. Really, I knew nothing of this man from Corydon, Pennsylvania.

In the 1880s, Corydon was a farming town south of the border of New York state, hard by the Allegheny River. It lay between two Indian reservations, the Seneca to the north and the Cornplanters to the west. Corydon proper was the home of a lumber mill, a gristmill, a livery stable, assorted blacksmiths and general stores, two hotels and two hundred living, breathing souls. Railroad tracks ran through the center of town. Before the railroad came, the link to the outside was a stagecoach from Steamburg, New York, passing through with passengers and mail. The town baseball team played its games on Saturdays, as in all other towns. Visiting teams arrived by stage or by train. Today there is no Corydon. The quiet town and its tree-lined streets were flooded in the 1960s behind the Kinzua Dam, so that today it lies at the bottom of a man-made lake.

April 26, 1888. The date did not mean much to the people of Corydon, but it was on that day that Ray Caldwell was born. At the turn of the century, baseball was the only sport at which a boy could make a name for himself, so in his late teens Ray Caldwell began playing town ball around the countryside. He was a willowy kid trying to earn a position in fast company, and he had to use his wits to convince people he could help the local nine on the diamond.

He wanted to play first base, but the boys voted him down. Another afternoon he stood in line during a choose-up game and asked to play. A burly team captain looked him over and said, "You're too skinny to make a ball player. Beat it!" But Ray stayed, and when the team's pitcher was knocked from the box early in the game, he went in and finished it, brandishing a blazing fastball in a 6–4 victory. The boys were impressed and allowed him to remain on the team. That was in 1908. The next year Ray played for semi-pro clubs in Bath, New York, and Kane, Pennsylvania. Duke Servatius, the manager of a minor league team in McKeesport, Pennsylvania, took a fancy to Ray's fastball and decided the kid could help his club. Ray played most of 1910 for McKeesport.

"What did I get for signing with McKeesport?" Ray recalled years later. "Well, a youngster had to do the begging back in those days, and I thank Duke for giving me a contract."

Back then, ball players often ascended to the major leagues in short order, and before 1910 was out, Ray had gained passage to the big leagues. The New York Yankees bought him for $1,500, a splendid sum in the day. Baseball in 1910 was closer in style to the humble game of the mid-1800s than to the game of today. The first World Series had been played in 1903. The American League had been organized in 1901, the National League some years before that. Until 1884, pitchers threw underhand. Unless you read the newspaper or lived in one of the ten cities that had a team, you knew little about major league baseball. All Ray knew about baseball was town ball and low-level minor league ball.

"I didn't know anything," Ray said of his first day in the major leagues. "I didn't even know what a catcher's mask was for. The manager gave me the ball, told me to warm up and that I was the starting pitcher. We were playing the Red Sox, and Harry Hooper was the leadoff batter. He hit my first pitch for a home run, and right then I learned there were hitters in the majors."

The day of the Dixie Series in 1931, Charles Stewart told me all about Ray Caldwell, about how he played his first big league game three weeks after Rickwood Field opened, that the Yankees were called the Highlanders back then, that Ray was tall and lank, and that he could throw the ball real hard.

"He was some pitcher, boy was he a pitcher," Stewart said, "'bout six-foot-two, 190 pounds. His fastball was a peach, and he had one of the best curveballs in the business."

But Ray Caldwell did not lead a picture-perfect life, and Stewart told me the whole story, beginning to end.

"Ray had arm trouble his first couple years in the big leagues," Stewart began. "'Twisted muscles' they called it. Ray's a real good hitter, and when he injured his arm they thought about making him an outfielder. But the heart of a ball club is in the pitcher's box, and Ray had one of the fastest balls in the loop, so they decided to keep him a pitcher.

"By and by, his arm got better, and in 1914 he had a good year. I was in New York that year on business—April, best I remember—and saw him pitch a game against the Athletics, who had won the World Series the year before. Ray could throw a knuckleball, and that day he pitched a gem, a three-hit game. I'll never forget that *sloow*, lazy ball he threw that day, the ball floatin' in the air like a driftin' summer cloud. He was something to watch that day. I still remember the way the newspaper described it: 'Caldwell teased the champs with a slow, hypnotic floater that dipped over the plate so easily the spectators could read Ban Johnson's signature on the leather.' Yep, that's what they wrote."

Stewart paused, ruminating about the gangling, gallant titan everybody called "Slim." "You see, the Yankees weren't very good in those days. Ray was their best pitcher, and he carried them on his broad shoulders. He had long, willowy arms and threw the ball so easily many folks thought he wasn't trying. In 1914, he won seventeen games. He threw five shutouts and completed almost every game he pitched, and still there were two months left in the season.

"Well, come August he lost a couple of games. Then he left the team, just up and disappeared. The long and short of it is, Ray had done things like that before. He was careless about keeping in condition. He was a restless spirit, a misfit, a sucker for old barleycorn—there's no dodging that fact. He never followed training rules, loved the nightlife, the big city. He was fun loving and had a way about him the ladies found attractive. The newspapers said he occasionally flirted with that which is amber and foamy, a nice way of saying Ray liked to drink."

Stewart cocked an eye at me: "You don't drink, do you, son?"

"No! Sir!"

"Smoke? Chew tobacco?"

"Yecchh!"

"Good. I'll tan your britches if you do. Now, where was I? Oh, yes, I remember, Ray's fun-loving ways.

"Anyhow, the manager was tired of Ray's 'Broadway training' and didn't like Ray being a ladies' man and all, so he fined Ray. It was the third time that season he had fined him. Ray didn't like it, so he up and left the team. In September, he hopped to Buffalo of the new Federal League. The league didn't last long—couple of years, maybe—but Ray never played a game for them. The Yankees hired a new manager. They offered Ray a three-year contract at a good salary, and he came back.

"The Washington Senators had a pitcher named Walter Johnson, a pleasant fellow with the longest arms you ever saw—arms like whips. I declare, he had this sidearm motion and would just whip the ball in there, just *whip* it." Stewart snapped his fingers as he said this. "Nobody'd ever seen anything like him.

Whenever he pitched, he bulked head and shoulders above the field. Why, he was one of the greatest who ever lived.

"Not many people know this about Ray, but he told me himself, so I know it's true. Before the 1915 season began, the Senators approached the Yankees about trading Walter Johnson for Ray. The trade didn't happen, but it shows you how much that team thought of Ray, that they would consider giving up the great Walter Johnson to get Ray. And guess what? The following spring Ray beat Walter Johnson on a two-hit shutout. Yes sir, Ray could climb into the ring with just about anyone. Ray won nineteen games that year, 1915, even though the Yanks were still a bad ball club. Now, listen up, I wanna tell you what he did in three straight games that year. The first day he hits a pinch-hit home run; the second day, another pinch-hit home run; the third day, he's the starting pitcher and — Wham! — out of the park, another home run. Three home runs in three games — how-de-do! Darndest thing I ever heard of.

"Anyway, Ray stayed out of mischief that year, but the next year was a different story. Late in the year he left the team again, and the manager suspended him. When the suspension was up, Ray didn't report back to the team, so they suspended him again for the rest of the season."

"How do you know all this?" I asked.

"I'm a travelin' man. I've been everywhere, seen everybody, done everything. It's been my fortune to see the Polo Grounds, Fenway, Detroit, Philadelphia, all the big, beautiful ball yards. I saw Ray Caldwell pitch when he was just a youngster blossoming out in the big leagues. I've talked to Ray, and he's told me about it. The things I could write about — oh, yes." He spoke with feeling as he said this, for baseball mattered to Stewart, maybe more than it should have, and when he got on his favorite hobby horse, baseball, I just sat and listened. As I recall, here's what he said that day in 1931:

"See, whenever time hangs heavy on my hands, I like to be in the great outdoors and go to a ball game. The young college man goes strong for football — the colorful crowd, the coonskin coat, the rah-rah student body, the gridiron. *Go! Go! Go! Fight! Fight! Fight!* Hip-hip-hooray — I can only take that stuff in small doses. You see, baseball is my one and only outdoor sport. I don't understand lots of plays in football, but you can bet I know everything that goes on in a baseball game.

"Ah, yes, baseball. Ol' Man Depression may be giving the game a blow to the chin whiskers about now. Its glories may fade for a time, but the game, Walter, it'll never die. And when this depression's over, it'll come back stronger and better than ever. You watch what I'm sayin'." Then he smiled.

When he played for the New York Yankees from 1910–1918, Ray Caldwell was known as "Slim." The Yankees were not a good team in those days, but Caldwell was their best pitcher. Pitching for the Cleveland Indians in 1920, he won 20 games.

"As I get older, I've found it's almost as much fun to talk about baseball as it is to watch it. We baseball people can go on forever talking and reminiscing. What happened yesterday is as important as what's happening today. Memories are sacred things, and we baseball people never forget anything—no sir, we don't forget any story about the old game. Big stories, little stories . . . one tale leads to another and—well—you can go on forever. Look at Ray Caldwell, forty-three years young, and he can't give up the game."

I WAS SLUMPED ON THE hard concrete floor in the shade of the grandstand, waiting for the Dixie Series to begin. My head dropped to my shoulder. It was the heat of the day, and the air was blast-furnace hot. My eyes fluttered open. I was roused from my reverie.

"I believe you nodded off," Stewart said. "Have I bored you?"

"No, I'm awake."

Stewart stretched his arms and flicked the ash from his cigarette. "I must finish my story. We left Ray in 1914, I believe. He'd won seventeen games that year and still there were two months left in the season. Remember me telling you that? Then he disappeared from the team for a spell. The manager fined him three times for doing things he shouldn't a' been doing. The next year he won nineteen games, and it looked like the sky's the limit for him. Then the year after that, 1916, he was suspended in August for the rest of the season. If only he were serious about the game, everyone said. About that time the newspapers said Ray had been a patient for alcohol treatment at a hospital in St. Louis. He was expected to join the Yankees for spring training in 1917, but he didn't report with the rest of the team."

The Washington Post wrote: "Caldwell is an example of a great pitcher going to ruin by his failure to take care of himself. The disciplining of Caldwell has gotten to be quite a hobby among baseball managers. . . . After his fall from grace last summer, this wonderful pitcher came to the owners of the Yankees and asked for one more chance. It has been granted him, and it is now up to Caldwell to show his appreciation of what was really a great kindness. Caldwell's presence on the Yankee roster means a chance for the pennant. His failure to report may mean that he will be out of baseball for good."

A writer in *The Sporting News* said, "This fellow Caldwell is a most peculiar chap. He is sensitive and boyish, although he is twenty-nine years old. He is good natured, intelligent, and nervy when he faces the opposing batsmen. But he lacks self-control when temptation is near at hand, and for that reason he has fallen from grace on several occasions."

Eventually, Caldwell reported to the Yankees training camp in 1917. Then in June, the day after a loss to the Boston Red Sox, Caldwell failed to return to the team's hotel. Nor did he show for the game the next day. Once again, he was fined and suspended. Caldwell's escapades often were followed by flashes of brilliance. After returning from the latest suspension, he pitched nearly ten innings of shutout ball. That night, he was arrested and charged with stealing a woman's ring worth $150. He returned the ring, and charges were dropped. Soon after, Ray's wife, Nellie, charged him with abandonment and sued for support for herself and their seven-year-old son.

In 1918, the Yankees assigned two private detectives to keep Ray out of trouble, yet he often eluded them. In August, he left the Yankees without notice and joined a shipbuilding company in New Jersey. It was during the World War, when the shipbuilding and steel industries were considered essential to the war effort. A number of players joined such companies to avoid the military draft and to play on company ball teams.

"Caldwell is a boy who really likes to play baseball," stated Walter Trumbull in the *New York World*. "When he is in condition, he is a great pitcher—one of the greatest in the game. Certain men, such as Ty Cobb and

John McGraw, cannot bear to lose. If it is only pitching pennies at a crack, they put their whole heart into it. If the soul of Caldwell ever burns with this flame, if he ever acquires this fierce ambition to be better than the best, he will make a name for himself that will last as long as the game endures."

IN ONLY TWO OF HIS ten years in the majors had Caldwell played for winning teams. Rarely did teams score many runs for him. During one stretch of forty-five innings, the Yankees supported him with only one run, and he made it hold up for a 1–0 win. And that run? It was scored by Caldwell himself. Connie Mack, the legendary manager of the Philadelphia Athletics, once said, "Put Ray Caldwell on a winning team and he would be one of the greatest pitchers of all time."

For several years, the Yankees had considered trading away Caldwell and his problems. Before the 1919 season began, while he was employed by the shipbuilding company, the Yankees did trade him to the Boston Red Sox, where his roommate was another lover of nightlife, Babe Ruth. By early August, the Red Sox had tired of Caldwell's behavior and released him. At the age of thirty-one, Ray's career was over. Or so it seemed.

Baseball proved kind to Ray Caldwell, however, and two weeks after the Red Sox released him, he got the chance to play for a winner. Ray was an acquaintance of Cleveland Indians Manager Tris Speaker, so he approached Speaker about a job. Speaker had a reputation as a kind and gentle soul who bossed his men with his heart as well as his mind. There was no question that Ray could help the Indians. The question was: Would Ray reform his ways?

"I won't drink anymore, Tris," Caldwell promised.

Speaker laughed at the tired line. "I'm not sure I want you if you *won't* drink anymore," Speaker said. Then, he handed Caldwell a contract. "Now I want you to read this carefully, Slim. Then if you want to sign it, okay."

Caldwell went straight to the bottom line, the salary, and his eyes absolutely popped. "This is more than I got at either New York or Boston," he declared. "Give me that pen. I'll sign!"

"I told you to read this contract very carefully," Speaker said. "You've looked only at the money. Now read every word in it."

Caldwell read the contract carefully, his lips forming the words:

After each game he pitches, Ray Caldwell *must* get drunk. He is *not* to report to the clubhouse the next day. The second day he is to report to Manager Speaker and run around the ball park as many times as Manager Speaker stipulates. The third day he is to pitch batting practice, and the fourth day he is to pitch in a championship game.

"You left out one word, Tris," Ray said. "Where it says I've got to get drunk after every game, the word 'not' has been left out. It should read that I'm *not* to get drunk."

Speaker smiled. "No, it says that you *are* to get drunk." Ray was baffled. "Okay, I'll sign."

I LOOKED AT CHARLES STEWART. "You sure know a lot about Ray Caldwell."

"I respect him," Stewart answered. "He's been playing the game a right smart while. Father Time came along and weakened his arm and slackened his pace. He knows the end of his pitching days is upon him. He's finally learned how fleeting is the fame of baseball and how meager its fortunes. His outlook is different now."

"Well, I'm hoping for his autograph," I said. "I don't have an autograph of a single ball player. My pal, Joseph, has autographs of big-leaguers. You know what? Babe Ruth signed Joseph's ball cap right here at Rickwood Field. There were a lot of little boys on the field that day, and Joseph shook Babe Ruth's hand right here on this field. And you know what Babe Ruth said to him? He said, 'Hey, keed, you're a handsome keed'—said it just like that: 'You're a handsome keed,' or something like that. Then he signed his cap, and then Babe Ruth shook his hand."

Stewart smiled. "I bet he could sell that cap to another lad."

"Well, if I had Babe Ruth's autograph, I wouldn't sell it."

People were streaming into Rickwood Field for Game One of the Dixie Series. Hot dog vendors milled about. The air shimmered with a smell of popcorn and melted butter, a hum of voices, and a patter of feet. Stewart walked proudly about, bowing here and there to acquaintances. One could sense the excitement of a big day. "I've a notion we're gonna have us a good crowd," Stewart said, "a *really* good crowd. Hey, let's us get some popcorn."

Stewart hailed a pop vendor. "Oh-ho! Soda pop boy! Give this lad a drink."

"Can I have a Dr. Pepper?" I asked.

"Whudever you say," the soda hawker replied, breathing hard, his shirt soaked. "That'll be five cents." Stewart pulled a change purse from his pocket, unclasped it, and handed the hawker a nickel.

"Plenty hot today," Stewart said, rolling his shirtsleeves to his elbows.

"Yes, yes, hot enough for me," said the soda hawker.

"Real baseball weather. Sold a lot of drinks, have you?"

"Yeah, almost fifty, and the game ain't even started yet."

"Have you now? Seems to me this heat's good for only two people: that would be you and the iceman. But this heat isn't nothing like what I've seen before. If you hark back six years, September of '25 — now that was some hot weather, hottest I ever did see." Stewart shook his head and studied his cigarette. "Intolerable heat all over Alabama. Five straight days over 104 degrees — in September, mind you. And drouth like you wouldn't believe — very little rain. Nothing you could do about it except walk on the shady side of the street and not eat too much. Odd weather for September, sure enough.

"I'm in the cotton business; I pay close attention to details like that. And I wanna tell you, in my business it's always something. First the boll weevil. Then the red spider mite — but that was only a scare. Then drouth and more drouth. Hailstorms. Yes, I'm in the cotton business — some people think the price of cotton'll go up; some think it'll go down. I do, too," he chuckled, "and I know this — whatever you do will be wrong. The price goes up after you've sold and goes down when you have more."

The soda hawker offered a polite nod. I cupped my chin in my hands and studied the two men. Stewart looked at me. "I was once a boy in knee trousers, just as you, Walter. There was a winding, shallow spring near our house, with water clear and cold. On hot days, I used to walk to that spring — barefoot, of course — and wade in, really cool off. Somehow, you don't see springs like that these days. I bet you don't have a spring like that at your house, do you?" I shook my head.

"Those hot afternoons when I was a boy I'd get a good-sized jug of fine, fresh buttermilk right out of the ol' cedar churn, put a little salt in it, take that jug down to the stream, and leave it in the water for two, three hours. I wish I could find some real buttermilk with yellow bits of butter floating around in it like I used to drink. None of this soft drink, ginger pop stuff for me. In the good ol' summertime, I'll have cold buttermilk, thank you."

Stewart grabbed me by the hand. "Alright, young man. We better make tracks to the field. Now where's that popcorn?"

IN AUGUST OF 1919, RAY Caldwell signed his generous contract with the Cleveland Indians requiring him to "get drunk after every game." In his first game, he was pitching against the Philadelphia Athletics. It was the ninth inning, and he was holding a one-run lead, pitching to the final batter with two outs, when it began to get dark and windy. A big rainstorm was about to kick up. Suddenly, there was a blinding flash — a lightning bolt right over the stadium.

"My, oh my," Stewart said to me, "it looked like the whole diamond was afire. Near as anyone can tell, the lightning had hit the metal button on top of Ray's cap and came out the spikes of his shoes. Regardless, Ray went down, right there in the pitcher's box."

As Ray Caldwell would remember, "I started to pitch, and the next thing I knew they were pouring water over my head. They said I had been struck by lightning."

"The shortstop, Ray Chapman, wanted to help Ray," Stewart said. "Chapman's leg was numb, and he almost slipped, but he recovered and went to Ray's rescue. Funny part of it was—not funny, but odd—a year later, almost to the day, Chapman was hit in the head by a pitched ball and died the next day.

"Anyway, after the lightning strike, Ray got up, finished off the last batter, and won the game, 2–1. But that's not the end of the story—not by a whole hatful. Two weeks later Ray faced his old team, the Yankees, and pitched a no-hitter. How-de-do! Can you believe it?"

In the final weeks of the 1919 season, Caldwell started six games for Cleveland, winning five, and the Indians almost won the pennant. In *The New York Evening Telegram,* Fred Lieb wrote: "Ray Caldwell is one of the marvels of the age. For years, he was in a class by himself for failing to take care of himself. Caldwell never looked better. He has his old smoke and his famous hop on the ball."

The next year, 1920, Cleveland won the pennant and the World Series, and Ray won twenty games for the first time ever. He had learned to throw a spitball the year before. The pitch was banned after the 1920 season, but he and sixteen other pitchers were allowed to continue throwing it for the rest of their careers.

One day during the 1920 season, a man saw Ray drinking in a speakeasy and mentioned the incident to a friend, a Cleveland banker. The banker, unaware of the special "drinking clause" in Ray's contract, thought he should notify the team. He visited owner Jim Dunn and Manager Tris Speaker and informed them that one of their players had been seen drinking quite liberally. Dunn and Speaker were concerned and asked who the player was. "Ray Caldwell," the banker answered.

Caldwell? Dunn and Speaker looked at one another, not the least bit concerned. Had it been one of the other players, it would have been a different matter.

"Did your friend know what Caldwell was drinking?" Speaker asked.

"No," said the banker.

"If he knew," Speaker retorted, "I would tell some of our other pitchers to drink some of the stuff. They're all five drinks behind Caldwell right now, according to our pitching records."

Ray spent most of the next season, 1921, in the bullpen. In September, he was suspended briefly for violating "rules of discipline." In the final days of the season, Cleveland and the Yankees were tied for first place when Ray was allowed to start a game against the Yankees. The Yankees scored five runs against Ray, and he got an early shower in the second inning. The Yankees won the game, 21–7. The Indians never recovered and lost the pennant. And Ray Caldwell never pitched another game in the big leagues. At thirty-three years of age, Ray was released at the close of the season. His name would disappear from major league box scores, no tears being shed save possibly his own. A hero one year, a hobo the next — that's baseball.

Like most ball players, Ray was not prepared for life without baseball. Major-leaguers of the day were not paid big salaries. Many worked in the off-seasons to make ends meet; few saved any money; none had pensions to look forward to; most had little education. Ball players made more money playing baseball than they could doing anything else and were not ashamed to finish their careers in the minor leagues. "What else am I qualified to do?" — it was a terrifying thought.

So what did Ray Caldwell do? He faded from the picture; spent the next twelve years in the outer darkness, the bush leagues; pitched three years for Kansas City, winning twenty-two games the first year, sixteen the next. Good enough for another shot at the big time? No. Major league teams were wise to his freckled past. He moved on to Little Rock of the Southern Association, where he played for three last-place teams. He lost — *lost* — twenty-two games in 1926 and twenty more in 1927. Memphis picked him up in 1928 — an aging forty-year-old — and he won ten games. The next year, 1929, he dropped down to Akron, a Class B team. Viewed as beyond repair, with a tired and worn arm, he was released after eight appearances. Shunted out of baseball for good. So it appeared.

The same year, 1929, Birmingham Barons Manager Johnny Dobbs went looking for a pitcher. He found Ray pitching and playing outfield for the Missouri Pacific Railroad, a semi-pro team in North Little Rock, Arkansas. Ray was back in business. He came to the Barons for the final month of the '29 season and helped the Barons win a pennant, then won two games in the 1929 Dixie Series. Rejuvenated, Ray won twenty games for Birmingham in 1930. The following year, 1931, he won nineteen, and the Barons won another pennant. Ten years after his last major league game, Ray Caldwell was back in the Dixie Series.

It sounded like a page from fiction: a baseball down-and-out . . . far from the glory of the bright lights . . . resurrected at age forty-three. One might argue that the years in Birmingham would be Ray Caldwell's greatest glory.

THE ROARING TWENTIES

CHAPTER 13

MONEY, MONEY, AND BURLEIGH

THE GREAT WAR ENDED IN November 1918. With the march to victory, America was bursting with patriotic pride. The world was safe for democracy, and the troops returned home to glorious celebrations. Americans were in high spirits, hopeful and upbeat. The United States soon would become the greatest of world powers. As a new decade opened, dramatic events were taking place. In January 1920, the Boston Red Sox sold Babe Ruth to the New York Yankees. Ty Cobb had just won his twelfth and final batting crown. In 1920, women won the right to vote, the prohibition of intoxicating liquors took effect, the first radio station began broadcasting, and the country learned that the 1919 World Series had been fixed. President Woodrow Wilson, who had brought the war to an end, was concluding his second term in office, bedridden by a stroke.

During the war and immediately after, the country had indulged in a prolonged spending spree. In Birmingham in 1920, demand was brisk for one hundred dollar suits, silk underwear, silk shirts, expensive shoes and hats, phonographs, pianos, motorcars, wardrobe trunks, watches, jewelry. Everybody was busy and happy, and everybody seemed to have money. Birmingham not only was prosperous, it *looked* prosperous, with streetcars moving in all directions, automobiles hurrying, people rushing. Delivery boys on bicycles scooted in and out among cars, cutting corners, and zigzagging from one curb to the next. Birmingham's growth in fifty years as a city had been remarkable. The city and suburbs were now populated by 238,000 people and were believed to be growing by an additional thousand each month. The town's business blocks pressed east, west, north, and south, "so that here before our eyes, like a miracle, appears a great city," declared a newspaper.

Birmingham was the industrial center of the South, its industries running to capacity. Enormous tonnages of steel, iron, coal, and manufactured products were being shipped to all parts of the Americas, Europe, and the Orient. Thirty ships made of Birmingham steel for the World War were floating the seven seas. The production of Birmingham steel mills increased from sixty-six thousand tons in 1900 to one million tons in 1920. Birmingham was one of the few cities of North America that could supply all major raw materials to construct an office building: Steel, brick, concrete, lumber, nails, water piping, and fixtures were manufactured at home, mostly from materials made from natural deposits nearby. Architects, contractors, labor, and, most important, the capital for new buildings could be supplied from home.

Merchants were doing their biggest business ever in 1920. People—black and white—were spending money on expensive finery they never had dreamt of. "I want the best," they said, and "the best" is what they bought. Thrift was being preached from housetops by a few courageous individuals, but the advice went unheeded. High wages were squandered for luxuries. Most of the reckless buyers were working people, not the wealthy.

"A week before Christmas, a colored woman bought a dress for eighty dollars," said a merchant. "She had been dealing with us for years and never had gone over thirty dollars. A clerk was taking a suit out of a box. 'How much is that one?' she asked. 'That's $395.' 'I'll take it,' she said. She took the cash from her pocketbook and paid for it on the spot."

Jewelry stores sold smoking pipes with solid gold stems and diamond-encrusted bowls—for the ladies—and cigarette cases priced from $300 to $3,000, also for the ladies. Another novelty: a cigarette holder with a clasp that could be fastened to a lady's hand when she was playing cards, or doing anything else with her hands. That was 1920, when people spent without thought of the morrow, when the country was prosperous. By 1921, as the country shifted from wartime to peacetime, the economy went into deep recession. Millions lost their jobs. In Birmingham, countless thousands who once had good jobs and a bankroll now were jobless and broke. "What has become of all the money?" they asked. "A while back there was lots of it."

The country struggled for normalcy, and by 1922 prosperity returned. A new president, Warren Harding, was in office. Americans were back at work. Industrial Birmingham entered the year 1923 under a full head of steam. The world was calling for production, and Birmingham was a producer. Steamships bearing Birmingham steel were leaving the port of Mobile every two months. The nation was riding a high tide of prosperity with no end in sight. By spring of 1923, three and a half million idle workers had been absorbed by industry in less

After one season with Pittsburgh, Burleigh Grimes was traded to the Brooklyn Dodgers in 1918. Brooklyn had a rough, rabid fandom. Prior to Burleigh's arrival, the Dodgers had played in only one World Series, but in 1920, Burleigh pitched the Dodgers to the pennant. He pitched in Brooklyn for nine years, averaging 17 wins a year, and became one of the best pitchers in baseball.

than a year and a half. Manufacturers competed for skilled and unskilled labor. A steel company in Pennsylvania offered a bonus of ten percent to anyone who worked every day of the month.

In August 1923, less than three years into his term, President Harding died. Harding was special to Birmingham, for in 1921 he had spent a full day there when the city observed its fiftieth anniversary. Word of Harding's death came shortly before ten o'clock in the evening. By ten-thirty, newsboys were on the street selling extra editions of the paper. In February 1924, former President Wilson died after lingering four years as an invalid. A month later, Birmingham experienced a snowfall of six inches, a record for the month of March.

Two years before the end of the Great War, Burleigh Grimes had graduated from Birmingham to Pittsburgh. His first full season with the Pirates in 1917 had been rotten: playing for a last-place club, fighting with his manager, and stumbling to a pitching record of 3–16. The Pirates quickly lost patience and traded him to the Brooklyn Dodgers, the Pirates receiving a popular but undistinguished outfielder named Casey Stengel. Burleigh was only twenty-four years old, Stengel twenty-seven. Stengel never would become an outstanding player; his fame came from managing the New York Yankees to championships in the 1950s. Burleigh, on the other hand, was about to become one of the best pitchers in baseball.

The Brooklyn team Burleigh joined was not a good one. Rarely had Dodger teams finished in the top half of the National League. They had played in only one World Series in their entire history, losing to the Boston Red Sox and Babe Ruth in 1916. Brooklyn, a borough of New York City, was considered Manhattan's bedroom, but if Brooklyn had been a city, it would have been the third most populous in the country. Brooklyn had a rough, rabid fandom. Outsiders thought the rabid Brooklynites talked funny. In Brooklyn, the word "earl" was pronounced *oil* and "oil" was *earl*. "Hey, Boily!" they'd yell. "Throw harder! We don't hear you gruntin'." Burleigh and Brooklyn were a nice fit: "Boily" was a blue-collar pitcher and Brooklyn a blue-collar town.

In 1920, Burleigh's acclaimed pitch, the spitball, was banned from the major leagues. The new rule forbade pitchers from applying a foreign substance to or defacing the ball. However, Burleigh and sixteen other pitchers whose primary pitch was the spitball were allowed to continue using it for the rest of their careers. Several reasons were given for the spitball ban: It was hard for pitchers to control and therefore dangerous; a wet ball was difficult for fielders to throw; and the spitball was unsanitary. The most likely reason for the ban, however, was that the spitball deterred hitting.

In 1919, George Herman (Babe) Ruth began to glorify baseball with the long ball. What once had been a game of batters slapping at the ball — playing for one run at a time — was now one of swinging for the fences. Long distance hitters sprouted like mushrooms. "It's no secret," columnist Heywood Broun pointed out, "that baseballs who want to travel have a new saying: 'Join Ruth and see the world.'" The spitball confounded home run hitters. Because of its downward movement, batters often topped the ball, hitting it on the ground, which was not what baseball owners and fans wanted to see.

The year of the spitball ban, Burleigh pitched the Dodgers to the pennant. He won twenty-three games and ranked high in every pitching category in the league, and he expected to be compensated handsomely. It was no surprise, therefore, when he returned the contract offered him, unsigned. Dodgers owner Charles Ebbets responded to the affront, sending Burleigh a letter demanding that he sign. Burleigh wrote back that he would rather stay home all season than pitch for the money the Dodgers had offered. Ebbets sent a telegram: "Very well. Stay there." The day before the season opened, Burleigh still had not reported, and no one had heard from him in months. Manager Wilbert Robinson told Ebbets, "I don't care how you get him. All I say is get him." The Dodgers gave in and offered more money. Burleigh signed and had another fine season, with a record of 22–13, but the Dodgers finished in fifth place.

In 1925 and '26, Burleigh had losing records. He had pitched in Brooklyn for nine years, averaging seventeen wins a year, mostly for second-division clubs. He was thirty-three, and the Dodgers feared he was losing his skills. Besides, management was tired of constant disagreements over salary, so they traded him to the New York Giants. As it turned out, some of Burleigh's best years lay ahead. He won nineteen and lost eight for the Giants in 1927 but snapped and snarled at teammates if they didn't give their best, and word was he didn't get along with Manager John McGraw—the same had been said about his association with Dodger Manager Wilbert Robinson.

"I didn't want to leave, but they wouldn't pay me what I wanted," Burleigh said of the Giants. "They offered me $15,000, and I wanted more. I would like to have stayed, but you've got to go where the money is, don't you?"

After one year with the Giants, he was traded back to Pittsburgh, where he won twenty-five games in 1928, the most in his career. Burleigh was now thirty-five. For the past decade, he had pitched more innings than any other pitcher. In twelve big league seasons, he had started and completed 260 games. Because of his age, people wondered how much longer Burleigh could endure, which puzzled him.

"They call me an old pitcher. Why should I be old? One of these physical culture experts told me that a man reached his prime in physical strength at thirty, but declined very little until he was forty or older. That's my schedule. I haven't quite as much stuff as I used to have, but I'm a better pitcher, if I do say it myself. Experience tells. I know the batters. I know how to pitch. I understand better what I can do myself and what the opposition is likely to do. A pitcher is like a good oak log. He needs seasoning.

"At the season's close, I'm a little stale, a little tired. So I go to a camp I own up in Wisconsin, where I spend the winter. There I'll hunt practically every day until Christmas. My rifle weighs ten or eleven pounds. Many players wouldn't carry such a heavy gun. I carry it because I think it's good for me. Lug a gun like that for ten or twelve miles through the woods every day, and keep it up for two months, and you're not going to puff much at pitching a few innings of ball. I tramp miles every day in the snow with my gun. I breathe crisp, frosty air many hours out of the twenty-four. I eat a lot of wholesome, well-cooked food. I go to bed early and sleep like a badger in a burrow. And next season I'm fit for whatever deviltry the batters can invent."

Burleigh believed the rugged conditions of his youth—hard winters and lumber camps—contributed to his conditioning. "We all had to work, and work hard," he said. "There were no luxuries in our home. We had a farm in Wisconsin and I was brought up to work. Our food offered no great variety, but it was wholesome and abundant. Hard work, fresh air, good food — those three things were the foundation of the physical condition which has enabled me to pitch all these years. Sometimes I think of that lumber camp when I hear pitchers complaining about overwork. Things are pretty relative in this world. Two hours in an afternoon every few days isn't what I would classify as the hardest kind of occupation. It has its strenuous moments, to be sure. But I prefer it to life in a lumber camp."

THOUGH BURLEIGH HAD WON TWENTY-FIVE games for the Pirates in 1928, his next season promised better. By mid-July 1929, he had won sixteen games and was the best pitcher in the league. He told himself, "If I get a lucky break, I might win thirty ball games this season." But a few days later, in a game against his old team, the Giants, a batter lined a bullet back to the mound. Burleigh threw up his hands to stop the ball, but it struck the thumb of his pitching hand. After that, he was not the same. He won one game the rest of the year.

After the season, he and the Pirates could not agree on a contract. Burleigh had won more games than any other pitcher during the decade of the twenties and wanted to be rewarded with one of the highest salaries in baseball. He asked for two years at $20,000 each, but President Barney Dreyfuss said his policy was to offer only one-year contracts. Burleigh said if the Pirates wouldn't give him what he asked for, he wanted to be traded. "If he turns me down, I will spend this year hunting and fishing in Wisconsin."

The Pirates did trade Burleigh — to the Boston Braves. And before 1930 was out, he was traded again — to St. Louis, where he helped the Cardinals win pennants in 1930 and '31. Both years the Cardinals faced the Philadelphia Athletics in the World Series. The Athletics had been managed since 1901 by Cornelius McGillicuddy, better known as Connie Mack. Mack was sixty-seven years old in 1930 and would manage the Athletics until the age of eighty-five. He was a prince of a man — considerate, conservative, and devout — never used profanity, never raised his voice. He directed the team from the dugout in coat and tie and derby hat. No one called him Connie; it was "Mr. Mack."

Burleigh pitched Game Five of the 1930 Series, belligerent as usual. Between pitches, he bantered with Philadelphia players and fans. He badgered Manager Mack. "Connie was pretty excited," Burleigh recalled. "He kept running up and down in front of the bench, and his collar was getting all wilted. I called his attention to the fact that his collar was getting a rough deal and made a few suggestions of what an elderly gentleman should do under the circumstances.

Perhaps that wasn't respectful to an elderly gentleman. Anyhow, as I was leaving the ball park in a taxicab, two women stuck their heads into the door and bawled me out. They said if I had kept my mind on my work instead of abusing Connie, I might have won the game."

Burleigh lost two games in the 1930 Series, allowing only five hits in each, and the Cardinals lost the Series. The following year, 1931, the Cardinals and Athletics again faced each other. Philadelphia had a team of powerful sluggers — Mickey Cochrane, Al Simmons, and Jimmie Foxx — and the best pitcher in the American League, Lefty Grove, winner of thirty-one games. The Athletics were expected to win their third straight world championship. They won Game One, the Cardinals Game Two. Burleigh took the mound for Game Three against Lefty Grove and held the Athletics without a hit for seven innings. He finished with a two-hitter and won the game. The teams alternated wins in Games Four, Five, and Six, and the Series was tied at three apiece. Burleigh would pitch the decisive seventh game with the world championship on the line.

During the final weeks of the season, Burleigh had pitched with an inflamed appendix but had refused an operation. Pitching in Game Seven, he had trouble with his appendix. As the game moved along, he took more and more time between pitches. He applied ice packs between innings. He was pitching brilliantly, though in pain, and held a 4–0 lead in the ninth inning. He walked the first batter in the ninth. The pain was intense. He retired the next two batters, then gave up a walk and two base hits. The Athletics trimmed the lead to 4–2. One out from victory, Burleigh couldn't finish. Manager Gabby Street brought in Wild Bill Hallahan to pitch the final out, and the Cardinals were world champions. The final putout was a fly ball to left centerfield caught by Pepper Martin. "I never knew a happier minute in all my life than when I got my hands on that ball," Martin said. "I sure would like to have kept that ball as a souvenir, but I had no right to it. Only one fellow had the right, and I gave it to him. That fellow was Burleigh Grimes."

Burleigh now was thirty-eight. The Cardinals were overstocked with pitchers and needed to make room for Dizzy Dean, their fine young pitcher from the Texas League. So for the sixth time in his major league career, Burleigh Grimes was traded. In 1932, he would be a Chicago Cub and make it to the World Series for the fourth time, this time against the New York Yankees. It was the World Series of Babe Ruth's legendary "Called Shot" home run. It was a mean Series, with lots of bench jockeying, some of it downright nasty. The first two games were played at Yankee Stadium — the Cubs and Yankees trading insults and catcalls throughout the games, with Ruth doing much of the yelling.

In Game Three at Wrigley Field, Chicago, Ruth hit a home run in the first inning. During the at-bat, lemons were thrown toward him from the stands. In the fifth inning, when Ruth came to bat, the game was tied, 4–4. Burleigh and the Cubs yelled at Ruth from the dugout, as did fans from the stands. Ruth responded by pointing and gesturing at the Cubs bench. A lemon rolled his way from the dugout. The first pitch from pitcher Charlie Root was a called strike. Ruth held up one finger as if to say: That's one strike. Root threw a second called strike. There was more banter from the dugout. Guy Bush yelled, "Now, you big ape, what are you going to do now?" Ruth held up two fingers: That's two strikes. He looked right at Bush and yelled, "I've still got the big strike left!" Then Ruth pointed. *Where he pointed* is the question. Legend says it was to centerfield. Years later, Burleigh told Charles Clark, the historian of Clear Lake, Wisconsin, that if Ruth had pointed to centerfield, the pitcher "would have knocked Ruth down with a pitch."

What did happen was that the pitcher, Root, threw a slow curve, and Ruth uncoiled a beautiful swing. The ball took off on a low line like a golf ball off a tee, leaving the park and skimming through a tree behind the centerfield bleachers. Little boys dropped from the tree like raindrops from the sky and went running after the ball. Ruth circled the bases with a big smile on his face: "Lucky, lucky, lucky," he told himself. Along the way, he made a derisive remark to each Cub infielder. Rounding third, he held up four fingers to the Cubs dugout and laughed all the way home. Seated in a box near home plate and also laughing was Franklin Roosevelt, a candidate for president against Herbert Hoover.

"He never pointed to center," Burleigh told Clark, the historian. "But he did in a sense call the shot because he was saying he had a third strike coming."

It was clear that Burleigh Grimes was near the end of his career. In 1932 and for the next two seasons, he pitched in relief as often as he started. During Burleigh's final two big league seasons, 1933 and '34, he drifted to three more teams — the Cardinals again, the Yankees, and the Pirates for the third time. On September 20, 1934, a month after turning forty-one, he threw his final pitch. It was the last game in which a pitcher would throw a legal spitball in the major leagues.

CHAPTER 14

HE BLEW IN LIKE A HURRICANE

ON A SUNDAY MORNING, MAY of 1924, Charles Stewart was up and about in his sitting room, reading the newspaper. The bay windows were open, lace curtains billowing in the breeze. His wife was seated by the light of the window, immersed in the latest craze: a crossword puzzle. In the next room, coffee percolated, and Stewart rose from his easy chair to get a cup, black. In 1924, the economy was flourishing. Americans had money to spend on wonderful, new products: mass-produced automobiles, telephones, electric phonographs, refrigerators, washing machines, and vacuum cleaners. Can't afford one? Americans now bought on credit. "Can't you make a small first payment and another payment once a month?" salesmen asked. "You'd be surprised the people who make purchases this way."

Everyone was excited about the new medium called radio. Three years before, a radio receiving set was a gadget built by a hobbyist, usually a bright boy in the home. Now, no home was truly modern unless it had a radio.

Stewart rubbed his hand against his freshly shaved face. His wife once told him that the scent of his shaving soap and the fragrance of his aftershave called to mind passing the open door of a barbershop when she was little. Stewart dropped the morning newspaper to the floor and took a package of Old Golds from his pocket. He leaned forward to speak to his wife, still occupied with the crossword. Through the open window he could smell the grass, wet with dew, and the honeysuckle and gardenia in a patiently tended garden. On the front porch a dog barked; down the street another dog answered. A whippoorwill called from a near wood. Somewhere a cock crowed. Lovely day, Stewart thought.

"Oh-ho, Kitten, I bumped into the owner of your beauty parlor yesterday," Stewart said to his wife. "She claimed her business over the past five months was better than it was all last year. Why? It's the flappers and their bobbed heads. She told me, 'We have to constantly cut and curl and trim their hair to keep it looking good.'"

THE YOUNG FEMALE "FLAPPERS" WERE the free spirits of the 1920s, their dresses rising above the knees of their pipe-stem legs, and their hair cropped close to the head like a man's. Stewart's wife, her eyes on the crossword, was exasperated. "Oh, this short, bobbed hair; it's a fad that will pass. A woman's long tresses used to be her crowning glory. Now no matter what subject one brings up at a dinner party, it always gets around to bobbed hair. Used to be only *little* girls wore their hair like that—or girls engaged in loose conduct. A fat woman looks fatter with a bob, and a thin woman looks positively haggard. Even Gloria Swanson is wearing a straight bob these days, and it's most unbecoming of her."

Stewart chuckled. "I'll admit, some of these girls look rather amusing with their little hats on the back of their bobbed heads."

Young people of the 1920s were a restless lot, reaching out for the jazzy freedoms of the new decade. The young woman—her vote in one hand, her pocketbook in the other—challenged accepted notions of behavior. Genus flapper was a brash, gum-chewing, ginned-up creature, full of animal spirits—using cosmetics and retouching her face in public. She rode a bicycle, drove a car, and enjoyed newfangled jazz music. She was out for a good time and not particular how she got it. Something new was under the sun—America's Jazz Age, the Roaring Twenties. "Nice" girls were smoking cigarettes and drinking whiskey, despite Prohibition. They swore a bit. They used slang. The flapper style was flamboyant and boyish—flat chest, broad shoulders, narrow hips. Dresses were slim and long-waisted, sheer and sleeveless; stockings sometimes were rolled below the knee. During the twenties, hemlines rose from a few inches above the ankle to just above the knee.

One Saturday afternoon in Birmingham in 1925, traffic ground to a halt. On the corner of Third Avenue and Nineteenth Street, a crowd of a hundred or more stopped and turned. The reason: a peppy young flapper, twenty-four years old, from Texas, in white linen knickers, flaming red sash, a man's sports shirt, black tie, silk hose, and black patent leather shoes. Around her waist was a brilliant red shawl and, on her head, a man's straw hat, trimmed and tilted after the fashion of a tango dancer. She minced along, daring the world to look. A traffic officer waded into the throng. The costume provoked a breach of the peace, he concluded. Followed by scores of the curious, he escorted the woman to headquarters, where she was ordered to return to her hotel and change clothes.

Stewart's wife put aside her crossword puzzle. "I'm just an old-fashioned woman, I suppose, but somehow I can't get used to seeing these young girls—and women old enough to know better—powdering and rouging in the streetcars and public places, smearing on lipstick as they walk along on high heels. Somehow the girls of today all look alike with their red lips and their ghastly white faces and their penciled eyebrows. I wonder, don't they realize that a girl with a natural complexion is so much prettier?"

She looked at her husband. Stewart drew thoughtfully on a cigarette, the smoke twirling and winding in a blue cloud to the ceiling. He looked at his wife through the smoke. "Well—" he hesitated. "Kitten, I'm strong for the flapper. They're nothing more than little girls grown up. The other day I saw a delightful little creature with a dainty, embroidered handkerchief tied about her wrist. And yes, she wore knickers. I said, 'Oh-ho. How'd you get hurt?' and she said, 'My goodness, I'm not hurt. It's the very latest thing, tying your handkerchief around your wrist.'

"'Beg pardon—my mistake,' I said. 'I suppose you're the modern girl I've been reading about. I don't keep up with all the fads.'

"'You should,' she said. 'Everyone should be up to date. No matter how old you are.'

"I must say, I like the spirit and independence of these girls today—they're afraid of nothing and nobody. They wear breeches, swim, hike, golf, drive cars, and study hard, right along with the boys. They can stand on their own feet and hold down a good job."

His wife frowned. "As I was telling the ladies at the literary club, these modern girls don't have two ideas in their head to rub together. They flock to dance halls wearing perfume, with lips redder than any red yet conceived. They should be at home sewing or—or—learning to play the piano. But, no, they go when and where they please and come home any hour of the night or morning, jaded and worn. And they won't bother with a boy who doesn't carry a flask on his hip.

"Once, it was a disgrace to go to a public dance. Now these girls dance with men they haven't even been introduced to. They may be in the arms of a thief or a bootlegger—it doesn't matter. Is it any wonder so many young girls have nervous prostration, considering they dance to such dreadful rhythms and smoke cigarettes? Not so many years ago a man would hardly think of smoking in the presence of a woman. If he did, he most certainly would ask permission. These days he doesn't ask permission; he says, 'Will you have a cigarette?' And her answer is, 'Yes, I am dying for one.'

"It used to be that men at a party withdrew to the pantry to take a drink. Now the women drink the men under the table. And you can be sure that a woman who smokes and drinks will take the Lord's name in vain. I've been told that girls not yet out of their teens tell men jokes which are of the most suggestive nature. And innocent girls of our leading families submit to caresses from men in whom they have little more than a passing interest. Yes, dear, I am a prude, but surely you will not tell me that a self-respecting gentleman believes that smoking and drinking and swearing add to the charms of a pretty girl. I leave it to you — is it this way now?"

Stewart flicked the ash of his cigarette into a coffee cup and stroked his face. "I think most girls do flapperish things like smoking and dancing and drinking because — well, just because. They do it because it's swanky and smart and up to date. These girls are young and gay — and maybe a little thoughtless — just as debutantes were in our day. Boys and girls today go joyriding, only they do it in automobiles, not in buggies as we did. They dance, but instead of dancing to 'The Blue Danube,' they dance to jazz. Our parents thought the same of our generation — we wouldn't amount to anything. But look at us; we turned out alright."

"Oh, I don't know," she said. "Don't you remember how we used to play in the yard as children? We played real games then — blowing bubbles, catching jacks, hiding the switch, dropping the handkerchief. Children today have been deprived of the simple pleasures of life by our modern ideas. We used to ride stick horses. Now they want automobiles. It's a sin-cursed world. Our morals are lax. Everything reeks of sex — jazz music, moving pictures, novels, even the comic strips. What a queer world. The modern girl has lost her curves and has become a fright. The women in New York are wearing very short skirts — fully fifteen inches from the ground, both the matrons and the misses. That is no exaggeration, for I have seen it with my own eyes. And have you seen the new red nail polish? Horrors."

A year later, in 1925, the Scopes human evolution trial would expose a conflict between science and religion. The Great Bull Stock Market would be in full force. In 1927, Lindbergh would fly the Atlantic, motion pictures would have sound, and speculation in the market would increase. By then, Stewart's conversation with his wife would go like this:

"Kitten, I've been thinking. S'posin', just s'posin' — how 'bout we take a flier in the stock market? You know, buy some stocks."

"Do you think it's such a good idea, dear?" his wife would say, and Stewart would reply: "They're calling it an 'office boy's market.' Stock prices have been going up. Everywhere you turn, people are giving tips on the market — office boys, shoeshine boys—quoting stock prices like batting averages. Besides, anybody can make money in a market like this. And, you know, we certainly can use the money."

"Whatever you think best, dear."

Early in 1928, the big Bull Market entered its sensational phase. Stories were told of fortunes reaped overnight. On a rainy day in March 1929, Herbert Hoover took the oath of office as president, and the "Hoover bull market" rushed merrily on. In October 1929, the Bull Market came crashing down. The Jazz Age was over. A new era, the Great Depression, would unfold.

CHARLES STEWART RESUMED READING THE newspaper. How large the Sunday paper was, he thought, the *two* Sunday morning papers, the sheer number of pages. Sometimes I wish they were smaller, not so much to read. He settled deeply into his chair. He loved the leather, how cool it felt to the touch. He sighed contentedly, lost to the world.

"Barons lost again yesterday," he muttered.

"What did you say, dear?"

Drearily, "We lost again, Kitten. We're in fifth place. But it's early still; the boys'll come around."

Every year since the war, the Barons had labored in the middle of the league standings. This year, 1924, they would fall to seventh place, with a record of 54–98, the most losses ever for Birmingham. The Barons' erstwhile manager, Carlton Molesworth, had quit his job in 1922. It happened this way: In early June the team was in second place with a winning record, but the season had been puzzling. Early on, the Barons had won eleven straight games, but they also had lost eight games after leading in the ninth inning. In late June, they embarked on a road trip to Atlanta, Mobile, and New Orleans, losing ten of thirteen games. The final day of the trip, a Sunday, they lost a doubleheader to New Orleans. After the second game, Molesworth sat for an hour in the clubhouse at Heinemann Park, his head in his hands, not changing his clothes, not speaking to anyone. The next morning after the team returned to Birmingham, he resigned.

Molesworth's withdrawal was a bombshell and the main topic of conversation in downtown Birmingham on Monday morning. Moley was an institution. To the people of that generation, the names *Molesworth* and *Barons* would be forever joined. Molesworth had managed the team fourteen years. He had shaped the destinies of a hundred—no, a thousand—ball players, those who had played for him and those he had let go. He said he had been on the job too long.

"The recent misfortune of the club in its ability to win ball games causes me to figure that maybe a new face as a manager would serve to help things along. I've always had the best interest of the club at heart, and figuring that a change might really help things, I decided to get out. Don't think, however, that I believe any man on the club has failed to give me the best he has in him. I love every man who has played baseball for me this year. There's not a man out there but would give his right arm to win a ball game for me. There never was a more loyal bunch gotten together than the men representing Birmingham on the baseball field this year. They're not yellow, as many fans have intimated. They're all wool and a yard wide.

"You can tell the world, though, that I'm not quitting baseball. I'm in the game to stick for years yet. . . . I wouldn't quit the grand old game for anything. It's part of me. I love it. And you can also tell 'em that I have no criticism to make over the way I've been treated in Birmingham. The fans have been more loyal than they themselves thought, and Rick Woodward has treated me like a prince ever since I've been connected with this club."

Molesworth had been in the Southern Association as a player or manager since 1901, twenty-two years. He joined Birmingham in 1906 as a thirty-year-old centerfielder, and became manager in 1908. Two dozen of his players had made it to the major leagues. During the Barons' middling years of the early twenties, a few individuals stood tall, and Molesworth managed them all. Stuffy Stewart, a second baseman and a fan favorite, played seven seasons in Birmingham and was among the league leaders in stolen bases every year. Dutch Bernsen, a first baseman, established a league record for home runs in 1921 with twenty-two. Three pitchers, Burleigh Grimes, John Morrison, and Earl Whitehill, had lengthy major league careers.

Then there was Pie Traynor.

"Oh-ho," Charles Stewart said with a laugh, "here's a spot of good news!" Gleefully, he clenched the newspaper in both hands and turned it so his wife could see. Across the page, a headline bore the words:

Mighty John McGraw Says Pie Traynor Greatest Natural Player in Big Tops; Expert Third Sacker Declares He Got Training in Birmingham

Pie Traynor, third baseman of the Pittsburgh Pirates, had played two full seasons in the major leagues and already was a star.

Stewart dropped the newspaper in his lap. "You remember Pie Traynor, don't you, Kitten? Beautiful boy, that. All arms and legs. And how he could run—style, dash, everything.

"And John McGraw—has there been a better manager, ever? Wins the pennant every year, seems. I've lost count the number of times his Giants have played in Birmingham."

Stewart returned to the newspaper, reading it aloud:

"He's the greatest natural ball player that has come up to the majors in many years," the great Giant leader, John McGraw, said of Traynor. "He has one of the greatest throwing arms in the infield today and the surest pair of hands in baseball."

The newspaper told of how McGraw had once hoped to sign Traynor. In 1920, the year before he joined the Barons, Traynor was twenty-one years old, playing for Portsmouth, a Class B team in the Virginia League. McGraw sent his scout, Art Devlin, to look over the youngster.

Stewart skimmed the newspaper column. His fingers rustled the pages.

"Devlin liked Traynor," said McGraw, "but the owners of the Portsmouth club were cagey and business-like. They set a price of $10,000. I don't know just what Devlin said to them, but he told them in rather plain grammar that no Class B recruit was worth $10,000."

But Pittsburgh Pirates owner Barney Dreyfuss met Portsmouth's asking price, and Traynor became the highest-priced player ever to come out of the Virginia League. Said McGraw:

"What always jarred me is the fact that I would have gone $5,000 higher than Dreyfuss did, had I been in the position to have made the offer. I don't suppose the Portsmouth owners dreamed of this, but nevertheless it's true."

Traynor left Portsmouth and played the final weeks of the 1920 season for the Pirates. The following spring he flashed promise in the Pirates training camp at Hot Springs, Arkansas. But he wasn't ready for the big leagues, not yet. So the Pirates sent him to Birmingham.

Stewart rattled the newspaper to get his wife's attention. "Kitten, it says here that Birmingham made Traynor the ball player he is today. Listen to what Pie says about this magic city of ours":

"I want to tell you about Birmingham, where I learned more about the baseball game than I had ever known. I was really disgusted the day I was sent to Birmingham . . . and I felt, regardless of what had been told me, that I was being let down.

"It was hard, breaking in at Birmingham. I went to Birmingham for experience, and I got it. When I started with Birmingham, some of the older players started to make my life miserable and at first it was discouraging. But I soon learned that the fans were alright, and I fought my way through. When I was recalled to the Pirates, I felt a pang at leaving Birmingham. I had learned to really like the city and its people. There are a lot of Northern folks there, but all Southern folks, too, were good to me.

"It was also hard for me breaking in with Pittsburgh as a rookie. The older regulars on opposing teams knew that I was a rookie and took advantage. When I started with Pittsburgh, some of the smart players on other teams made my life miserable, and more than once I wished that I was back in dear old Birmingham."

Here, Stewart put down the newspaper and sank into his easy chair. He closed his sixty-year-old eyes. In his mind's eye, he pictured young Pie Traynor, tall, confident, and dashing, playing shortstop for the Birmingham Barons in 1921. At six feet, 170 pounds, Pie Traynor was large for a shortstop. One newspaperman observed that he had hands "as big as Tennessee hams." And fleet afoot? "When he stretches out on the base paths, he looks like a greyhound in motion." Although Traynor was twenty-two years old when he came to Birmingham, he claimed to be twenty-one. Fibbing about one's age was not uncommon for ball players of the day. Many believed that being younger made them a more attractive prospect.

As Charles Stewart lay in his chair, he recalled vividly the spring day Pie Traynor blew in.

On the morning of Saturday, April 16, 1921, a storm was brewing near Rickwood Field. Farther west, tornadoes were poised to strike Alabama and four other states. Around eight o'clock in the morning, the heavens blackened, and the storm broke in all its fury. Tornado-like winds and blinding rain swept through Central Park on the western edge of Birmingham. The windstorm rushed eastward into West End, hitting hard at Rickwood Field. It gathered strength and moved northeast into Graymont and Owenton, then hopped to Fountain Heights and Norwood. During its surge eastward, the storm took in a small area of downtown Birmingham. Plate glass windows were smashed. Signs were hurled upward. Store awnings were torn, and book and newspaper stands destroyed. Throughout the city, whole rows of giant shade trees went down, trees that had withstood the weather ever since there had been a Birmingham. Hundreds of homes were wrecked or damaged. That day, tornadoes killed nearly one hundred people in Alabama, Mississippi, Tennessee, Arkansas, and Texas. Fourteen people died in Alabama. In the opinion of weather forecaster Edgar Horton, however, Birmingham received not a tornado but a straight, hard blow, a "thunder squall."

On Saturday, April 16, 1921, a windstorm swept through Birmingham, tossing aside Rickwood's bleachers and board fencing. That afternoon Pie Traynor played his first game for the Barons in Nashville, Tennessee. The next day, Sunday, workmen erected a new fence, and Traynor played his first game at Rickwood the following day. He had three hits, a walk, and a stolen base.

The groundskeeper at Rickwood Field, Bill Walker, was at work under the rightfield stands when the gale blew through. He and his helper, Frank Smith, hugged a concrete post to keep from being blown away. In the groundskeeper's house, back of the rightfield bleachers, Mrs. Walker and her child were in hysterics as the wind blew away much of the roof. Rickwood's wooden bleachers along the left- and rightfield lines were picked up, bodily, and slammed down. Bleacher posts were snatched out of their concrete moorings. Most of the ball park's board fencing tumbled down, including an outfield scoreboard that posted major league scores. Two big trees guarding the entrance to the ball park were blown to the ground. Also down was a grove of oak trees beyond the rightfield fence. From the boughs of these spreading oaks, young boys had watched hundreds of ball games through the years. Left standing were the Southern League scoreboard in centerfield, the grandstand, and the baseball diamond. Sunday, the day after the storm, more than a hundred workmen labored all day to erect a new fence around Rickwood because the Barons had a game scheduled for the next day.

Saturday, the day of the storm, was the day the Pittsburgh Pirates dispatched shortstop Pie Traynor to Birmingham. More precisely, they sent him to Nashville, where the Barons were playing their fourth game of the season. He blew in like the storm in Birmingham, banging out a double and three singles in five trips to the plate. The newspaper account of the game described him thusly: "The newcomer, Traynor, is a rangy, big fellow with a stride like Man o' War and an underhand peg to first that sends a ball like a rifle shot."

Two days later Traynor made his first appearance at weather-beaten Rickwood. He walked in his first at-bat, hit a triple to the fence in rightfield, singled and stole second base, and singled again. At shortstop, he fielded a ground ball and started a double play, lightning-like, whipping the ball in a flash to Stuffy Stewart at second, Stewart whipping it to Dutch Bernsen at first. The runner was out easily. After the game a newspaperman wrote, "He cost the Pirates $10,000 but looks like he is worth a million."

CHARLES STEWART OPENED HIS EYES.

"You were asleep, dear," his wife said, smiling.

"I was just thinking."

"About some ball player, I presume?"

Stewart smiled.

"The Traynor boy?" she asked.

Stewart nodded.

"He was such a good boy," she said, "the sweetest, dandiest, loveliest boy. I really liked him."

"Everybody did," Stewart said, remembering. "A prince of a fellow."

"He told me once why everyone calls him 'Pie,' " she said. "When he was a little boy, all the stray dimes that came his way, he spent on pie, so they started calling him 'Pie.' "

Stewart chuckled. "That's part of it. Every week his mother would send him to the store with a grocery list. The last item was always pie, so it became a bit of a joke to folks in the store. And there was a priest who organized baseball games for boys in the neighborhood. After every game, the priest would treat them to whatever they wanted. Most wanted ice cream, but not Harold Traynor. He'd say, 'I'll have pie, Father.'

"Doesn't the name suit him just perfectly," Stewart went on, "his spirit and personality and all? He has one sweet disposition, and he loves playing ball. He'd rather play ball than eat."

Harold Joseph (Pie) Traynor grew up in the city of Somerville, Massachusetts, near Boston. He never was particularly interested in what went on inside a schoolhouse and left school after the eighth grade. There were seven children in the family, and the family was struggling. He felt it his duty to help keep food on the table. That was in 1915. For three years, he worked odd jobs to help out at home. In 1917, when the United States entered the war, Traynor tried to enlist in the army but was turned down — too young. Eager to aid the war effort, he left

Pie Traynor was a lithe, graceful shortstop who made one-handed catches that took your breath away. Here he is with the Pittsburgh Pirates in the spring of 1921. A few weeks later, he reported to Birmingham. After his first game with the Barons, a reporter said, "Traynor is a rangy, big fellow with a stride like Man o' War and an underhand peg to first that sends a ball like a rifle shot."

home early in 1918, taking a job at a gunpowder plant in West Virginia. The day of the Armistice, November 11, 1918, was Pie's birthday. He turned twenty.

The following summer Traynor played baseball for the town of Falmouth on the southern shore of Massachusetts. Falmouth was an amateur summer team on Cape Cod that played town teams from the Boston area. That was in 1919. The next spring he secured a workout with the Boston Red Sox, who recommended that he sign a professional contract with Portsmouth, Virginia.

"When I was eight years old, I determined to become a professional ball player and I was positive that someday I would be a major-leaguer," Traynor said. "But that chance never came at Falmouth, at Portsmouth, or Pittsburgh, as has so often been written, but at Birmingham in Alabama."

At Birmingham in 1921, Pie Traynor became a truly marvelous player. He was one of the top batsmen and base runners in the league. He always hustled, no matter the score, was always the first man in uniform for batting practice and the first to return to his position after the side had been retired. He was modest and sincere, without frill or fuss in his makeup, and a boy that flattery and acclaim never affected. From his shortstop position, he wheeled and circled like a gull at the seashore, going hard after every ball and pegging swiftly and surely to first base. Lithe and graceful, leaping into the blue, he made one-handed catches that took your breath away.

"I shall never be satisfied, however, until I am a well-rounded ball player," he said, "a good fielder, a good base runner, and a good batter. I may never get there, but that is my aim."

Ah, Traynor—the classic striver . . . it made him one of the most beloved men and the sweetest shortstop ever to wear a Barons uniform. One month after Traynor reported to the Barons, New Orleans Manager Johnny Dobbs made a prediction: "This Traynor is going to make a great ball player. I like his looks; take it from me, he is going to make a name for himself in the big leagues."

Never has a greener but more willing player ever reported to the Barons than Pie Traynor, said *Birmingham News* sports editor Zipp Newman. He made errors by the dozen, mostly on throws to first base.

"No fan dares to knock Traynor when he boots one, for they know he is out there hustling," Newman said. "For every boot he makes, he will pull three spectacular plays to make up for it. Traynor has made a number of errors this season, but most of them have been on throws, taking desperate chances on getting his man."

Newman said never would he forget Traynor, "not so much for his playing but for his gameness." During a road trip to Mobile and New Orleans in late July, "This writer saw Traynor play through the entire series with a raging fever and ptomaine poisoning. Each day Traynor would leave his room a half hour before game time, play through the game, and return to his room. He was advised to stay in his room, but Traynor said 'no' and Moley [Carlton Molesworth] knew the kid meant it."

Pie Traynor finished the 1921 season with a batting average of .336 and forty-seven stolen bases. The Barons won ninety games, good enough to lead the league in many years, but Memphis won a record 104 games and led the league from start to finish.

Pie Traynor made his final appearance at Rickwood Field on a Saturday in late August. Three weeks remained in the season, but the Pirates were ready to call him north to Pittsburgh to play out the major league season. The fans knew it would be Pie's last game, and they cheered him wildly every time he handled a chance in the field or came to bat. In the first inning, Pie made a play to thrill the crowd. With a runner on third base, a batter hit a high, bounding ball everyone thought would bounce over Traynor's head into leftfield. Did the ball go through? Not with Traynor on the job. Pie leapt high, snared the ball, and snapped a throw to the plate to catch the runner trying to score. When the game ended with a Birmingham victory, fans rushed the field to shake Pie's hand. Hundreds more cried his name as they departed the park. Traynor accompanied the Barons to Memphis and played two more games. Then he was done, never again to play in the minor leagues.

To say that Pie Traynor instantly became a major league star would be untrue. The Pirates had a shortstop, a waifish, clownish fellow named Walter (Rabbit) Maranville, who was having a Hall of Fame career. The Pirates, therefore, moved Traynor to third base in place of another former Baron, Clyde Barnhart. The new position did not come naturally to Pie. He worked tirelessly, but in his fourth game with the Pirates, his throwing error allowed the winning run to score. The Pirates lost faith, and Barnhart returned to third base. Just how good is Pie Traynor going to be? the Pirates wondered. Manager George Gibson left no doubt where he stood. When the season was over, he said he would be willing to trade any man on his club but one — Pie Traynor.

"He's one of those old-fashioned ball players who take a real delight in playing ball," Gibson said. "Baseball is the only thing in life worthwhile to him. When he isn't playing ball, he's talking about it, and I believe he dreams about it at night."

Gibson reflected on Traynor's first spring training with the Pirates in March 1921 before he joined Birmingham. Whenever the team went back to the hotel for lunch that spring, Traynor often continued working on his own, usually asking an experienced teammate to tutor him. Once, after Gibson told Traynor that he had a habit of running the bases flat-footed, Pie asked outfielder Carson Bigbee to stay through lunch and teach him how to run bases. When Gibson returned to the park in the afternoon, Bigbee said:

"That kid Traynor is a glutton for punishment. He came to me and asked if I would show him something about running the bases. Said you told him he was flat-footed. I told him I didn't know much about running the bases, but I'd show him as much as I could. So I told him what his faults were, and he started to run around the sacks. Well, sir, he ran those bases for thirty minutes without a letup, and when he got through — I had to stop him or he'd be running yet — he asked me to hit grounders to him. I hit 'em to him until I've got blisters on both hands. If you don't steer him away from me, I'll be a wreck."

"That," said Gibson, "should give you some idea of Traynor."

The following season, 1922, Traynor established himself once and for all as the team's third baseman. His presence of mind was on display one day in late August. Pie was playing third base with a runner on first. The batter hit a fly ball into short leftfield, and Pie raced to make the catch with his back to the infield. The base runner on first, believing Pie would be off-balance and unable to make a play, tagged up and prepared to sprint for second as soon as the ball touched Pie's glove. Pie, thinking as he ran, made the catch and tossed the ball to leftfielder Bigbee, who relayed it to second for the putout.

The next season, 1923, his second full season in the big leagues, turned out to be one of the best of Pie Traynor's career. He hit .338 with 12 home runs and 101 runs batted in. He and teammate Max Carey led the major leagues with nineteen triples. Honus Wagner, an old Pittsburgh Pirate and one of the greatest ball players ever, had retired by the time Pie Traynor came along. In 1923, Wagner said:

"This young fellow Pie Traynor is sure to be one of the greatest ball players in the world. He can't miss because he simply thinks and lives baseball. Often I have passed the park and seen him working out there in the morning with a single companion. One day I saw him all alone in the rain, throwing a ball against the grandstand and fielding it as it bounced back. 'Gee,' he said one day, 'I wonder when we are going to play another doubleheader.' Most ball players look on a doubleheader with dread—a double day's work for no more money. That boy Traynor would play three if they could crowd in the time some way."

PITTSBURGH IN TRAYNOR'S DAY WAS a paradox: a city of wealth and prosperity but, in many ways, a dreadful place. With 700,000 citizens, it was a city three times the size of Birmingham and, like Birmingham, an iron and steel town. Its industrial economy was the envy of the world, but the air was choked with thick, black smoke. Jobs in mills and factories were plentiful, and mill owners and managers amassed stunning fortunes. But for the toiling masses, Pittsburgh was a place that resembled "hell with the lid off." In 1927, social critic H. L. Mencken presented a distressing view of the city:

> Here was a scene so dreadfully hideous, so intolerably bleak and forlorn that it reduced the whole aspiration of man to a macabre and depressing joke. Here was wealth beyond computation—almost beyond imagination—and here were human habitations so abominable that they would have disgraced a race of alley cats. I am not speaking of the mere filth. One expects steel towns to be dirty. What I allude to is the unbroken and agonizing ugliness, the sheer revolting monstrousness, of every house in sight.

Into this town came Pie Traynor, a gregarious, jovial, affable human being. He possessed a dashing style of play and a personality that made him a favorite of Pittsburgh fans. In September of 1923, Traynor and two teammates attended an amateur sandlot game in Pittsburgh. Pie stayed around long after the other two had left, signing autographs and talking baseball with children. His attention to children—to people in general—was a matter of course for Pie Traynor. After games at his home stadium, Forbes Field, he often stopped to speak to the populace. One old fan recounted: "And long after the other players and the ushers and the crowd had left, he'd still be talking to the kids and the old Italians from Boundary Street and the traffic cops and the guys who'd come out of 'Put' Tierney's saloon." A fan from Brooklyn recalled standing outside Ebbets Field with his autograph book when he felt a tap on his shoulder. "Would you like me to sign?" When he looked around, he was face to face with Pie Traynor. Another young Dodgers fan struck a casual friendship with Traynor. "He'd walk with me all the way to the Franklin Avenue subway when the Pirates were in town."

The Pirates won the World Series in 1925. It was Traynor's fourth full major league season, and he had come to be regarded as one of baseball's best players. In September that year, John McGraw, the Giants manager, said of Pie, "He will go down in history as one of the really great third basemen."

In the late 1920s, Pie shared a heavy, forty-two-ounce bat with teammate Paul Waner. The pair had "borrowed" the bat a few years earlier from another player. "We had taped it and nailed it together as long as we could," Pie said. He told a sportswriter in 1931 that he had not used a brand-new bat since his rookie season. "I liked to get old ones, with the lumber well seasoned. . . . They had more oomph and drive in them."

Traynor often wandered over to the opposing team's dugout, and if he found a good heavy bat, well, he would just . . . take it. "I'd find one that suited me in the Giants' [bats], for instance, and I'd tell [Manager] Bill Terry I was taking it. What could he say but, 'Sure, go ahead, Pie'?"

Traynor played the 1931 season with a torn ligament in his right shoulder, and from then on injuries slowed him. For the first time in seven years, his batting average fell below .300, though he drove in more than one hundred runs for the fifth straight year.

Pie Traynor was remarkably likeable and engaging. Not once did he hold out for more money, though his salary was at the low end for major-leaguers. He was grateful, in fact, for every paycheck. "We're so lucky to be making a living this way," he would say, as the country was enduring the Depression and after he himself had faced deep losses in the stock market.

In 1934, Traynor was named manager of the Pirates while still a full-time player. In many ways, he was psychologically unsuited for the new role. Authors James Forr and David Proctor, in their biography of Pie Traynor, describe him as a worrier— sensitive, neurotic, and averse to confrontation. During stressful moments, he might smoke an entire pack of cigarettes, even between games of a doubleheader. Beneath his affable persona, Pie was intensely ambitious. His drive, it seemed, was fueled by a deep-seated fear of failure. Even after he had become one of baseball's best players, he allowed batting slumps to eat away at him.

"I always worried a lot as a player, but now I'm worse than ever," he said after becoming manager. "I can't shake myself of that habit of worrying, worrying, worrying."

Authors Forr and Proctor say Pie was a caring, decent man, too kind and softhearted to be a manager. His reputation was that of a pushover, someone who was hesitant to come down on players who drifted out of line. He sulked and grew deeply pessimistic when his team struggled, to the point where it became a drain on his own physical and emotional health and possibly affected his team's performance. Before the 1936 season, Traynor retired as a player. The previous season had been his worst as a hitter. He had batted .279, and his arm was worn out. The next year, 1937, injuries on the team forced him back into the lineup for a handful of games. After that, he was finished as a player. The Pirates placed third in the National League in 1937. Forr and Proctor say that after the 1937 season, Traynor received a telegram from Chester Washington of the black newspaper *The Pittsburgh Courier*. The telegram began:

KNOW YOUR CLUB NEEDS PLAYERS. HAVE ANSWER TO YOUR PRAYERS RIGHT HERE IN PITTSBURGH.

Washington went on to say that catcher Josh Gibson, first baseman Buck Leonard, outfielder Cool Papa Bell and pitchers Ray Brown and Satchel Paige were "all available at reasonable figures. . . . What is your attitude? Wire answer."

Just who were these guys that Chester Washington wrote about to Pie Traynor? They were Negro League players at or near the peaks of their playing careers. They all played their home games in Pittsburgh. Eventually, all would be named to baseball's Hall of Fame. Traynor appreciated the talent in the Negro Leagues. "I have seen countless numbers of Negro ball players who could have made the grade," he once said. He also said he was not reluctant to use black players, if only he could. "Personally, I don't see why the ban against Negro players exists at all."

Authors Forr and Proctor wonder: Could Chester Washington have delivered these Negro Leaguers to the Pirates? Regrettably we will never know, for Traynor never answered the telegram. Had he responded and had Pittsburgh signed the players, the Pirates would have been a force in the National League for years. More important, Pittsburgh would have imported the first black baseball players into the white major leagues in the twentieth century. It would be ten more years before the Brooklyn Dodgers broke the color line with Jackie Robinson.

Traynor managed the Pirates for two more seasons, the team finishing second in 1938 and sixth in 1939. Then Traynor resigned. He served as a scout for the Pirates for a couple of years before finally moving on from baseball. In 1945, Traynor began a radio broadcasting career in Pittsburgh. He delivered a fifteen-minute sports broadcast each night that continued for twenty-one years and helped secure his place as one of the most admired athletes in Pittsburgh history. In 1948, Traynor received major league baseball's highest honor—induction into the Hall of Fame as only the second third baseman to be chosen. He was enshrined with four other players and received the heartiest reception of the day. His acceptance speech of forty words was over in seconds.

PIE TRAYNOR HAD BEEN A beloved ball player during his one season in Birmingham, but his popularity in Pittsburgh was fifty times greater, *fifty* being the number of years he lived in Pittsburgh. Throughout his adult life, he mixed and mingled with the citizens of Pittsburgh. Rare was the day that he turned down a speaking request or failed to treat a stranger with respect. Pie Traynor never learned to drive a car. He went everywhere, almost any distance, on foot. Once when he was in New York City to report on the World Series, he walked from his hotel on Thirty-fourth Street to Yankee Stadium on 161ˢᵗ—a distance of 127 blocks. It took him three and a half hours.

Said Pirates pitcher Nellie King, "He would stop everyplace and meet people and talk to them. It seemed kind of odd for a person of his stature." One day in 1955, a newspaper reporter followed Pie as he walked from his home to the radio studio. First, he stopped at a seamstress shop to ask about someone who had been ill. Then he dropped in on a businessman: "How are you? How's business?" It compelled the reporter to ponder, "One wonders how many times over the years Pie has thrust his head in that doorway to inquire how things were going—and how it must have brought a moment's brightness to some bleak days."

Children called to him as he passed on the sidewalk. Strangers rolled down car windows to speak. This was not unusual. It was routine. And it was Pie Traynor's life. He mingled with people of the city hour after hour, day after day, year after year. He was more than a public figure; he was public property. His habit of walking allowed Traynor to remain graceful and athletic as he aged. He could have passed for a film star—six feet tall with a healthy tan and silver hair, carefully combed and parted. Even in his seventies, he was elegant and handsome. He took pride in his appearance regardless of the occasion, splendid-looking in

Pie Traynor always hustled, no matter the score. He was the first man in uniform for batting practice and the first man to return to his position after the side had been retired. In his only season with the Barons, Traynor batted .336 and stole 47 bases.

dark suit and tie. Traynor smoked cigarettes, a common practice for men of his day, and he lived in Pittsburgh, where heavy industry had fouled the air. As a result, he was afflicted with lung problems for years. He was first hospitalized for breathing difficulties in 1958 and later diagnosed with emphysema. By the early 1970s, his emphysema was acute. When questioned about his illness, he denied it. Until the day he died, he never appeared to be ill.

In April 1971, Traynor was admitted to a hospital for respiratory trouble. During late summer and fall of that year, he pushed himself hard with public appearances. In August, he appeared at the Baseball Hall of Fame. Later that month, the Pirates honored him at Pie Traynor Night at Three Rivers Stadium. In October, he received a rousing ovation when he threw out the ceremonial first pitch before Game Three of the World Series. In November, the Baseball Writers Association of America honored him at a banquet. The sportswriters sent him a check from the proceeds of the event, but he refused it. "That night alone," he said, "was a whole lot more than any person could have expected."

Two weeks later, Traynor's respiratory system foundered again. He was rushed to the emergency room, where he almost died. The following spring, March of 1972, he made his annual trip to Bradenton, Florida, at the age of seventy-three to take part in the Pirates spring training camp. Wearing a Pirates uniform, he interacted with fans and rode the team bus to exhibition games. Though he had been ill for years, the end came suddenly. He left Bradenton to return to Pittsburgh for an engagement. A few days later, on March 16, he collapsed while visiting an acquaintance. Minutes later, he was pronounced dead from cardiac arrest due to severe pulmonary emphysema.

WHAT IS PIE TRAYNOR'S LEGACY? In their biography of Traynor, published nearly forty years after his death, James Forr and David Proctor wrote:

> One could argue that he was the most popular athlete in the history of Pittsburgh sports. He was the face of the Pirates during an era when the team was an annual pennant contender and when baseball was far and away America's most culturally relevant sport. But he grew into an even more beloved figure after his retirement, with his appearances on radio, on television, and on the streets.

Historian Jim O'Brien told the authors that Pie Traynor became a "Pittsburgh guy." Pittsburgh guys are down-to-earth, hardworking, unpretentious; people like Art Rooney, Arnold Palmer, Bill Mazeroski, Hines Ward. It is a town that does not tolerate self-aggrandizing, prima donna nonsense. O'Brien said the city's attitude is rooted in its DNA. "Pittsburgh was definitely a working man's town in [Traynor's] days. Nobody thought they were a big shot because they were reminded every day when they came home dirty. Even the white collar workers came home with soot on their white shirts."

Rabbi Solomon Freehof conducted the funeral service for Pie Traynor, saying, "As for you, Pie Traynor, you began in Framingham, Massachusetts. You earned your first living in baseball in Portsmouth; and your great career was here in Pittsburgh. Now, at the age of 72, you are released. But your name will appear in another lineup written in letters of light. Here among us, your baseball achievements are recorded in the record books. But your human attainments are written forever on the tablets of our hearts."

Throughout his adult life, Pie Traynor was steadfast in the fib about his age, maintaining he was a year younger than he actually was. Baseball record books—even Traynor's gravestone—list his birth year as 1899. However, his birth certificate, his World War I draft registration card, and U.S. Census records indicate he was born a year earlier. Even Rabbi Freehof unknowingly misstated his age.

LET US CLOSE THE CHAPTER on Pie Traynor by returning to the late-August day in 1921 when Pie Traynor played his final game at Rickwood Field. The Barons had just defeated the Chattanooga Lookouts, 3–2, the game ending when a Chattanooga batter watched a third strike go by. As twenty-two-year-old Pie Traynor walked from his shortstop position to the clubhouse, hundreds of spectators called his name from the grandstand and bleachers. Many rushed onto the field to shake his right hand. Pie, in his scuffed shoes and smudged uniform, removed his cap and smiled humbly as he accepted their good wishes.

Rick Woodward, owner of the Birmingham baseball club, witnessed the stirring scene and, with pen in hand, recorded his thoughts for the newspaper the following day:

"When George Cunningham stood with his bat on his shoulder and took the third strike in the ninth inning, it meant the end of Pie Traynor's days in Birmingham. It meant the end of the miraculous stops and throws that this boy has made look easy all season as one of the brightest stars the Southern Association has ever possessed. Pie's sole thought since joining our club has been to keep himself in such condition that he could always give his best efforts to win games and to win them the right way. . . . It was a great ovation the fans gave him, and he richly deserved every hand and good wish that went forth to him as he stood in his sweaty uniform and gave us the best he had. God bless you, Pie, old boy, and may Dame Fortune continue to smile on you to the end of your days."

CHAPTER 15

1925: JOHNNY COMES TO BIRMINGHAM

ON SEPTEMBER 30, 1924, THE first chill of winter had descended on Birmingham. People buttoned their coats and hurried along downtown streets as the mercury dipped into the forties. In front of their shops, the butcher and greengrocer called out their wares. A popular song floated from the window of a record store. Cantaloupes and tomatoes were piled high on a wagon. Streetcar bells clanged. A traffic cop blew his whistle. The courthouse clock chimed the afternoon hour. People, people everywhere, their hurrying feet resounding on the avenue. Birmingham's population was growing faster than that of any other Southern city. New buildings were everywhere; one could scarcely walk the streets for the construction debris.

On this September day in 1924, there was great joy in the streets, a lighthearted spirit not seen in a long, long time. People shouted to one another. On every corner, newspaper boys—hands full of afternoon papers—chattered the news:

"Rumors true! Meet the new boss! Read about Johnny Dobbs!"

The headline atop the front page told the story: Dobbs To Pilot Barons in '25. Johnny Dobbs, one of the most successful managers in minor league baseball, had accepted his dream job—Johnny Dobbs was coming to Birmingham. Rumors had persisted for a week that the parties had reached an agreement. Dobbs had wanted to manage in Birmingham since 1907, his first year as a manager. The feeling was mutual. The Birmingham Baseball Association had hoped to hire Dobbs, going back a number of years, but conflicting contracts on both sides had prevented their discussing business. Then, shortly before the 1924 season ended, Dobbs passed word to Birmingham ownership that

Johnny Dobbs belonged not to one team in the Southern Association but to the entire league. He managed in six different cities—seven if you count Chattanooga, which was not a league city when he managed. Dobbs led Birmingham to two pennants during his five years, the Barons' first championships in fourteen years. He left for Atlanta at the peak of his popularity. During his career, he managed six pennant-winners.

he was available. It seemed a curious time for Dobbs to leave his employer, the Memphis baseball club. He had just piloted the Chicks to the Southern Association pennant, winning a remarkable 104 games. At the very moment his hiring was announced by Birmingham, Dobbs and his Memphis team were in Fort Worth, Texas, playing in the Dixie Series. Yet given his history, the move from Memphis to Birmingham should not have been a surprise, because Johnny Dobbs seldom stayed in one place for long.

When he was a wee lad visiting playmates in his neighborhood, his mother would caution: "Now, Johnny, remember, don't stay until they ask you away; then you'll receive another invitation." That admonition accounted for the wanderlust that carried him from port to port in the Southern Association. Dobbs generally moved out of a city at the height of his popularity—and, as

Johnny Dobbs was a centerfielder in the major leagues from 1901–1905 with Cincinnati, Chicago, and here, with Brooklyn.

he said, "I feel, not boastfully, that I could go back to any of those cities if I so desired."

In seventeen years, Dobbs had managed in five different cities. Birmingham would be the sixth. He had won four pennants, and his clubs were continually near the top of the standings. In nine years at New Orleans, for example, he never finished below third place. Birmingham, meanwhile, had been wandering the baseball wilderness, afflicted with poor ball clubs. The team had not won a pennant in ten years, had not even been a contender for the past three seasons, 1922–23–24. "What's the matter with the Barons?" was a worn-out line, no longer funny.

The 1924 Birmingham club had finished with one of the worst records in team history—fifty-four wins, ninety-eight losses, and next to last in the league standings. Dobbs' Memphis club had won nearly twice as many games that season. Yet Birmingham was a good sporting town, with a population large enough to support a winning team, and Birmingham ownership was willing, nay eager, to spend money for ball players. No set of players in the history of Birmingham baseball had been paid more in salary than the woeful club of 1924. One of the local newspapers declared:

"The time was when Rickwood was the scene of lively gatherings, and Birmingham enjoyed prosperity in baseball circles. Now, a few fans, with no other amusement available apparently, occasionally wander out to the park to watch the daily beating for the locals." The day after the foregoing statement appeared in print, the Barons lost to Nashville, 18–3.

Despite the futility, many fine ball players passed through Birmingham in the early and mid-1920s—players with long, worthy records in the major leagues: pitchers Earl Whitehill, seventeen seasons, 218 wins; Walter Stewart, ten seasons, 101 wins; Eddie Wells, eleven seasons, 68 wins; Alvin (General) Crowder, eleven seasons, 167 wins; Irving (Bump) Hadley, sixteen seasons, 161 wins, helping the Yankees win four consecutive pennants; and Whitey Glazner, the National League leader in winning percentage in 1921. Others from the twenties who became major league stars included outfielders George (Mule) Haas, twelve seasons and a World Series hero in 1929, Sam West, a .300 hitter for eight seasons, and, of course, Pie Traynor. Haas, Traynor, and four other former Barons played on the 1925 world champion Pittsburgh Pirates.

With these events as backstory, John Gordon Dobbs was hired to bring the Barons out of the weary wasteland. He was given complete charge of the club at the highest salary ever paid a manager in the Southern Association. Barons President W. D. Smith was succinct: "It will be entirely up to Mr. Dobbs to hire, fire, and dispose of the players as he sees fit. We have hired him to give us a winning ball club."

Dobbs' hire would become the most fortuitous in the history of the Birmingham Baseball Association.

I HAVE ALWAYS WANTED TO live out on one of the hills around Birmingham," said Johnny Dobbs. "The hills have always appealed to me. When I used to come here with the New Orleans and Memphis clubs, it was one of my hobbies to ride around among the hills. No place in the country has prettier homes than Birmingham, and I am sure the hills have something to do with it."

Birmingham craved a pennant contender in 1925—not a pennant winner, necessarily, just a contender. Dobbs made a promise: "If the fans will just stick with us until we can get started, everything will come out alright."

The fans believed. As Opening Day approached, dozens of towns within seventy-five miles of Birmingham announced that many of their citizens would travel by automobile and by train to attend the home opener. Downtown Birmingham merchants agreed to close their establishments for the afternoon so employees could attend the game.

"Now has baseball assumed the prominent place on the stage," wrote the sports editor of *The Birmingham Age-Herald* on Opening Day. "Thousands and thousands of people are talking the game this morning at the breakfast table. The same thousands will continue to talk it until the leaves turn yellow in the fall.

"It is just the beginning," the sports editor continued. "The season continues for six months longer. The showery days of April will lengthen into the blossomy days of May, and still baseball will be the subject of conversation. May will give place to June, but no one will dare suggest that any other topic can be as interesting. July and August will follow, and the fan will be found still unsatisfied and still enthusiastic. And September will come with its calm to close it all—will come too soon for a great many."

Those words were written by Hugh Roberts on Opening Day, 1910. Now, fifteen years later in 1925, the notion still prevailed. For the next six months, baseball would rule the land. There would be days when tennis, golf, boxing, or horse racing would draw the public's attention for a few hours, but those days would come and go. For the next six months, John Henry Baseball would be king. At the home opener at Rickwood Field on April 16, more than fourteen thousand people paid to see the game despite the team having lost its first two games on the road. It was the largest crowd ever to witness a baseball game in the state of Alabama. Throughout the game, Johnny Dobbs stood on the first base coaching line and led the fans in cheers and ovations.

Just who was this Johnny Dobbs, anyhow? He enjoyed managing baseball teams in the big cities—Nashville, New Orleans, Memphis, Birmingham—but what he savored was life in the country. As soon as baseball season ended, he repaired to his farm, an out-of-the-way place at Ringgold, Georgia, near Lookout Mountain, Tennessee. He liked to kid himself about being a farmer of the earth, but he did little farming, really. The farm was where he kept his bird dogs and a kennel of the finest foxhounds one cared to see. He spent his entire baseball off-season at Ringgold, hunting. As a boy, Johnny loved hunting and horses and dogs and sports. The first game of baseball he ever saw, he rode an old horse to the baseball grounds in his hometown of Chattanooga and watched the game from over the fence. That was in the late 1880s.

Johnny Dobbs began his professional baseball career on Alabama soil. The Spanish-American War had yet to crank up when an old man by the name of John Nicklin heard tell of young Johnny Dobbs. Nicklin had served in the Union army during the Civil War and was president of the Southern League in the 1890s. He told Johnny he could get him a job as a baseball player in Mobile.

"How much would you want, son?" Mr. Nicklin asked.

"Well, do you think sixty-five a month would be too much?" Johnny asked meekly.

No, the old man didn't think it was too much. In fact, he didn't think it was enough, so he arranged for Johnny to sign for seventy-five dollars each and every month. That's how Johnny Dobbs, not yet twenty, became a professional baseball player in 1895. Johnny went on to play at Mobile, Alabama; Chattanooga, Tennessee; Springfield, Ohio; Wheeling, West Virginia; and Utica, New

Johnny Dobbs savored life in the country. When baseball season ended, he repaired to his farm near Lookout Mountain, Tennessee, where he hunted with his bird dogs and foxhounds.

York, before making the big show with the Cincinnati Reds in 1901. He was a centerfielder, an instinctive "fly chaser," who made chances look easy. His salary with the Reds the first year was $1,500. He thought surely the Cincinnati management had made a mistake, that it was too much money. Every payday he expected to be told that, yes, a mistake had been made and some of the money would have to be returned, but such was not the case. Imagine his surprise when he received even more money the following year.

From Cincinnati, Johnny regularly sent to his family in Chattanooga a copy of the newspaper so they could keep up with his ball playing. His father knew little about sports but was aware of his son's fondness for horses — how he always tended to them and wanted new ones. Glancing over the Cincinnati paper one day, his father noticed a headline stating that "Johnny Dobbs was out of the game because he had a charley horse." The old gentleman thought hard for a moment, turned to his wife, and said, "Now what the hell do you suppose Johnny wants with another horse?"

Johnny grinned at the thought. "Later during my vacation time, I went back to the farm and took my horses and entered them in various fairs. Once when I was in Savannah attending the annual fair and was about to leave for the fair in Jacksonville, Florida, I wired my father that I thought my horse would win at Jacksonville. He wired back: 'Better ship horses home; you are faster than they are.' And later when some fifteen or twenty of my horses were turned over to my dad to look after while I was playing ball, he decided to dispose of them. No more fox hunts and riding and sports of that sort it looked like, and sure enough when I got back home he had swapped all the horses for a lot of mules, and he suggested I take a couple of them and go to plowing."

Dobbs was in the big leagues for five seasons with Cincinnati, the Chicago Cubs, and Brooklyn. "Then I retired for a year and went into the dairy business. But getting up at one-thirty a.m. and driving a milk wagon was a harder life than baseball. And besides the latter was in my blood, and I again listened to the call and went to Nashville—back to my first love, the Southern League."

That was in 1907, when Dobbs was player-manager for Nashville. There, he displayed a marvelous ability to judge young talent that stood him well in later years. Then it was on to his hometown, Chattanooga, in 1909, Montgomery in 1911, and New Orleans in 1914. In nine years at New Orleans, he won a pennant in 1915 and placed second in 1916 and 1917. In 1918, when the league disbanded at mid-season out of respect for the World War, New Orleans was in first place. Birmingham struggled in the post-war years, but Dobbs' teams at New Orleans and Memphis finished first, second, or third every year from 1914 through 1924. Dobbs was not only an outstanding game manager but a wonderful leader. He believed in leading, not driving, his men.

"He did not ride his players," said the team's trainer, Mickey O'Brien. "He was a great fellow, but once on the field he was battling every minute. He fought for his men."

Dobbs' personality, the ever-present smile—win or lose—the sunny, amiable disposition, inspired his men to play their heads off for him. He made sure his players were well paid and when necessary would step into the owner's office in support of their salary rights. He was one of the best-dressed men in the league, easily mistaken for a banker or a lawyer around hotel lobbies. But he also was a salty, lusty chatterbox with a knack for razzing opposing players from the coaching lines.

Said a veteran pitcher, "Dobbs never says anything unbecoming a gentleman, but he keeps right on saying the same thing over and over, and if a pitcher has a rabbit ear, it gets on his nerve. Anytime Dobbs can get the pitcher to paying attention to him he won't last long in the box. He begins to think about what Johnny is saying and forgets what he should throw the batter."

Which brings us to the present, 1925. The fans of Birmingham had never seen such a human pepper pot, or heard such come-on chatter from their manager. They watched Dobbs coach from the sidelines, not sit placidly on the bench. They watched him mix with fans. For the first time, they heard and saw all sorts of things on the coaching lines—and they loved it. It became a familiar sight: The opposing team has a big lead when Johnny Dobbs steps from the dugout and starts clapping his hands, coaching his batters, ragging the pitcher. There's Johnny, calling to the stands for a few yells, cupping his hand to his ear, awaiting a response. He asks the bleachers how many runs they want. They tell him. Sometimes the fans ask him how many runs the Barons will score in the inning, and Johnny will indicate the number with his fingers. Johnny claps his hands—loudly, like the backfire of an old Ford. He signals the batter. He pulls for a rally. He annoys the enemy pitcher with his biting tongue—shaking, unnerving him. Assisted by razz from the stands, Johnny Dobbs sent many an opposing pitcher scrambling to the safety of the showers. It was startling how he and the fans together could start a rally. The fans believed they were vital to the team's success when, in fact, they had nothing to do with it. That as much as anything accounted for Johnny's success.

Dobbs was popular in Atlanta. There, the fans imitated his hand-clapping, clapping in concert with him. Their intention at first was to rattle him, but Johnny turned the tables. He began leading the Atlanta grandstand, shouting to the fans and clapping with them until, eventually, they began to kid and clap with him.

Tuesdays and Fridays were Ladies' Days at Rickwood, and a thousand women, give or take, attended games at reduced prices. To draw attention from male fans, ball players often had to make dazzling plays or timely hits. Not so with the females. A routine play in the field or a batted ball—safe hit or not—drew squeals and applause from the ladies. They enjoyed the spirit of the game and loved to see male spectators razz the visitors, as long as nothing untoward was said. In the excitement of the game, men often forgot themselves and let their tongues slip. When that happened, apologies followed and everyone was happy.

"Women are the best supporters the Barons have," Dobbs declared. "They keep right on pulling for the Barons, regardless of the score."

IN DOBBS' FIRST YEAR WITH Birmingham, the country was riding a tide of prosperity. It was 1925. The great Wall Street boom was in full swing. Farm crops were abundant. Business was good everywhere. Shrewd observers said the stock market had produced the greatest number of personal fortunes in history in so short a time. Never before had there been as many speculators on Wall Street as now.

"Ain't she a sweetie!"
"She's mine. I saw her first."
"I'll match you for her."

Remarks such as these—and others unprintable—were heard on downtown streets every day in 1925. Police officers working downtown beats were enforcing a "move on" law directed at men who loitered on sidewalks and made suggestive remarks to women. The popular area for the street corner loafers was the square block between Second and Third avenues and Nineteenth and Twentieth streets, the block everyone called the "chicken run" or the "race track." *The Birmingham News* likened the street corner loafer to the vagrant and the petty criminal. In the frank language of the day, the newspaper called the loafers "ordinary young smart alecks who hang around poolrooms, visit blood-and-thunder movies, and perhaps read the 'penny dreadfuls'—the cheap, trashy magazines glorifying the 'two-gun man,' and such other blithering rot.

"Where have these husky young men been working?" the newspaper asked. "Not at all—they are poolroom loafers, sidewalk ornaments, such as may be seen every day, especially along the 'race track.' Cigarette hanging from pendulous lip, cap pulled low, eyes leering at every attractive female who passes, and frequently addressing remarks to them. Fairly well dressed, yet never working; living by their wits, shooting craps a bit, matching coins, maybe doing a bit of quiet bootlegging. . . . Put them to work, on the chain gang, or on the train [out of town]. The town is infested with them."

On a Saturday night in February 1925, one hundred Ku Klux Klansmen in full regalia swooped down on a dance hall in the town of Brookside on the outskirts of Birmingham. The chief klavalier stood on the orchestra platform, raised his hand, and demanded silence. "There will be no more dances in this hall on account of immorality," he commanded. "That's final."

The Klansmen left the hall, ignited a large cross outside the building, and moved off into the night. Sheriff's deputies accompanying the Klansmen arrested four men for violating the Prohibition law, for drunkenness, and for carrying concealed weapons.

THE BARONS OF 1925, DOBBS' first team, proved to be a snapping, fighting ball club. In the middle of May, they were tied for first place. The best players were second baseman Stuffy Stewart and outfielders George (Mule) Haas, Ernest

(Tex) Jeanes, and Foster (Babe) Ganzel. Alvin (General) Crowder, the best relief pitcher in the league, was always ready to pitch. Whenever the starting pitcher was getting hit all over the lot, Crowder grabbed a ball and asked Dobbs to let him go in. Five warmup pitches was all it took, and Crowder was ready to face his first batter.

In July, Dobbs purchased a new catcher, Yam Yaryan, one of Dobbs' players at Memphis. Yaryan, from Knowlton, Iowa, was a slow runner who seemingly hit every ball on a line. Whether it went for a hit or not, the fans thrilled to see the ball travel. Before Yaryan's career was over, he would become one of the greatest hitters in Birmingham history, and one of the most popular. The baseball season was a long one, and Dobbs' 1925 Barons were unable to endure the grind. They fell out of the race by summer and at season's end were seventh in the standings.

"Hottest weather I ever saw"—all of Birmingham was saying that. The 1925 baseball season closed with Birmingham in the throes of the longest, hottest, driest heat wave in its history—seven straight days over one hundred degrees and widespread heat and drought from the Mississippi River to the Gulf of Mexico to the Atlantic seaboard. For four days, September 5–8, the temperature reached 104 degrees or higher. On September 10, the heat wave ended, the mercury peaking at ninety eight.

On Friday evening, October 30, 1925, the people of Birmingham turned out in large numbers at the Terminal Station to welcome a train carrying screen stars of the silent drama "Men of Steel," which would be filmed in Birmingham's mines, furnaces, and steel mills. It was the fast-stepping tale of a virile "he-man," an untamed creature of the iron ore fields, embroiled in a thrilling romance. It would be the second feature motion picture ever filmed in the city.

OVER THE NEXT TWO YEARS the Barons made notable progress under Dobbs, finishing third in the league in 1926, with a record of 87–61, and second in 1927, 91–63. Total attendance at Rickwood Field in 1926 was 237,000. President W. D. Smith, who had been associated with the Birmingham baseball club since 1907, said, "Back in 1907 if the attendance throughout a season in Birmingham amounted to seventy or eighty thousand, we thought it splendid."

The Barons' high standing in 1926 was due to the slugging of catcher Yam Yaryan and the pitching of Alvin Crowder. Yaryan hit .369, led the league in home runs, and was voted by fans, overwhelmingly, as their favorite player. Crowder, a reliever in 1925, a starter in 1926, had a pitching record of 17–4 for the first three months of 1926 before being sold to the Washington Senators in July. He pitched for eleven years in the major leagues.

Johnny Dobbs possessed an ever-present smile and a sunny disposition. In 1925, he took over a beleaguered Birmingham club that had lost 98 games the year before and made steady progress in league play: seventh in 1925, third in 1926, second in 1927, before winning pennants in 1928 and '29. He had total control of the team. Whenever he needed a player, he bought one—that was his style, and Birmingham ownership accommodated him.

In 1926, THE WORLD SERIES was broadcast on radio for the first time in Birmingham. WBRC, fifty watts, barely a year old, was Birmingham's only radio station. The studio was located on the twenty-third floor of *The Age-Herald* newspaper building. Announcer D. J. (Dud) Connolly identified the station over the air in the following manner: "This is station WBRC, of Bell Radio Corporation, broadcasting from *The Age-Herald* studio, atop the tallest building in Dixie."

Connolly broadcast the 1926 World Series from the telegraph room. Wearing earphones, he received Associated Press dispatches by telegraph wire of the games between the St. Louis Cardinals and the New York Yankees. As the wire ticked off the details, Connolly reported the action. "This is called play by play," *The Age-Herald* newspaper informed its readers. Connolly's play by play also was relayed through loudspeakers to an anxious crowd outside *The Age-Herald* building. More than three thousand people jammed Twenty-first Street between Second and Third avenues to hear Connolly announce Game One. Two traffic officers closed the street to motor traffic. The eyes of the crowd were on a huge scoreboard high on the building that featured the diagram of a baseball diamond. A man at the scoreboard listening to Connolly's account of the game chalked up each ball and strike, and indicated on the diamond the location of each base runner and the place where every batted ball was hit. Many radio dealers also tuned in to WBRC and relayed Connolly's play by play to excited crowds in front of their stores. The next day for Game Two, the streets were alive again, as former Baron Billy Southworth hit the game-winning home run for the Cardinals.

CHAPTER 16

1927: A GREAT RACE

BIRMINGHAM HAD LAST WON A Southern Association championship in 1914. Since then, the pennant had flown all around the league but not in Birmingham. The populace had endured twelve years of mediocre baseball. After the Barons' third-place finish in 1926, fans were stirred up over the team's chances in 1927 — and who could blame them? Thirteen thousand attended the opening game at Rickwood, a 3–2 win over Nashville in ten innings.

Ten days before the season opener, Dobbs had traded two players to Chattanooga for a big, blond outfielder named Elliot (Sandy) Bigelow. Bigelow was a lefthanded batter and thrower, not a polished fielder, without much of a throwing arm, but, oh, could he hit. Over his previous six seasons in the minor leagues he had batted .315, .343, .322, .388, .349, and .370. With the trade for Bigelow, the Barons of 1927 took the field a stronger club than the year before, even though only three starters returned: catcher Yam Yaryan, shortstop Grant Gillis, and leftfielder Babe Ganzel.

The Barons battled for first place in April and May of 1927, while in New York City, a tall, serious young man was preparing to fly alone, nonstop, to Paris. By May 15, Charles Lindbergh was ready to fly, but the forecast called for several days of stormy weather over the Atlantic Ocean. Four days later, on May 19, light rain was falling in New York, but the weather was clearing over the Atlantic. At midnight, Charles Lindbergh decided to fly the next day. Earlier that afternoon at Rickwood Field, Yam Yaryan hit a grand slam home run in the eleventh inning to beat the Little Rock Travelers, and the Barons were in first place by a game over Memphis.

On the early morning of Friday, May 20, 1927, Charles Lindbergh folded his long legs into the cramped space of his *Spirit of St. Louis*. The single-engine monoplane was loaded with more than a ton of fuel. Lindbergh buckled his seat belt, pushed cotton into his ears, pulled goggles over his eyes, and put a leather helmet on his head. He eased the throttle open, and the plane crept forward, picking up speed, bumping and bouncing for nearly a mile down the narrow runway. Slowly, by feet, *Spirit* began to rise, barely clearing telephone wires and trees at the end of the runway. That afternoon, as Little Rock defeated Birmingham, 11–2, Lindbergh was eleven hours into his journey, approaching the southern coast of Newfoundland at a speed of one hundred miles an hour. Despite the loss to Little Rock, Birmingham held a one-half-game lead in the league standings. Spirits were rising.

At sunset Friday, Lindbergh had passed Newfoundland and was flying over the dark Atlantic in a poorly equipped plane, navigating by the stars, sometimes no more than ten feet above the water. He would endure the monotony of open ocean for sixteen hours. For nearly twenty hours after he left the coast of Newfoundland, little was known of Lindbergh's progress. During the late afternoon of Saturday, reports trickled in that he had crossed the ocean, that he had passed over Ireland, over England, and was approaching France. For two full days and a night, Lindbergh had listened to the rush of the wind and the beat of the motor; sat alone in the tiny cabin; relaxed for never a moment; flew for thirty-three hours; struggled to stay awake; went without sleep for nearly sixty hours.

All day Saturday in downtown Birmingham movie houses, announcers read cablegrams from the stage, informing audiences of Lindbergh's progress. Shortly before ten p.m., Paris time, Lindbergh spotted the Eiffel Tower and the revolving searchlight of Le Bourget airfield ten miles away. Pulling back on the stick, he closed the throttle, cut his speed, and descended slowly, landing gently out of an inky black sky. Despite the hour, tens of thousands of French men and women surged onto the landing field, eager to salute him, to see his face, to touch his flying coat, to lay a hand on the wing of his plane. The crowd swarmed and pulled him from the cockpit, lifted him above their heads, and carried him away. Two French aviators eventually escorted him to safety.

The afternoon of Lindbergh's landing, Saturday, May 21, at Rickwood Field, the Barons were engaged in a doubleheader with the Little Rock Travelers. The pitcher in the first game for Little Rock was Ray Caldwell, and Caldwell was proving tough to beat. In the top of the ninth inning, Caldwell's team led, 3–2, but the Barons scored twice in the bottom of the ninth to win, 4–3. Moments before the winning runs scored, Lindbergh had been swept up by the frenzy at Le Bourget. Two hours later, the Barons won the second game of the doubleheader

Eddie Wells pitched for the Detroit Tigers from 1923–1927 before coming to the Barons in July 1927. He quickly became the class of the Southern Association. During a four-game stretch in August 1927, he pitched 28 consecutive scoreless innings. In his half season with the Barons in 1927, he had a pitching record of 13–1.

to remain atop the standings. Ball players and spectators at Rickwood probably did not learn of Lindbergh's safe landing until they returned home after the second game. They likely received the news over the grapevine from people who owned radios or from theatergoers who had heard the announcements. Others received word from special edition newspapers on the street. In Paris, Charles Lindbergh went to bed early Sunday morning and slept for ten hours. He awoke as the most famous man on the planet.

THE BARONS CLUNG TO THE league lead for the remainder of May, lost the lead, and dropped to third place before embarking on a nineteen-game win streak—*nineteen straight*—on June 9. The streak ended June 27 with a 2–1 loss in eleven innings to Nashville. When the streak began, the Barons were in second place, two and a half games back of Nashville. When it ended, they were in first place, seven games ahead of New Orleans. Days after the streak ended, the Barons traveled to Atlanta and lost two games. The evening of the second loss, a local man, a baseball fan, was seated on a stool at a drugstore counter.

"I see they lost another," the man grumbled. "I knew they couldn't keep it up. By George, they're no ball team. Going over there and losing two in a row." "But they won nineteen in a row," his companion replied.

"That's true, but they've let the Crackers wallop them twice. I tell you, if we don't start getting some pitchers we're going to —."

Pitching help was indeed on the way. The Barons had a working agreement with the major league Washington Senators that allowed players to be transferred frequently between the two cities. In July, the Senators obtained a pitcher from the Detroit Tigers named Eddie Wells and immediately turned him over to the Barons. Wells had pitched in Birmingham in 1923 with modest success, but this year, 1927, he would become the class of the league, winning thirteen games and losing one, with a 2.13 earned run average. Over four games, from August 19 to August 30, he pitched twenty-eight consecutive scoreless innings.

The Barons were in second place on July 24, as Wells traveled all night on a train. He met his new team the following afternoon in Chattanooga and pitched a complete-game victory over the Lookouts. The Barons regained the league lead on August 4. Only three games separated the top four teams, but soon it became a two-team race of Birmingham and New Orleans. On August 20, New Orleans nosed the Barons out of first place. Three days later, New Orleans and Birmingham began a six-game series — the first five at Rickwood and the finale at New Orleans. "If we can't beat New Orleans for the pennant we don't deserve it," said leftfielder Babe Ganzel on the eve of the series. New Orleans players felt the same way.

The series began with Birmingham a game back of New Orleans. The Barons, however, won all five games at Rickwood to take a four-game lead. Fifty-one thousand fans witnessed the five games. Had more grandstand seating been available, attendance likely would have been sixty thousand. The day after the five-game series ended, the teams traveled to New Orleans, where they played a single game in front of fourteen thousand. New Orleans won the game. A week later the two teams met again in New Orleans for four games over Labor Day weekend. The Pelicans won three of four, and the race was tied with twelve games to play. The season was headed for a fabulous finish.

What a rivalry. Birmingham and New Orleans — and their fans — had fussed and fought for years. The previous ten games had drawn one hundred thousand customers, and every possible instrument had been used to create every possible noise. Fans at Rickwood agitated New Orleans hitters and fielders with sirens, horns, and cowbells; New Orleans fanatics did likewise on their home grounds. During the games in New Orleans, thousands of Birmingham fans attended baseball matinees — re-created games — in venues around town. Others followed the progress of the games in hotel lobbies, barbershops, restaurants, and telegraph offices. Citizens discussed the games in theater waiting rooms, office buildings, and streetcars. Telephone operators at Birmingham's three daily newspapers answered thousands of phone calls from fans requesting updates.

What a race. The first week of September, Birmingham found itself heading the parade, down the stretch, for the first time in thirteen years—ahead in the standings by three full games with seventeen to play. The Barons had fought the good fight, but in the final two weeks New Orleans rushed to a spectacular finish. Beginning in the waning days of August, New Orleans won nineteen of its final twenty-one games. With nine games to play, the Pelicans led the Barons by a single percentage point, .608 to .607. The Pels lost only one of their final nine. The Barons, meanwhile, lost eleven of their last seventeen. One of the defeats, 1–0, the final week of the season was to Whitey Glazner, a former Baron pitching for Mobile. The loss to Glazner crippled the Barons' chances, putting them two games back of New Orleans with six to play. The 1927 race was over. New Orleans had won.

Johnny Dobbs' managing style was to constantly look for players—experienced players—who could improve his club. Players came and went. If a player didn't produce, he was replaced. Dobbs made plenty of changes in 1927, but he never assembled a great pitching staff. He opened the season with seven pitchers and experimented all along, bringing in nine more pitchers during the season; yet at no point did he have more than two good ones. The Barons contended because of their hitting; they were, in fact, the best hitting team in the league with an average of .306. The stoutest hitters were Elliot Bigelow (.361), Babe Ganzel (.349), and Yam Yaryan (.336). Bigelow was second in the league in batting, and he led the league in home runs, runs batted in, and runs scored. Yaryan was hobbled the last month of the season with a pulled tendon in his leg, an injury that may have cost the Barons the pennant. Yaryan's troubles continued in the off-season, when a ruptured appendix all but cost him his life. In early November, he was in TCI Hospital in grave condition. Recovery was a long way off. Ten weeks later, January 9, 1928, Yaryan finally was released from the hospital.

Boosted by large crowds during the final weeks of the season, Birmingham led the league in attendance at home and on the road in 1927. The 299,150 full-price home admissions broke the league record held by Atlanta. If reduced-price tickets sold on Tuesday and Friday Ladies' Days had been included, Birmingham's official home attendance would have been approximately 350,000.

THE *1927 WORLD SERIES*, FEATURING the New York Yankees and Pittsburgh Pirates, opened on Wednesday, October 5. Pittsburgh fanatics stood in line all night

They sighted him flying over North Birmingham. "Lindy! Lindy!" the people shouted. Charles Lindbergh circled the city twice and turned his *Spirit of St. Louis* west to Birmingham's landing area, Roberts Field. Lindbergh spent two full days in Birmingham, October 5–7, 1927, on his tour of the country to promote aviation.

waiting to purchase bleacher seats. The jam at the gates was terrific, and a colorful crowd of forty-one thousand packed Forbes Field to the edges.

To the south, in Birmingham, blue skies painted a perfect October day. People were walking with their heads up, looking skyward, looking for Lindy. They sighted him first flying low over North Birmingham. Soon the *Spirit of St. Louis* spun into view over the heart of the city, its silver-gray sides glistening in the sun. As Colonel Charles Lindbergh dipped the wing of his plane, onlookers could see his face in the cockpit. "Lindy! Lindy!" they hailed him. Lindbergh circled the city twice and turned the nose of the plane west toward Roberts Field, Birmingham's landing area.

Lindbergh was near the end of a three-month tour in the *Spirit of St. Louis*, hoping to kindle interest in aviation and promote the potential for transport of mail, freight, and passengers. The tour covered eighty-two American cities. Modest and bashful, Lindbergh had become a demigod since landing in Paris. *The New York Evening World* had called his flight "the greatest feat of a solitary man in the records of the human race." Whenever he appeared in public, thousands of adoring men, women, and children endeavored to see him. On his tour of cities, an estimated thirty million people, one quarter of the nation, turned out to salute him.

Birmingham's thousands had waited all morning for their moment. Above Roberts Field they heard the steady drum of an approaching engine; detected a glint of silver in the sky; finally saw his fabric-covered plane appear over the treetops. A swelling murmur started from the crowd. Lindbergh descended, bullet-like, to within six feet of the grassy field, stirred the dust, and nosed back into the air. He circled the airfield and descended again. Gliding, he throttled down the engine. With a flash of silver and a whir, *Spirit* came to a gentle landing, precisely on time. Two o'clock.

In Pittsburgh, meanwhile, World Series Game One was in the seventh inning. Babe Ruth cracked a single to centerfield, his third base hit of the game, and the Yankees won, 5–4, over the Pirates. "The guy can really hit," Pittsburgh customers were saying of the Babe.

As Lindbergh landed in the swirling dust and heat of Roberts Field, the Birmingham Police and Avondale Mills bands played. Smiling, Lindbergh stepped into a large touring car. Hundreds of small boys swarmed the automobile, leapt upon the running boards, and swung on the spare tire as the car moved off. Under a radiant sky at Fair Park, Lindbergh addressed thousands of schoolchildren. The party proceeded five miles to the Tutwiler Hotel downtown, with Lindbergh perched atop the rear seat of the car. Parked automobiles lined the streets. Sidewalks and intersecting streets held cheering spectators. Lindbergh wore a loosely fitted business suit of gray tweed. People noted his blue eyes, his ruddy face, his sandy, disheveled hair, and his ready smile. Too good to be true, they thought. From upstairs windows and rooftops, folks called lustily: "Lindy! Lucky Lindy!"

Along the route, they cried:

"Lindy needs a haircut!"
"All this to-do over one little fellow!"
"Ain't he cute? Oh, ain't he precious?"
"Oh, AIN'T he darling!"
"Why, he didn't even speak to me!"
"Do you think he'll ever marry?"
"They say those French girls kissed him something awful!"

No one knows how many people greeted Lindbergh that day, but everyone agreed it was the largest gathering Birmingham had ever seen. Thousands shrieked when he landed at Roberts Field. Thousands more saw him at Fair Park. Tens of thousands lined the thoroughfare to the Tutwiler Hotel, waiting, watching, waving. That evening Lindbergh spoke to thousands more at Municipal Auditorium:

"Starting in 1928 we will probably see the greatest progress commercial aviation has ever known," he said. "It is obvious that the more people see airplanes the more confidence they will have in their performance. To this end it is most important that well-equipped airports be established. Eventually, centrally located municipal fields will assume the status of our present railroad terminals, which are merely points for boarding and leaving trains."

Lindbergh predicted a notable increase in air transportation, that the country would soon be a network of airlines. The morning after his reception, Lindbergh rested in his suite at the Tutwiler. During the afternoon, he motored about the city with his personal aide. If anyone noticed him, they didn't make a fuss. The following morning at ten-thirty, a roar ripped the air at Roberts Field. Thousands witnessed Lindbergh race the engine and warm up the plane, watched as he rumbled down the grassy runway and rose into the air. Lindbergh circled the field twice, gliding above screeching automobile horns and a cheering crowd. He flew to the heart of the city, circled the downtown district twice, and returned to Roberts Field for a final good-bye. Nosing the plane down as if to land, he swooped gracefully over the field and ascended steeply in flight. *Spirit* performed beautifully, rearing her wings and sailing into the blue beyond.

CHAPTER 17

THE SMASHING BARONS OF '28

In 1928, Johnny Dobbs entered his fourth season in Birmingham. Steady progress had been made. His first three clubs had finished seventh, third, and second in the league. Still, no flag had flown over Rickwood since 1914. The people of Birmingham had come out in record numbers in 1927, only to witness the team falter in the final two weeks of the season. Some fans had become jaded. After the Barons finished the 1927 season in second place behind New Orleans, one Dan Heaton wrote a letter to the editor of a Birmingham newspaper:

> Now, Mr. Editor, you probably will say that I am a poor sport. Well, perhaps I am, but I am fed up on this "We will win a pennant next year" stuff. I have waited patiently for 14 long years and have heard the same old story every year until I am fed up to the gills. What I would like to see is the old pennant at Rickwood. Other clubs win pennants, why not the Barons? . . . I have been paying for a pennant on the installment plan for 14 years. What I want to know is when am I going to get the darn thing paid for?

Mr. Heaton, luck is bound to turn, sometime.

As players arrived for spring training at Rickwood Field in early March 1928, the scene resembled more a boomtown than a baseball plant. Workmen were putting the finishing touches on a remodeled Rickwood, now with an entirely new look. Plaster art had been applied to the front of the park, giving it the Spanish-style gateway it retains to this day. Fourteen new ticket booths had been constructed, with a suite of offices overhead. Patrons in years past had been greeted by roadways of dirt and dust leading to the park. Now, roads from the main avenues to the park entrance had been paved. The outfield was bounded by a concrete wall, painted green, to replace a tall wooden fence. The vast spaces of the outfield were even more expansive than before—five feet farther to the rightfield wall, twenty-five farther to centerfield, and ten feet farther to left. The dimensions were 334 feet to the rightfield wall; 470 feet to center; and 405 feet to left. A handsome new scoreboard had been erected in front of the concrete wall in left centerfield, 411 feet away.

Remodeling had begun the year before when a roof was placed over the third-base concrete bleachers, extending the grandstand along the third-base line. This year, 1928, the grandstand on the first-base side was extended. Second baseman Stuffy Stewart had played on teams in the American and National leagues. Amidst the pounding of hammers and the rasping of saws, he remarked, "I can tell you there are a number of clubs in the major leagues which would be proud to sport such a baseball plant as Rickwood now boasts, or will boast, just as soon as the finishing touches are applied."

The cost of remodeling was estimated at $200,000. The cost of the scoreboard alone, it was said, was more than the original investment in Rickwood Field. The park was now a modern baseball plant, with ten thousand grandstand and box seats and seven thousand bleacher seats. When needed, temporary seating could be placed in remote areas of the outfield, bringing overflow capacity to approximately twenty thousand.

On Friday, April 6, 1928, the opening game in Chattanooga was four days away. That morning, Manager Johnny Dobbs was at his desk in his new second-floor office at Rickwood Field. A cold rain fell outside. An exhibition game between the Barons and Montreal Royals had been called off. Dobbs rested his head in the palms of his hands and looked up and down his roster of twenty-three players. He tapped his right foot on the hardwood floor. "Twenty-three men," he said to himself. "Gotta cut it to eighteen." Dobbs spent most of the day alone. He reflected on the performance of each player during spring workouts and intra-squad games. He recalled how each of his pitching prospects had handled himself under fire. He liked every youngster and every veteran on the team. Dobbs had spent lavishly during the off-season to build the best club the city had ever seen. The Birmingham Baseball Association had spent a large sum remodeling the park. Dobbs knew this was the year to reap rewards. The Barons had done well in spring exhibition games against major league clubs, losing to the St. Louis Browns but beating the Cincinnati Reds and Washington Senators—twice beating the Senators, in fact. In the second win against the Senators, the Barons scored six runs in the late innings to win, 10–8.

Rickwood Field was remodeled in 1928 with a Spanish-style gateway, tan in color. Though the façade today is green, the entrance retains the same appearance it did immediately after the remodeling. This scene is from a Black Barons game in 1942.

Dobbs studied the roster. He had practically overhauled the club. The team was well balanced, solid in experience. He would begin the season with an entirely new infield, two new outfielders, and two new starting pitchers. Returning from last year's club were rightfielder Elliot Bigelow and centerfielder Max Rosenfeld, who had been moved to the outfield from second base. When Dobbs finished deliberating over the roster late Friday, April 6, he was no nearer a decision than when he had started that morning. He spent three restless nights mulling over his ball players. The night before the opening game, he gave the good news — and bad — to his boys. He had pruned his roster to eighteen — selling or farming out the final five players.

One player not on the Opening Day roster was hard-hitting catcher Yam Yaryan. Yam was thirty-five years old, in his twelfth season of baseball. After his appendix operation of November, he looked finished. He had been in the hospital for two months. Newspapers went as far as to prepare his obituary. In spring workouts, Yam looked helpless: couldn't hit, couldn't throw, confidence

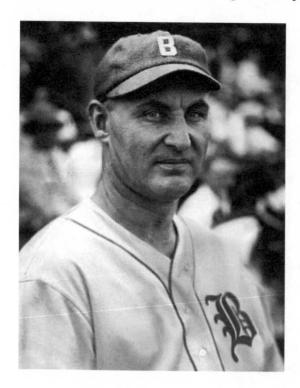

Catcher Yam Yaryan played for the Barons from 1925–1930. In 1926, he hit .369, led the league in home runs, and was voted by Birmingham fans as their favorite player. Two years later he escaped a calling with death to bat .389.

gone. Fans doubted his future. A sore arm kept him off the Opening Day roster. Even if the arm were to heal, it was uncertain if he would make the team. Yam was an easygoing soul, but he didn't quit. He tried and kept trying. He shook off the mental burden of his tender abdomen. The third week of the season, sore arm or no, he was added to the roster. In June, he was hitting .400. By July, his confidence was back—so was his poise. The steam returned to his throwing arm, and he hit as no other catcher ever had hit for Birmingham. He escaped a calling with death to bat .389 for the season.

For the infield, Dobbs had selected two other aging ball players that Birmingham knew well—second baseman Stuffy Stewart and third baseman Jimmy Johnston. John Franklin (Stuffy) Stewart, Birmingham's second baseman for six years from 1920 to 1925, had led the Southern Association in stolen bases four times and would do so again in 1928. Stewart was a bright, happy character with an abundance of personality, truly the life of the team. He'd been called "Stuffy" since high school, fans shouting "That's the stuff!" whenever his speed turned an infield rap into a safe hit.

Stuffy joined the Barons from the Philadelphia Phillies in 1920. The story was this: The Barons and Phillies were sharing Rickwood Field for spring training that year. Stewart, a twenty-six-year-old rookie from Lake City, Florida, was

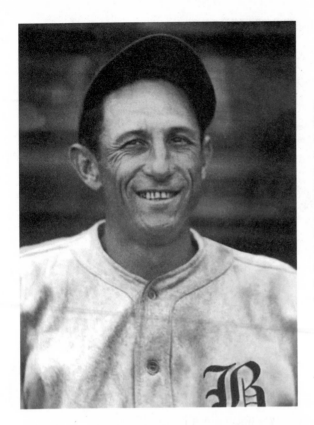

Stuffy Stewart, a bright, happy character, led the Southern Association in stolen bases five times as Birmingham's second baseman in the 1920s. He played for Pittsburgh, Brooklyn, and Washington in the major leagues. When Stewart was in high school, fans shouted "That's the stuff!" whenever he beat out an infield hit, thus the name "Stuffy."

nothing more than an extra infielder for the Phillies, but he was a peppy player who had made a big impression on Birmingham fans and Manager Carlton Molesworth. One afternoon, W. D. Smith, president of the Barons, bumped into Phils Manager Gavvy Cravath in the lobby of the Hillman Hotel, and they began discussing players. The Barons had a catcher by the name of John Peters, and Cravath liked his throwing arm. "I like this boy Peters," Cravath told Smith. "He has shown me one of the greatest whips I have ever seen."

Smith knew that Stuffy Stewart had won the hearts of Birmingham fans with his play for the Phillies that spring, so Smith asked Cravath what the Phillies were going to do with Stewart. Cravath then asked Smith what he would take for John Peters. Smith told Cravath that Peters would cost him $5,000 — and Stuffy Stewart. The two men agreed on the deal. Peters would report to the Phillies at the close of the season; Stewart would report to the Barons immediately. Stewart promised the Birmingham owners that he had given up on being a major-leaguer and was ready to serve the Birmingham club.

That year, 1920, Stewart became the Barons second baseman — and the soul and spirit of the team. Standing five-foot-nine, 165 pounds, he moved like a hunted rabbit on the bases and in the field. He was an outstanding fielder—fast and sure—streaking between first and second, handling hot smashes, one flashy play after another. At bat, he was one of the fastest men in the league, often beating out infield taps. Opponents feared seeing him on base when the Barons needed a run. His derring-do on the base paths absolutely demoralized the other side. He could do more to unsettle a team than a slugger could with his bat. When he took a big lead off first base, the other team tightened up. And he worried the poor pitcher until he no longer paid attention to the batter.

Stewart explained his style of play: "I owe what credit I have been given for being a peppery player to the Birmingham fans. I couldn't loaf if I wanted to, for the fans are always encouraging me to turn a-loose. Sometimes I am so tired I can hardly field a ball or run out a hit, and just about the time I begin to think how tired I feel, some fan will break loose with a yelp, 'Give us a little pep, Stuffy,' and a player can never refuse to give his best when the spectators are encouraging him."

In his second season with the Barons, 1921, Stuffy was a star, hitting .323 and waging a battle with teammate Pie Traynor for the league lead in stolen bases. Stewart won with sixty-six steals. The Pittsburgh Pirates purchased both Stewart and Traynor after the season. Stewart was set to be a utility player for the Pirates in 1922. Rather than sit on the bench, he asked to return to Birmingham. Back with the Barons, he batted .300 and again led the league with forty-seven stolen bases. After the season, he was drafted by the Brooklyn Dodgers. The Dodgers kept Stewart for the first month of the 1923 season, then worked out a deal to send him to the Phillies. Once again Stuffy said he preferred to return to the Barons. Why? Stewart said he had spent some of the best years of his career decorating major league benches when what he yearned for was to be in the action.

Stewart was back playing second base for the Barons in 1923, hitting .306 and stealing forty bases, but more important, his piping voice was back at Rickwood, chanting over the field: "What's the matter with you guys? Get in there and play ball!" And buoying the pitcher: "Bear down, Red! Bear down!"

That season, in the middle of June, the Barons were next to last in the standings, ten games under .500, when Manager Joe Dunn resigned. Dunn had replaced longtime manager Carlton Molesworth in July the year before. Stewart, at age twenty-nine, was named player-manager, replacing Dunn, and he proved as popular a manager as he was a ball player. The Barons were in a demoralized state when he took over, but he turned them into a popular ball club with the fans. The team finished fifth in the league standings but third in attendance, drawing 199,000.

STEWART RETURNED AS PLAYER-MANAGER in 1924. Interest in Birmingham baseball had never been higher, and Stewart was on the playing field, clapping his hands, pepping up the infielders, encouraging the pitcher. No manager had ever started a season with fans behind him in such numbers. Individually, Stuffy Stewart had a fine season in 1924, batting .326 and stealing sixty-seven bases, but the team was one of the worst in the history of Birmingham baseball with a record of 54–98. Around the first of August, Ty Cobb, player-manager of the Detroit Tigers, urged Stuffy to finish out the season as Detroit's second baseman, but Stewart would not desert the Barons. "I like to play ball here, and I am going to stay just as long as they want me. I could have stayed with Pittsburgh the last time I was sent up, but I chose to return to Birmingham. I tell you, I simply love to play ball for Birmingham. It is no easy task managing a losing club, but with all the worries I had much rather be here than with Detroit."

As the season neared a close, the Birmingham Baseball Association began negotiating with Johnny Dobbs to become the manager. When the deal was done, there were no hard feelings. Stuffy Stewart would return in 1925 as the Barons second baseman. He would hit better than .300 and once again lead the league in stolen bases, earning a promotion to the Washington Senators in 1926 and '27 before returning to the Barons in 1928.

Across the diamond from Stuffy Stewart, playing third base in 1928, was a seasoned ball player with blue eyes, a florid face, and a shock of reddish-blond hair. Jimmy Johnston was his name. Johnston, thirty-eight years old, stood a shade under five-foot-ten and weighed 165 pounds. He had the most wonderful legs in baseball. Now in his twenty-first season of organized ball, he could outrun anyone on the club, with the possible exception of Stuffy Stewart. To take the strain off Johnston's aging legs, groundskeeper Bill Walker, before every home game, watered the hard-baked infield thoroughly around third base.

Early in his career, Johnston had played centerfield for the 1912 Birmingham Barons as a teammate of Pop Boy Smith. The Barons won the Southern Association championship that year, and Johnston established a league record with eighty-one stolen bases. Beginning in 1916, he spent ten seasons with the Brooklyn Dodgers, playing every position on the field except pitcher and catcher. The Jimmy Johnston of 1928 could still run. In a game against Mobile, he stole second, third, and home in the same inning. The next day in New Orleans he stole home on the front end of a double steal. Two years later at the age of forty, playing for Atlanta, he circled the bases on an inside-the-park home run at Rickwood Field, scoring standing up. In 1928, Johnston was expected to be a utility player for the Barons, but he crossed everybody up. He

Jimmy Johnston returned to the Barons in 1928 after 10 years with the Brooklyn Dodgers. Birmingham fans voted him the team's most popular player in 1928. With the Dodgers, Johnston played every position except pitcher and catcher. He had the most wonderful legs in baseball.

did play every position on the infield, but primarily he was the starting third baseman. After the season, he was voted by fans as the team's most popular player. A scout with the Boston Red Sox, Pat Monahan, said, "If I could find two ball players this year with the fight, hustle, and speed of Johnston, I would consider myself having dug up two great major league prospects. The young players of today lack what Johnston still retains after twenty years in baseball."

WITH FOURTEEN THOUSAND FANS HOWLING in the stands, Birmingham owner Rick Woodward stood in the dugout on Opening Day, 1928. He watched as pitcher Eddie Wells homered into the rightfield bleachers to give the Barons the lead in a win over Nashville. "This is the best ball club that has ever represented Birmingham," Woodward remarked. The 1928 team had it all: the league's

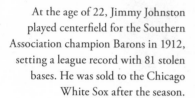

At the age of 22, Jimmy Johnston played centerfield for the Southern Association champion Barons in 1912, setting a league record with 81 stolen bases. He was sold to the Chicago White Sox after the season.

best hitter, Elliot Bigelow; the best pitcher, Wells; and the best base runner, Stuffy Stewart. The entire Birmingham lineup could hit—from leadoff man to pitcher. Even the infield was full of hard hitters: Johnston hit .338, Stewart, .318, shortstop Ernie Smith, .306, and first baseman Ernest Raeford (Mule) Shirley, .342. Shirley had a league-leading 133 runs batted in. The batting order—third through seventh—was a Murderers' Row: Johnston, Shirley, rightfielder Bigelow (.395), centerfielder Max Rosenfeld (.344), and catcher Yaryan (.389). On days that Wells or Ralph Judd pitched, the lineup consisted of nine .300 hitters. Judd's batting average as a pitcher and part-time outfielder was .437. The bountiful offense led the league in team batting, runs, hits, total bases, and stolen bases. The defense led in fielding.

In the real old days of baseball, before Babe Ruth began hitting home runs, if two teams played to a score of, say, 6–4, they had engaged in quite a hitting affair. Not anymore. If the 1928 Barons were behind by multiple runs in the seventh inning, the game was not over. Base hits and runs fell like raindrops from their bats. Fourteen times they rapped eighteen or more hits in a game, with highs of twenty-nine, twenty-six, and twenty-three. Their hitting led to game scores of 19–0, 16–4, 15–2, 21–15, 17–4, 19–6, 15–1, 18–2, and 20–1. Yet, along with their power, the swashbuckling Barons employed the bunt and stolen base to confuse the opposition. Here was a club that sacrificed 208 times

Elliot Bigelow swung freely from the left side of the plate with a powerful snap of his broad shoulders. He was not a home run hitter; normally he rifled low line drives that terrified infielders. In 1928, however, he hit a ball in New Orleans that hit the top of the centerfield scoreboard and bounced over, 450 feet from home plate. His batting average over 12 minor league seasons was .349. Here he is in 1929, the year after he played for Birmingham.

and stole 185 bases. Opposing managers didn't know whether they were going to blast, sacrifice, or steal.

Indeed, good ol' 1928 was the year when all the Barons could hit—even the pitchers. But one batter did it better than the rest: the rightfielder, the big, blond Bigelow. Elliot Bigelow did not have good foot speed, he was not a graceful fielder, he did not have a good throwing arm, but this guy, Bigelow, was a professional hitter. His career batting average over twelve minor league seasons was .349. Only once, however, would he be offered a chance to play in the major leagues, that in 1929 when he was thirty-one. His trial with the Boston Red Sox lasted one year.

Bigelow grew up in Tarpon Springs, Florida, where he was a lefthanded pitcher and outfielder on the town baseball team. He had a good fastball and a quick-breaking curve. One spring day when he was about fifteen, he pitched in a

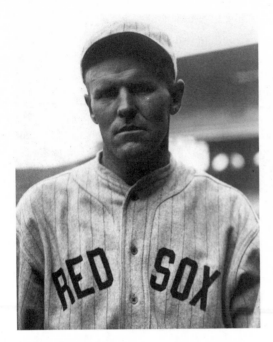

Elliot Bigelow doesn't appear to be happy in this picture from 1929, when he played for the Boston Red Sox. Perhaps he suspected his tenure with the Red Sox would be brief, or maybe he missed dear ol' Birmingham. After hitting .361 and .395 for Birmingham in 1927 and '28, Bigelow received his only opportunity to play in the majors at the age of 31. His trial with the Red Sox in 1929 lasted one year. Bigelow retired from baseball at age 34 to become a full-time fisherman in his hometown of Tarpon Springs, Florida.

cold, drizzling rain and hurt his throwing arm. The arm remained a liability the rest of his career. Bigelow batted from the left side of the plate and swung freely with a powerful snap of his big shoulders. Everything he hit was a line drive. He did not lift the ball; he rifled low line drives that terrified infielders or crashed against the fence. He was not a home run hitter, but he did lead the league with nineteen homers in 1927. One April day in New Orleans in 1928, Bigelow hit a ball harder and farther than the people at Heinemann Park had ever seen, the ball hitting the top of the centerfield scoreboard and bouncing over. The scoreboard was twenty-one feet high, four hundred and fifty feet from home plate. Had the ball cleared the board cleanly, it would have traveled another thirty to forty feet. The scoreboard had been standing fourteen years, and no other batter had ever cleared it, not even Babe Ruth, who had played there numerous times.

For the first time in its history, the Southern Association in 1928 divided the season into two halves. The winners of the first and second halves would play for the league championship at the end of the season. The split season fell short of expectations. The flow of the pennant race was interrupted, and fan interest diminished in the second half. The split season experiment lasted one year.

Birmingham won the first-half title by three and a half games but sagged badly as the second half began. On July 25, twenty-five games into the second half, the Barons were in seventh place, a game under .500. From that point, they won thirteen of their next fourteen games to take over first place on August 1.

Bigelow, meanwhile, was threatening to hit .400. His batting average in mid-July was .444, better than any other hitter's in the twenty-two minor and major leagues across the country. A month later in mid-August, he was hitting .438. On September 1, with fifteen games to play, he was at .423. On September 12, he was still hitting .400, but over the final three games of the season his average fell to .395.

Bigelow's disappointment at not hitting .400 was no match for the grief borne by third baseman Jimmy Johnston. As the Barons wrapped up the first-half title the last week of June, Johnston's fourteen-year-old daughter in Spring Hill, Tennessee, lay sick with typhoid fever. Johnston was called away from the team on July 2. Two days later young Dorothy died. Johnston returned to the lineup five days later. Sharing the grief with Johnston over the death of Dorothy, the Barons in late August led Memphis in a tight pennant race for the second-half title. The Barons won twelve of their final sixteen games, but their lead diminished by the day: to three games on August 31, to two games on September 5, to one game on September 7. The two teams were tied on September 11 with four games to play. Memphis won its final eighteen games of the season to pull off the most sensational finish in the history of the league, and won the second-half title by two games. The first- and second-half winners, Birmingham and Memphis, would meet in a best-of-five series to decide the 1928 Southern Association title.

The championship series resulted in a three-game sweep for the Barons. Eddie Wells won the first game at Rickwood, 3–2, Elliot Bigelow driving in the deciding run with a triple. Birmingham won the second game behind pitcher Lute Roy, 10–4, at Rickwood, that guy Bigelow going four for four, with three doubles and a triple. It was Roy's sixteenth straight win at Rickwood; he finished the season with a record of 19–5. The two games at Rickwood drew a total of twenty-five thousand fans. The final game of the championship series was played in Memphis, Barons winning, 5–0, for the title. Manager Johnny Dobbs had come to Birmingham in 1925, and the team began a steady climb in the standings—seventh place, third, second, now first. Birmingham, champion of the Southern Association, would face Texas League champ Houston in the Dixie Series.

IF JOHNNY DOBBS HAD A favorite book, one would guess it to be *Robinson Crusoe.* Crusoe could not have survived without his man Friday. Neither could Dobbs have survived the pennant race without Eddie Wells, the man Friday who brought Birmingham a championship with his pitching. Wells finished the regular season with a record of 25-7 and would pitch the first game of the

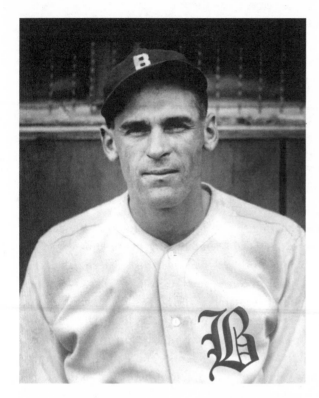

Eddie Wells, king of Southern Association pitchers in 1927 and '28, brought Birmingham a pennant with his remarkable pitching in 1928. In his season and a half with the Barons, he posted a record of 38–8. After the 1928 season, he was sold to the New York Yankees where his locker stood between that of Babe Ruth and Lou Gehrig. He pitched four years for the Yankees and two years for the St. Louis Browns.

Dixie Series against Wild Bill Hallahan—like Wells, a past and future major-leaguer. Wells pitched a shutout, 2–0, at Rickwood. The Barons also won Game Two, 5–3, behind Ralph Judd's seven shutout innings in relief. Jimmy Johnston scored the deciding run, stealing third and home in the seventh inning. Though the Barons were up two games to none in the series, Houston stormed back to win four straight and take the Dixie championship.

For the season, the Barons set a record that would never again be matched in the Southern Association—a team batting average of .331. It was a mark that would stand up to that of any other league, of any year, ever. The Baltimore club of the International League had hit .318 in 1920. Three years later, Kansas City of the American Association hit .316, and Salt Lake City of the Pacific Coast League hit .327. The smashing Barons of 1928, with their .331, had swung the mightiest bat of any team in minor league history.

CHAPTER 18

1929: TWO IN A ROW

JOHNNY DOBBS AND W. D. SMITH, together, would accomplish quite a feat in 1929. After the pennant-winning year of 1928, Smith and Dobbs came back with a brand new championship combination. Dobbs, as field manager, was responsible for selecting the ball players on the field. Smith, as president of the Barons, controlled financial affairs. Smith traded and sold players to generate revenue and procured the players Dobbs wanted. Smith, sixty-two years old, was a genial, friendly spirit whom people naturally gravitated to. He was part owner of the Barons, though Rick Woodward was majority owner. If Woodward could be called the godfather of the Barons, Smith was Woodward's balance wheel. Baseball to Woodward was his amusement, his adventure. His pleasure came from owning a championship team, no matter the cost. He was a spender. He would buy an entire big league club, if possible, and bring it to Birmingham for a championship. Smith, though, preferred to *build* a championship ball club and sell the best players to the highest bidder. His association with the Birmingham Baseball Association went back to 1907, when he was treasurer of the club.

Baseball was a hobby, not a business, for both Smith and Woodward, each the owner of large interests in other fields. Before the turn of the century, Smith had been a grocer. He owned a farm in Springville, Alabama, and through the years had purchased downtown property and other real estate. By 1929, he had collected enough worldly goods to take care of his needs for life. His passion with the Barons was searching for youngsters in the "bushes" and watching them develop into finished ball players. He developed, traded, and sold players wisely to keep the club's books clear of red ink. It was a game within a game, and one in which he excelled. Back when Smith was selling groceries and trading in real estate and marketing farm commodities, he learned the secret of being a master trader—sitting pretty when you had something the other fellow wanted and making it appear you had rather keep than sell.

W. D. SMITH AND JOHNNY DOBBS bargained fast and furiously to replace star players from 1928 who had been purchased or drafted by other clubs—Elliot Bigelow, Eddie Wells, Stuffy Stewart, Max Rosenfeld, Mule Shirley, Lute Roy, Ralph Judd, and Jimmy Johnston. Johnston had joined Chattanooga as field manager. Birmingham had lost all its outfielders, three infielders, and its two best pitchers from the championship team of 1928. The only starting position players returning were shortstop Ernie Smith and faithful catcher Yam Yaryan. Yam, now thirty-six, was returning for his fifth season.

During Johnny Dobbs' long reign in the Southern Association, he likely uncovered more good young players than any other manager in the league. He believed that youngsters inspired the old heads and that the wise old heads taught the youngsters the fine points of the game. But in 1929 Dobbs stocked the lineup not with youngsters but with minor league veterans: Guy Sturdy at first base, Bill (Jiggy) Black at second, Urbane (Brute) Pickering at third, John (Moose) Clabaugh in rightfield, Andy Moore in center, Art Weis in left, and Frank Gibson behind the plate. Gibson was recruited to alternate with Yaryan at catcher. He was a thirty-eight-year-old Texan who had spent seven years with the Boston Braves. He joined the Barons shortly after the season began, hoping to play on his first championship club.

Urbane Pickering, the third baseman, thirty years old, was called "Brute" for his stocky build of five-ten, 180 pounds. As Zipp Newman of *The Birmingham News* described him, "Pickering is as big as all outdoors, but he gets around third base like a ballet dancer over a polished floor." Pickering would have two fine seasons for the Barons, then become a full-time third baseman for the Boston Red Sox in 1931 and '32.

Jiggy Black, the new second baseman, was a hearty, happy, hail-fellow-well-met, much like the man he replaced, Stuffy Stewart. Here was a man from Philadelphia whose best days were behind him. His ten years in professional ball included a brief sojourn with the Chicago White Sox, but at twenty-nine, he had no hope of returning to the big leagues. Art Weis, the leftfielder, age twenty-eight, had played parts of four seasons with the Chicago Cubs in the early twenties. Returning to the minor leagues in 1924, he led the Texas League with a batting average of .377. Weis not only could slug the ball but he could field and throw. In 1926, playing for Los Angeles of the Pacific Coast League, he went 150 consecutive games without committing an error.

Art Weis played parts of four seasons with the Chicago Cubs in the early 1920s. Returning to the minor leagues in 1924, he led the Texas League with a batting average of .377. He played for the Barons from 1929–1931 and 1933–1934.

Andy Moore, whom Dobbs said had the perfect hitter's swing, was the new centerfielder. He had been a football quarterback at the University of Georgia, where his tenacious play earned him the nickname "Scrappy." Moore and Weis were two of the finest defensive outfielders in minor league baseball.

Moose Clabaugh, twenty-seven, with powerful, tattooed arms, had hit sixty-two home runs for Tyler, Texas, in 1926. He began the 1929 season with Mobile but was struggling at the bat. Dobbs, an unexcelled judge of aging ball players, acquired Clabaugh in early May to be his rightfielder. Two weeks later Clabaugh had boosted his average more than one hundred points, as the Barons climbed into first place in the standings.

The year Clabaugh hit sixty-two home runs for Tyler, Guy Sturdy hit forty-nine in a small ball park in Tulsa. A lefthanded batter and thrower, Sturdy was by all accounts the best-fielding first baseman who'd ever worn a Barons uniform. He flagged thrown balls with ease—scooping them from the dirt, stretching for wide ones, and climbing for high ones. He also was a bearer of good fortune. In 1921, his second professional season, he won a pennant with Chickasha, Oklahoma, of the Western Association. In 1922, he went to Joplin, Missouri, winning another pennant. In 1923, Joplin played a split season, winning neither the first nor second half, but producing the league's best overall record. Sturdy broke his leg in 1925 and played less than a full season, then won another pennant with Tulsa in 1927. With all the flags, Sturdy must have thought this baseball business was some sort of parade. He went to the majors in 1928, to a seventh-place club, the St. Louis Browns. The Browns finished third in 1928. Now Sturdy was with Birmingham, and more pennants lay in his future, with Birmingham in 1929 and Houston in 1931.

Heading the Barons pitching staff in 1929 were Dick Ludolph and Bob Hasty. Ludolph, a lean righthander, was twenty-nine years old, a career minor-leaguer who would win 241 games in seventeen professional seasons. Hasty, thirty-three, had been purchased from a team in the Pacific Coast League the previous August, in time to help the Barons win the 1928 pennant. He was a broad-shouldered righthander with long arms and size 13DD feet. He stood six-feet-four, weighed 220 pounds, and threw the ball hard.

Bob Hasty grew up in rural Cherokee County, Georgia, one of twelve children. His father was a prosperous farmer who believed sports were a waste of time and refused to buy his son a baseball. Bob learned to pitch by skimming rocks across the river. He played his first game of organized ball at the age of twenty-two, pitching for an army team at Camp Gordon, Georgia, during the World War in 1918. The following year he pitched for Mobile and Atlanta in the Southern Association. As a young player, Hasty was an awkward, overgrown country boy who didn't know how to wind up or hold runners on base or mix up his pitches. Yet Connie Mack, manager of the Philadelphia Athletics, was impressed with his size and his fastball and purchased him from Atlanta. He went to the majors, still green, and pitched five full seasons for the Athletics. According to the Hasty family, Bob's major league career was sidetracked and ultimately ended after a dispute with Connie Mack, who sold his contract to the Portland Beavers of the Pacific Coast League. He remained on the West Coast for four years, where he pitched for the pennant-winning Oakland Oaks in 1927, coming to Birmingham in 1928.

Hasty was quiet and unassuming—he had a wonderful disposition—not the type of pitcher who would aim at a batter's head. On one occasion he faced fellow Georgian Ty Cobb and threw a pitch Cobb had to sidestep to avoid being hit. Thinking Hasty had purposely thrown at him, Cobb marched to the mound, spitting fire. Stoically, Hasty allowed Cobb to rant. When Cobb threatened to punch him, Hasty responded, "These people paid money to see a baseball game, so we need to finish the game. After it's over, you and I can just step into the alley, and you can take a swing at me if you want to." Cobb was not a small man, but Hasty was much larger. Cobb backed down: "Hey, now, I was just kidding, Bob! Us Georgia boys gotta stick together!"

THE SEASONED BALL PLAYERS THAT Johnny Dobbs and W. D. Smith assembled in 1929 were the class of the league. The Barons began climbing in the standings

W. D. Smith's association with the Birmingham Barons began in 1907 as treasurer of the club. He served as president from 1915 until his death in 1932. Baseball was a hobby, not a business, with Smith and Rick Woodward; both men owned interests in other fields. Smith's passion was searching for youngsters in the "bushes" and watching them develop into finished ball players.

The Birmingham Barons were Rick Woodward's pride and his joy. He operated the team for amusement, not financial gain, spending whatever necessary to produce winning teams and never drawing a cent in profit. "Rick Woodward was the most glamorous owner in baseball," said sportswriter Zipp Newman. "He loved baseball and spent fabulous sums for players and entertaining guests."

Bob Hasty from Cherokee County, Georgia, married Wilma Butler of nearby Marietta in 1923 when he was a member of the Philadelphia Athletics. Bob and Wilma were each from families of 12 children. Bob's father was a prosperous farmer, Wilma's a prominent businessman who owned several businesses.

soon after Moose Clabaugh joined the club. On May 24, six weeks into the season, they moved into first place. By June 28, they had built a lead of eight full games over second-place New Orleans. In early June, Morgan Blake, sports editor of *The Atlanta Journal,* wrote: "Dobbs has again collected a gang of baseball murderers, a lineup that is dangerous from top to bottom. And it is a better balanced club in all departments than the champions of last season. To stop them is a problem this writer would hate to have the responsibility for."

By the first week of July, Dick Ludolph and Bob Hasty each had twelve victories. The Barons were leading the league in team batting. Art Weis was the leading individual hitter and Ludolph the best pitcher. A baseball season, however, is full of fortune and misfortune. On the first of July, second baseman Jiggy Black broke his thumb. On July 14, the Barons were no-hit by Memphis. The next day, Birmingham led Atlanta, 6–3, in the eighth inning but lost, 9–6. Four days later Manager Johnny Dobbs used all seventeen men on his roster in a 13–12 loss to Atlanta. Three weeks into July the pitching staff was shot to pieces, the infield was crippled, team morale was low, the lead had dwindled from eight games to three and a half, and the Barons had four powerful clubs on their coattails—New Orleans, Nashville, Atlanta, and Memphis. By July 30, the lead was down to one game over New Orleans, and the Barons were being called the "sinking champions." Four days later, five teams were bunched near the top of the standings, and fans were disgruntled. Johnny Dobbs, desperate, went looking for help. The trail led to North Little Rock, Arkansas.

In early August, Ray Caldwell was toiling for a semi-pro team in North Little Rock called the Missouri Pacific Boosters. After his long major league career, he had spent seven years in the minor leagues. Dobbs was familiar with Caldwell, having seen him pitch numerous times for Little Rock and Memphis over the previous four years. With Memphis in 1928, Caldwell had won ten and lost seven. Two of his wins were over the champion Barons. But Caldwell wasn't completely healthy. In August of 1928, he had sought a doctor to cure nerve inflammation in his left arm, neuritis. The following February, Memphis judged Caldwell to be irredeemable and released him. He caught on with Akron, a mid-level minor league team, but made only eight appearances before being let go. Viewed as beyond repair with a tired and worn arm, Caldwell was out of organized baseball for the first time in twenty years and, it appeared, out of baseball for good. Then destiny came calling.

In need of work, Caldwell had taken a job with the Missouri Pacific Railroad in North Little Rock on June 15. In reality, he was hired to manage and pitch for the company baseball team. The first week of August the Barons were clinging doggedly to first place, and Johnny Dobbs was sorely in need of pitching. Dobbs had always been strong for the old heads of the game, and he signed Caldwell. He also bought Elmer (Bunny) Hearn, a five-foot-seven, 168-pound lefthander.

About this time, the Barons had begun turning around their season, winning a doubleheader at Chattanooga on August 4 and a single game on August 5. Their one-game lead of the week before was now three and a half. The next day, August 6, 1929, Ray Caldwell made his first appearance for the Barons, pitching and winning the second game of a doubleheader at Chattanooga. The team won another doubleheader the next day—its seventh straight victory—and suddenly the lead was five and a half games. Ten days later Caldwell pitched a stint in long relief: eight and a third innings, allowing one run, but the Barons lost the game to New Orleans. Their lead was down to a game and a half in a three-team race among Birmingham, Nashville, and New Orleans. The Barons had been leading the league since late May, had endured a long slump in July, and had crept along at a .500 pace for six weeks in late July and August. On August 28, they dropped out of first place for the first time in three months.

"I know that every player on the club is giving his best efforts," Dobbs said. "In fact, the boys have been trying too hard. They have been under a terrific strain for nearly three months, with every club in the league shooting its best pitchers at them. I know my boys too well for them to give up just because they are out of first place."

DURING THE FINAL DAYS OF August, Birmingham and Nashville were in and out of first place, with New Orleans close behind. Ray Caldwell continued doing his part. On August 23, he pitched seven innings, allowing one run. On August 28, he pitched against his former team, Memphis, without any run support, losing, 2–0. On the first of September, more than seven hundred Birmingham supporters traveled to New Orleans for a Labor Day weekend series, the beginning of a seven-game stretch that would decide the pennant. The Barons won two of the three games in New Orleans, then came home and won two straight doubleheaders over Mobile on September 3 and 4. In four days, the Barons had won six of seven games. Bob Hasty had won two games with two days' rest in between. In the second game of the Mobile doubleheader on September 3, Caldwell entered the game in relief in the seventh inning, facing the bases loaded and nobody out. He retired the side with no one scoring; Birmingham won the game and reclaimed first place.

Zipp Newman wrote in *The Birmingham News:* "These be stirring days in Birmingham, Nashville, and New Orleans. With eleven days to go, the three managers are putting the spurs to their pennant contenders, urging them on down the home stretch. Dobbs got his horse out in front by jockeying his pitching staff through seven games the Barons looked on as their hardest spot in the schedule."

The seven games Newman referred to were those against New Orleans and Mobile the first week of September. As the 1929 pennant race tightened, so did the batting championship. With ten days left in the season, three players contended for the league lead: Jim Poole of Nashville, .341, Tex Jeanes, Memphis, .339, and Art Weis, Birmingham, .339. In early September, the Barons began playing like champions once again. When hits were needed, they got them; when pitching was needed, Caldwell and others supplied it; and when double plays were needed, they materialized. Caldwell no longer threw pitches with blinding speed; still he showed he could pitch, not only with his arm but with his head. Against Caldwell, batters would get nothing good to strike at and they knew it. Caldwell won his final two games on September 6 and 11. On September 12, the Barons won the Southern Association championship with a

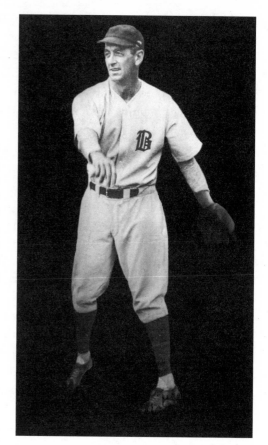

In the summer of 1929, Ray Caldwell was toiling for a semi-pro team in North Little Rock, Arkansas. Manager Johnny Dobbs, desperate for pitching, signed Caldwell to a contract in August. Caldwell helped the Barons win the pennant and won two games in the '29 Dixie Series.

doubleheader victory over Chattanooga at Rickwood Field. Johnny Dobbs had won his second straight pennant.

"You have accomplished your greatest piece of managing a ball club," owner Rick Woodward told Dobbs. "You and your players refused to give up, putting up a fight against odds that deserves the congratulations of every fan in Birmingham. My hat is off to you, Mr. Dobbs."

It had been one of the most gripping August-September campaigns ever staged in the Southern Association. The Barons had been in first place since May 24. During August, the Barons were challenged for the lead day after day. On September 1, the top three teams were separated by a half game. On September 3, with thirteen games to play, the Barons reclaimed the lead, and this time it held. They charged down the stretch, winning sixteen of the final twenty-one games to take the pennant. The Barons would not have weathered the storm without Ray Caldwell. He joined them in early August when they were being challenged for the league lead, when the doubters, behind smirks, were calling the Barons the "sinking champions." He had indeed been a gift of the baseball gods and had secured a place on the team for next season. At no time within the last sixty days was it a dead sure thing the Barons would win the pennant, declared *The Birmingham News* in an editorial. "But something there was in the indefatigable personality of Dobbs and his men through the whole season that merits the respect of the community, and not least the dominating personality—dominant without arrogance—of Manager Dobbs."

T. G. Holt, writing in *The News,* observed that "the team started strong, hitting with as much power as last year's devastating machine, grabbed an eight-game lead by July, then was thrown off stride . . . losing the lead twice to Nashville and New Orleans, only to set a torrid pace during the past month that left the Vols and Pels hopelessly beaten and wondering what came over the champions. . . . Just what made the titleholders spurt toward the close is rather a mystery. The best explanation is—they had the stuff."

The Birmingham fans voted shortstop Ernie Smith as their favorite player. Smith had played a leading role in the Barons' pennant march in 1928. This year, 1929, he was head and shoulders above other shortstops of the league and one of the most dangerous batters with men in scoring position, driving in ninety-two runs and hitting .309. Pitcher Dick Ludolph led the league in winning percentage with a record of 21–8. Bob Hasty won twenty-two and lost eleven. Art Weis, playing much of the season with a bat purchased in a drugstore, led the league in hitting with a .345 average, edging Tex Jeanes by one percentage point.

Weis explained how he acquired his potent bat: "One day I was in a drugstore and saw a bat I admired for no reason at all. I think I gave twenty-five cents for the bat, and never did I enjoy such a batting streak. It was the secret of my hitting."

Frank Gibson, the Texan who alternated at catcher with Yam Yaryan, was full of emotion the day the Barons won the pennant. He had dislocated his thumb the final week of the season but played on. He would turn thirty-nine in two weeks and finally had won a championship.

"It is the first time in seventeen years that I have ever played on a pennant winner," Gibson said. "I have been on teams that came close, but this will be the first time I can go back to Texas and tell them I was on a championship club. And, baby, I mean we are going to bear down on the Texas champions. I have always wanted to play in the Dixie Series. Gee, it feels great to be on a winning club that won because it had the staying powers. Don't worry about my dislocated thumb."

The Roaring Twenties had been a blast for the Birmingham baseball club. In the early years of the decade, Birmingham had wandered the baseball wilderness, cursed by poor ball clubs. By 1929, people no longer were saying, "What's the matter with the Barons?" They were saying, "How does Johnny Dobbs do it?"

How does he do it? That was the question managers around the league asked. When Dobbs broke up his smashing Barons of 1928, there was great rejoicing around the league. But the 1929 season was hardly underway before Dobbs had another wrecking crew on display.

Zipp Newman, the sportswriter, said, "Dobbs has always been regarded as the best teacher of hitting technique in the Southern League. Year after year he turns out a hard-hitting club, taking mediocre batters and making good hitters out of them. For the past three years, Dobbs has turned out the best hitting team in the league. A common expression among Southern League ball players is 'If I could get under Dobbs for a few weeks, he would have me hitting .300.' Dobbs has an eagle eye for batting faults."

Morgan Blake of *The Atlanta Journal* wrote: "Dobbs is a positive genius for assembling talent . . . and when he gets them he knows how to get the best out of them. Without a question, Johnny Dobbs is the outstanding figure in the league."

As the 1929 baseball season came to a close, the Roaring Twenties roared loudest on Wall Street. The stock market, going heaven knows where, looked like Alice in Wonderland. From 1924 to 1929, the Dow Jones Industrial Average had quadrupled. From June through August 1929, stock prices had reached their highest levels ever. But the Bull Market was perilously close to danger. Remember the day, September 3, when Ray Caldwell entered a game with the bases loaded, nobody out, and allowed no one to score? That day the market peaked. Two days later a breathtaking correction occurred in the final hour of trading. The next day "bull" forces regained the saddle and charged ahead with renewed vigor. For now.

For the Barons, it was on to the Dixie Series.

THE SERIES, FEATURING DALLAS AND Birmingham, opened Wednesday, September 25. Games One and Two at Rickwood Field were played to thrilling, one-run conclusions. In Game One, the two teams were hitless until the sixth inning, scoreless until the seventh. In the third inning, with a runner on second base, Dallas batter Sy Rosenthal drove a hard fly ball to right. At the crack of the bat, Birmingham rightfielder Moose Clabaugh broke to his right and ran hard. The ball was hit impossibly far, it seemed, but on his last stride, Clabaugh leapt and reached across his body with his gloved left hand. He lost his balance and somersaulted along the ground, then jumped to his feet with the ball in his hand. He had made the catch and saved a run.

Throughout his career, fly balls were risky for Clabaugh. He blamed his eyesight. "I talked to the major league scouts," he said years later. "They all told me the same thing. They said my fielding was holding me back. . . . I couldn't get a good jump on the ball because of the problem I had with my eyes. I'd make easy plays look hard."

In the seventh inning of Game One, Clabaugh made another play, and it brought victory. Reaching base on a walk, he advanced to third base, with teammate Herschel Bennett on at first base. The two players engineered a double steal. As Bennett dashed for second and the catcher threw, Clabaugh ran home with the only run of the game. In the next inning—the eighth—Clabaugh preserved the victory when he backed into the overflow crowd standing in front of the rightfield fence and caught a fly ball to save a run. The Barons won Game One, 1–0, with only three base hits; Dallas had two.

"There were just enough men getting on the bases to keep your nerves at the bursting point," one observer said. By the end of this day, September 25, the stock market was in despair bordering on panic, as declines carried leading stocks well below their highs. United States Steel, which had sold for 261 dollars a share earlier in the month, dropped to 226.

Game Two at Rickwood was in doubt until the final out. Dallas jumped on pitcher Bob Hasty for four runs in the second inning. When Dobbs realized Hasty wasn't right, he nodded to Caldwell on the bench, who rose and made a beeline to the bullpen. Moments later, still in the second inning, Caldwell entered the game and pitched the rest of the way. In the ninth, Birmingham led, 7–6, with two outs and two Dallas runners on base. The final Dallas batter was thrown out at first base, with the tying runner headed to the plate and the go-ahead runner on the way to second. Dallas had used five pitchers in the game. The battered and broken Dallas pitching staff and the demoralized Steers left for Texas, down two games to none. The stock market regained its poise that day, and prices rallied. The day after, as the teams traveled to Texas, the market experienced one of its most drastic declines of the year.

"I'm glad the two games of the Dixie Series at Rickwood have been played and that the Barons are away for a while," said a fan. "I went out to see the first game and never was quite so nervous over anything in my life. That night I swore I would not go again; it was too trying on the nerves, but Thursday found me among the first arrivals at Rickwood. I just couldn't keep away."

As the Series moved to Dallas, hundreds of people in Birmingham crowded around loudspeakers in front of drugstores, furniture stores, and restaurants. Because most people didn't have radios in their homes, they gathered on the street and listened as sportswriter Henry Vance, in a studio at WAPI Radio, broadcast the road games from telegraph reports. Dallas won Games Three and Four. The Barons, trailing 4–2 in Game Three, threatened to take the lead in the eighth inning with the bases loaded and two of their best hitters coming up. Clabaugh, however, swung viciously at a third strike and struck out, and Art Weis grounded to short to end the inning. In Game Four the Barons trailed, 6–1. In the ninth inning, they scored four runs to close within 6–5, but the tying run was thrown out at the plate. The Series was tied at two games apiece.

Pitcher Ray Caldwell and first baseman Guy Sturdy were the heroes of Game Five in Dallas. It was a bizarre game in which the Barons took the lead early, dropped behind twice, and scored four times in the final three innings to win, 8–4. In the top of the seventh, Sturdy hit a ball to the fence, foul by two feet. On the next pitch, he smacked the ball with every ounce of his power, and the ball sailed over the fence for a home run. It was the longest hit of the Series and the deciding run of the game, and it broke the spirit of the Dallas club. Though there were still three innings to play, Dallas players knew they had no chance against Ray Caldwell. For Caldwell, it was his second win of the Series. "I am now pitching for a manager who understands me, and I understand him," Caldwell said.

That afternoon stock market traders continued liquidating their holdings on a broad scale. The teams boarded a train to Birmingham to play Game Six, with the Barons needing one more win to take the Series. Two hundred fans had traveled to Dallas with the Barons. On the trip home they reached into their pockets and collected eighty dollars to reward Ray Caldwell for his efforts. Ray's eyes grew moist as he accepted the money: "This is the first money I ever received from fans in my life, and after all these years in baseball, you don't know how it touches something around my heart."

Bedlam and chaos — that's what Rickwood Field became late on the afternoon of October 2, 1929, with thirteen thousand people raising a ruckus and a racket. Moments earlier, the Barons had won Game Six, 7–5, to become Dixie Series champions, breaking out of a 4–4 tie in the sixth inning. In the top of the eighth, relief pitcher Bunny Hearn entered the game with two runners on base and nobody out. Not only did he stem the rally, but in the ninth he struck out the final two batters to end the game. What a scene in the growing dusk: thousands of fans throwing seat cushions and straw hats into the air, people swarming the field. Fans hugged players and Manager Johnny Dobbs. They pulled owner Rick Woodward and President W. D. Smith through the milling mob. They clutched the hand of reliever Bunny Hearn. The Barons had stolen seven bases and worked double steals twice to score runs. And in the clubhouse afterward, the ball players were rip-roaring crazy over being crowned Kings of Dixie.

OVER THE NEXT TWO DAYS, October 3 and 4, enormous losses were registered in the stock market. Panic-stricken speculators threw their holdings overboard for whatever they would bring. Small traders who had held onto stocks through earlier declines were unable to pay margin calls, and brokers closed their accounts. Two weeks later, Saturday, October 19, a violent storm of selling occurred, followed by another collapse on Monday, October 21. Investors large and small rushed to dump stocks at any price. Wall Street buzzed with stories of huge fortunes at stake. Big traders, the millionaires of yesterday, lost millions. Small traders were wiped out. Thursday night, October 24, Wall Street was alive with workers and ablaze with light. Stock prices had plummeted that morning, but the panic subsided in the afternoon when powerful interests hurled buying orders at the market. It was the busiest day ever on the stock exchange. In brokerage offices, every employee, from junior partners to switchboard girls and messenger boys, was ordered to work all night if necessary to restore order. Four days later, Monday, October 28, the stock market fell again. In the final hour of trading, the scramble to unload stocks was staggering. Thousands and thousands of shares were dumped on the market with little thought of what they would bring.

The next day was October 29, Black Tuesday, the most terrifying day in stock market history. All trading records were broken. A steady stream of liquidation in early trading carried prices down ten to seventy dollars a share before stocks began turning upward in the afternoon.

IN BIRMINGHAM LATE THAT AFTERNOON came a report from Atlanta—an out-and-out total surprise to the Birmingham Baseball Association: Johnny Dobbs was to be named manager of the Atlanta Crackers. President W. D. Smith said, "We have an oral agreement with Dobbs to manage here in 1930, but if Johnny can benefit by piloting the Atlanta team, we will not stand in his way."

That day, Johnny Dobbs was at his farm in Ringgold, Georgia. There being no telephone in his house, the Atlanta report could not be confirmed. "It is all news to me," said W. D. Smith the next day, October 30. "We have an oral understanding with Johnny to manage the Barons next year, and until I hear from him, I can't say more." As if the events of the past two days weren't enough to frighten the populace, the next day was Halloween.

Remember the admonition of Johnny Dobbs' mother? "Johnny, don't stay until they ask you to leave; then you'll receive another invitation." Johnny obeyed that advice. On November 2, he publicly confirmed he was leaving Birmingham to head a syndicate of eleven Atlanta businessmen to buy fifty thousand shares of stock in the Crackers. Dobbs signed a three-year contract to manage the team. He made clear he had never been treated so kindly as in Birmingham, that he was leaving with regret, and he would forever hold a warm spot in his heart for Birmingham. Johnny Dobbs knew that a manager could linger in one place too long. It remained to be seen whether the move to Atlanta would be a wise one.

THE 1931 DIXIE SERIES

CHAPTER 19

DIXIE SERIES PRELUDE

"WALTER, THIS PLACE IS STARTING to fill up," Charles Stewart said to me. The gathering crowd awaiting the start of the Dixie Series had spilled into the temporary bleachers in front of the outfield fence. It was September 16, 1931, and for the twelfth straight year, the Dixie Series was being contested for supremacy of Southern baseball: the Birmingham Barons of the Southern Association and the Houston Buffaloes of the Texas League, best four games out of seven.

"The Birmingham sports crowd is turning out for this game," Stewart said. "There is this thing called *depression* that makes a man pause before laying down a dollar for a bleacher seat. But look at all these folks, they're paying it because everyone wants see this young fellow, Dizzy Dean."

Jerome (Dizzy) Dean, a hard-throwing righthander, would oppose Ray Caldwell in the first game of the Series. Dean was of the country, of Arkansas stock, a lean and wiry youth with four grades of schooling. When his mother died at the age of thirty-three, Diz, his father, and two brothers became itinerant farmhands, traveling from one backbreaking job to the next—picking cotton for fifty cents a day. Later they sharecropped in Arkansas, Oklahoma, and Texas, living rent-free on farms and keeping a share of the profit.

Diz's ability to play baseball was about the only thing he owned. Unusually intelligent, he had a sharp wit and a fondness for people. He possessed a swaggering manner but a good nature. At the bottom of his heart, he had an honest desire to work his head off for people, a desire to please.

"He was always a little stubborn," said his father, Pa Dean, "but if you would brag on him, he would work his head off. You couldn't ever get anywhere with severe methods. When he was a youngster, I'd tan him until his back was on fire, but he would just get white-mouthed and wouldn't whimper. He had to be smoothed down."

Dizzy was christened Jay Hanna Dean, but he didn't like his middle name. While in the army in 1927, he took his half-brother's first name, Herman, for his middle name, unofficially becoming Jay Herman Dean. Two years later, pitching for a semi-pro team in Texas, he took the name of his best friend, Jerome, as his first name and became Jerome Herman Dean. Nobody ever taught Diz how to play baseball, and he never had to learn. He was doing what came naturally when a scout for the St. Louis Cardinals discovered him playing semi-pro ball in San Antonio and signed him to his first contract. That was in the fall of 1929 when Diz was nineteen. Tall and lanky, he had a long stride and a smooth, overhand delivery. In the course of a single year, he would go from the sandlots of Texas to the major leagues.

In the spring of 1930, the Cardinals instructed Diz to report to Houston of the Texas League. Houston farmed him to St. Joseph, Missouri, where by mid-summer he had won seventeen games and lost eight. Recalled by Houston, he won eight of ten games. At the end of the 1930 season, the Cardinals brought him up to the majors, and he threw a three-hit game against Pittsburgh. In the Cardinals spring training camp in 1931, Dizzy "acted up" and threatened to jump the club if they didn't treat him like a star, unsuitable behavior for a prospect trying to make the team. On the first of May, the Cardinals sent him back to Houston, hoping he would "get some sense." Diz did well. His pitching record was 26–10, and his 303 strikeouts set a Texas League record. He was acknowledged as the best player on the club. Not only was he good but he readily plead guilty to the charge. It was his nature to boast, and boast he did in the weeks leading up to the 1931 Dixie Series. The newspapers were full of accounts of Dizzy Dean.

Talking to a reporter over breakfast one morning, Diz said, "See that grapefruit? Well, do you see that grain of salt? That grapefruit represents how big the baseball looks to the batter before I turn loose my fast one, and that grain of salt represents the size of the ball as it looks to him while speeding across the plate."

Diz was young and strong and good enough to back it up. Later in life, his creed was "It ain't braggin' if you can back it up." The night before the Dixie Series, stepping from the train in Birmingham, Dizzy said of the Barons, "I will give them a hard one, come back with a harder one, and show them the hardest fastball in captivity. The Series is as good as in the bag. The Barons really have my sympathy. Bring along a pair of magnifying glasses if you want to see my fastball."

The next morning the public saw another side of Dizzy Dean. In the lobby of the Thomas Jefferson Hotel in Birmingham, he explained to a female reporter what he, Dizzy Dean, was about:

"I'm just an ol' country boy who can play ball. If I didn't think I was good, why would I be wasting my time trying to play ball? The game won't be a walk-away. Judging by the way we have been playing, we'll get, say, six or seven runs. I'll pitch—and yeah, I guess the Barons will score. They may get a couple," he said, grinning. That was not bragging; it was the way he talked when he was feeling good. Said Diz:

"Baseball's a game. I get fun out of it. When I get out on the field, I'm feeling good, and I like to kid the fellows—all in good fun. I don't pretend to be the best player that ever lived, but I am big league stuff. I don't care if the public kids me back or gives me the razzberries in a friendly way, just so they like me. I like everybody, and I don't want folks hating me 'cause I'm a conceited guy. I'm not—just going strong. I'm going back in the big show next February, and I'll show 'em I can play. I thought they were making a mistake when they sent me to Houston, but now I can see the good experience it was for me. I made a gorgeous record last year, and I did again this year."

At that moment, a pretty, brown-eyed brunette stepped into the interview. "Now don't you be popping off, Dizzy," cautioned the girl. It was Pat, his wife of two months. She had just eaten scrambled eggs and toast in the hotel coffee shop and came in search of Diz, who'd forgotten his breakfast. Pat admitted Diz was really a sweet boy at home, where they keep house in an apartment.

"He washes dishes for me, picks up his clothes, and does anything about the house I want him to," Pat said. "When I'm sick, he fixes a tray for me and brings it to the bedside. He's very temperamental, but he's always good natured. He 'pops off' a lot, but I'm glad he has enthusiasm for what he's doing. That's the only wifely duty I don't have to perform—keeping Dizzy encouraged. He gets enough momentum from his own confidence to keep him going," she said with a smile.

Pat Dean was girlish but gracious, even when the subject of female fans came up. "He gets letters, telegrams, telephone calls. Girls ask him for dates, even. But a wife has her advantages," she laughed, then ducked as Diz took a playful swing at her.

"Everyone calls you Dizzy," the reporter said, "but what is your given name?"

"Jerome Herman," he told her, but added, "say, don't call me Jerome Herman Dean. I'm just plain Dizzy Dean."

Still, Diz had talked too much, and his bravado had helped make this game the biggest sporting event in Birmingham's history. Charles Stewart refused to give Diz his due. "Dizzy's half Ray's age, but he's not half the pitcher Ray is,"

The St. Louis Cardinals discovered 19-year-old Dizzy Dean pitching for the semi-pro San Antonio Public Service Utilities in 1929. Diz pitched for St. Joseph, Missouri, in 1930 and Houston in 1931 before being promoted to the Cardinals.

he said. "Diz is a good pitcher alright enough, but Ray was a marvel before Diz learned to walk. Say what you will, but Ray's pitched against many great pitchers, and Dizzy Dean will not faze him one bit—oh, no."

As a boy, I loved walking through the gateway to Rickwood Field, advancing through the turnstile—the click-click of the rotating wheel—and proceeding up the gentle slope of the concourse toward the drink stand. Then a choice: left or right? *Right*, I decide, up a steep incline and a turn to the left. Suddenly, sunlight. A wide expanse before me: the emerald green of the diamond, the raked dirt of the infield, the rich loam of the base paths, the white chalk of the base lines, the sweep of the playing field, the broad outfield wall—not an advertising sign on it—and blue sky beyond. Game One of the 1931 Dixie Series would soon begin.

I was relaxing on the hard concrete floor of the grandstand. Overhead, dusty little sparrows swooped and flocked beneath the grandstand roof, chirping and searching for crumbs. Rays of afternoon sunlight filtered through the framework of the grandstand, casting delicate patterns of light and shadow on the concrete walk. Suddenly a clatter of footsteps and a tang of boot polish filled the air.

"How 'do, fellows!" a man said. His voice had sort of an oily whine, and I looked up to find the biggest, tallest man I'd ever seen. He looked like a prize ox, this man. Big and strong and prosperous, he smelled of a fresh barber shave, a pleasant, lavender scent. He wore dark, high-heeled boots with fancy stitching, and his feet seemed, oh, 'bout a foot long. On his belt was a big buckle, shiny as a silver dollar. Around his neck was a string tie and on top of his head a big Western hat, pulled low. Rugged looking he was, with whiskered jaws and sideburns down below his ears. I looked at the man curiously—a stranger, I thought—someone from far away.

"Pleasedtomeetcha," the man said in a voice that rang like a temple bell. "Just blew in from the truly great state of Texas. What a fine, growin' town Birmingham is. Lots bigger than the last time I was here."

"The Magic City, we call it," Stewart said proudly.

"Magnificent baseball plant you have here," the big one observed genially.

"Thank you. We're right proud of it. Yes, sir, this is the greatest town in the country. Got everything—positively every, little, thing." Stewart hopped readily into baseball talk: "Babe Ruth called this a fine ball park. Please, I'll offer you the grand tour. And you'll not have to take a single step. Shall we?"

With a sweep of his hand, Stewart directed the Texan's attention to the playing field below. In the distance, mountains loomed dark and green.

"Look out beyond the outfield. See those mountains?" Stewart asked. "Well, sir, the iron ore that went into building this ball park came from deep beneath those mountains." The Texan peered long and earnestly in the direction of Stewart's outstretched arm.

"Now over to the west—look." Stewart gestured with his silver walking stick. "See the smoke rising from that furnace? That's where the ore was smelted and turned into iron. Now, just beyond that point, notice those towering stacks and all the black smoke? That's where the iron was made into steel. On some days, standing here you can almost smell the coal burning, making the steel. Beyond the steel mill is another mill where they fabricated the steel into girders used in this very ball park."

A glint of sunlight shone through the steel rafters, and the Texan stroked his whiskered chin. "Well, I'll be dog-gone."

"Bear with me, please." Stewart paused for a breath and drew at his cigarette. "Just a few miles from where we stand is a network of coal mines. The coal from those mines was the fuel for the furnaces that turned the ore into iron and the iron into steel."

"You don't say," drawled the Texan.

Beyond the outfield wall, a high-pitched whistle and a low rumble rent the air. Stewart paused as the two men watched a steam engine and a line of boxcars grind to a halt, wheels gnashing on steel. The engine exhaled a cloud of wet steam and a plume of oily smoke.

Stewart continued: "Now, my fine friend, take a look at the grandstand before you and the bleachers along the base lines—all made of concrete. That mountain where they dug the iron ore? Just beyond that mountain is one of the greatest cement manufacturing plants in the South. The whole thing is this: All the materials in this huge baseball plant were produced within a few miles of where we stand."

"By golly. In Texas we often hear of Birmingham, but this I was not aware of."

The Texan removed his big Western hat and mopped his brow with the crook of his elbow. "Tell me, cuz, is it always this hot here?"

"We've been havin' a spell."

"Well, your town's not a bad one to be hot in if one must be hot someplace. Say, I walked through your business district this morning. Everyone's talking up the game, but the wise money is on Houston. We won 108 games this year. No ball club anywhere won more'n that. Lots of people were flashing the long green in the hotel lobby this very morn. I saw a bet of $7,000 to $5,000 roll out of a Houston pocketbook."

The Texan smiled, showing his teeth. "You know who's pitchin' for us, don't ya? A gent by the name of Jerome Herman Dean. Ol' Diz. He says Houston'll take it in five. Diz talks a lot, but as the man says, it ain't braggin' if you kin back it up. Your man Cardwell, excuse me, *Cald-well*, he was a good 'un back in the day, but prob'ly he don't have much of a arm left."

"Oh, he had a fair year," growled Stewart through the smoke of his cigarette. After a pause, "I guess you'll be going back to Houston right after your club wins this game?"

"Yep. It's tough for me to get away, even for a day or two. I got a big ol' stretch a' oil fields and pastured cattle to look after."

"Big place, that Texas," Stewart acknowledged.

"I'll say. Git this," declared the cocksure Texan, "if you combined all the cows in Texas into one big ol' cow, the tip of one horn would reach the Atlantic shore and the tip of the other would touch the Pacific. And that cow's tongue would lap the waters of the Gulf of Mexico, and his tail would swat flies off the North Pole."

Stewart drew his lips together in a long whistle. "Is that a fact? Say, bub, you remember all those hills and valleys outside the window of your railway train as you whistled into li'l ol' Birmingham? Well, you'd just crossed a mountain of iron, and there's enough ore in them hills to make a kettle to cook that cow in!"

The Texan roared. "By thunder, that's a good 'un! You got me there, cuz!" And with that he turned on his heel and stalked off, his laughter echoing off the steel and concrete of Rickwood Field.

"And you have a nice afternoon, too," Stewart muttered through gritted teeth.

"I didn't like him very much," I said.

"Him? Oh, I've seen his kind before, drat his hide. He don't mean no harm. Probably not an acre of land to his name. And those cattle and oil fields? More'n likely he's got a barn and a couple of milk cows."

Stewart pulled a gold chain from his vest pocket and looked at his watch. "Come along, it's time we went down to the field. Let's you and I go meet Ray Caldwell. You've gotta ask him to sign your mitt."

I wrapped my arm around one of the steel pillars supporting the roof of the grandstand. Relaxed, I allowed my body to swing forward, lazy-like.

"Ouch!"

"What happened?"

"I whacked my knee on that hard seat. It hu-u-rt!"

"Alright, you're a big boy; no need to cry. Now shake a leg. Let's get down to the field before you do serious damage to yourself—or to that seat."

Stewart took off his hard straw hat and put it playfully on my head. Together we walked down the steps of the grandstand with our bags of popcorn.

ON THE SUNNY GREEN GRASS, a short man with dark, close-cropped hair was talking to one of the ball players. "That's Bull Connor," Stewart said.

"The HOG CALLER??!!"

"That's him. The Plantersville hog caller."

"Why do they call him that?"

"Because he's from Plantersville."

"No, why do they call him 'the hog caller?' My mama says it's 'cause he fancies himself a farmer."

"Could be. But more'n likely it's because when he broadcasts a ball game it reminds folks of a man calling hogs. You know, the way he calls the balls, strikes, hits, and o-o-u-u-t-t-s. He makes the game come alive."

The Plantersville hog caller, Eugene (Bull) Connor, was the Barons radio announcer. Other than the players on the field, Connor may have been the most admired man in town. Whenever he broadcast a baseball game, people brought him watermelons, peaches, dinners, cigars—brought them right to the studio. He was thirty-four years old, stood five-foot-eight, and owned a booming voice and a knack for chatter. He grew up poor, never completed high school, and was blind in one eye from a childhood accident. He had been reluctant to take the radio job a few years back, thinking he "would get up there and talk like a country man and have people laugh at me." During broadcasts, he filled the dead air time between pitches by "shooting the bull" in his Alabama twang, and people began calling him "Bull." And he became extremely popular. Stewart explained:

"You see, Bull's down-to-earth . . . a self-made man . . . natural and straightforward. People like that about him. And he likes people. I hear he may go into politics some day."

"Can he still do the games and do politics?" I asked.

"I reckon."

"Maybe I should get his autograph. He might be famous some day. I wisht I could go to every game like he does. That would be keen."

"Well, he doesn't actually go to the games."

Stewart explained that baseball announcers of the day, sitting in the studio of a radio station, re-created games from Western Union ticker reports. A Western Union operator at the game, tapping a telegrapher key, transmitted each pitch in Morse code back to the radio station: every ball, every strike, every hit, every out. The same method had been employed by Commodore Orcutt for his baseball matinees back in 1910.

The dots and dashes of Morse code were printed on a ticker tape in the radio studio. Someone in the station familiar with Morse code translated the dots and dashes into a script for the broadcaster, who re-created the game for listeners. It cost less to do a game this way than to pay for a telephone line and have a broadcaster call the game from an out-of-town locale. Only the road games were broadcast. Baseball people feared that if home games were broadcast, fans would stay home and listen on the radio rather than come to the park. Bull Connor's first job in life was as a railroad telegraph operator, using Morse code to coordinate the arrival and departure of trains. Because of his railroad background, he could call the game by reading the Morse code without a transcriber. He held the ticker to his ear and announced each play as soon as the pitch was thrown.

"Bull's so good, some people don't realize he's not at the game," Stewart said. "He fooled you, didn't he?"

ON THE FIELD, BALL PLAYERS stretched and limbered up a final time. Off to the side, baseballs popped into leather gloves as players threw back and forth to each other, swapping small talk. They were all out there—Weis, Hasty, Bancroft, Cortazzo. Suddenly Stewart caught sight of Ray Caldwell.

"There he is, yonder. Over by the dugout. Oh-ho, Ray! Say, Ray!"

Caldwell looked up, tall, erect, and bronzed, with the sun in his face. I was in awe of the rugged face, lean and lined, the big, vigorous body, and the arms, tanned by the suns and winds of twenty-two summers. "Hiya, Mr. Stewart. Where you been keepin' yourself?"

"Oh, around and about."

"Well, glad you're here. I'll be right with ya."

I ran a few steps to get close to the ball player. "Slow down," Stewart said. "I'm tellin' you, I don't move as fast as I used to. Get your mitt ready. Here, take my fountain pen."

Ray walked toward us with a slight lean and a limp. He was a little weary about the eyes. The clubhouse boy—the mildly crippled Edward (Crip) Whitley—ran out and placed a fresh towel around Ray's neck.

Stewart squinted into the sun from beneath his hat brim. "How's things, Ray?"

"The leg's been nagging me—water on the knee." Ray leisurely wiped his face on the towel with its lemony, tonicy, barbershop scent. "Missed a turn last month. Other'n that I feel good."

I noticed how seriously the men talked. I looked at Ray's arms and smelled the eye-watering liniment on them. I'd never been up close to a ball player before and was struck by the ruggedness of the man. I was surprised at his arms, how long they were, and at the hair and the sweat on his arms and the way the brown turned to white under the short sleeve of his woolen baseball shirt.

Stewart nudged me: Go to it, my boy.

"Mr. Caldwell, will you sign my baseball glove?" I looked at him hopefully. "You're my favorite player. Your name's Ray and so's my grandpa's."

"You don't say. Well, well, that's a popular name, it appears. I played with a 'Ray' in Cleveland, Ray Chapman. Poor boy was hit in the head by a pitch. It appeared he ducked right into the baseball. Died the next day." Slowly, sorrowfully, Ray shook his head and handed me the mitt with his signature.

"Do you remember who the Cleveland Indians called up to replace Chapman?" Stewart asked. "Joe Sewell from Titus, Alabama. He'd been playing in the minors less than a year—under Johnny Dobbs at New Orleans. Before that he played at the university in Tuscaloosa, and during the summers played on a City League team in Birmingham. Fine brand of ball, that City League." Stewart offered Ray a stick of Beech-Nut, and the player took it gratefully.

"Ray, you been pitching for twenty-two years—longer than Dizzy Dean's been alive. How do you do it?"

Ray lifted the bill of his cap and brushed his hair with the fingers of his right hand. "In a word—it's *control*. When you're young and can throw hard, you try to blow the ball by hitters. As you get older, you learn it's control that counts, and you gotta tinker and add to your repertoire.

"I'll tell you a story. When I was young, my idea of a well-pitched ball was one that I threw by the hitter. I had a big hop on my fast one, and when anybody got a hold of it I thought he was just plain lucky. Then one day an old pitcher come up to me and he says, 'Boy, keep some of those fast 'uns for a rainy day. Hook 'em and slow up on 'em and save yourself.'

"But I just kept on rearin' 'em through. Finally, that old pitcher got sore at me and comes to me and says, 'You're just a damned fool,' and he hardly ever spoke to me again. Then one day, a big rube, fresh from the bush leagues, came up to bat against me. I had a contempt for him and sort of lobbed one up—didn't think he could hit it. Well, it came back at me like a rifle shot. I didn't have time to move, and it took me full on my pitchin' arm. I tried to stall through, but I couldn't. My arm was numb to my shoulder. The nerve had been injured. The club kept me the rest of that season and another one, but my big league days was over. I got so I could pitch to the batters a little, and I could cut loose about a dozen fast ones in batting practice. That old pitcher came up to me one day and says, 'Bo, your days are numbered up here, but you still got quite a time in the minors if you'll listen to me. You gotta outguess 'em from now on. Gotta save yourself,' he says. 'I'm gonna give you the tip-off: You watch their feet, and it'll surprise you how often you can tell when they're gonna swing. They sort of tighten up, and you wanna put a little extra on that one. And then when you see they're gonna just look at the pitch, save yourself and just toss it over.'

"So that's what I do now. I've slowed it down, and I use my head instead of my arm—throw a lot of off-speed stuff and try to put the ball in good spots. It's somethin' young Diz'll have to learn."

"Indeed he will," Stewart said.

Caldwell combed his fingers through his graying hair. He had the look of a man who'd seen it all. "I'd like to have all those years back with what I know now. Can't allow myself to get old. Age is always fatal, so I'm just turnin' back the clock, stayin' as young as I can."

"Don't we all. Say, Ray, it's some kind of hot today."

"Ain't it the truth?" Ray shrugged his shoulders. "Nothing I can do about it. I'll go out there and do my best, same as I been doing fer all these years."

"What are your plans for the off-season, Ray? You sold radios last winter, did you not?"

"Yep, for Jimmy Morgan's radio store in West End — me, Yam Yaryan, Clay Touchstone, Whitey Glazner, Ben Chapman. And Bull Connor.

"Have you anything lined up this winter?"

"I'm lookin'. Just got married for the third time." He pointed to the third-base stands. "The missus is over there with Diz's new bride."

"You gonna be back with the Barons next year?"

He shrugged. "If they want me. I'd like to be back, powerful well. I had a fair year."

"I'll say you did. Nineteen wins against seven defeats. Ray, I need someone to buy cotton. It's not a hard job, but you *will* have to work. I can use you all the way to spring training. Here's my card. Look me up when the Series is over.

"And, Ray —" Stewart paused. "We're depending on you today. God be with you, my boy."

Ray tucked the card in his hip pocket. "Hey, better go warm up. Don't want 'em to start the game without me." He grinned and turned to leave.

"Mr. Caldwell," I said.

Ray looked back.

I waved my hand: "So long. Good luck."

CHAPTER 20

A GREAT RUSH

TO RICKWOOD THEY CAME—BY streetcar, by taxi cab, by motorcar, by shoe leather. From homes of the rich and poor, black and white, high and low, chic and plain. They came in dozens, in hundreds, in thousands; the working people, the unknown people; the babbling voices of working girls and clerks; ministers, bank presidents, and bank messengers; doctors and lawyers; young men with their best girls; fathers with families; men in coats and ties and narrow-brimmed straw hats; sweet smiling ladies in swirling skirts and patterned hats; people who'd never before seen a baseball game. They flowed through the gates in a brook-like throng, a steady stream of humanity, eager voices echoing through the portals of the grandstand.

The town had worked itself into a high pitch. Newspapers had made a fuss about Game One of the Dixie Series, and folks carried on like it was the World Series. Rickwood Field was running over with people on a ninety-six-degree day. Everyone was curious about this Dean person—who was this loud, confident fellow? What did he look like? Dizzy Dean, a big, strong righthander, was twenty-one years old. He would be Houston's pitcher in Game One. His opponent, Ray Caldwell, was forty-three, a grandfather. Dean would rely on his humming, whirring fastball, Caldwell on his control and experience. Every day for a week, the showman Dean had issued challenges in the papers—claimed he would strike out twelve Barons each game he pitched, that Houston would win the Series in five games, that if he didn't beat the Barons every game, he would grow a beard and never, ever, shave it off.

"That beard would help hide my blushes of shame," he said.

Dizzy Dean had talked too much. His boasts had stirred civic pride. The buzz-buzz of gossip said the town was ready to put the upstart in his place. Extra streetcars had been deployed with open-air trailers hitched behind. And people came from all over in a great rush.

That morning, Billy Bancroft, Birmingham's second baseman, awoke at his usual time—eight o'clock—to the smell of bacon, eggs, and biscuits. He and his wife, Sammie, talked about the game, but not for long, for he had to be at the park by ten for a team meeting. Bancroft lived in the suburb of East Lake, nine miles from Rickwood. At two minutes past nine, driver's cap on his head, Bancroft jumped into his Ford roadster. With the car top thrown back, the breeze in his face, he headed west down First Avenue toward town. His Model A skimmed the road. He cut across from First to Third Avenue, and from there, it was a straight shot to the ball park. Bancroft made the meeting early.

From the moment Dizzy Dean walked onto the field, the big, eager crowd eyed him curiously. Before the game, they laughed at him and he laughed back. So did his wife of two months, Pat, seated in the third-base box seats. The people of Birmingham presented Dizzy with a gift. He grinned and threw back his head. He thanked them with a laugh.

"What is it? I can't see!" I cried.

"It looks like a regular nosegay of carrots, cabbage, and cauliflower, with ribbons and such," said Stewart. "And onions! Lots of onions! Now, that's a corker! The people of Birmingham are mocking him for his big talk—oh-ho."

Houston, winner of 108 games during the season, was a ten-to-seven gamblers' favorite to win Game One, but the Barons were a fine team, also. Before the season, nobody expected these Barons to be a championship ball club, but on the tenth day of the season they moved to the top of the standings, and there they remained. By the end of May, their lead was eight full games. From mid-July to the middle of August, they won twenty-four of twenty-eight games, extending their lead to sixteen and a half games. Their final record was ninety-seven wins and fifty-five losses. They won the pennant by ten and a half games. It was Birmingham's third pennant in the past four years.

Johnny Dobbs, the manager who brought Ray Caldwell to Birmingham in 1929, had moved on to Atlanta. This was now Clyde Milan's team. Milan, a mild-mannered, modest man, was forty-four years old. In 1931, he was in his second season managing the Barons. Milan had been a major league outfielder for sixteen seasons with the Washington Senators. He and the great Walter Johnson had begun their careers together with the Senators in 1907, became hunting companions, inseparable friends, and the team's best players. Milan had introduced Johnson to a debutante in Washington society, Hazel Roberts, in

1913. Milan had met her previously, had danced with her at the Hotel Dewey, where some of the Washington ball players lived. She was to become Walter Johnson's wife.

As a player, Milan owned the fleetest pair of legs in the American League. People said he was faster even than Ty Cobb, and they gave him the nickname of "Deerfoot." In 1912, he stole eighty-eight bases, a record Cobb later would break. Milan was born in the Smoky Mountains of Tennessee—town of Linden—in 1887, a few years after outlaw Jesse James had robbed and terrorized the Wild West. His parents—his father was a blacksmith—must have decided the boy was going to lead the league *stealing* bases, for they chose Jesse as his first name: Jesse Clyde Milan. He was such a demure little chap, however, that most folks called him by his middle name, Clyde. When the boy was eighteen, his father called him into the family living room for a heart-to-heart:

"Son, I would like to send you off to college, but I haven't the money, so make up your mind what profession you wish to learn."

"I want to play professional baseball," Clyde said, though he had not played more than a dozen games of baseball in his life. His sporting interests were hunting quail and wild turkey, but he was sure of what he wanted to do with his life.

"Didn't I tell you I didn't have enough money to send you to college, and now you expect me to pay your expenses all over the country to play baseball?"

Seeing that his father was displeased, Clyde explained that professional clubs paid all traveling expenses and offered good salaries. Having heard about the strong semi-pro baseball teams in Texas, Clyde left Linden and traveled to Blossom, Texas, a town of one thousand inhabitants in the northeast corner of the state. He walked into the ball park and asked for a tryout. Naturally, the first question the manager asked was how much professional experience he had.

"None," Clyde answered, "and I couldn't get any recommendations that would impress you. All I ask is to let me show you I can play the outfield."

Milan made the team but later ended up playing for Blossom's rival, nearby Clarksville, Texas. The league disbanded in mid-July during an epidemic of yellow fever. Milan began the following season, 1906, with Shawnee, Oklahoma, but this club also disbanded. He played the rest of 1906 and '07 with Wichita, where he drew the attention of the Washington Senators. An injured Washington player, Cliff Blankenship, was ordered to travel to Wichita to sign Milan and proceed to Weiser, Idaho, to sign a pitcher named Walter Johnson. Washington paid one thousand dollars for Milan; for Johnson they paid one hundred dollars plus train fare.

Manager Clyde Milan and his family lived in Birmingham during the baseball season but returned to their hometown of Clarksville, Texas, for the winter. Here is the Milan family in Birmingham (L-R): wife Margaret, Clyde, and daughters Elizabeth and Eugenia.

In his final major league season of 1922, Milan was the Senators player-manager. The job gave him ulcers, the team finished sixth, and he was fired. "He was too good a fellow to manage a ball club," Walter Johnson said. "The fellows took advantage of his good nature, and that hurt."

When his playing career ended, Milan managed Memphis for three seasons, went back to the Senators as a coach for two years, and came to Birmingham from the Washington coaching staff in 1930. By then, Walter Johnson was the Senators manager. After Milan left Washington for Birmingham, Walter's wife, Hazel, wrote to Clyde's wife, Margaret: "Every once in a while Walter gets to grieving over Clyde's departure. He will miss him terribly."

Before Milan's first season with Birmingham, someone asked him: "Were you anxious to come to Birmingham?"

"Was I!" he exclaimed. "Well, I could hardly wait to get my release [from Washington]. Birmingham showed me back in 1927 that it was the best baseball center in the minors—a city that stuck by its clubs whether they were winning or losing. And when players on the Washington club heard they were being released, they all wanted to come to Birmingham. Why? Because they knew they would get a square deal from the fans."

Milan spoke with a firm but friendly voice. He had a ruddy face, coal-black hair, and a twinkle in his brown eyes. His figure was straight and upright. The build, the coloring, the dark eyes implied that Milan was of Indian blood.

"My ancestors were Indians, I'm proud to say, and I've got the Indian fighting blood in my veins. My native state is Tennessee; my hometown, Linden, which you have to look mighty close on the map to find. In fact, it would almost take a microscope to locate it. But it's there, miles from any railroad; about ninety miles to the southwest of Nashville and sixty-seven miles from Jackson, near the Tennessee River."

One of his players said, "Milan never scolds—he tells you about your faults and how to correct them. He is very patient, never resorts to abuse to get you to play better ball . . . a gentleman in every sense of the word. He insists on the game being played as it should be. Ball players are always anxious to play for him."

Milan explained: "Ball players are temperamental and human, just like singers, artists, and other folk. I never offend a player or hurt his feelings by criticism administered in a harsh, unkind manner unless it happens to be a type that can't be managed otherwise. Always firm, yet considerate, is my motto, for as a ball player myself I know that nine out of ten ball players like to be treated before the public like you'd like to be treated yourself."

Milan's first Birmingham team in 1930 returned most of the regular players from Dobbs' championship team. One of the players was *old reliable*, catcher Yam Yaryan, back for his sixth season. Finally, it seemed, Yaryan was in good health, his best shape in three years. After appendix operations following the 1927 and '28 seasons, he came through the winter in good health and reported to spring training ahead of many teammates. Two weeks into the 1930 season Yaryan was batting .420. Then Lady Luck spit in his face. In a game in New Orleans on April 27, a base runner attempting to score collided with Yaryan at home plate. Yaryan was carried from the field with two broken bones in his left leg. He was out of the game for three months.

In April and May 1930, the Depression was closing in. "Hard times are upon us" were popular words in the American vocabulary, yet people from foreign shores still viewed America as a land of promise. President Herbert Hoover, speaking to the United States Chamber of Commerce on May 1, asserted that the worst effects of the stock market crash were past, that renewed prosperity lay ahead.

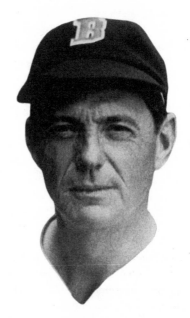

Mild-mannered Clyde Milan was an outfielder for 16 seasons with the Washington Senators, where he was best friends with the great pitcher Walter Johnson. In this photo, Milan is 44 years old and manager of the 1931 Barons. In June of 1935, the Barons were in sixth place with a losing record when the Birmingham board of directors released Milan as manager. He finished his career with the Washington Senators, coaching first base from 1938 until his death in 1953.

Weeks came and went in 1930, and Clyde Milan's crew staggered helplessly, losing as many as they won, hovering around .500 and looking the part of amateur sandlotters. They lost 15–2 to Little Rock on May 19, with Ray Caldwell giving up nine runs and eleven hits in three innings. That day the Barons stood fifth in the standings, closer to last place than to first. "The Barons are running around like an old hen looking for her chicks," said sportswriter Zipp Newman.

Employment conditions in 1930 were growing more serious by the day. Strolling around town, one noticed large numbers of unemployed men standing about, wondering what was the matter with the country. A black laborer from Talladega, Alabama, after searching for work in Anniston, Gadsden, and Chattanooga, said hopelessly, "There ain't no work to be had nowhere. They's got a bread line in Chattanooga, and I was told there'd be a bread line in Gadsden in a few days."

Milan's old club, Memphis, was running away with the 1930 pennant. Only two teams in the league were above .500 on July 4, and Birmingham was not one of them. By mid-July, Memphis was ten games ahead of second-place New Orleans, though Birmingham was advancing steadily in the standings. In early August, the Barons were in a fierce fight with New Orleans for second place. In a game on August 20, the Barons trailed Memphis, 9–0, but scored eleven runs in the seventh inning to win, 11–10. The next day Ray Caldwell shut out Memphis, 12–0, for his seventeenth victory of the season. Caldwell had become a grandfather in late July when his son's wife gave birth to a daughter. That very

Billy Bancroft   Shine Cortazzo

Playing at five-foot-six, 145 pounds, Billy Bancroft became the Barons starting second baseman at mid-season 1930 and held the position through the 1933 season. Shortstop Shine Cortazzo was acquired from Minneapolis in mid-1930. Cortazzo was a hustler, a hard loser, and tough to pitch to in a pinch. He and Bancroft fit together, hand in glove, at second and short.

day at Rickwood Field, Caldwell celebrated by winning his fourteenth game and driving in four runs with four base hits. Memphis won the pennant comfortably in 1930. Birmingham finished third. On the next-to-last day of the season, Ray Caldwell won his twentieth game.

All along, Clyde Milan had been putting in place the team that would win the championship in 1931, acquiring shortstop John (Shine) Cortazzo from Minneapolis, pitcher Clay Touchstone from the Boston Braves, and catcher Bill Eisemann from the New York Yankees, late of Albany. Milan had worked newcomer Billy Bancroft into the lineup at second base in place of Bill (Jiggy) Black. When the calendar turned to 1931, he re-signed pitchers Ray Caldwell and Bob Hasty and leftfielder Art Weis. Then he added two players who had been with the Barons in the spring of 1930 before they were farmed out to other minor league teams: first baseman Pete Susko and outfielder Woodley Abernathy.

Billy Bancroft, the new second baseman, stood five-foot-six, maybe five-six-and-a-half, and looked like another Stuffy Stewart running the bases. "Look at those legs go!" cried pitcher Ray Francis in the spring of 1930. "Believe me, I have seen lots of speed in my life, but that Bancroft can pick 'em up and lay 'em down faster than any little short-legged fellow I ever saw. The trouble with lots of short-leggers is that they run too much in the same place, but not this Bancroft. When he cranks up those legs of his, he covers more ground than a lion."

BANCROFT HAD BEEN MARKED AS the team's infield utility player in the spring of 1930. Early on, he played shortstop and third base, going long periods without seeing the field. In mid-June, second baseman Jiggy Black went out with an injury, and Bancroft seized the position. In his first game as the starting second baseman on June 18, 1930, Bancroft got four hits. On July 5, an hour before a game against Nashville, he became the father of a baby boy. He celebrated the arrival of William, Junior, with a triple, a single, and a scoring fly ball. He missed a home run on the fly ball when the Nashville leftfielder caught the ball over his shoulder, ten feet from the distant wall. The next day, Manager Clyde Milan gave the new dad the day off. Jiggy Black spent hours with Bancroft, teaching him to play second. Black was interested in Bancroft's career, saying, "I hope I don't get back on second—not that I don't want to play—because it would rob one of the pleasures of seeing a great kid going like a house afire."

Shortstop Shine Cortazzo, acquired by Milan on the first of June, 1930, was the most spectacular player in the league. He, like Bancroft, was a mite of a man, a hustling player, a hard loser, a tough baby to pitch to in a pinch. Bancroft and Cortazzo fit together, hand in glove, at second and short, and Jiggy Black never returned to the lineup. Yam Yaryan missed two-thirds of the 1930 season with his broken leg yet hit .340. Clyde Milan wanted a young catching staff to start the season of 1931, and in January, he sold Yaryan to Fort Worth. One of the most beloved players ever to play for Birmingham was gone. Rickwood Field would not be the same without him.

CHAPTER 21

PLAY BALL!

IN THE DAYS LEADING TO the 1931 Dixie Series, Manager Clyde Milan said, "We have heard much about Dizzy Dean's prowess as a hurler, and we are anxious to face him. If we get good pitching, we have nothing to fear from the Buffs. They made a wonderful record in the Texas League, and we made a pretty fair one in the Southern League. The Barons played their best ball when they had to win, and long before the season started people told us we didn't have a chance to win the pennant. My boys didn't take any stock in that, and they haven't paid any attention to all this talk about Dizzy Dean and the Buffs."

The Barons possessed four reliable workmen on the pitching staff: Ray Caldwell, Bob Hasty, Jimmy Walkup, and Clay Touchstone. Caldwell was the sturdy oak, forty-three years old, twenty-two professional seasons, a winner of 289 games. Hasty and Walkup were thirty-five years old; Touchstone, twenty-eight. Hasty and Caldwell were roommates on the road by order of Clyde Milan. Hasty was in bed every night by nine o'clock. Some nights he didn't see night-owl Caldwell until the following morning. Throughout his career, Hasty had been a fastball pitcher and his fastball helped him win twenty-two games on Birmingham's pennant-winning club of 1929. The next year, 1930, an arm injury forced him to use all his resources—fastball, curve, control, and finesse. In 1931, Hasty's pitching record was 21–13. Even at his age of thirty-five, one scout said of Hasty, "He belongs back in the majors." Hasty, however, never again pitched in the big leagues, and by 1933, was out of professional baseball.

Walkup—little Jimmy Walkup—was a timid country boy with an Arkansas drawl. A lefthanded pitcher, five-foot-eight, 150 pounds, he was nearing the end of his baseball career. Except for two games with the Detroit Tigers in 1927, all his baseball years were spent in the minor leagues, where he won 259 games. Walkup was mild-mannered and soft-spoken but enjoyed a good laugh. He liked to fill a drinking straw with gunpowder, light the end, and watch his homemade missile frighten teammates. Walkup didn't have a fastball—he threw a slow ball and a soft, sweeping curve. One April afternoon in 1928, he used the curve against the greatest slugger of the age, Babe Ruth. Walkup's team, the Fort Worth Panthers, was playing an exhibition game against the New York Yankees. It was the spring after Ruth had hit his record sixty home runs. Walkup threw Ruth nothing but slow curveballs and struck him out three consecutive times. Ruth was furious. "Put enough on the ball for a man to hit!" he bellowed, pounding the plate with his bat.

The youngster on the Barons pitching staff was a blond, rotund curveballer from Moore, Pennsylvania, named Clayland Maffitt Touchstone. Clay Touchstone had pitched briefly for the major league Boston Braves in 1928 and '29. In 1930, he won fifteen games for the Barons and fifteen more in 1931. He was powerfully built through the chest, shoulders, arms, and legs. After coming to Birmingham, he perfected a crossfire delivery—a throwing motion across his body—and he was a better pitcher in 1931 than he had been with the Boston Braves. By 1933, he would become one of the best pitchers in the Southern Association, and major league scouts began watching him closely. A dozen years would pass, however, before he made a brief return to the majors in the war year of 1945, when the best major-leaguers were serving in the military. He finished his career with 272 victories, all in the minor leagues.

The Barons' best all-around player was leftfielder Art Weis. In 1929, Weis won the league batting title. In 1931, his .369 average, twenty home runs, and defensive play won him the award as the outstanding player of the Southern Association. A player for the Little Rock Travelers said, "Name a ball player in the league who can run, throw, field, and hit with Art Weis. No, you can't name anyone who can do everything a good player is supposed to do as well as Weis."

"WALTER, LET'S FIND A SEAT," Stewart said, as we waited for the game to begin. Across his arm swung his silver walking stick. "My, I've never seen so many people. Let's sit in the bleachers, whaddya say? That's where the real baseball fan sits, not in the grandstand. Seems more like real baseball out there. You're right in the middle of the game, rootin' for the home team—the cheering's the loudest, so's the hazing of the other team. Everyone's analyzing the play, sizing up the next move. And then a foul ball comes your way, and what fun it is to scramble for the ball, even if you do fall under the seats trying to get it. Let's sit in the bleachers. Huh? Whaddya say?"

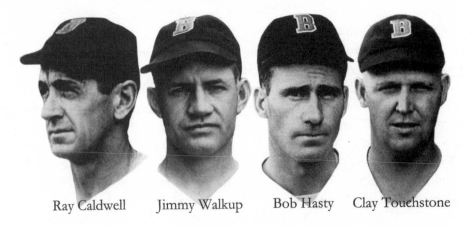

Ray Caldwell   Jimmy Walkup   Bob Hasty   Clay Touchstone

Here are the four workmen of the 1931 Barons pitching staff: Ray Caldwell, 43 years old, had played 22 professional seasons, winning 289 games. In 1931, Jimmy Walkup and Bob Hasty were 35 years old. Walkup was a career minor-leaguer, winning 259 games. His record for the 1931 Dixie Series champion Barons was 20–5. Hasty was quiet and unassuming off the field but a fireballing pitcher on. He won 22 games for Birmingham's pennant-winning team in 1929 and 21 for the Dixie Series champions in 1931. Hasty won Game Seven of the '31 Dixie Series with relief help from Caldwell. Clay Touchstone won Game Five of the '31 Dixie Series, preventing Birmingham's elimination from the Series. A portly, crossfiring curveballer, Touchstone won 272 games during his career, all in the minor leagues.

The blazing sun of a September afternoon beat down from a cloudless sky. Men removed their coats without apologizing. Long sleeve shirts clung damply to arms. Women's dresses hung limp and disheveled. People clutching scorecards crowded under overhead fans in the grandstand. Those wearing eyeglasses constantly wiped them off. People across the social spectrum bantered with one another and sat shoulder to shoulder—captains of industry next to laborers next to merchants. The grandstand was stacked and jammed until not a single square inch of space was left. The air smelled sharply of hair oil and sweat and perfume and men and women. When ticket sellers yelled that the grandstand was full, society women and shop girls took seats in the bleachers under the merciless sun.

Extra bleachers had been placed on the grass in deepest centerfield. When the bleachers became a sea of white shirts and straw hats, the crush surged onto the field in front of the leftfield and rightfield walls. The fortunate sat on the grass in front of the first-base box seats. Many were denied entrance to the ball park. Thousands watched from vantage points outside. Beyond the rightfield wall on the tracks of the Atlanta, Birmingham, and Atlantic Railroad, hundreds of people sat atop idle boxcars. At least two thousand customers had been turned away from box office windows. Clearly, this would be the largest gathering in the history of Birmingham baseball.

The best all-around player for the 1931 Dixie Series champions was leftfielder Art Weis. His .369 average, 20 home runs, and defensive play won him the award as the outstanding player of the Southern Association in 1931. Though he didn't win the league batting title in '31, he did win it in 1929.

The pre-game hubbub had died down. Rick Woodward, owner of the Barons, took his customary seat in the first-base dugout. It was his birthday. On the bench, he edged up to Ray Caldwell, who was lacing up his black spiked shoes. "Ray, this is the old man's fifty-fifth birthday, and I'm asking for a big birthday present. I want you to win this game."

As chairman of Woodward Iron Company, Rick Woodward was one of Birmingham's leading industrialists and a patron of sports. In the morning, he conducted business at Woodward Iron as A. H. Woodward. In the afternoon, he dropped the *A* and the *H* and went to the ball park, where he became plain Rick. He liked nothing more than to don a uniform, jam a cross section of plug-cut in his jaw, put a mitt on his hand, and toss a ball with the players. Then he watched the game from the dugout. To see him on the field, you would never take him for one of the most successful businessmen in the South.

Home plate umpire Lee Ballanfant of the Texas League tore the wrapper from a shiny, new Southern Association baseball and put it in his pocket. Twenty years before, it had been common practice to play entire games with four new balls and four used ones. Today, two dozen brand-new balls would be at the ready.

Ray Caldwell stepped from the dugout. Sunshine flooded the park, as rays of gold splashed the baked clay of the pitcher's box, the billowy white base bags, and the yellow-green of the infield grass. A man came out with a rake and combed the surface around home plate. Another man carefully chalked the foul lines. A photographer lugged a heavy camera to a shady spot and squatted in front of the grandstand.

Caldwell stood on the mound and waited for the umpire to call for the first pitch of the game. His teammates jogged to their positions—Joe Prerost in rightfield, Woodley Abernathy in center, Art Weis in left, Pete Susko, first base, Billy Bancroft, second base, Shine Cortazzo, shortstop, and Charley Gooch, third base. The first batter, Houston third baseman Eddie Hock, climbed the steps of the third-base dugout and strode to the plate. Charles Stewart and I watched every movement, intently clutching our bags of peanuts.

Umpire Ballanfant, dressed in a dark blue suit and dark cloth cap, tossed the game ball to the pitcher, and Caldwell threw the final warmup pitches to his young catcher, Ellis Taylor, whom no one called "Ellis." Taylor's older brother, Zack, was a catcher for the Chicago Cubs, and players had taken to calling Ellis "Little Zack." During the season, Taylor had split catching duties with Bill Eisemann, but Taylor was Caldwell's preferred catcher.

Ballanfant bent over and vigorously dusted home plate with his whisk broom. Then came the shout that reverberated about the park: "PL-A-AY B-A-A-LL!" It was three o'clock, Wednesday, September 16, 1931. The game was on.

Inning one. Caldwell gazed across the sunny diamond. Leadoff batter Eddie Hock dug his spikes into the red earth around home plate. Caldwell checked the positioning of his infielders. Over at third base stood Charley Gooch, purchased from the Kansas City ball club the first week of the season. Charley was the cousin of Johnny Gooch, a Barons catcher from ten years before who had played with Pie Traynor at both Birmingham and Pittsburgh. Temperamentally, Charley Gooch could be hot-headed, but he was a hard-hitting third baseman who proved to be the final piece that made these Barons a championship ball club. Caldwell nodded at his infielders and looked in at the batter, Hock. He got the sign from Ellis (Little Zack) Taylor and threw the first pitch of the game. Hock surprised Caldwell with a bunt, but the ball bounced right back to the mound, and Caldwell threw him out.

"Oh-ho, Ray!" Stewart whistled through cupped hands. "Sweet!"

"Great work!" yelled the fans.

Forty-three-year-old Ray Caldwell and 21-year-old Dizzy Dean pitched against each other in Games One and Four of the 1931 Dixie Series. Here, they meet before Game Four in Houston, won by Dean, 2-0. Note the glove in Caldwell's hip pocket.

"Oh-ho. They tried to catch the old man sleepin'!"

The next batter, Earl Smith, singled off the glove of Barons second baseman Billy Bancroft. Houston's second baseman, Carey Selph, followed with a single to leftfield. Two runners on base and Caldwell faced Joe Medwick, the Buffs' nineteen-year-old centerfielder and cleanup hitter. Medwick's baseball shirt was cut off at the shoulders, presumably to give his arms more freedom of movement, exposing his biceps and forearms. When Medwick dug in at the plate and raised his bat, his muscles rippled. He liked to be called "Muscles," but his teammates called him "Ducky," a name he deplored. Medwick lived for moments like this. He had led the Texas League in runs batted in during the season, and now he had two runners on base with a chance to drive them home. Woodley Abernathy knew Medwick was a powerful hitter and moved back a couple of steps toward the crowd in centerfield. Abernathy, from nearby New Castle, Alabama, had played freshman ball at Auburn University. He'd tried out for the Barons in 1930 but failed to make the club, playing for Montgomery instead. An outfielder by trade, he'd been the starting first baseman early in the 1931 season when Pete Susko had the flu. Abernathy played so well, Susko didn't get his job back until mid-June.

Caldwell looked at the batter, Medwick; and came in with the pitch. Medwick let fly with both barrels and hit a smoking liner on the nose to left centerfield. At the *cr-a-a-ck* of the bat, centerfielder Abernathy took to his heels. The ball sailed high and far to his right, and the two base runners headed for home. Abernathy ran like a streak. The stands groaned, not a ghost of a chance did he have of reaching the ball — a double for sure, maybe a triple. Abernathy raced to the ball. The crowd drew a collective breath. At the last instant, Abernathy threw his left hand across his body and stretched. The leather fingers of his glove squeezed the ball — a backhanded, running catch. The entire ball park let out a roar.

"Whee-e-e!" I whistled.

"Dingdong it!" Stewart cried, slapping his hat against his leg.

Medwick rounded first base and kicked the dirt. *What's the use to sock it on the kisser if they're gonna play that kind of ball?*

Stewart looked at the faces around him. "Oh-ho, I say, oh-ho! What'd you think of that catch!?"

"He saved the day!" I shouted at the top of my voice.

"Whew, boy, and how!" Stewart yelled, waving his cigarette. "If the ball 'ud been two feet further, they'd have scored two runs. And I just scattered all my peanuts. Kindly hand me the smelling salts!"

Across the aisle, a man in a wrinkled suit wagged his finger at us and blurted: "Fly ball! F-to-8! That's all 't is! — nuttin' more." He scrawled the play with a pencil on his scorecard.

Stewart roared with delight. "You betcha, old-timer, alright, alright. Okay, Ray, pin your ears back! Get the next man and you're out of the inning!" Caldwell obliged. The batter grounded to third for an out. Caldwell tossed his glove behind the mound and walked off the field — a curious custom, but from the earliest days of baseball, players had left their gloves on the field at the end of each half inning. Infielders dropped their gloves on the edge of the outfield grass; outfielders left theirs in the wide-open outfield.

Dizzy Dean's fastball was singing in the air, and his wide-breaking curve and changeup were working fine. He retired the Barons, one-two-three, in the bottom of the first.

Inning two. The first batter to face Caldwell in the second inning was first baseman Guy Sturdy. Caldwell and Sturdy had been teammates with the Barons the past two seasons, but this year Sturdy was back in his native Texas, playing for Houston. The crowd gasped as Sturdy hit a screamer that hopped over Caldwell's head, headed for centerfield. Second baseman Bancroft darted to his right and lunged, snaring the ball in his bare right hand near second base. Off balance and falling toward centerfield, he looped the ball in the direction of first base. First baseman Susko stretched as far as he could and caught the ball an instant before the batter touched the bag. The umpire whipped his arm up and over his head—"YE'RE OUT!" The play might have been a game-saver: Two Houston batters followed with hits. If Bancroft had not made the play, one run, possibly two, would've scored. Caldwell, however, escaped the inning with no one scoring.

Dizzy Dean walked the leadoff batter in the second, but a double play ended the inning.

Inning three. In the top of the third, Ray Caldwell worked the corners of the plate and retired the Buffs, three up, three down. "Sock it at him, Ray!" the fans cried. The man in the wrinkled suit sharpened his pencil, scratching it back and forth on the concrete walk, and recorded the outs on his scorecard. In the bottom of the third, Dean put down the Barons in order.

Ray Caldwell was near the end of his playing years. Here was a pitcher cool and confident, a master of the situation, pitching with savvy and patience. At age forty-three, his pitches no longer had zip or snap, but he threw the ball where he wanted. Above all, he had a head on his shoulders. He baffled batters with his curve, his slow ball, and his head. He studied every pitch, worked every corner. On the mound, he toyed with the ball and the resin bag until he chose his pitch. He threw sidearm on one pitch, overhand on the next—a knuckleball here, a fastball there, a change of pace, maybe a moist one. He worked hard at his trade, thinking ahead of the hitters, coming inside to the hitters, moving the ball around.

"Ray cuts the corners and changes pace so easy," Stewart explained to me. "See how he uses the same motion every time he throws? That keeps the batter off his stride. He doesn't have overpowering stuff anymore, but he makes batters swing at balls they swear they won't swing at. That's what you call pitching. Now watch him move his fielders around for every batter. He's not just throwing; he's thinking about what he's doing. He doesn't seem to have much on the ball, but with his control he makes the batter hit the ball where he wants him to. Frankly, I'm worried about the fans standing there in the outfield. Ray's not a strikeout pitcher; he's a 'fly ball' pitcher. Those Houston batters might lift the ball into that crowd."

Innings four and five. Caldwell allowed two hits in the top of the fourth—but again, no runs. In the bottom half, Dean allowed the Barons their first hit, but a double play ended the inning.

"Ray's been a little shaky, but he'll settle down," Stewart said. "Dizzy Dean's pitching like a ragin' prairie fire."

In the fifth, Caldwell retired the Buffs, three up, three down. When Caldwell struck out the last batter in the fifth, the crowd let out a mighty roar. "You own this game, Ray!" Stewart cried. Halfway through the game, still no score.

Stewart stole a glance at the press box atop the grandstand roof. "Oh-ho, we got ourselves a game. The well known twins, Nip and Tuck, are watchin' this 'un. So are the boys in the sporting press—they're lovin' it."

Inning six. Joe Medwick opened the top of the sixth with a single through the pitcher's box and reached second on a sacrifice bunt. Houston fans cheered loud, but Caldwell snuffed out the next two batters to retire the side. Dean breezed through the bottom half of the inning. He had waded through the Barons all game long, allowing but one hit. The sixth moved into the seventh, the teams still deadlocked.

Inning seven. Houston's leadoff batter in the seventh reached base when Caldwell overran a bunted ball. But once again he escaped. A murmur went through the crowd—no score, still. In the bottom of the seventh, the Barons got their second hit of the game—the first solid lick off Dean. It came with two outs when Pete Susko slapped a ball through the pitcher's box. Susko stole second base, Dean intentionally walked the next batter, and the next hitter popped out to third base to end the inning. A stony calm settled over the park. This game would not be decided until the final round.

RAY CALDWELL HAD PITCHED A season full of games, taking his turn every fifth day, hurling his head off. Here was an old man as baseball reckons age, but almost every time out in the fierce summer sun, through a season's worth of games, Caldwell had pitched a full nine innings. He was like a devoted draft horse. Willing. Now, he tapped a wellspring of strength. Inning after inning, he climbed the mound. And inning after inning he walked back to the bench without allowing a run. Surely by this point in the season the old man was weary. The wise old men of the press box, perplexed by the warrior, peered over their spectacles.

"You say this chap's been doing this all year?"

"Yep, been doin' it goin' on twenty-two years."

The game wore on.

Inning eight. Yonder stood Caldwell, hanging on by the hardest, earnest as ever. In the top of the eighth, he retired Houston's top three hitters on two strikeouts and an infield pop-up. He tramped off the mound like a dusty old coal miner at the end of the day. Still no score. I had shouted myself hoarse. I looked at Stewart with a schoolboy grin:

"Some game, ain't it, mister?"

In the bottom of the eighth, Barons fans began calling for a rally. Dean retired the first two batters. The next hitter was catcher Little Zack Taylor. Dean got two strikes on him. Then, just like that, Taylor singled sharply to rightfield. Caldwell was due up next—no pinch-hitter for Ray; he would bat for himself. Caldwell, a lefthanded batter, drew a bead on one of Dean's fastballs and slashed a grounder through the dust around second base, base hit. The base runner, Taylor, headed for third and made it—runners on first and third. Next up, second baseman Billy Bancroft, and the issue rested squarely on his shoulders. A din of cheering started as Bancroft walked to the plate.

Cheers. William Henry Bancroft had heard them often in his young life. Reared in Birmingham's East Lake section, he was one of the greatest athletes the city had ever produced, a high school and college star in football, baseball, and basketball. Old-timers said he was some pumpkin on the gridiron, and a finer boy you wouldn't meet in a Sabbath Day's journey.

To HIS MOTHER HE WAS William; to everyone else, Billy. Billy Bancroft was a quiet, courteous boy, born in Livingston, Alabama, the youngest of three children. His father was a doctor, and in 1905, when Billy was six months old, the family moved a hundred miles northeast to Birmingham and settled in East Lake. At Barrett Elementary School, Billy didn't particularly distinguish himself. "I just plugged along and passed; that's about all," he would say. In the ninth and tenth grades, Billy attended Paul Hayne High School, where again he was just another boy—an able, sound fellow and little more. In his junior year, 1922, Billy entered Woodlawn High School, and that's when the fireworks began. He played quarterback on the football team, catcher on the baseball team, and forward on the basketball team. Weighing 120 pounds, he was the fastest and best football player in the city. By his senior year, he had filled out to 145 pounds and was captain of the football team. Solidly built, fast as a streak, with the nerve of a tiger, Billy was gifted with the ingredients of a great athlete, a spectacle not to be forgotten—barking signals, punting, kicking field goals, running interference, side-stepping and twisting through enemy lines.

Newspaper columnist James Saxon Childers said that Billy Bancroft was responsible for his team's victories, game after game. The followers of the old yellow and white of Woodlawn High spoke of a game when Bancroft led his team, Moses-like, to victory. Entering the final minutes of play, the Colonels were sixteen points behind. From his forty-yard line Bancroft went around end for a sixty-yard touchdown run. He kicked the point-after. Moments later, he ran ninety yards for a touchdown. Again, he kicked point. Finally, from his own twenty-yard line, he went sixty yards before being stopped. Then, on the final play of the game, he stepped back and dropped kick the three points needed for victory.

After graduating from Woodlawn, Billy applied for a scholarship from *The Birmingham News* and won it easily. In 1924, he entered Howard College, where he became one of the finest all-around football players in Dixie. No man who had ever been at Howard was as beloved as Billy Bancroft, columnist Childers said. He was the idol of the campus, and justly so. Undergraduates and professors at Howard spoke his name as boast. They talked about his demon-like play in athletic contests, about his amazing successes and the successes of his teams. But most of all they talked about his sportsmanship.

"You see," said one professor, "out at Howard we were eager to win, naturally, and we were eager to see the school achieve the success in athletics that it has achieved in scholarship; but we didn't want that athletic success unless it came untarnished by unfair play or by quarreling and bickering with officials. And that was our greatest glory in Billy. Never during his really remarkable career did anyone question his absolute sportsmanship, never was there the slightest suspicion that he had taken unfair advantage, and never did he quarrel with officials or question their decision. So long as the play was on, Bancroft was the center of it; but the instant the whistle blew he faded out of the picture with that shy modesty which has characterized him from the first moment he stepped into the limelight."

In Bancroft's first year on the varsity, Howard played heavily favored Auburn University. The year was 1925. The Howard team fought from start to finish, but Auburn won, 7–6. Bancroft accounted for Howard's six points by kicking two field goals. The next year the two teams squared off at Rickwood Field. That afternoon Bancroft was a marked man. Auburn, with its relentless, smashing attack, was playing Bancroft as much as it was playing Howard College. People said they never saw a man take punishment like Bancroft took that day. Whenever he touched the ball, Auburn's heavy, rangy fighters hit him from every sector, four and five tacklers each. They hit clean, of course, but hit viciously. Whenever Bancroft ran interference, he was swept off his feet — two and three men taking him out. All afternoon, again and again, Auburn piled on him, hard. Everyone in the stands knew the boy must be finished, but after every play he was back on his feet, among the first trotting back to his position. Never once did he call time. Never once did he whimper. Howard led by 14–6 at intermission, but Auburn won the game. Before the game ended, Bancroft walked off the field,

At Birmingham's Woodlawn High in 1922 and '23, Billy Bancroft was the best football player in the city. Fast as a streak and with the nerve of a tiger, he played at 120 pounds as a junior, filling out to a solid 145 pounds as a senior.

No man who ever attended Howard College in Birmingham was as beloved as Bancroft, the captain of the football team and one of the finest backs in Dixie in 1927. One Howard professor said, "Never during his remarkable career did anyone question his absolute sportsmanship, never was there the slightest suspicion that he had taken unfair advantage, and never did he quarrel with officials or question their decision. . . . And that was our greatest glory in Billy."

groggy from the terrific punishment. After it was over, they picked him up, carried him home, and put him to bed. He stayed there three days.

THOUGH BILLY BANCROFT WAS A man's man on the gridiron, he was his mother's pal at home. Mrs. Bancroft, a widow, adored Billy, and he adored her. Mrs. Bancroft watched every Howard football game, not from the grandstand but from the players' bench on the sideline. Billy knew she was there, rooting for him and believing in him, and he played better for it.

"Since Billy was a little fellow, I've never attempted to order him to do anything. I've merely tried to direct him," Mrs. Bancroft said. "Even when he graduated from Woodlawn High School and was considering what college he would attend, I did not interfere. Several schools were after Billy, and I greatly wanted him to go to Howard, but had he decided upon Auburn or Alabama, I would have cheerfully let him go. When he finally chose Howard, I was lots more pleased than I've ever admitted to him."

Before his final football game at Howard she said to Billy: "I've been a pretty good sport, don't you think, because I've never run on the field during all these years. I'm looking forward to Saturday's game, but I'll be glad when the final whistle blows. It's a great nervous strain, especially in the Birmingham-Southern game because we're all so anxious to win."

Billy Bancroft's final game was against Birmingham-Southern in 1927, the day Birmingham's Legion Field was dedicated. The Howard-Southern game was the classic of the Birmingham gridiron, the city's private football feud. The rivalry stood knee-deep in greatness, and every year, the morning of the game, students staged a parade through downtown streets. Men and women who had little interest in football, who never went to any other game, looked forward to this one, the most colorful game of the year. And during the years of 1925–26–27, the games were dominated by one boy, Billy Bancroft. He was preeminent in giving Howard its splendid victories. Before the Birmingham-Southern game in 1927, Zipp Newman of *The Birmingham News* wrote an introduction for each player on the two teams:

"Captain Billy Bancroft . . . his flying feet have caused thrill after thrill for football followers during his four campaigns, and he has been mentioned at least twice for All-American honors. His heady generalship has been the talk of sportswriters all over the South, and his ball carrying is a feature of almost every game. He has run little with the ball this year, however, giving the other backs a chance to work . . . He may carry the ball halfway down the field to the shadow of the goal post and give a fellow back the honor of going through for a touchdown."

Into the story, now, comes someone who has been in it all the time. In high school, Billy met a girl named Claudie Mae Hoover, a girl everyone called "Sammie." All through high school, as he crashed into defenders and delivered base hits for Woodlawn, he did it for glory, for his mother—but most of all he did it for Sammie Hoover. About this time, Billy wrote a little piece called "My Ideal Girl." It was genuine, and it was an indication of his character. It went like this: "To build somewhere in the world the sheltering walls of a home, however humble and obscure, is part of my creed. Everyone knows that the happiness of a home depends entirely upon those who make it up. The home of my dreams would be ideal and, to be such, it would be necessary to have an ideal mother."

It continued: "For my ideal girl to be pretty or beautiful, I would much prefer the pretty one. It seems to mean more than just physical beauty. Over all the beauty in the world rules a good, pleasing disposition. I don't mean the weak, cling-vine type, but one who is capable, industrious, ambitious. This girl whom I call ideal is not the flapper type who has only the thought of a good time in her head. Although she is capable of dancing, swimming, playing bridge or being hostess at any sort of entertainment, or out-of-door girl if that occasion arises, or an indoor-girl if necessary. Then over this girl's life there is the consciousness of the one guiding hand, for the mightiest of all forces holding a home together is the reverence of God in the home."

In 1928, Billy married Sammie, the girl he had loved in high school and college. After graduation, he signed with the Barons for a thousand dollars. He didn't make the team, instead being sent to the low minors for two years. In the 1931 Dixie Series against Dizzy Dean and the Houston Buffaloes, Billy Bancroft was completing his second season with the Birmingham Barons. He was twenty-seven years old and looking forward to a long career in baseball, "but I want to coach, too," he said, "and they interfere with each other. I don't know what I'll do about it. Guess I'll wait and let things work themselves out."

Stewart smiled at me. "Billy Bancroft's as steady as an eight-day clock. You're about to witness something big, right here. You can bet your last copper cent on that."

Bancroft walked over to the bench for final instructions from Manager Clyde Milan. Like an old football coach, Milan said this:

"Listen, Billy, there are only three minutes to play, we're behind, and a dropkick will pull this ol' game out of the fire. Let's get that ball between the bars." Then, with two outs, he sent Bancroft to the plate. And Billy gave us a moment for history.

Bancroft gazed over the greensward, at the clutch of spectators standing against the fence in leftfield. He scooped up a handful of dirt and dusted his hands. Then he walked to the plate. He stepped into the batter's box with the bat on his shoulder. His eyes moved from spectators, to base runners, to pitcher. He wrapped his hands around the bat and took a practice swing. He tapped his bat on home plate and moved in close, crowding the plate, daring young Dizzy Dean. The infielders, who had gathered around the gawky frame of Dean, returned to their positions.

Diz rubbed the ball in his glove and looked hard at Bancroft. The pitcher held the ball in his right hand, looked at his catcher, checked the runners. He threw the ball in a blur. Bancroft swung and missed—*Strike one.* The crowd quieted, and they all eased back in their seats. Bancroft reminded himself: *Keep your eye on the ball. See the ball. Hit the ball.* He squared his shoulders and practice swung two, three times. He was not much to look at, this Bancroft—he took another practice swing—not much bigger than a pound of soap, a bantam-size contact hitter, a shade over five-foot-six, 145 pounds. Bancroft set his feet and stared out at Dizzy Dean.

The people stirred anxiously. "Look 'em over, Billy, look 'em over!" Fans sitting behind the grandstand pillars craned their necks so as not to miss a beat of action. "Wait on 'em, Billy!"

Dean went into his stretch, checked the runners on first and third, and threw again. Bancroft watched a fastball go by. The umpire threw back his head: "ST-R-I-I-I-KE TWO!"

The people rose to their feet, shoulder to shoulder, a sweltering mass. A vibrant rumble went through the park, rolling from grandstand to bleachers, hoarse and pleading. Everyone waited breathlessly, standing, shifting from foot to foot. Two strikes. Two outs. Two base runners. Scoreless game. Every eye in the park turned upon the pitcher. Charles Stewart shot a wink at me. The umpire glanced at his indicator: *No balls, two strikes.* The batter gritted his teeth and dug his spikes into the soil. The pitcher stepped to the mound and looked at the batter. The catcher waggled his fingers with a sign. Then young Diz made a mistake.

"He threw a curveball," Bancroft recalled years later. "It hung up there, or something. It wasn't a very good curveball. I guess he thought he was going to fool me, or maybe he thought he would waste it."

Diz threw, and the ball came in chest high. Bancroft stepped forward to meet the pitch. *BANG!* He caught it squarely on the nose. At the flash of the bat, the voice of the crowd became a rolling roar. "There it goes!" shouted the thousands. "He knocked the hide off the ball!" The ball arched high and far, beyond the leftfielder into the beautiful blue yonder—bounding into the hard-packed crowd in front of the fence. Base runner Little Zack Taylor scored. The fans fought for the ball, and Bancroft pulled into second base, heart pounding, face shining in triumph.

Billy Bancroft had swatted a double!

Billy Bancroft had swatted a double that scored a run!

Billy Bancroft had swatted a double that scored a run to put the Barons ahead!

There was a great carrying on throughout the park. Every person there felt he had made that hit and scored that run. People hugged one another and slapped each other with hats and newspapers. I jumped up and pounded Stewart on the back and shoulders.

Praise God! There's your run, Ray! Make it stick! And for one blissful moment, everyone relaxed.

Inning nine. Ray Caldwell walked to the mound for the final act of this epic. "He looks old, doesn't he?" said someone from the stands. Early on, with the hot, Alabama sun beating in his face, Caldwell was in trouble almost every inning. He looked a pathetic figure, this Caldwell—cheerless, dogged, each pitch slow and deliberate, an old man struggling in a young man's game.

The Houston ball club, young men in their gray, traveling uniforms, thought Caldwell would tire before the finish. Yes, he wobbled early on, but he seemed to draw strength as the game went along. Somewhere around the fourth inning, he acquired full command of his repertoire and began cutting the corners of the plate. He was pitching with his heart, his head, and his arm, and the batters were falling like ripe grain before the scythe. They couldn't hit him for shucks, and it was startling to watch. After the fourth inning, Caldwell gave up only one hit and walked not a single batter—never even went to a three-ball count. Only one batter reached third base in the game. Caldwell struck out three of the last six. It was then that the crowd began feeling sorry for the young men of the game, the Houston ball club in traveling gray.

Ninth inning, the sun sinking low. A gray haze sifted over the playing field. For a moment, the crowd hushed. Once again, Ray Caldwell shuffled out to the hill in the center of the diamond, his tread deliberate, people on the edges of their seats. Ray Caldwell, baseball in hand, considered his twenty-two years in the game—the good, the bad . . . the no-hitter, the lightning, the twenty wins, the World Series . . . the mistakes, the suspensions. The press box hummed with the tap-tap-tapping of typewriters.

Caldwell considered the stories about his drinking. *That's not true. I was sore about them. I was always ready to pitch.* Caldwell pounded the ball in his glove.

He considered the years in the bush leagues, hanging on for dear life. *Please, Lord, just one more year. Lemme pitch just one more year. One!*

The boys in the press box loosened their ties and began pecking out the story wrought by the forty-three-year-old:

> "The very crafty Caldwell, who a fortnight ago was married for the third time, had the Buffs breaking their backs on his tantalizing curves and deceptive knuckle ball . . . After he had a chance to look over the Houston hitters, the smart old fellow had them at his mercy. He gave up only one hit after the fourth round and fanned five in the last five stanzas."

> "Ray Caldwell was slow in getting started. The Buffs nicked his delivery for six hits in the first four innings and then Caldwell found the cunning of yore in his arm."

Caldwell tightened his cap down over his eyes, shading them from the afternoon sun. Facing the first batter, he lifted his weary right arm, and threw a slow one. The batter rolled a ground ball to first base, and a mighty cheer went down the line. *One out.*

The newspapermen, heads down, puffing cigarettes, pounded their battered typewriters:

> "Long before game time Rickwood's seating capacity, increased to more than 15,000 by temporary bleachers thrown up around the outfield, was completely sold out, with the gloomy prospect of not witnessing the ball game facing several thousand who had been unable to buy tickets . . . All these thousands came to worship at the shrine of Dizzy Dean, even though fondly hopeful at heart of a Birmingham victory—a victory they were afraid to expect against the glamorous young fireball artist, but they left Rickwood marveling at the apparently undying efficiency of the Grand Old Man of the Mound, who outdazzled Dean from start to finish."

Sweat and dirt streaked the pitcher's face and arms. Quickly, he had the next batter in a jam. Two strikes. Working carefully, ready now, the pitcher wound and fired. The batter swung and missed—*Strike three.* Another din of cheers. *Two outs.*

Houston Manager Joe Schultz called for a lefthanded pinch-hitter, Jimmy Sanders. Caldwell stepped from the mound. The umpire removed his mask, looked to the stands, and growled in a large voice: "Sanders now batting for Carey!"

Sanders scuffled to the plate, and Caldwell stepped to the hill. A moment of tense silence. Charles Stewart wiped his brow with a handkerchief. Soda vendors and peanut boys halted in their rounds. The staccato clacking of typewriters continued:

> "No pitcher could have shown a greater fighting heart. He was slow in getting started, but once he started trimming the corners of the plate, he was superb. And after all there is only one Ray Caldwell in baseball — THE MAN WHO CAME BACK."

Caldwell kicked the spikes of his dusty shoes against the rubber slab of the pitcher's box. He turned his back to Sanders. Forehead glistening with sweat, he wiped his whiskered face and turned to face Sanders. He threw the first pitch: swing and a miss. *Strike one.*

> "Billy Bancroft furnished the knockout blow, and he pulled the fielding masterpiece of the game. No finer play has ever been seen than Bancroft's stop of Sturdy's hopper over Caldwell's head with his bare hand. And what a throw the youngster made, while off balance, to Pete Susko, who took the ball with his gloved hand while stretched out six feet from the bag."

Caldwell lifted his long, beaked cap, now gray with dust. He wiped a hand across his forehead, and looked up at the high cloudless sky. Dog tired, he worked deliberately. He could hear the threshing of feet in the grandstand, as everyone now was standing. He looked at the batter, Sanders, through a haze of cigar and cigarette smoke that had settled over the field. He held the ball behind his back and felt for the seams. Once again he unleashed the pitch: swing and a miss. *Strike two.* The catcher dropped one knee in the dirt and fired the ball back. The batter clawed at the dirt with his cleats. He fouled off the next pitch, then another, each time the ball landing on the grandstand roof with a resounding *thump.* The pitcher looked in at his catcher.

> "With the game in his big right hand, Caldwell pitched like the Caldwell budding into major league fame long before Dean was born."

The dying shadows of a September day crept across the field. The crowd sensed the moment. The great throng rose to a pitch of excitement. The men in the press box looked up from their typewriters. The umpire adjusted his mask with his right hand and peered at the pitcher. The fielders crouched, hands on knees, awaiting the pitch. The pitcher pulled on the peak of his cap, glancing in every direction, at the defense of every fielder. The umpire stooped low behind the plate. The batter licked his lips nervously. Then silence. Silence.

As if in a dream, the pitcher leaned forward and peered at the catcher, read the sign, and took a deep breath. He wound, his hands rose and fell, and with all the guile remaining in his forty-three-year-old right arm, he threw the final pitch of the game.

Swing. The batter struck the ball: a ground ball to first. Cheers. The earth seemed to rock. The first baseman scooped up the ball and ran to the bag. *Out! Game over!* Everyone was frantic, hysterical. From the grandstand, shouts of "Ray! Ray!" rang out. Spectators streamed the field, lauding his name, surging in a human tide. "Yonder he is! There's Ray!"

Every player, it seemed, every spectator wanted Ray, wanted to call his name, to shake his hand. The players hoisted him to their shoulders; cheered for him, and for each other, as did the fans.

> "When you stop to consider that Ray Caldwell struck out three of the last six men to face him and that he retired a half dozen of the last six men to face him in order, winning one of the greatest victories of his long career by a count of 1–0, you will no longer wonder that the frenzied populace went collegiate for a few moments and picked the veteran up, placed him on its collective shoulders and carried him to the dugout."

Rise up on your hind feet and inform the whole cock-eyed world: The old man had faced a kid pitcher young enough to be his son; had given the Buffaloes but seven hits; had struck out five and walked nobody; had pitched a 1–0 shutout in an hour, forty-five minutes. Somewhere in the world there may be a better pitcher than Caldwell. Somewhere, maybe. But not this day.

> "Uncle Ray Caldwell, granddaddy that he is, showed Dizzy Dean a few things about this business of pitching baseball Wednesday afternoon, beating the sensational Houston hurler in the opening game of the Dixie Series. No finer pitching efforts have ever been uncorked on the same day in this historic post-season clash between the Southern Association and Texas League champions."

And Dizzy Dean? He lived up to his billing, using sweeping curves and changeups more often than his fastball. He allowed only five hits but did not strike out a single Birmingham batter.

"Congratulations, Dizzy Dean! You are much better than anyone has ever claimed you were. You showed them you could use your head as well as your good right arm. And you showed all those people that you could take a bitter defeat."

Newspaper reporters rushed from the press box through the grandstand. Cheers rang out, and people milled about the aisles. Men and women shed shameless tears. No one wanted to go home.

"Why are they crying?" I wanted to know.

"The old man, Walter. It's for the old man. Someday you'll understand."

People clustered about the clubhouses beneath the grandstand. Outside the park, automobile horns honked. Charles Stewart laughed: "By jingoes, it's been some day. Can't nobody say there ain't some excitement in li'l ol' Birmingham now!"

Outside the Barons clubhouse, Stewart and I were in the middle of a swirling, shoving crush of men and women, lighting cigarettes for each other, all laughing, yipping, and backslapping. Behind the clubhouse door, the Barons were celebrating, happy as catfish in a muddy river. Stewart spotted a familiar face:

"There's my friend, Henry Vance, the newspaperman. Oh-ho, Hy, are you going inside?"

"Yes, I am!" the reporter hollered. "Come on. I'll get you in."

"That, by God, was a really good game! Shame somebody had to lose. Ray showing his battle spirit—by golly, his whiskered old face. Don't it make you glad you were here? Look, I'm trembling like a leaf, goose flesh all over me."

"If you can write this story without a tear in your eye, you're a better man than I," Henry Vance said.

"Agreed," said Stewart. "You should write that in the lead of your story."

Stewart spoke to me under the noise. "See, even a hard-boiled old newspaperman can be sensitive." Then he looked at Vance. "What a crowd, Hy! How many were here?"

"Twenty thousand and seventy-four; that's 2-0-0-7-4. And two thousand more turned away at the gate. You count those people on railroad cars and elsewhere outside the park, I'd say twenty-five thousand people were at Rickwood Field today."

"Oh-ho, I believe it. Who says we're in a depression? All these people. And for a weekday game. Imagine if it'd been a Saturday."

"Yeah, they'd have turned away *ten thousand*," the reporter smirked.

The home clubhouse at Rickwood Field steamed with heat and noise and the smell of soap and sweat. Smiling ball players stripped off their uniforms.

Newspapermen, pads and pencils poised, crowded around the Barons manager, hanging on every word. Above the shouts, Clyde Milan could barely be heard: "That Dean is really great. His fastball was everything I heard it was. And he pitched plenty smart. I didn't expect him to have such an assortment of stuff. His change of pace was great. He doesn't belong down here with us fellows."

Then Milan called for Caldwell. "Ray! Come over here and give the boys a statement."

Caldwell, stripped to the waist, walked to the center of the noisy, steamy room. "Ray, what'd you think of Dizzy Dean?" a reporter asked eagerly.

In twenty-two years of professional baseball, Ray Caldwell had seen it all. He could afford to be modest. "Dizzy Dean is a great pitcher. I got the breaks, and he didn't. The score could very easily have been the other way." That's all Ray said.

Stewart looked at Vance. "Hy, have you been in the other clubhouse?"

"Yes, their players were gracious. They said Ray deserved to win."

"Did they now?"

"They couldn't believe Diz didn't strike out a single batter. First time that's ever happened."

"What did Diz say?"

Vance looked at his notes. "Let me see . . . where is it? Here it is. He said, 'Boys, that was the greatest game I ever pitched. I can't explain it, but I'm telling you my fastball vanished. I had no fastball. . . . Without my fastball working in anything like normal fashion, I considered myself lucky to hold the Barons to five hits and one score. If I had been at top form with my fast one, it would have been just too bad for the Barons.'"

"Oh-ho," Stewart laughed.

"Wait," the reporter said, "that's not all. Diz said, 'My next venture against them should be as easy as rolling an empty wheelbarrow.'"

"H'm! We'll see about that, won't we?" Stewart said, laughing. "What a day!"

"What a night it'll be," the reporter answered. "I imagine Ray'll be out bending an elbow tonight."

"That he will."

Outside the park, Houston's ball players waited for taxicabs back to the hotel. The street was crowded with creeping, honking automobiles. A good-natured crowd gathered 'round Dizzy Dean, razzing and ragging him. Diz smiled and bantered back. With traffic blocked in front of Rickwood Field, the police had to rescue Diz.

"Ya'll come over to the hotel, and we'll continue the conversation there!" he hollered to the fans.

The end of a perfect day.

CHAPTER 22

THE DIXIE SERIES CONTINUES

THE NEXT DAY, THURSDAY, WAS much like the first: A pitiless sun beat down, batters didn't hit, and a pitcher threw a shutout. Houston won this one, however, 3–0. The Barons had but four hits, of which pitcher Jimmy Walkup had three. The Barons and Buffaloes continually swung at first and second pitches, not making the pitchers work. Both teams played with haste for good reason: It was even hotter than the day before—ninety-eight degrees. The game was over in an hour and twenty-one minutes.

That night the Barons and their backers left for Houston on an L&N and Missouri Pacific special. On board was the forty-five piece Birmingham Police Band. Due south lay the route, past fields where goldenrod bloomed, to Montgomery for a brief stop, then southwest under a cream-white moon. Small towns flashed by in the night—Greenville, Georgiana, Flomaton; a stop in Mobile, then west along the coast—Pascagoula, Biloxi, and Gulfport. Early Friday morning, September 18, the Baseball Special whistled into New Orleans and lingered through a two-hour delay. Once again, the mighty locomotive hurtled westward with the strength of ten thousand horses, thick, black smoke curling from its engine.

What a glorious feeling, the pulsing of the great steam engine. Shining rails—ribbons of steel—stretched to the horizon. The engineer, monstrous goggles over his eyes, pushed the throttle with his great gloved hand, and the steel monster climbed to a speed of seventy-four miles an hour on the best of the roadbed, the telegraph poles looking like a picket fence. Inside the train, the heat was intense. Card games—bridge and rummy—occupied the baseball party as the Special rolled over the marshlands of Louisiana and the plains of Texas, onward to Houston. After a twenty-one hour journey, the train hailed its arrival with a clanging of bells and a hiss of steam. The brakeman shouted: "All out for Ho-u-u-s-ton!"

It was Friday afternoon, and a large crowd jostled about the railway station. The Birmingham Police Band in its navy blues disembarked, drums rattling, horns wailing. A crowd of fifty former Birmingham citizens greeted Caldwell, Bancroft, and the rest with well wishes. After hearty handshakes, the Barons trickled through the depot gate to the sidewalk. The Police Band stormed the Rice Hotel with the team. Over the next three days, the band gave a spirited concert at a wrestling match, conducted recitals over two radio stations, performed a musical at a church, and played at all three games in Houston.

Game Three of the Dixie Series was on Saturday night. A light rain fell most of the day, breaking an intense heat wave in Texas, but back in Birmingham, the temperature was 102 degrees. Game Three featured a Texas-size version of Ray Caldwell: forty-two-year-old George Washington Payne, Houston's starting pitcher. Payne was in his eighteenth minor league season, with his fourteenth different ball club, but his arm still contained mileage. He would pitch eight more seasons, until he was fifty-one, appear in nine hundred career games, and earn 348 victories. Seated next to the Barons dugout, the Police Band whooped up the crowd. George Payne pitched a masterpiece, throwing curveballs, screwballs, and an occasional head-high fastball to loosen up hitters. He allowed only one hit — a single to Billy Bancroft on the third pitch of the game — and beat Barons pitcher, Bob Hasty, 1–0. Houston scored the only run of the game in the sixth inning when Joe Medwick doubled and Homer Peel singled him in. The game was played in an hour and a half.

Sunday's Game Four again matched Caldwell and Dean. Clyde Milan had planned to give Caldwell another day of rest, but Caldwell pleaded to pitch. Before the game, the brass-buttoned Police Band stepped lively to the Houston dugout and played "The Eyes of Texas Are Upon You" to a roaring crowd. Next, the blue coats paraded to the Birmingham dugout and burst forth "Dixie" to another ovation. Caldwell pitched masterfully but received little support from his teammates. Houston made seven hits, but four were infield taps that could have been handled by Birmingham fielders, and Dean won, 2–0. After the final inning, Caldwell walked from the diamond to thunderous applause from the Houston crowd, head held high. In two appearances in the Series, he had allowed just one earned run. The Series had turned into a pitching carnival, with shutouts in each of the first four games. The Barons were in a woeful batting slump — thirteen hits in four games. With the Barons losing Games Two, Three, and Four, the Series count stood at three victories for Houston, one for Birmingham. The Barons were one loss from elimination.

BEFORE GAME FIVE, MONDAY, SEPTEMBER 21, Manager Clyde Milan reminded the team, "We haven't lost four games in a row all year." Later that evening, a burly righthander warmed up for the Barons. "Say, who is this Touchstone the Barons are going to start against us?" asked Houston fans near the press box.

"Clay Touchstone, a curveball pitcher," replied a Birmingham reporter. "He can tie righthanded batters in knots with his crossfire, and his curveball breaks like the surf in an angry sea."

"Well, he won't last long against us tonight," declared the fans.

The Barons jumped to a lead with a run in the first inning—their first run in twenty-eight innings. They scored two more in the fourth when Art Weis, Pete Susko, and Charley Gooch rapped out sharp blows in succession. Meanwhile, pitcher Clay Touchstone put down the first ten Houston batters he faced, with only two balls hit to the outfield. Houston fans demanded to know more about this pitcher, Touchstone.

"Twenty-eight years old and already he's won ninety-six minor league games," the reporter told them. "Purchased by the Barons from Newark of the International League on the recommendation of New York Yankee scouts."

The fans—eyes large—nodded their heads. Houston hitters couldn't touch Touchstone in the critical moments of the game. In the final five innings, seven Houston batters reached base yet only one runner scored. Houston's only run came in the sixth on a single, two infield outs, and an infield hit. Touchstone won the game, 3–1. The Barons victory put a new complexion on the Series. Though they still trailed in the Series, the difference now was one game—three games to two. Back to Birmingham they went. The two clubs rode the same train, Houston's two cars in front of the Barons string of cars. The train pulled into Birmingham Tuesday night, with Game Six scheduled the next day. It felt good to be home, to see what the morrow might bring.

Wednesday morning the sun cast a blazing, steaming sheet upon the city, and Birmingham steeled itself for another scorcher. At nine in the morning the temperature was eighty-seven degrees—by game time, ninety-nine. Though the Barons trailed the Series three games to two, the fan in the street believed if the Barons continued hitting as in Game Five, they would win Game Six and force a seventh game. The first five games of the Series had been low-scoring. Every pitcher but one had thrown a complete game. Houston's starting pitcher for Game Six, George Washington Payne, had pitched a one-hitter against the Barons four days earlier. But, for Game Six, Manager Clyde Milan had a buckeye in his pocket.

Before Game Five in Houston, Milan had left his hotel room to go to the ball park when he remembered: The night before, a fan hoping to pull the Barons out of their hitting slump had given Milan a nut from a buckeye tree. Folk tradition has it that a buckeye in one's pocket brings good luck. Milan put the buckeye in his pocket.

"I thought of the buckeye that was in my street clothes," Milan said. "I rushed back to the room and got the buckeye and we won Game Five. I left it in my road uniform when we came back to Rickwood. I thought of it again just as Billy Bancroft was coming to the plate in Game Six. I stopped him and told him not to go to bat until I came out of the clubhouse."

Milan held up the start of Game Six until he could retrieve the buckeye and put it in the pants pocket of his home uniform. Maybe the buckeye would bring the Barons luck. With it, they had won Game Five in Houston.

In the first five games of the Series, the Barons had scored a total of four runs. Then in Game Six, with the buckeye again in Milan's pocket, the Barons roused their slumbering bats. Trailing 3–2 in the fourth inning, they hammered pitcher George Washington Payne as if he were a carpet tack, hitting safely seven consecutive times for six runs. They finished the game with twenty-three hits and won the game, 14–10. Together, the two teams combined for forty-one hits. Houston Manager Joe Schultz used five pitchers. Birmingham's Art Weis had five hits in five at-bats, including two doubles and a home run. Billy Bancroft drove in four runs. The three ball games at Rickwood had drawn forty thousand people, and now the Series was tied at three games apiece. The teams headed back to Texas for the deciding seventh game.

In 1931, as this Dixie Series was being contested, the economies of the Western world were in decline. The Roaring Twenties had been a decade of wealth and excess, but lifestyles had changed for the better. People had more money than ever before, and spent it: on automobiles, radios, appliances, entertainment, and sporting events. Ordinary Americans had speculated in the stock market, borrowing more and more money to invest in higher and higher share prices. Real estate values peaked in 1925. By the summer of 1929, sales of luxury goods dropped. In October, the stock market crashed, the symbolic onset of the Great Depression. The next few years were hard for Americans. In 1930, banks began failing, and people lost their money. By 1933, the trough of the Depression, one-quarter of the work force was idle. People stopped spending money, deepening the crisis.

On the day the Barons and Buffaloes rode the rails to Houston for Game Seven, the New York Stock Exchange dropped to its lowest point in six years.

The market eventually would lose ninety percent of its value. The Depression and its aftermath lingered until 1941, when the United States began mobilizing for World War II. The stock market did not fully recover its losses until 1954.

The Barons and Buffaloes arrived in Houston, Thursday night, September 24. On the platform of the Missouri Pacific station, Dizzy Dean told the Houston fans to go home and sleep well. "Leave it to the great Dizzy Friday night!"

In his two appearances in the Series, Dean had pitched during daylight hours. His normal pitching motion was to throw from over the top, using mostly curveballs and slow pitches. Now for Game Seven, a night game, he planned to use a sidearm delivery and lots of fastballs.

"I'm going to pump 'em in so fast they can't see 'em, and there will be plenty of moaning and striking out." As for his sidearm delivery, he said, "I try to come down just as close to the green turf as possible to give the batter less time to follow the ball, as it must come out of the shadow before he can get ready to swing. The Barons didn't see me at my best in the daytime, no fooling. Nighttime is my time in the box."

"BULL CONNOR'S ON!" MY MOTHER called.

The Plantersville hog caller, I told myself. Yeah, the hog caller. "I'm coming!"

The rays of a setting sun were falling upon Birmingham. Boys were shooting marbles under street lights; girls were playing jacks in alleyways: games like Ladies over the Fence, Putting Horses in the Stables, and Peas in the Pot. It was Friday, no school tomorrow. I lived in a comfortable home on Seventh Avenue West—a house of red brick, one story, with a large yard in which a boy could play. When my mother called me in for the game, I ran to the back of the house, swung open the garage door, stomped up the basement steps, and ran through the kitchen, pausing to rub the head of my cat, Smarty. I slumped lazily into a big chair in the den. Then I noticed:

"Ma! You got a new radio!"

"Your friend, Mr. Stewart, brought it. You were outside, playing. It took two men to bring it in the front door. They hooked it up to an aerial. The reception is quite good. By the way, your father starts work Monday for Mr. Stewart, maybe Ray Caldwell, too."

I sat down on the floor beside the new Philco. The radio in its wooden cabinet was the size of a chest of drawers. "Ma, this must a' cost a lot."

"Your Mr. Stewart is a very nice man."

The room was dark, and the lighted dial of the radio cast a warm, cozy glow on the wall. I lay my head on the baseball mitt signed by Ray Caldwell and closed my eyes.

Eugene (Bull) Connor broadcast Birmingham Barons games on the radio from 1930–1937. Connor and other radio announcers of the day re-created games from telegraph reports while sitting in a radio studio. Only the road games were broadcast.

This is Bull Connor behind the mike, coming to you from the studio of WKBC Radio in the Birmingham Athletic Club at the corner of Third Avenue and Twenty-third Street. I'll be calling the game for you tonight—the Birmingham Barons and the Houston Buffaloes from Houston, Texas. This game is for all the marbles, the championship of the 1931 Dixie Series. Stay with us—I'll be right back.

"So, Bull," said a man visiting the WKBC Radio studio, "tell me about yourself."

"Ain't nothin' to tell," Bull stated flatly.

Eugene (Bull) Connor was relaxing in the studio—his coat off, his tie loosened, pushed far down his neck, the top buttons of his shirt unfastened. He leaned back in his chair and propped his feet on the desk. The visitor continued:

"You're the most popular radio announcer in the South. You're quite an act. You've been announcing the Barons games on the radio for two years now. People who don't care a thing about baseball listen to the games because of you. They love the way you say: 'He-e-'s O-o-u-u-t-t!'"

"I'm just a good old country boy," Bull drawled.

"You mean you really are from the country—that isn't just a lot of talk?"

"Who me?" He looked puzzled. "You mean you can't tell I'm from the country? Why, man, I'm from so far back in the country that I get homesick every time I see a mule."

Theophilus Eugene Connor was indeed from the country. He was born in 1897 in Selma, Alabama, where his father worked as a railroad dispatcher. When Eugene was eight, the family moved to Atlanta. Shortly after, his mother died of pneumonia, four months after giving birth to her fifth son. Eugene went to live with an uncle in North Birmingham.

"In North Birmingham I started to school," he reminisced. "Yeah, believe it or not, I been to school; though to hear me talk, you'd never believe it."

Soon, Eugene moved to Plantersville, near Selma, to live with an aunt. There, he learned about farming and how to follow an old gray mule up one furrow and down the next.

"In Plantersville I got a whole lot better acquainted with a hoe handle than I did with books; I learned all about chopping cotton, even if I didn't find out the difference between a participle and an infinitive. In Plantersville, too, was when I went crazy about baseball. I was going to the Dallas County High School whenever I could get away from the farm, and I played second base on the high school ball team."

Bull laughed. "I suppose one reason I like little Shine Cortazzo so much is that I know how he, a little man, feels playing baseball. Even now I'm not much bigger than Shine, and in those days I was really small. I know how it feels to play against men so much bigger than me. A lot happened to me in Plantersville; I mean, a whole lot, because it was in Plantersville that I met my wife. I married her there—after we'd been going together nine years."

Beara Levens, the daughter of a timber company vice president, married Bull in 1920. "I tell her all the time that if she didn't know any better than to marry me after going with me for nine years, then she deserves everything she's getting today."

Eugene did not complete high school. By the time he married, he'd begun working as a railroad telegrapher, and when a job opened in New Orleans, he took it. Railroad people moved around a lot, and the New Orleans position was the first of many jobs and many cities for Eugene and Beara during their first year of marriage.

"We been married eleven years," Bull told his studio guest, "and now we have a little three-year-old daughter, Jean, and I'm tellin' you that she's the greatest kid that ever lived. Next year I'm goin' to let her broadcast baseball. I mean it. Already she can call 'em out as good as I can, and I figger I might as well get her started young."

"Tell me, Bull," the visitor asked, "how did you get into broadcasting?"

"Well, you see, my father being a dispatcher, I naturally hung around telegraph offices, and naturally I picked up telegraph. After I got big enough to start out on my own, I left Plantersville and began to travel around the country. I went from coast to coast and from the Gulf to Canada, working as an operator. I always was that way, always wanted to be roaming about. Why, my wife and I lived in seven different states during the first year we were married."

Not long after they were married, the Connors were living in Dallas, Texas. Bull regularly attended the local team's baseball matinees, where an announcer called the games from the telegraph wire.

"The first game I ever called was just luck," Bull admitted. "I loved baseball, and so every afternoon I used to go to the matinee. One day I was sitting there when the man came out and asked if there was an operator in the audience. I hung back—you know, modest like, that's Bull all the time—but when didn't nobody else go up, then I did and told him I was an operator. He said he was sick and couldn't stand up and would I call the game. I told him I couldn't do that, but he insisted and said he'd give me five dollars. Well, five dollars was a lot of money in them days, so I said I'd do it—least I'd try.

"Well, the man who had been calling the game was doing it from a written account given him by the operator—you know, the operator would receive the message, type it out, tear out the piece of paper and give it to the announcer, who would then call it. I said I couldn't do all that; I said I'd call direct from the ticker; I'd read the message as it came in and then call it direct. So I went out on the stage, scared to death, and held the ticker to my ear and called the game. I'm still modest, but I'm tellin' you I made a big hit. The next day when the other man came out to call the game, the fans yelled for me. They kept on yelling until the other man asked me to come on up and work again. That day he gave me ten dollars. And after that he hired me regular. That was the first baseball calling I ever did. Some time afterward I drifted back to Birmingham and opened up a baseball matinee of my own."

That would have been around 1922 when Bull was twenty-five. He charged customers thirty-five cents to attend his matinees but was barely making ends meet financially. Back then, it was illegal to present any form of entertainment on Sundays, not just in Birmingham but in many cities across the country. No baseball games, no movies. Most people felt Sundays were for the Lord and little else, not for enterprises interested in a profit. Though Sunday baseball games were not allowed in Birmingham, some cities of the Southern Association did allow games on the Sabbath, so the Barons traveled to another city every Sunday to play. People worked at their jobs six days a week, Sunday being their day of leisure. Because there was a ready clientele looking for entertainment on Sunday afternoons, a friend suggested that Bull hold baseball matinees on Sundays when the Barons played on the road.

"I knew I couldn't do that," Bull said. "It was against the law. Then I thought of the fact that it *wasn't* against the law for me to entertain all my friends by calling the game for them; it *wasn't* against the law if they wanted to drop a free will offering in the box for ol' Bull. So that's the way I worked it, and everybody dropped in their thirty-five cents, and I was making plenty of money. Then I got a job working on the telepic—the machine that sends pictures by telegraphy—over at *The News*. They had just installed the equipment, and they hired me to operate it. I didn't know much about it, nor did anyone else, for the thing was new, so they sent me to Chicago to study. When I came back I ran the telepic machine for a while, and, if I do say it, there are some letters at *The News* right now from newspapers all over the country saying that the pictures we sent out were better than any others sent from this part of the country. The reason was that I worked carefully and did the best I could."

Beginning in 1926 and continuing through 1928, Bull operated his matinees in a room at 206½ North Twentieth Street. "Eugene Connor will conduct baseball matinees with full detail play-by-play," stated *The Birmingham News* in May of 1926. In 1929, he moved the operation to the Club Florentine on Twenty-first Street. People anxious for the score of a game either attended a matinee or received the news by word of mouth. They also could receive baseball scores by telegraph in approximately a dozen venues in the city or wait until the newspapers published their late afternoon editions. Those who owned radios could catch final scores on a scoreboard show at nine o'clock.

During this period, Bull Connor also worked at radio stations in Birmingham, taking sports results from the telegraph wire and handing them to the announcers. There were three stations in Birmingham in the late 1920s: WBRC, WAPI, and WKBC.

"My job was to take the details of different sporting events. I'd sit at the typewriter and take down the message coming in over the wire, write it out, and give it to the announcer to call. And then came my big chance." It occurred on a Sunday afternoon in late June 1930 when the Barons were playing a game in New Orleans. Bull Connor was about to call his first game on radio.

"I went to work at the studio of WKBC. I got my little table and my typewriter all ready. I put my paper there for me to work with. I lighted up my cigarette and was all ready to go, when in came [studio manager] Dud Connolly, and Dud asked me how I was. Right away I got suspicious because ordinarily an operator don't get asked how he is. But I told him I was alright, then I waited.

"Then he told me, 'Bull,' he said, 'you're gonna call this game this afternoon.'

"'Oh, no, I ain't,' I said, and lighted another cigarette. 'I got a wife and baby, and I don't want to get killed.'

"'But you know baseball better than anybody around here, Bull, and you can call it alright.' I told Dud that nobody would understand my language, and I wasn't gonna get up there and talk like a country man and have people laugh at me. Dud told me I was all wrong, that what everybody wanted was to hear about the baseball game, not get a lesson in grammar. That sounded reasonable to me, and I told Dud I'd try, provided he didn't announce my name.

"And that's how I started. When I started to call the game, I was scared to death. Every time I'd try to say anything I'd choke up and I expected any minute for that mike to swing out and sock me on the chin. After a few innings had passed, the telephone began to ring and we began to get dispatches. People began to kid me, and I kidded back with them and things got hotter and hotter until by the end of the game I was really enjoying myself. The next Sunday I went on the air again and though I was shaky at first, I soon felt alright, and ever since then I haven't worried."

Because the telegraph ticker was noisy, Bull had to scream to be heard, and his raspy voice became the talk of the town. He learned to "shoot the bull," and steadily he became more popular.

"Well, I ain't saying I haven't made a lot of friends, because I have. Lots of people send me dispatches and write me letters, and I know that some of them like the way the game comes to them. The reason is that I read the details direct from the wire. So many other announcers have to wait for the operator to get the message, write it out, and hand it to them before they broadcast it. I save a lot of time by reading the play directly from the ticker. I figure that I get the play on the air within five seconds after it is over. Suppose, for instance, a man grounds out. The detail man at the park begins his message with the word 'out.' Well, there isn't any other word in the detail that begins with 'o.' The minute I hear that letter, I announce 'OUUUUUUUUT.' Then the details of how he went out come in and I announce them. That's the reason people like my calling—I get on the air just a fraction quicker than some of the other announcers."

"What sport had you rather broadcast, Bull?" the visitor asked.

"Baseball. That's my favorite game, and I'd rather call it, though I never miss a prize fight and I love to call them, and football is another game I enjoy and enjoy calling. I have called basketball, but it's almost too fast, and I don't like to do it. When I was in New Orleans not long ago I broadcast the [horse] races. I've tried most of the sports, though I still stay by my old favorite and prefer baseball."

"Say, Bull, do you expect to stay in Birmingham next year and the year after that, or do you want to go to bigger cities and broadcast in the big leagues, perhaps?"

"I don't much care. Birmingham is plenty good for me. I'm one of these fellows who takes what comes when it gets there and never asks many questions. I hope I'm still here in Birmingham next spring. If the fans want me, and if I can hold my job, I plan to stay here."

CHAPTER 23
THE DIXIE SERIES CONCLUDES

"*I THINK BULL CONNOR IS* simply marvelous," my mother said. "The way he says 'OUUUUUUUUUT!' is just a scream!"

I looked up from beneath the four-legged Philco radio. "Hey, Ma, listen to me doing Bull: 'Now you pitchin', Candy Kid! Th'ow that onion, boy, th'ow it!'"

"Now you goin', chilluns, now you goin'!" my mother cried.

"The ball's up against the rightfield wall for one-two-three bags!" I screamed. "Billy Bancroft sittin' on the bench, fannin' himself with his cap."

My father stuck his head in the door. "Hey, what's all the commotion?"

"Bull's on, Pop."

The father smiled at the boy with the baseball mitt on his hand. "That was my mitt when I was a boy," he said to himself. "And before that, my father's. Not much left of the old glove, all battered and beaten—surprises me Walter even wants it, but I'm honored he does. I remember the day Rickwood opened—yes, I do, I do. I was just a boy, a young boy—liked baseball a lot, just like Walter—a hot day, real hot—lots of people, thousands on the field watching—Coveleski pitched, got in a fight. I went to the game with my father, went to all the games with my father—took that old glove with me, took it everywhere."

My father grew up and got married. Not long after the war, I came along. My father worked six days a week, just like everyone else. No time for baseball anymore. No money. Times were hard. "One of these days I'll go back," my father promised. "If only I can get caught up and see my way clear."

I looked at my mother. "That makes Birmingham, one, Memphis, *goose egg*." They all shared a laugh.

"And that makes my friend, Ruby, furious," said my mother. "Ruby says radio is being run into the ground. Wherever she goes, it's running full tilt, too loud and too much static, people always turning the dial, 'fishing' for something. Ruby lives in an apartment and she'll tell you she can't get away from the radio—radios beneath us, radios above us, on either side of us, and across the street, sometimes two or three on the same station, sometimes each one on a different station. Radios turned on far into the night and long before she's ready to get up in the morning.

"That's Ruby for you, always complaining. 'Why do they have night baseball?' she'll say. 'And why do they have that Bull Connor calling the game? A terrible fellow. His grammar is simply horrid,' she says.

"I'll confess," said my mother, "I didn't like him at first—his bellowing the outs, his rooting for the home team, his coaching from the radio studio, inventing most of the action. But that's changed. I declare, I absolutely love him now and the way he calls 'em: He-e-'s O-o-u-u-t-t! I absolutely love it. He's so natural, so honest and sincere, I feel as if I know him. And he's endeared himself to the people across the state. Why, they even stop by the studio with candy, cakes, cigars, bananas, and chicken dinners."

Now you know what we thought of Eugene (Bull) Connor before the police dogs and the firehoses. Birmingham loved Bull; he entertained us. Years later, the Chicago Cubs had a broadcaster—maybe you remember Harry Caray. Every game, seventh inning, he sang over the loudspeaker, "Take Me Out to the Ball Game." They would show him singing on television, the crowd smiling and enjoying it. If I was feeling poorly, watching Harry Caray sing that song during the seventh inning stretch brightened my day. That's kinda the way we were with Bull on the radio. He made us feel good about ourselves.

> Bull Connor back with ya, ball fans, for the seventh game of the Dixie Series. It's been a hot and sultry day in Houston, Texas, ideal weather for makin' hay. Dizzy Dean's gonna hurl tonight for the Houston club. Young Dean is a big, gangling, grinning country boy, noisier'n a two-dollar radio. It's been a fine Series for Diz. As you recall, he lost Game One to Ray Caldwell before that whopper of a crowd at Rickwood Field, but Diz pitched a gem that day. Some would say Diz outpitched Ray. Then in Game Four, Mr. Dean got revenge. He beat Ray, the score being Houston two, Birmingham, goose egg.

Every now and then crackles of static punctuated the call of the game. These were, after all, the early days of radio. The first radio broadcast in the country occurred in 1920. Two years later more than two hundred licensed stations were on the air. Soon, families would gather 'round the radio for their nightly entertainment. In the early years, radio stations broadcast for only a few hours each evening. There were no rules, no regulations. Radio reception was unreliable—sometimes the signal faded; sometimes tuning in was difficult, as other stations crowded the dial. The first licensed radio station in Alabama was WSY, broadcasting from a small studio on Powell Avenue in Birmingham. Originally, the station had been established by the Alabama Power Company to communicate with line crews in isolated areas. As radio gained favor, the equipment was converted to transmit entertainment programs and went on the air in April 1922. The station's range was around two thousand miles.

"This is WSY, broadcasting services from the Heart of Dixie," was familiar in the early 1920s to listeners as far away as Canada and Cuba and to ships at sea. Birmingham residents—the few who owned radios—heard programs from Chicago, Pittsburgh, Minnesota, New Hampshire, Texas, Oklahoma, Florida. A typical program on WSY included baseball results from the major leagues and Southern Association, vocal and piano solos, comedy by local artists, and stock market and commodity quotations. Farmers in remote areas learned the value in the Birmingham market of their fruits, livestock, beef, hides, tallow, and poultry. Programs sometimes were ad-libbed, with droppers-in furnishing talent. One evening in 1922, the entertainment included two cages of canaries singing their hearts out. A woman in Columbiana, Alabama, said:

"Our little town sits up every night to hear the music, lectures, and what-not sent out by the broadcasting station of Alabama Power. Some bright boys have made their own receiving sets, and sitting around and sharing the messages from Birmingham has become a regular family evening's entertainment. The young people like to get the baseball returns, and all the merchants want to hear what the price of cotton is. We older people take a great interest in the short sermons of the Birmingham pastors. I have seen many inventions come during my long lifetime, but none seems to be more capable of carrying messages of good cheer and enlightenment to places where most needed."

Bull Connor, too, belonged to the early days of radio.

Back with you, fans. Bull Connor here. On the hill tonight for the Barons will be the man with dynamite in his long, right arm — hard-throwin' Bob Hasty. Bob's a big ol' farm boy out of Cherokee County, Georgia. He'll be looking to pin back the ears of the Buffaloes. You remember, he lost a heartbreaker, 1–0, to George Washington Payne in Game Three. Bob's catcher tonight will be the Dutchman, Bill Eisemann. Bill was a basketball player at Syracuse University a few years back. After college, he signed a baseball contract with the New York Yankees. Before coming to the Barons, he played with Hartford and Albany in the Eastern League, then the Yankees sent him here last year. The Barons've never had two finer gentlemen than Bill Eisemann and Bob Hasty. Quiet, easy-going, and conscientious, those two boys are.

I read in the paper where Dizzy Dean told the Houston fans to go home and sleep well; he was planning on winning this final tilt. That bird, Dizzy Dean, is a confident fellow, certainly. What d'you folks at home think of Dizzy Dean? Come on down to the studio here on Twenty-third Street North and tell me. A few Barons fans are already here. I see 'em — they're shakin' their heads and givin' Diz the razzberries. I don't think they care very much for Mr. Dean, d'you?

Alright, here's what's happened so far in the Series: Birmingham, behind Ray Caldwell, won Game One, 1–0. Houston came back and won the next 'un, 3–0. Then we went to Houston, where the Buffs won two more to lead the Series, three games to one. It looked like a Buffalo stampede. Birmingham was about to be eliminated, sure as you're born. But the Barons came back and won the fifth game behind the hurling of Clay Touchstone. Our boys were still behind in the Series, three games to two, when the teams went back to Rickwood for the sixth game. The Barons fired both barrels and won Game Six, 14–10, to tie up the Series. Now we're back in Houston — each club has won three games — and as I said, the winner of tonight's game will be the Dixie Series champions.

I've got the dope right here on Ray Caldwell . . .

I jumped off the floor, eager to hear what Bull would say about Ray.

I've been told that Ray is feelin' top notch and is available to pitch in tonight's game, if needed. Ray Caldwell has told Manager Milan that if Bob Hasty gets in serious trouble, he is willing and able to pitch in relief. Let's hope that's not necessary. Ray's gotta be one tired boy at this point in the Series.

Alright, ladies and gentlemen, under the floodlights in Houston, the ball diamond inside Buffalo Stadium looks like a green carpet . . .

"Hey, Ma! Golly, did ya hear that? Bull said Ray's gonna pitch tonight."

"No, young man, I don't believe that's what he said. He said Ray *could* pitch if they need him to."

"Oh-h . . . okay."

In the kitchen, steam rose from a sauce pan—fresh vegetables on the boil.

"Say, Ma, whacha doin'?"

"Shellin' butter beans. The ladies at church are donating fruit and vegetables to the Red Cross for needy families this winter. I pledged twenty quarts of butter beans and black-eyed peas. Times are bad. The majority of working men in town are laid off or on short pay. Business ever'where is down. I hear there's twenty thousand men in town without jobs. Will Rogers says ten men in our country could buy the world—and *ten million* can't buy enough to eat. The women shopping in the markets all talk of hard times and what's going to become of the country—and when will hard times end?" A pause and then, "So help me, why can't something be done now before thousands of lawful citizens turn into thieves and bootleggers and find lawless ways to support their families? Does it take a smart man to see if conditions remain like they are, conditions more horrible than we can imagine will spread over the country? Someone said what we need to bring prosperity is a good, big war. Our city has felt this depression as much as any city and a little more than most. You should be grateful we don't have to accept charity."

"I'm grateful."

"Well, don't forget it when you say your prayers tonight."

THE GREAT DEPRESSION HIT BIRMINGHAM early and hard. In Birmingham, as nowhere else in the world, were all the minerals needed for iron-making: iron ore, coal, and limestone. Iron ore was smelted into pig iron, which could also be processed into steel. Pig iron piled up and went unsold; steel production slowed down. The city lived and died with its blast furnaces, but one by one the furnaces went out. Layoffs started in 1927. Banks began failing in 1929. During the thirties, employment dropped from 100,000 to 15,000 full-time workers, and Birmingham was called the hardest hit city in the nation. One-third of its people were at the mercy of over-burdened private welfare. The Red Cross Family Service, which had aided just five hundred families in 1927, tried to help twenty-three thousand families in 1933. Murders and robberies rose, and the city faced financial ruin. In 1933, the First National Bank lent the city one million dollars to keep it operating. An old Birmingham adage seemed to be true: Hard times come here first and stay the longest.

Bull Connor back with you, ladies and gentlemen. The Barons are wearing their gray, traveling uniforms with BARONS across the shirt. Our boys are batting in the top of the second inning and Houston's leading, 1–0. Dizzy Dean poured everything he had across the plate in the first inning. He fanned all three batters with his blindin' speedball. Art Weis now leading off the second inning for the Barons. He bats lefthanded. Art's the main cog in the batting order; that bat of his big as a bass fiddle. He hit .369 this year. Art takes a toe-hold in the batter's box. Make him pitch to you, Art, make him pitch. Dean winds up — *here's the pitch:* Weis smacks a vicious liner into rightfield, bouncing into the stands; it's a long, hard two-bagger. What a shot that was. That's the sixth straight hit in this Series for Art Weis.

Now coming to bat for Birmingham is Pete Susko, another lefthanded batter . . . *Here's the pitch,* and Pete hits a hard ground ball to the second baseman, who throws him out. One away, and Weis moves to third. Charley Gooch, the burly third sacker, comin' up. *Here's the first pitch:* He takes a called strike . . . *Next pitch to Gooch:* another strike — no balls and two strikes. *Next pitch* . . . Swiiiing and a miss! Stee-riike three! And how-de-do. Dean gets him — two away. Whew! Diz is slinging a wicked ball tonight, folks.

Shine Cortazzo, the Dazzlin' Italian, now up for the Barons . . . a gritty little shortstop, righthanded batter . . . a bouncin' little Leprechaun, he is. The Southern League's never known a fiercer player. *Shine batting with two outs.* He would tackle a buzz saw to help win a game — you can bet your last streetcar ticket on that. *Dean throws:* ball one. Shine's size is the only thing keeping him out of the big leagues. *A man on third, Barons down, 1–0.* As a fielder, Shine's a Fancy Dan. He gets the ball out of his glove quicker'n the eye can follow. *Next pitch to Shine:* There's a strike. Come on, Shine, we need a hit. *There's another strike.* Dean has Shine in a hole, one ball, two strikes, two outs. *Art Weis, the base runner on third.* Shine has a chance to do some business. *Here's the next pitch:* Dean throws a fastball, and Shine wallops the ball — over the shortstop's head . . . BASE HIT INTO LEFT CENTERFIELD! Shine rounds first base and goes into second. It's two bags for Shine. He knocks in the run, and the Barons tie the game, 1–1. Attaboy, Shine, our Italian friend!

"WHAT DO YOU WANT FOR supper?" my mother asked.

I thought for a moment. "Snap, crackle, pop! Mm-m-m."

"If you want Rice Krispies, you can fix it yourself. Sh-h-h-h . . . listen."

Ball fans, this is Bull, and I have an important message. The food conservation campaign will be ending this month. Miss Roberta Morgan, director of the Red Cross, says they've reached their goal of 100,000 pint containers of food. Now they've doubled the goal to 200,000 containers. People across this land have heard what we're doing here, and they're taking "the Birmingham idea" and using it in their cities. To the people of Birmingham, I want to say thank you, truly. Please, continue your efforts until all your garden and orchard crops have been exhausted. Bring all canned fruits, vegetables, preserves — whatever you have — to the Red Cross food depot at 1720 Second Avenue North. God bless you.

Dizzy Dean was sailing along. In the first, third, and fourth innings combined, the Barons hit only one ball out of the infield — *one.* Meanwhile, Bob Hasty was pitching with men on base every inning. After Houston scored a run in the first, Hasty gave up a base hit in the second, another in the third, and two more in the fourth. Still, the game was tied, 1–1, in the fourth.

Bottom of the fourth inning, ladies and gentlemen. Score tied, 1–1. The leadoff batter, Joe Medwick, up for Houston. The Houston fans give him a wild cheer. He is certainly getting *some* hand from the populace. Joe's their money player. He's s'pose to be some pumpkins when it comes to driving in runs — it's a fact he led the Texas League knockin' in runs this year. *Hasty throws a ball to Medwick.* Bob Hasty's been learnin' the game of golf lately. *Strike to Medwick.* You'll be seein' Bob around town this off-season. He plans to spend the winter here and will be back with the Barons next year. *Medwick steps out of the box.* Many of the boys'll be back on the team next year. Hasty and the rest of the pitchers will be back — little Jimmy Walkup, Clay Touchstone, and Ray Caldwell. Ray'll be forty-four next year. Shine, Billy Bancroft, Woodley Abernathy, Bill Eisemann — I'm goin' on faith ever one of 'em will be Barons again next year. Manager Clyde Milan has already agreed to his contract. Art Weis will probably move up to a higher league, where he can make more money. *Here's the pitch to Medwick:* He drives the ball, a low liner to rightfield. Abernathy darts in, quick as a flash, and dives headlong for the ball . . . sliding on his stomach . . . skidding on the grass. Did he catch the ball? Hold yore breath, fans! YES — THANK HEAVEN! — HE HOLDS THE BALL HIGH FOR EVER'ONE TO SEE! HE CAUGHT THE BALL OFF THE TOP OF THE GRASS! THE BATTER'S OUT!! HIGHWAY ROBBERY, PLAIN AND SIMPLE!

With nobody on base, Homer Peel followed Abernathy's catch with a double into the leftfield stands. Guy Sturdy singled, and Abernathy made a fine throw to the plate, holding Peel at third. The next batter hit the ball back to Hasty, who threw out Peel at the plate. Despite two hard-hit balls in the inning, Houston failed to score. Abernathy had saved one run in the inning with his diving catch and maybe another with his throw to hold Peel at third base. The score was still tied, 1–1.

Yessir, Ab's the fielding hero of this Series. What a fly hawk that boy is. He grew up near Birmingham, ya know. Remember the first game of the Series in Birmingham when he made the backhanded catch to steal a triple from Medwick? That was nine days ago. Oh brother, with ever'thing that's happened in this Series, seems like a month ago. Know what I mean?

Bob Hasty's been plenty tough tonight. The fourth stanza was a tough racket for the ol' righthander. He gave up two hits, but nobody scored. Then in the fifth and sixth, he gave up base hits, but his mates helped save him each time. Now, Charley Gooch, the third baseman, leads off the seventh for the Barons. Gooch has his bat on his shoulder. The score's still tied, 1–1. *Dean winds up and fires:* Charley lines a ball off Sturdy's glove at first base — AND THE BALL ROLLS DOWN THE RIGHTFIELD LINE! Charley Gooch chugs around first and goes into second base for a two-base hit. Nobody out and Shine Cortazzo's coming to bat. Shine, the dazzlin' Eye-talian. He can run faster than a bad rumor. Shine had a double in the second inning to knock in the Barons' only run and a single in the fifth. *Strike one to Cortazzo.* Dizzy's still hummin' that pea. Shine's a fire-eater who gives his best effort on every play. The boy's got color, gobs of it. *Alright, here's Dean's one-strike pitch to Cortazzo:* Shine hits a hard ground ball to second base. Selph fields the ball and throws him out, but Charley Gooch goes to third. Way to move him over, Shine. One away. Bill Eisemann, the catcher, is next. *Dean throws:* Ball one. The Dutchman looks out at Dean and waits for the next pitch; *here it is:* He hits a hard smash between third and short, on the nose, boy, on THE nose . . . it's *through the infield* . . . BASE HIT! Gooch comes home, and the Barons lead for the first time tonight, 2–1. Yow!

The lead didn't last long. The Buffaloes scored in the bottom of the seventh on a walk, a sacrifice bunt, and a single to tie the game at two. In the top of the eighth, Abernathy singled with two outs, bringing Art Weis to bat. The first two pitches to Weis were balls.

Dizzy Dean is clearly worried about Art Weis. Count of two balls and no strikes on Art. King Art is a stellar hitter . . . voted best player in the Southern League this year. *Dean throws a strike.* Two balls and a strike. Two years ago, Weis led the Southern League in batting average. Tie game, 2–2. *Dean winds and throws again:* strike two; two and two. Back in 1924, Weis was the Texas League batting champion, playing for Wichita Falls. *Next pitch:* B-A-A-A-L-L T-H-R-E-E-E! Full count to Art Weis, and a hush hits the crowd in Houston. Somethin's gotta give, ball fans: top of the eighth, tie game, three balls, two strikes, two outs. The umpire adjusts his chest protector. Abernathy leads off first base; he'll be running when Dean throws this pitch. *Here it is:* Weis swings and hits a low line drive, OVER second base, INTO centerfield — BASE HIT! Abernathy rounds second and heads for third. He's runnin' with the muffler wide open! Medwick fumbles the ball in center! Look a-here, Ab's gonna try to score! LO-O-O-OK at that boy go. He's in a fearful hurry. Go it, boy, go it! Run, boy! Ab's roundin' third and comin' home, and — YES! — he makes it standing up. Ab scores all the way from first on the hit by Weis after the ball went through Medwick's legs in centerfield. The Barons take the lead, 3–2! That is championship play, gentlemen, championship play!

In the Houston half of the eighth, Medwick led off with a double. After an out, another Houston runner reached base on an error. Hasty retired the next two batters on a fly ball and a ground ball, and the inning was over, Birmingham still leading, 3–2.

In the top of the ninth, the Barons scored three runs to increase the lead to 6–2. The bottom of the ninth would prove a fitting finish for this remarkable Series.

Ladies and gentlemen, Bull back with ya. The howl around here is that the Birmingham Chamber of Commerce has sent a wire to the Barons ball club right now informing them of a welcome home party when they return Sunday morning. Here's what I've heard: The ball players will depart Houston tomorrow morning — that's Saturday — on the Pan American — nineteen Barons bound for Birmingham, nineteen Barons and true. They're due at the L&N station Sunday morning at 7:30. There'll be a brief celebration at the station. Then the boys'll dust the train smoke off their civvies and head over to the Thomas Jefferson Hotel for a breakfast in their honor. I know the boys'll appreciate everyone being there to greet them. Remember, keep the Sabbath holy, and don't be too noisy Sunday morn when the Barons come blowin' into town. We'll keep our fingers crossed, but it shore do look like they'll be coming home as Dixie Series cham-pee-uns. Our boys came to play ball tonight!

"Ma, Bull Connor says everyone can go meet the team at the station Sunday morning, and eat breakfast with 'em. Can we go, Ma? Can we go?"

"I'll be in Sunday school. You'll have to ask your father."

Whooo-oo, whoo-who – whooo-ooo. Outside a whistle wailed from a far-off train.

"Ma, I seen some bums riding on top of the train today."

"What bums?"

"The bums who catch a ride on freight trains. They sit on top of the boxcars, and when the train slows down they jump off."

"Walter, those men are not bums. You can call them 'hoboes' but, *please*, don't call them 'bums.'"

"Yes'm."

"Times are bad, and those men are down on their luck. Some are just boys, so help me. They come by this house ever' once in a while lookin' for work — say they'll do anything for a meal. I don't have any work for 'em, but I still feed them — ever' one of 'em — black or white, it don't matter. They come through town from all over — North, East, West — some from big cities. They think they's jobs here, but when they get here, they find out the jobs are filled. Not much hirin' going on here or anywhere else. My friend, Ruby, won't have a thing to do with 'em . . . won't feed 'em a lick. So they come over to this house. I don't turn down a single one.

"The other morning a woman came by. The charities were doing all they could, but there wasn't money enough to help her. She had two children, and they were all hungry. She had some meat someone had given her, a cabbage from someone else. I gave her a loaf of bread. One afternoon in town I walked along behind an old man selling chewing gum and candy from a basket. You could see he had no experience selling. He scarcely asked anyone to buy, but people passing him would stop and make a small purchase. They saw he needed it, and they did what they could. How can we let people starve in this land of plenty? We thought we gave 'til it hurt during the war, but we didn't know the meaning of the word 'hurt.' We're mighty blessed. As long as there's food in this house, I'll share with those in need."

Fans, bottom of the ninth, the Barons three outs away from winning this game and the Dixie Series. Bob Hasty made another brilliant stand in the bottom of the eighth. Houston had two runners on base with one out, but once again, Bob lassoed the Buffaloes with his long right arm, and no one scored. This veteran has pitched jamb-up ball tonight. And don't forget our manager, Clyde Milan — let's give him credit for the job he did this year. Before the game tonight in Houston, the ball players had a ceremony and presented ol' Deerfoot with a handsome wristwatch. That shows you what the boys think of him.

Alright, Jimmy Sanders, lefthanded batter, leading off the bottom of the ninth for Houston, batting for Dizzy Dean. The park is silent. Hasty stares down at Sanders. Can you hear the chatter in the Barons' infield? I can. They're encouraging Hasty, reminding him just three more outs. Absolutely, I can hear the sing-song voices of Gooch and Bancroft. *Now, here's Hasty's pitch:* Sanders pops up. Charley Gooch, the third baseman, moves into foul territory and catches the ball. *One away in the bottom of the ninth.*

Third baseman Eddie Hock now the batter. He takes a toe-hold in the dirt. *Hasty winds and pitches: ball one.* Hock's a lefthanded batter, in his fifth year with the Houston club. *Hasty grips the horsehide and throws:* Hock bunts the ball in front of the plate. Hasty fields it and throws to first, but Hock is safe. The ball gets away from the first baseman, and Hock hustles to second. A runner at second base and one out for Houston in the bottom of the ninth. Now Earl Smith, the rightfielder, at bat. He's a dangerous switch-hitter — already with three hits in the game. They tell me Ray Caldwell is warming up in the bullpen; Ray is gettin' warm. Hasty's been in trouble every inning. His curve has refused to break tonight. *Here's the pitch:* Smith hits the ball into centerfield, base knock. Hock comes around from second base and scores. Houston cuts the Barons' lead to 6–3. And Ray Caldwell continues throwin' in the pen.

Selph, the second baseman, now batting for Houston. *Hasty throws to Selph — ball one.* Bob Hasty's pitchin' his heart out. *Here's the next pitch:* Selph hits the ball into leftfield, another base hit. Runners at first and second, only one out, Barons leading, 6–3. Hasty's in a peck of trouble now. I believe by this time Ray is warm and ready.

Where's the ball? Give me the ball. I'll go out there, Ray Caldwell told himself.

And here comes Clyde Milan to the pitcher's box. What's he aimin' to do? He's gonna take Bob Hasty out of the game. It's good doings to yank Bob. Yes, the boy's plum' wore out. Bob has labored this entire ball game, struggled out of many difficulties. He was on the firing line for eight and a third innings and gave up thirteen hits, but his teammates gave him beautiful support. Now Bob is walking slowly and sadly to the showers, and he gets a round of applause from the Houston fans. Hold your head up, Bob; hold it high, boy.

Ol' Deerfoot, Clyde Milan, will put the game in the able hands of the old warrior, Ray Caldwell. The players all turn and watch Ray walk to the mound. Here he is now, ambling in with all the nonchalance in the world. Has he not been in situations like this before? Course he has. All those years in the big leagues, the World Series. You think Ray's scared? Course not. There's no man in the world I'd rather see out there right now than Ray Caldwell.

Clyde Milan hands Ray the ball, and Ray starts his warmup tosses. Ray's an old horse with a arm of iron. He don't throw hard like he used to — he's lost that snap. These days he throws mostly slow stuff, but he's got a head full of pitching tricks. With his control, he can shave the eyebrows off a gnat. A few years back people had given up on Ray. Remember when he was an ace pitcher for the New York Yankees of long ago? Many a run has crossed the plate since then. If Ray could come in here and set down this Houston threat, what a story it would be.

Just a few days ago, the Barons couldn't buy a base hit. They were shut out three straight games and were on the brink of defeat, down three games to one. But they fought back and tied this Series. Tonight they've played with pep and vinegar, and now they've got the lead in the ninth inning of Game Seven. Can Ray Caldwell stamp out this threat by the Buffs? We're gonna find out.

Back home in Birmingham, everyone took a deep breath. This game's more thrilling than a six-reel Western, Bull told 'em.

Alright, one out, bottom of the ninth, two runners on base, Barons leading, 6–3. Cries of "Play ball! Play ball!" come from the crowd. Ray Caldwell facing Joe Medwick, the centerfielder. Joe's a tough customer — has two base hits tonight. *Ray throws a strike to Medwick.* Just imagine, Ray was pitchin' in the World Series eleven years ago. Now, here he is. Ray hitches up his pants, tugs at his cap. Tough moment here. Shake it up out there, you Barons! Make some noise! Let's hear some chatter! Help Ray out! Okay, I hear ya. Now you goin', chilluns, now you goin'!

Ray's workin' a little slow; rubs the baseball on his trousers to get a better grip. *Ray looks in for the sign from the catcher and throws:* ball. The Barons got Ray off the scrap heap two years ago, August of '29 when the stock market was roarin' and everyone had plenty of money. The Barons needed pitching that year, and Ray had an aged but able arm and helped us win the pennant. *Ray throws again:* Medwick swings and misses, strike two. Now you pitchin', brother. Don't shilly-shally and dabble about it. Th'ow that onion, boy. TH'OW IT!

Everyone still remembers the two games Ray won in the '29 Dixie Series when the Barons beat Dallas. Okay, the count is one ball and two strikes. *Here's the pitch to Medwick:* SWING AND A MISS, STRIKE THREE!! No dice, Medwick! Ray threw 'im a curveball. It rolled off his fingertips. I declare, it broke a foot, and Medwick couldn't touch it! Oh, brother, Ray Caldwell's one out away from saving this ball game. Whew!

Eleven thousand pop-eyed Houston fans have worked theirselves to a frenzy. Cool 'em off, Ray, cool 'em off! Two outs . . . bottom of the ninth. Runners on first and second. Ray Caldwell now pitchin' to Homer Peel. Ray looks at his infielders; he motions for his third baseman, Gooch, to move back a couple of steps. A fluke hit or a bobble could spell victory or defeat. The crowd's buzzin' — the score is 6 to 3 against them, two outs, bottom of the ninth. *Ray throws . . . there's a strike to Peel.* Peel was voted by the Houston fans as their favorite player this year. Ray adjusts the cap on his head. Caldwell takin' his time now. Each ball is thrown with utmost care. *Next pitch from Ray:* Strike two! The old grandpa, Ray Caldwell, ain't he somethin' tonight? Caldwell raking the dirt in the pitcher's box with his foot; wipes his face with his shirt sleeve. *Next pitch: Ray throws a ball.* One ball and two strikes. It's been a pippin of a game. Both teams on their toes every minute. Ray reaches down and rubs his hand in the dirt, hitches up his pants, fiddles with his cap. Fans are on their feet in Houston now. Two outs, runners on first and second. The umpire is ready; the catcher is ready. *Ray's arm goes up; the ball comes in; here's the pitch:* a ground ball to third base. Charley Gooch picks it up and throws to Bancroft at second. He-e-e's O-o-u-u-t-t!! The runner's O-o-u-u-t-t! The game's over!

Clyde Milan runs out of the dugout, and the players rush to shake his hand. Milan and the players grab hold of Ray Caldwell — slap him on the back, congratulate him. It's some scene on the field, I wanna tell you. Ray Caldwell — joy pouring outta every wrinkle in that forty-three-year-old face — has done it again. What else can a man do? Ray Caldwell and the Barons finish in a blaze a' glory. The Barons will come back to Birmingham, champions of Dixie! Ball fans, we's in high cotton tonight!

Ladies and gentlemen, I've been doing these games for a few years now, and I am so proud right now, proud I could bring you this moment. Ray Caldwell, Man of Destiny, a grandfather, forty-three years young. His feats will live in the minds of baseball fans for as long as they play this great game. There's nothing in fiction to rival what he has done. As long as they talk baseball, they'll talk of Ray Caldwell! What a pitcher! What a man!

THE HOUSTON PLAYERS WERE GRACIOUS in defeat. "We were licked by a great ball club," said Carey Selph, the second baseman. "The Barons deserved to win, and I salute them as the team that should have won."

The Houston manager, Joe Schultz, said, "I want to congratulate a great ball club and a great manager. We had our chance, and the Barons showed they were

The Dixie Series champions step from the train at the L&N station, Sunday morning, September 27. Shown here are Manager Clyde Milan (left) and his wife, Margaret, and Ray Caldwell and wife Dorothy, along with other members of the team.

a great club in coming from behind to win the Series." Dizzy Dean declared: "I thought I had too much speed for the Barons. They are a great bunch of players, and they got me by hitting my fastball."

Clyde Milan said, "It has never been my lot to know a gamer ball club than the Barons. They demonstrated it in winning this Series after it looked awful doubtful, and they proved they could play ball under pressure. They won the pennant under pressure, and they won this Series after some bitter disappointments in three shutout games. They beat a great club with as fine a pitching staff in minor league ball — next to those men who pitched for the Barons."

SUNDAY MORNING, SEPTEMBER 27, THOUSANDS of people, buzzing with championship talk, gathered in the yards of the Louisville and Nashville station. When the Pan American steamed in with the Dixie champions at 7:24 a.m. — hot, black, and sooty and on time — there wasn't room for another soul. It was an orderly, respectful audience in honor of the Sabbath. The ball players, slap-happy after a night celebrating, stepped to the station platform and gave their clothes a good brushing. The Birmingham Police Band performed, and people shuffled forward, hoping for a glimpse of Hasty, Weis, Bancroft, Caldwell, and others. Some had never before seen their heroes in civilian clothes. Photographers snapped pictures. Someone had brought a coffin: "Here Lies the Great Dizzy Dean." A welcoming committee from the Chamber of Commerce escorted the champions three blocks to the Thomas Jefferson, tallest hotel in the South, for breakfast and accolades. Players made brief remarks.

Bob Hasty, the pitcher who won Game Seven with relief help from Ray Caldwell, said the championship game was the most important game he had ever pitched because "I wanted to show my appreciation of a great club owner, a never-give-up manager, and a city that always backs its ball club. It was the one opportunity I had to show my appreciation of the fine support Rickwood fans have always given me."

Ray Caldwell admitted, "I got just as big a kick out of beating Dizzy Dean as I ever got from winning any game in my major league career. The biggest thrill for all the boys was when that third putout was made in the ninth inning Friday night."

When the celebration concluded, the jubilant masses headed to their churches and their homes. *Well, that was fun. I'm glad we came. Someday we'll tell our grandchildren we were here at this moment.* The Dixie Series of 1931 was, for them, a marvelous, magnificent memory that would live not for an hour, not for a day, not for a year — but always.

AUTHOR'S NOTE: *EUGENE (BULL) CONNOR, ONE OF* the most notorious figures in Birmingham's history, played a prominent role in the final episode of this book. One of my editors said to me, "The tone of the Bull Connor story seems as if you are trying to ameliorate his image, and that bothers me." Someone else had a starkly different view: "I think the portrait of Bull Connor will be a revelation to many readers. They know of him only as Birmingham's villain during the Civil Rights era. It will cause a lot of them to say: *What??? This can't be right, can it?*" Yes, the good ol' country boy and the Connor of thirty years later are one and the same.

Another reader said, "The 'ol' country boy' was more ambitious than he let on. If one reflects on it, it's not hard to understand how this country boy and the infamous Bull Connor could be one and the same. He greatly enjoyed public adulation and didn't like to have his decisions questioned, which is a common trait among those who acquire, or long for, power."

This book portrays the Bull Connor of the 1920s and '30s, when he was an icon of the Birmingham sporting community. Readers can make their own judgments, their own connections between the latter day Bull and the "heeeee's ouuuut!" Bull.

EPILOGUE

AND THEN . . .

THE DIXIE SERIES PROVIDED AN heirloom of memory for participants, management, and spectators. All had stories to treasure and hand down to future generations. The hard work and the toil, they would tell you, had been worthwhile. And the names of the men who comprised the 1931 champion Barons, and who covered themselves in glory, will live on in baseball lore.

IT WAS A SAD DAY for Birmingham when **Carlton Molesworth** resigned as Barons manager in 1922. Fans around the league looked at Moley as a Birmingham landmark—he had been with the team as player or manager since 1906, sixteen years. Seated in a cane-bottom chair at the end of the players' bench, arms crossed and cap bill pulled low over his eyes, Molesworth managed the Barons for fourteen years. His teams won more than a thousand games.

Molesworth's final month in Birmingham played out this way: In early June of 1922, the Barons were second in the league standings, two games out of first place, when the ides of June hit. Over the next three weeks, the team lost nineteen of twenty-five games and fell to fifth place. On Monday, July 3, the team returned home from a thirteen-game road trip, losers of ten games. Molesworth resigned that morning. "I feel that it is in the interest of baseball here, as I believe I have been here too long," he said.

It was quite a scene at the team's headquarters on Third Avenue North. Ball players stopped by, one by one, and heard the news from Molesworth himself. Every man was stunned—unable to believe Moley was no longer with the club. "You can tell the world, though, that I'm not quitting baseball. I'm in the game to stick for years yet. . . . I wouldn't quit the grand old game for anything. It's part of me. I love it."

The Barons had a game to play that afternoon, but the cane-bottom chair would be empty. It was a dreary, soggy day at Rickwood Field. Most of the fans remained in town, thinking the game would be called off by rain. Molesworth watched the game—and every game that week—from the press box, rooting for the Barons. Then he left for his home in Maryland. For the first time in twenty-six summers, he didn't have a baseball game to fret over.

Back in May 1908 when Harry (Dad) Vaughn was deposed as manager, the Birmingham Baseball Association took a gamble, anointing the team's centerfielder, Carlton Molesworth, as his replacement. The owners didn't know if Molesworth would succeed, but they had no one else to turn to. Molesworth did so well he was retained for the next season, the next, and the next. A decent man, Molesworth took his job seriously. He played each game in his mind for hours beforehand and again after it was over. When a ball player blundered, he didn't make crude remarks—he remained silent. When a player came through with a crucial base hit or displayed coolness under fire, he acknowledged it with a smile.

Birmingham owner Rick Woodward said, "I never saw a more square, more honest, or more conscientious man than Carlton Molesworth. If he ever pulled a dirty deal, lied about anything, or failed to deal fairly with a man or an employer, I have never heard of it. You can bet that Moley's severance of relations with the Barons was nothing personal, and we have been and are such good buddies that I expect to continue hunting and fishing with ol' Moley as long as he lives."

Sportswriter Henry Vance began covering Birmingham baseball in 1912. "When I came on the job as a sportswriter, I was pretty green and pretty raw," Vance said. "Ol' Moley took me under his wing during those days when I was just a cub, and he has been a friend ever since. He always toted fair with me, and I know that if Carlton Molesworth ever told me anything, it was just that way. We've had our arguments and debates over certain players, and I've been forced to hop on his club at times when they were in the rut, but Moley has been a real friend."

After leaving Birmingham, Molesworth managed the Columbus, Ohio, Senators for three years. In his final season, the team finished last in the American Association.

Remember the spring of 1911? The Philadelphia Phillies were training at Rickwood, and Clarence (Pop Boy) Smith, in his first year as a professional, was trying to make the grade with the Barons. The Phillies had a young prospect from Elba, Nebraska, a big, freckle-faced kid, that Molesworth liked, and he asked the Phillies to let the youngster pitch for Birmingham that season. Philadelphia agreed. The Phils broke camp and left in two squads. Manager Red Dooin asked Molesworth to let him take the young prospect as a member of the second squad.

In an exhibition game against the world champion Philadelphia Athletics, the prospect pitched five scoreless innings. When Molesworth wired for the prospect, he was informed that he was the most promising pitcher on the staff. The prospect's name was Grover Cleveland Alexander. Alexander won twenty-eight games for the Phillies that season, and 373 wins later he was in the Hall of Fame. That was Molesworth for you—able to spot young talent.

While managing Birmingham, Molesworth established a wonderful working relationship with Pittsburgh Pirates owner Barney Dreyfuss. Dreyfuss had entrusted the development of many young prospects to Molesworth, including Pie Traynor. Year after year, the Birmingham club sold talented players to the Pirates, and when Molesworth resigned as manager of Columbus, Dreyfuss hired him as a talent scout. Molesworth spent four months of each year scouting. The rest of the time he farmed, fished, and hunted in Frederick, Maryland, his boyhood home.

Molesworth grew up poor. He quit school after the third grade to help on the family farm. He hunted for food to provide for the family. "Mr. Woodward calls me a 'pot hunter,'" Moley often would say. "He's right. I had to hunt deer, squirrel, quail, and turkey to fill a pot at home for hungry people."

During his long baseball career, Molesworth regularly set aside a portion of his earnings into his modern farm and was comfortable financially for life. "I remember the first year I started in the game in 1898, I was playing with Elmira, New York," Molesworth said. "I started in at eighty-five dollars a month, but times were so hard owing to the Spanish-American War that my salary was cut to sixty-five dollars. Did I quit? I should say not. I stuck out the season and by some hook or crook I managed to put twenty-five dollars in the bank that year. I have not missed a season since then of laying aside some money. All ball players should do this."

In August of 1928, Molesworth made his first visit to Rickwood as a Pittsburgh scout. He attracted as much attention as the players. Fans recognized him as soon as he strolled into the park; they spoke to him and shook his hand. He looked younger than he did six years before, confessed Zipp Newman, sports editor of *The Birmingham News*. He had lost weight. "Farming did it," Molesworth said, displaying a set of arm muscles.

For twenty-one years, Carlton Molesworth traveled the country scouting for Pittsburgh. His wife, Sarah, died in 1939. At the close of the 1947 season, Molesworth retired to his farm. He was seventy-one years old and had spent fifty-three years as a player, manager, and scout in professional baseball.

"After he retired, he didn't do much except be retired," recalled his grandson, Carlton Molesworth III. "He sat on the rocker on the front porch a lot, and he tended his chickens. I would sometimes help him butcher the chickens when I was a boy. He had a 1931 Chevrolet that he kept until about 1954, when he traded for a 1950 Chevy with an automatic transmission. Later, when his memory began to fail, he would drive the car downtown to get a haircut, or whatever, and ride the city bus home, forgetting that he had driven his car. That evening the police would call my dad [Molesworth's son] to let him know where the car was parked. Dad and his brother, my Uncle Tommy, would drive into town and bring the car home."

When Molesworth's health began to fail in 1956, he entered a nursing home in Frederick. He died five years later, eighty-five years of age. His ninety-thousand-dollar estate was left to his five children.

In 2005, a committee of Birmingham media, historians, and Barons executives selected the inaugural class of the Birmingham Barons Hall of Fame. Prerequisites for induction included outstanding achievement, good character and reputation, and devotion to the ideals of sportsmanship. Among those up for consideration were Pie Traynor, Burleigh Grimes, Satchel Paige, George (Mule) Suttles, Reggie Jackson, and Rollie Fingers, all members of the National Baseball Hall of Fame. Those greats would have to wait another year for induction, but Molesworth would not. Eighty years removed from Rickwood Field, Carlton Molesworth joined Willie Mays, Negro Leagues star Lorenzo (Piper) Davis, and Barons owner Rick Woodward in the first class of the Barons Hall of Fame. Great-grandson Jesse Molesworth traveled from Maryland to represent the family at his induction.

WHEN CLARENCE (POP BOY) SMITH pitched batting practice to the Barons in 1910, catcher **Harold (Rowdy) Elliott** told Manager Molesworth, "I think the kid can win." Elliott, who grew up an orphan, played two seasons for Birmingham in 1910 and '11. In 1914, he was Pop Boy's teammate at Venice, California, of the Pacific Coast League. Rowdy Elliott made it to the major leagues with the Chicago Cubs in 1916 and '17 and served in the military during the war in 1918. He was back in the big leagues with Brooklyn in 1920 and that year caught the major portion of a twenty-six inning game against Boston. Over the next nine years, he played for ten different minor league teams, but within five years of his final game, Rowdy Elliott was dead.

Elliott had moved from Birmingham to Nashville following the 1911 season because of trouble with Manager Carlton Molesworth. His personal problems continued at Nashville. Team officials there alleged that Rowdy fully lived up to his nickname, accusing him of "not doing his best, dissipating, playing off sick, leading younger players astray, and doing nearly everything else not intended to promote the best interests of a club."

Year after year, newspapers told a similar tale: "Elliott is not a scholar in the use of refined English. He was not always in that ideal condition which assures the best work and presents a fine example for other, and especially younger, players. . . . He failed last season to give the club his best services every day and promised to do no better."

"With a little highbrow conduct he probably could land a berth in the majors."

"Maybe if Rowdy Elliott had taken better care of himself when he was with the Barons, he would still be under the Main Tent."

". . . suspended for the remainder of the season for misconduct and insubordination."

"He's a hustler and a fighter for his club when his heart is in his work," said New Orleans Manager Charlie Frank. "He knows more baseball in a minute than most minor league catchers could learn if they lived as long as old man Methuselah himself."

In the early morning hours of February 12, 1934, Rowdy Elliott was picked up by police in a vacant lot on Eddy Street in San Francisco and treated for bruises at Central Emergency Hospital. He said he had fallen from the first story window of an apartment. Doctors were unable to detect a serious injury, and Elliott was booked for drunkenness at City Prison. A few hours later he was taken to Harbor Emergency Hospital for treatment of acute alcoholism. There, his condition turned for the worse, and he died at seven o'clock that night. He was forty-three. No surviving relatives were located. Donations from friends prevented his body from being interred in Potter's Field.

EARL FLEHARTY, THE NOISY KANSAN who taught Clarence Smith to pitch, left Birmingham after the 1911 season and pitched two seasons for Nashville. He was a teammate of Clarence and Rowdy Elliott at Venice in 1914. His baseball record after that is spotty, but we do know he was reunited with Clarence in Sweetwater, Texas, in 1921. It appears that he played the 1923 and '24 seasons in the Class D West Texas League in the cities of Marlin, Austin, and Temple. After baseball, Fleharty settled in Nevada, Missouri, where he was an auctioneer. He died in 1956 of an apparent heart attack. Survivors included four sisters and two brothers.

RAY BOYD HELPED CLARENCE SMITH refine his pitching technique in the spring of 1912. Boyd was twenty-five years old that season and helped the Barons win the pennant with his pitching record of 23–11. The following season, 1913, he had a sore arm and pitched hardly at all. Rick Woodward recalled that Boyd "had the longest little fingernail on his right hand that I have ever seen. He did not make any display of it, and, of course, one secret of his success was that he was roughing the ball, which gave him a sinker that was almost unhittable."

Possibly, Boyd never recovered from his sore arm in 1913. Here was a pitcher who had won a hundred games in four seasons, 1909 to 1912. Beginning in 1913, he pitched five more minor league seasons, never winning more than nine games a season. He finished his career with Bloomington, Illinois, in 1917, the year America entered the war. He spent the next two years working on his mother's farm near his hometown of Hortonville, Indiana. In early February 1920, Boyd became ill with influenza. His wife, Evangeline, and one of his two children also were seriously ill. Ten days later Ray Boyd died of pneumonia. He had just turned thirty-three.

ROY ELLAM, *THE SHORTSTOP WHO* was jeered early in his career for miscues in the field, played with the Barons from 1909 to 1915. After leaving Birmingham, he became player-manager for Nashville in the Southern Association. In the 1920s, he managed Galveston and Atlanta and in the Florida cities of Lakeland, St. Augustine, and Tampa. He finished his baseball career managing the Montgomery Lions in 1929 and '30. He won pennants with Nashville and Montgomery in 1916 and 1929. Ellam had major league trials with Cincinnati and Pittsburgh in 1909 and 1918 but had one major weakness: he couldn't hit. He appeared in thirty-six major league games, batting .143.

While playing baseball, Ellam worked as a master plumber during off-seasons. In 1948, he was sixty-two years old and the owner of a plumbing business in his hometown of Conshohocken, Pennsylvania. At the noon hour of October 28, he prepared to inspect a job completed by his workers on the top floor of a three-story building. Finding the downstairs door locked, he decided to climb the fire escape. The bottom stair of the fire escape was suspended in the air by a balance weight. As Ellam pulled down the stair to mount the bottom step, the cable holding the balance weight snapped, and the two-hundred-pound weight fell on him. Though the weight had been deflected by Ellam's body, its impact was still strong enough to demolish the bottom step of the fire escape. Ellam was killed instantly.

JOHNNY DOBBS *LEFT BIRMINGHAM FOLLOWING* the 1929 season to manage the Atlanta Crackers. He received a three-year contract at a salary of $9,000 a year, but his stay in Atlanta was not a happy one. Dobbs' first Atlanta club in

1930 finished fourth in the league. The following year, as Birmingham won the pennant and Dixie Series, Atlanta placed sixth. That year Dobbs' Crackers hosted Birmingham in the first night game played in Atlanta: May 25, 1931. In the second inning of the game, the Atlanta shortstop hit a ball that rolled under a signboard on the centerfield fence. The Atlanta player rounded the bases with what appeared to be a home run. Birmingham outfielder Andy Moore was unable to retrieve the ball from under the sign, and the umpires ruled the hit a double. Dobbs contended the ball had not rolled under the sign but had stopped dead in the outfield grass. He protested vigorously and the umpires banished him from the game.

Dobbs and Umpire Eddie Goes had been at odds all season. Dobbs said Goes cursed him during the argument, and in the heat of the moment, Dobbs punched Goes in the jaw. When the case went before League President John Martin, fans and news reporters were under the impression that Dobbs faced a minimum suspension of ninety days for striking an umpire. Birmingham fans, still fond of Dobbs, sent a petition to Martin urging him to treat Dobbs leniently. President Martin stated that baseball rules did *not* specify a minimum penalty for hitting an umpire. He said that a bulletin issued by Commissioner Kenesaw Landis in 1927 had established a mandatory minimum of ninety days but that the National Baseball Association later determined the penalty was discretionary.

Nick Dobbs, Johnny's son, was nine years old at the time. "Judge Landis called my father and bawled him out about that fight," Nick recalled. "My mother thought Landis would throw him out of baseball. Everyone in the league was afraid of Landis."

League President Martin considered the "long and honorable career" of Dobbs, calling him a "real sportsman," and ruled that Dobbs would be suspended for thirty days for striking the umpire. Dobbs said, "I regret the unfortunate incident very much, which was simply a case of losing my presence of mind. It is just one of those things that happen now and then during a heated baseball contest." Everyone around the league felt that the penalty was fair and just. Regarding the petition sent to Martin by Birmingham fans, Dobbs said, "I want to say that I will always have a warm spot in my heart for Birmingham. The fans were always my friends, and when they had a chance to show me a favor, they did unhesitatingly."

By the end of the 1931 season, Dobbs and the directors of the Atlanta ball club were publicly sparring over his future—but not because of the umpiring incident. While managing Birmingham, Dobbs had been given near total control of the purchase and sale of players. Rick Woodward had told Dobbs to spare no expense—money was plentiful and players could be had. Whenever the team needed a ball player, Dobbs bought one—it was his management style and Birmingham ownership was happy to accommodate him. In Atlanta, however, Dobbs' style met with disfavor. Buying ball players cost serious money, and the Atlanta management considered Johnny Dobbs an expensive manager. During the off-season of 1931, Dobbs and Atlanta management clearly had tired of one another, and rumors of his future swirled about. In November of 1931, Dobbs confessed that "I've heard the rumors, it is true, and there may be something to them—that efforts are being made in Atlanta to oust me as manager—but I have a three-year contract, and before the Atlanta club can dismiss me they must pay me $9,000.

"They thought so much of me that they offered me my choice of a three-year or a five-year contract. I accepted the three, explaining that we might not find ourselves suited to one another and they might wish to hire a new manager. I was well set in Birmingham, having just won two pennants and a Dixie Series, and the club had begun to make some real money for the first time. I never liked to stay anywhere, so I snapped up the chance to move over to Atlanta. But in the light of what I hear is going on, it looked as if I made a mistake."

In early January 1932, Dobbs admitted he did not want to return to Atlanta under existing circumstances. His hands, he said, were shackled to a certain extent, that he "was told what to do" instead of having baseball matters left to his own judgment. "I would rather sit on a fence on my farm over at Ringgold than go through with that again."

Dobbs said that when he took the Atlanta job he had been promised sufficient resources to obtain needed players. Soon after, however, he found himself being forced to take chances with free agents and "drifters" because the club was not willing to spend money for real talent. He also implied that, after twenty-one years of managing, it had been humiliating to have his baseball judgment questioned and to be interfered with by men who were constantly reminding him of what "he did not know." He said he did not want to return to Atlanta unless he were given capable players. He also said he was disappointed at his failure to accomplish more for the team and that he hated to leave Atlanta with such a record.

A week after making these remarks in mid-January 1932, Dobbs was replaced as manager of the Crackers. He would be paid $9,000 for the remaining year of his contract. A statement from the board of directors asserted in part that "Our problems have been the subject of many conferences between Mr. Dobbs and our officers, extending over a period of several months. . . . It has been the considered judgment of all concerned that a complete reorganization was the best thing that could be done for baseball in Atlanta. Mr. Dobbs will be paid in full for the unexpired portion of his contract."

Dobbs remained at his Ringgold home, out of baseball, through the 1932 season. In the spring of 1933, he bought the franchise of the Charlotte club of the Piedmont League, with Wilbert Robinson as his partner. Robinson had managed the Brooklyn Dodgers for eighteen years, retiring after the 1931 season. A year after investing in the Charlotte ball club, Wilbert Robinson died suddenly. One month later, September 8, 1934, Johnny Dobbs was in Atlanta consulting with attorneys on matters concerning the team. That night he rushed by train back to Charlotte to make arrangements for a post-season series with Norfolk to decide the league championship. Just before two o'clock in the morning, en route from Atlanta, he suffered a stroke. He died twelve hours later in Charlotte. He was fifty-nine years old.

Johnny Dobbs belonged not to one team in the Southern Association but to the entire league. He managed in six different league cities—seven if Chattanooga is included, which was not a league city at the time he managed. Zipp Newman, the *Birmingham News* sports editor, had known Dobbs for twenty years. "There has never been a greater personality in the Southern League than Johnny Dobbs," Newman said. "He was a mighty driving force, terrific in its intensity, friendly in dealings off the diamond. . . . He was a showman, and he knew what the fans wanted was a driving ball club. The great personality of the man was contagious.

"Johnny Dobbs believed in moving around," Newman said. "And everywhere he went attendance picked up. Montgomery, New Orleans, Memphis, Birmingham, and Atlanta fell under the spell of his personality. . . . Birmingham will always hold Dobbs in high esteem. . . . During his tenure here, Birmingham broke one attendance record after another. He brought Birmingham its first pennant in fourteen years and left at the peak of his popularity. Hail and farewell, Johnny. You were a great pal."

CLARENCE EVERETT (YAM) YARYAN, THE beloved catcher from Iowa whose appendix surgery nearly cost him his life, was sold to Fort Worth in 1931. He continued playing minor league ball until he was forty-seven years old. Yaryan began his professional career in 1917 with Wichita. Four years later, at the age of twenty-eight, he received a tryout with the Chicago White Sox. He thought so little of his chances, he didn't even carry an extra shirt to spring camp. When he found out he had made the team, he told Manager Kid Gleason he had to go home and get his clothes. That's not necessary, Gleason said, the clothes can be shipped. "Oh, no, they can't," Yaryan said. "Nobody but me knows where they are." Afraid somebody would steal his clothes, Yam had buried them out in the woods. Sure enough, he had to go home and get his clothes.

Yam was dear to the hearts of Birmingham fans for his ability to hit the ball and hit it hard. Witness his batting averages of .369, .336, .389, .335, and .340. Yaryan was slow of hoof, which was a break for Birmingham; otherwise major league scouts would have grabbed him. Yaryan had the ideal build for a catcher—sturdy and thick set—yet he was meek and mild, the salt of the earth. He was considered the strongest man in the league, said Zipp Newman, the sportswriter. "If you have any doubt, ask some of the men he has blocked off the plate and some of the players he has knocked cold simply running into them."

Because of Rickwood's distant left- and centerfield fences, Yaryan averaged only twelve home runs a season for Birmingham. Newman said Yaryan would have hit forty to fifty homers a year if he had played at modern day Rickwood Field with its compact dimensions. Yaryan finished his career in the late thirties, playing for and managing minor league teams in Andalusia, Gadsden, Anniston, and Brewton, Alabama, and hitting .300 at the age of forty-seven. At Andalusia, he was the catcher for Virgil Trucks, a future major league pitcher. From February 1941 until his retirement in January 1959, Yaryan was a successful salesman at Sears, Roebuck in downtown Birmingham. He died in 1964 after a brief illness.

EDDIE WELLS, THE KING OF Southern League pitchers in 1927 and '28, brought Birmingham a pennant with his remarkable pitching. During his season and a half with the Barons, he won thirty-eight games and lost eight. After the 1928 season, Wells was sold to the New York Yankees where his locker stood between that of Babe Ruth and Lou Gehrig. He pitched four years for the Yankees, then two years for the St. Louis Browns. Wells possessed a better than average fastball but only a fair curve, a shortcoming that may have limited his success in the majors. His major league record was 68–69. After his big league career ended, he returned to the minors for two seasons in the Pacific Coast League.

Wells pitched for the Detroit Tigers early in his career. In June of 1926, a year before coming to Birmingham, he pitched an amazing string of thirty-three consecutive scoreless innings. One of the games during the streak was a 1–0 defeat of Walter Johnson.

Wells was a native of Ashland, Ohio, but he married a Birmingham girl, Annie McConnell, and made Birmingham his off-season home. After baseball, he moved to Montgomery to work in the oil business with his brother-in-law. He retired from work in 1972 and died of a heart attack in 1986 at the age of eighty-five.

Late in life, Wells recalled playing with and against Babe Ruth: "He never hit a home run off me. I never gave him a good fastball. Babe was simply born a natural baseball player. He was a smart ball player. I never saw him throw to the wrong base from the outfield. Babe simply had the most natural equipment, both physical and mental, for a baseball player that I ever played with or against.

"Babe was a great man; he loved kids and would go to hospitals to see them when sick. I dressed beside Babe in the Yankee Stadium locker room. Naturally, I knew him very well. People loved him; Babe loved people. We got so we were pretty close. I liked him, and I know he liked me. My wife and I would be guests in Babe's and his wife's apartment now and then, and everything was very enjoyable. I sure did enjoy my baseball career. I was far from a star pitcher, but I gave what I had."

John Franklin (Stuffy) Stewart, the peppy second baseman on seven different Birmingham teams, led the Southern Association in stolen bases five times from 1921 to '28. During those years, he also served five stints in the major leagues, mostly as a pinch-runner and late-inning substitute. After his final season in Birmingham, he completed his career by playing in twenty-two games for the Washington Senators in 1929, then three more years in the minor leagues.

Stewart's asset was his foot speed. "That's all I really had. I had to develop everything else I played with." In 1979, a year before he died, he reflected on his career: "Baseball is still the same game, but it is moving more and more toward showmanship. They want to make a circus out of it. It used to be the game was enough. Babe Ruth, Ty Cobb, and Tris Speaker, now those were some ball players. They don't make ball players like that anymore. That was the thrill I got out of playing baseball. It was playing with all those great baseball players—with me and against me."

Stewart recalled the first time he met Cobb: "It was the summer of 1911. I was working up there in Washington (D.C.). My uncle got me a job, although I didn't work much because I was always out at the ball park. I saw Cobb in a hotel lobby one day, and I went up to him and asked him to show me how to steal bases. Before long he was showing me how to steal bases by him actually sliding into his chair in the hotel lobby. A lot of people that day were wondering what we were doing."

After retiring from baseball, Stewart worked a series of jobs: at an illegal horse racing track in New Jersey, at Gulf Oil for ten years, and as a Florida Racing Commission judge at the Clay County Kennel Club in Jacksonville. His final years were spent in Lake City, Florida, where he was raised. He died at the Veterans Administration Hospital in Lake City at the age of eighty-six. Asked to name his proudest achievement, Stuffy said, "Just being able to play was a thrill every time I took the field, and to be just one of the boys was reward enough."

JIMMY JOHNSTON, WHO PLAYED ON Birmingham's league championship teams of 1912 and 1928, left the Barons after the 1928 season to become player-manager of the Chattanooga Lookouts. The following season, 1930, at the age of forty, he played for Johnny Dobbs in Atlanta. He coached his old major league team, the Brooklyn Dodgers, in 1931, managed Montgomery in 1932, then retired from baseball. Johnston farmed until 1941, then moved to Chattanooga as park superintendent at Engel Stadium, home of the Lookouts. In 1959, he became the starter at Brainerd Golf Course and was one of the town's most affable senior citizens. He died in 1967 after a series of strokes.

The Great Depression hurt Johnston. "I'd always wanted a farm," he once said. "I took what I'd saved over the baseball years and bought a beautiful farm in middle Tennessee. I bought at the peak of the market, and in no time the Depression wiped me out. I lost my shirt."

Johnston was a teammate of Casey Stengel with the Dodgers in 1916 and '17. "He was a very good player and a teammate player," Stengel recalled. "They used to alternate me and him in the big league because I was a lefthanded batter and he was right. He was fast on the bases and could hit the ball for a triple or a home run. An outstanding, great player, and he was never in any kind of trouble that you ever heard of."

BIG, BLOND OUTFIELDER ELLIOT (SANDY) **Bigelow,** who hit .361 and .395 for Birmingham in 1927 and '28, was given one shot at the major leagues: In 1929, he batted .284 in 100 games. The Boston Red Sox released him after the season. He played the 1930 season for two teams—Chattanooga and Mission, California, hitting well above .300.

Bigelow was adrift in baseball at the start of the 1931 season. He visited Mobile, Nashville, Atlanta, and Birmingham looking for a job, but all turned him down. Eventually he caught on with Chattanooga, the town that had sent him to Mission the year before. With Chattanooga in 1931, he dealt misery to his old teammates, the Barons—three singles and a home run beat Ray Caldwell, 4–2; four RBI's helped beat the Barons, 10–9; and a double, homer, and single beat the Barons, 6–4. For the season, he hit .371. The following season, his last in baseball, he hit .327 for Knoxville.

Zipp Newman recalled that "Bigelow was known among his craft as a 'great guy.' He had no enemies. There was always a smile on Sandy's face, and he spoke no evil. He took life as it came without offering any alibis about his play when he booted one or failed in a clinch. There was always a next time with Elliot. He would often say 'Those were good years I spent in Birmingham,' as he polished a bat and laughed at some incident that happened while under Dobbs' banner. There was something of the sailor in him. He liked adventure. When there was a lull in baseball conversation, he would spin a yarn about deep sea fishing."

Bigelow grew up in Tarpon Springs on the west coast of Florida, a fisherman all his life with his brother. The fortunes of fishing and baseball were on his mind as he reflected on hitting .395 for Birmingham: "You know, I started out hitting everything in 1928, and I believe I would have finished above the .400 mark had I not gotten out of the lineup for a brief vacation [missing three weeks in June, injured]. But down the home stretch I got to where I couldn't even get a good foul tip. Something happened to my timing, and before I got out of my slump I had lost a golden opportunity to hit above .400.

"I never could understand why it was so easy for me to hit when I was going good nor why it was so hard for me to get a base hit after I went into a slump. The days you are hitting you are up there taking a free, easy cut, not worrying at all. If you ever try to bear down too hard, you are hopeless. Well, fishing is like hitting. Brother and I were worrying one winter about making enough out of our season's catch to pay off the debts on our new boat. We tried out all kinds of ways, but they didn't increase our catches. One day we went out in an indifferent mood and came up with a catch that netted us a thousand dollars. We accidentally ran into a big school of fine pompano—paid off the debts on the new boat and received five hundred dollars for my share of the profits."

Bigelow was thirty-four when he retired from baseball to fish full time in Tarpon Springs. Less than a year later, in August 1933, he complained of a headache but didn't think it serious, this after a recent operation on an infected ear. His condition, however, became grave, and he was rushed to a hospital in Tampa. He died two days later of cerebral meningitis.

AFTER **BURLEIGH GRIMES'** *PITCHING CAREER* ended, he remained in baseball for another thirty-five years. He succeeded Casey Stengel as manager of the Brooklyn Dodgers in 1937. Financially, the Dodgers were nearly bankrupt; on the field, they finished sixth and seventh in the National League in Burleigh's two years as manager. Later he managed for twelve years in the minor leagues and served as a major league scout. His career in baseball spanned six decades.

During his playing career, Burleigh Grimes was a determined negotiator with his employers, which sometimes meant being traded but also earned him a higher salary than other players of his day. As a rookie, he earned $2,600 dollars. At the end of his career, he was making $25,000 a year, one of the highest salaries in baseball. In contrast, Urban (Red) Faber, a Hall of Fame pitcher and a contemporary, likely earned no more than $10,000 a year.

Burleigh had no hard feelings about those whom he worked with and for. "I spent nine years in Brooklyn. Many newspaper stories have leaked out that I didn't get along well with Manager [Wilbert] Robinson. Perhaps I did cause him unpleasant moments, but I have no unfriendly feeling whatever toward Robbie. I'll say of him, he's a good man with his pitchers. His record shows it. Perhaps he's a little too good, a trifle too considerate for his own selfish interests. True, we had our disagreements, but that's ancient history. Baseball is a rough-and-ready, give-and-take proposition. It's not a game for weaklings. You talk plainly sometimes, but what of it?

"Robbie traded me to the Giants. I was glad to go to the Giants. True, they didn't keep me very long, but that's their business. Stories have flitted around that I didn't fit in to [John] McGraw's system. That's not true. I admire McGraw's ability as a manager and obeyed his instructions always. I had no trouble with McGraw. I did have an argument with the club over salary matters. It seemed to me I was worth more money than I was getting. The owners didn't view the matter in that light, but what of that? I had no hard feelings. Baseball is my business and baseball is their business. If we don't both look out for our own interests, I don't know who else will, so they traded me to Pittsburgh.

"There's been a lot said about my temperament. Some sportswriters have written stories about my prima donna emotional outbursts. Maybe I have got hot under the collar more easily than I should, but I think those stories have been exaggerated. The point is, I was always a hard loser. When I'm on the mound working my head off to win, I want to feel that the fellows behind me are carrying their share of the load. Ball players get disgruntled easily. They may be sore at the owners or sore at the manager. If they get a couple of hits, they feel they've done well. If they boot one, that's all part of the game. But booting one may cost a pitcher a well-earned victory, and victories are the only sales talk he can give the owner when salaries come up for discussion. More than once in my career I've made remarks to fellows who didn't seem to me to be hustling, and I'd do it again.

"In some cities I've been in bad with the crowd, but that never bothered me. In fact, I rather like to have the crowd ride me. It keeps me on my toes. It's a kind of inspiration. The crowd pays its good money to see an exhibition. If they want to do a little yelling, I don't begrudge them the privilege. Why should anybody else?"

Burleigh Grimes lived a long, productive life. He was a toddler when Babe Ruth was born, ten years old when the first World Series was played, and a teen the year the Titanic went down. During Burleigh's lifetime, Henry Ford rolled out his first automobile; the Wrights flew their first airplane; America fought two World

Wars, a Cold War, and a Great Depression; man walked on the moon; a president resigned; and a movie actor became president. Burleigh was a young man when people first listened to radio, middle-aged when they began watching television, and a senior citizen when computer technology reshaped the world.

He played baseball when it was segregated and witnessed its integration. He lived during the Spanish-American War and the Vietnam War, the Roaring Twenties and the Swinging Sixties. He observed flappers, beatniks, peaceniks, hippies, and draft dodgers. He journeyed a long road: from a town ball team in Clear Lake, Wisconsin, to the minors, the majors, and back to Clear Lake for the final years of his life. He played during the bygone days of Wagner, Ruth, and Cobb and marveled at the later generation of Mantle, Mays, and Aaron:

"I can remember some of the clubhouses used to have one or two light bulbs in the whole place, and they smelled like old socks. Little-bitty stalls—you didn't have room enough to hang your clothes. I was in a big league clubhouse last year, and each player had a great big locker, and the room was air-conditioned, and the floor was carpeted, and there were leather-upholstered chairs all around. There was music playing, and half the fellows were blow-drying their hair. And I said, 'Boy, this is the life.'"

Burleigh Grimes won 270 games in the major leagues and eighty-six more in the minors. He won thirty-seven games in two seasons for Birmingham. His career was long enough and rich enough that thirty-six of his teammates were named to Baseball's Hall of Fame. He himself was elected to the Hall of Fame in 1964. Burleigh Grimes died of cancer in his hometown of Clear Lake in 1985. On his headstone is an engraved symbol of the Hall of Fame. He lived to be ninety-two.

THE THIRTIES: THE SOUTHERN ASSOCIATION championship won by the Barons in 1931 was their third in four years. It would be twenty-seven years before they won another. For sixteen seasons—1932 to 1947—they never finished higher than third in the league; often they stood sixth or seventh.

The thirties were troubled times for America. Men sold apples on street corners for a livelihood. People waited in charity lines for soup or dry bread. Desperate people foraged through garbage cans for food. Children went hungry. Beginning with the stock market crash in October 1929 until President Roosevelt's inauguration in March of '33, the U.S. economy slumped nearly every month. Hourly wages dropped sixty percent. People lost their pride and sometimes their hope. Still, minor league baseball was played in towns and villages across the country.

The thirties were grim for the teams of the Southern Association. Ordinary people could no longer afford to attend games. Many clubs reported healthy losses in 1931. By 1932, losses were dire, with four teams combining to lose more than $120,000. Before the Depression began, at least one million fans had attended Southern Association games every year from 1920 to 1931. League attendance dropped to 793,000 in 1932 and 633,000 in 1933. The Birmingham Barons drew only seventy-one thousand in 1933, a quarter of its attendance in 1927.

At the beginning of the 1933 season, many clubs feared they wouldn't survive a full season. Between 1930 and 1933, nine thousand banks failed across the country. People lost confidence in banks and withdrew their money. Club owners could not borrow money because banks had none to lend. Atlanta, backed by the Coca-Cola Company, was the only team with financial security; the rest got along by cutting corners. Player salaries and roster sizes were reduced and operating expenses cut. Every club wanted to sell players, but few had money to buy.

Yet President Roosevelt was confident in 1933, telling the American people: "We are on our way." Indeed, in Birmingham that year the Christmas shopping season was the best since 1929. Men and women who had been out of work for three years were back in their old jobs or in new ones. By 1934, the national economy showed signs of improvement. Baseball owners were optimistic about conditions for the season ahead, and Americans were looking forward to a "new deal." As the Birmingham Barons prepared for the 1934 season, there was little money in the club treasury, certainly not enough to assemble a competitive team. Many of the players were castoffs from other teams, and the wins and losses reflected it—a record of 64–90 and a seventh-place finish in 1934.

The economy improved between 1934 and 1936. Then, as full recovery seemed near, the economy slipped again in 1937; the stock market lost almost half its value; unemployment rose again; industrial production dropped by a third. The Great Depression would linger for more than a decade.

*In 1924, **Rick Woodward** was* tired of losing. His Birmingham Barons had not won a pennant in ten years. What's more, the '24 club had finished with the worst record in club history. In August 1924, Woodward asked sportswriter Zipp Newman to suggest someone to be the new manager. Zipp said, "Well, you like Johnny Dobbs and I think he would make you a good manager."

"See what kind of contract Johnny wants," Woodward responded.

Woodward's remark illustrates how he ran his pride and his joy—his baseball team. Woodward entered baseball solely from sporting instinct. Baseball was his hobby; he operated the team for amusement, not financial gain; he gave liberally of his time and wealth; he enjoyed seeing a championship team on the field and spent whatever necessary to produce winning clubs; he never drew one cent in profit; and he took the ups and downs of the Barons more seriously than did the fans.

"Rick Woodward was the most glamorous owner in baseball," Zipp Newman often said. "He loved baseball and spent fabulous sums for players and entertaining guests." He enjoyed the association with players, managers, scouts, and executives.

"He liked to warm up the pitchers, sit around in a uniform, and speak the language of the ball players," said Newman. "Many would see the young Baron owner and take him for some new husky recruit reporting to the team. He loved baseball with a passion. He traveled with the team but always as one of the team. He fished, hunted, and played golf with the most famous of ball players; he and Ty Cobb were very close friends. He was one of the most glamorous and unforgettable characters the game of baseball will ever know."

Baseball to Woodward was an adventure. In his baseball memoirs, penned in 1934, Woodward recalled his first year as owner of the team: It was 1910, and "I had visions of a pennant! Three weeks after the season opened, we were hanging on to seventh place by an eyelash. Something had to be done!" Woodward was thirty-three years old and had never met or conversed with a single major league owner or manager. So, "I went to Cincinnati in fear and trembling and visited Harry Vaughn, who had formerly managed Birmingham. He was tending bar, and, after buying a beer or two, I mustered up courage and asked him about players, and he recommended Harry Coveleski. I bought Coveleski from old man Garry Herrmann [of the Cincinnati Reds], paying one thousand dollars for him. It was a huge price!

"From there, I went to Chicago and met Mr. Comiskey." Charles Comiskey owned the Chicago White Sox. "I was very anxious to get an outfielder, and Mrs. Comiskey, who was present, prevailed on 'Father,' as she called him, to let me have Bob Messenger for another thousand. It seemed to me that I had spent a fortune for ball players, because the attendance in those days was decidedly limited. These two men made the club, and we finished the season in second place."

From 1912 to 1931, Birmingham won five league championships. In the Johnny Dobbs' era of the late 1920s, the club reaped huge financial dividends from record-setting attendance and from the sale of players to major league clubs. Then came the Depression. Operations in Birmingham's iron and steel industry were drastically curtailed. Woodward Iron Company suffered financially and entered bankruptcy reorganization. Fortunes of the Birmingham Baseball Association slumped as well. Rick Woodward was sixty-one years old in 1937. Poor attendance and heavy operating losses over several seasons had created sizable indebtedness, and Birmingham baseball operations, in effect, passed into the hands of the First National Bank.

Birmingham's attendance declined sharply from 1936 to 1937. In late 1937, rumors began circulating about a possible sale of the ball club. In January 1938, a local businessman, Ed Norton, explored the idea of buying Woodward's controlling interest in the team. Norton had business connections in real estate, radio, and banking and was actively involved in local civic affairs. He was informed that Woodward would like to see the holdings of the Birmingham Baseball Association sold to a local person such as Norton. Around the first of February, 1938, Norton entered into negotiations for ownership of the Barons. The franchise, ball players, and Rickwood Field were valued at $340,000. On February 7, the sale became official, with Norton paying something less than full value. For the first time since 1910, Rick Woodward no longer owned the Birmingham baseball club.

Said Woodward, "I have had $250,000 worth of pleasure out of owning the Barons and broken even. Mr. Norton is a young sportsman, and I do not know of anyone with more enthusiasm for baseball nor better qualified to own the club."

The Birmingham News declared in an editorial, "For twenty-nine years, baseball in Birmingham has meant Rick Woodward. The seasons have come and gone, championships have been won and lost, but it was ever Mr. Woodward's enthusiastic sportsmanship that made the Birmingham Barons a fighting team. . . . It will be hard to think of the Birmingham Barons without Rick Woodward in the dugout and as the team's No. 1 rooter."

Some thought Woodward sold the team to devote more time to his hobbies—golfing and fishing—but Zipp Newman insisted that "Rick quit because he couldn't give Birmingham the club he thought the city was entitled to after the lean years."

Fandom took the change in ownership in style—wistful that the Woodward era was over but optimistic over Ed Norton's enthusiasm and investment in the Barons. The day Norton bought the club, field manager Fresco Thompson said he needed a good-hitting outfielder and a pair of pitchers. "Well," said Norton, "I suppose the first thing we should do is try and find the outfielder we need and ascertain just what price tag he has on him. Then, after that is done, we better go into the market and buy a couple of pitchers that can win in this league."

Indeed, the Birmingham Barons were ready to move on.

In June of 1935, the Barons were in sixth place with a losing record when the board of directors released **Clyde Milan** as manager. Milan and the Birmingham

Baseball Association admired one another. The team's management gave him a farewell banquet at the Tutwiler Hotel, and the players presented him with a handsome hunting ensemble of knife, jacket, and boots. Milan said, "Our losing streak was due to something impossible to be helped under conditions brought on by the Depression. The fans of Birmingham have been loyal, and my only regret is that I couldn't have given them better clubs. I think they all understand the handicaps under which the entire management of the club has striven to give them good baseball since the Depression hit back in 1932."

Three weeks after he left Birmingham, Milan was hired to manage the Chattanooga Lookouts, another Southern Association club. He stayed for two years, then returned to his old team, the Washington Senators, from 1938 to 1952, coaching first base and hitting fungoes to infielders before games. In spring training, 1953, Milan was one of the most active members of the Washington training camp in Orlando, Florida. On March 3, three weeks shy of his sixty-sixth birthday, he insisted on hitting to the infielders in both the morning and afternoon workouts. Afterward, he walked to the Washington dressing room and collapsed. An ambulance took him to Orange County Hospital, where he died an hour later. It was a fitting way to go out for a man whose whole life had been baseball.

Clyde Milan regretted that he didn't live out his life in Birmingham. After he was relieved as manager in 1935, two friends offered to buy the Barons and make him part owner. "I never have regretted anything more in my life than in turning down the chance to become a Birmingham owner," he said later in life. "It was during the Depression, and the club could have been purchased at a reasonable price. I should have stayed, for my wife and I loved the people in Birmingham, and they had been good to us. It was one of the saddest days of my life when we left."

ART WEIS *WAS THE OUTSTANDING* player in the Southern Association for the Dixie champion Barons in 1931. His record that year—.369 average, 20 homers, 122 RBIs—warranted a trial in the major leagues, but not a single team bid for him. Instead, the Double A Louisville Colonels drafted him off the Barons roster. The following season, Weis dislocated a vertebra and had a mediocre year for Louisville. At the end of the year, Louisville sold him to Atlanta. He never got going for Atlanta and was shipped to Knoxville. Knoxville returned him to Atlanta, then Atlanta released him. The Barons reacquired him in June of that year, 1933.

In Birmingham, Weis had always been a favorite of small boys, who swarmed the field and escorted him to the dugout after every game. He played a full season for Birmingham in 1934 and hit .324. He had another good season at Fort Worth in 1935, hitting .331 — seemingly, he always hit .300 — but 1935 would be his last big year. He played sparingly in the seasons to follow, finishing his professional career in 1938 with St. Paul. Weis then began playing semi-pro ball with the Belleville, Illinois, Stags, financed by Stag Beer. "Anytime I could get a ball in my hands on the field and swing a bat, it made me happy," he reminisced toward the end of his life. After his ball playing days, Weis worked as a clerk for the U.S. Postal Service in Webster Groves, Missouri, a suburb of St. Louis.

Early in his professional career, Weis played four seasons for the Chicago Cubs of the early 1920s as a part-time outfielder. For a time, he roomed with one of baseball's greatest pitchers, Grover Cleveland Alexander, who was epileptic and alcoholic. "I don't know how he ever pitched, drinking like that," Weis recalled of Alexander. "Overall, though, he was very quiet. He was a wonderful, wonderful person. We'd have our supper together, I'd take him out, and then I'd bring him back to put him to bed. He did a lot of sleeping and went to bed early."

Though Weis was born and raised in St. Louis, he wore a Cubs cap around the house until the day he died. He lived to be ninety-six.

JIMMY WALKUP, THE GRACEFUL LITTLE lefthander who pitched Game Two of the 1931 Dixie Series, played two more seasons for Birmingham but was unable to equal his success of 1931, when he had a pitching record of 20–5. He finished his professional career in 1934, pitching in the Texas League for Tulsa and Fort Worth. No matter where he played during his seventeen-year pro career, Walkup always led the league in best humor. No one ever reported seeing him angry.

In 1935, Walkup joined a semi-pro team in Oklahoma City and the following year went to work for the Halliburton Company in Duncan, Oklahoma. He played three years for the Halliburton Cementers, one of the best semi-pro teams in the country. He pitched his final game at the age of forty-two but continued working for Halliburton for twenty-five years.

Jimmy Walkup's idol was Babe Ruth. He fanned the Babe three times in an exhibition game while playing for Fort Worth in 1928. The fans hooted and jeered Ruth. "I'll tell you one thing," growled the Babe. "I'm in the big leagues, and he ain't." After the game, Jimmy took the Babe home to meet his two kids. Ruth grabbed them, one in each arm, and made for the nearest ice cream joint.

Jimmy Walkup died in 1990 at the age of ninety-four.

CLAY TOUCHSTONE, WHO WON GAME Five to prevent Birmingham's elimination from the 1931 Dixie Series, remained with the Barons through the 1933 season. Over the next nine years, he pitched for Memphis, Oklahoma City, and Dallas.

He was managing the Oklahoma City Indians when the league closed in 1942 for the Second World War. Touchstone was out of the game in 1943 and '44, but with many major-leaguers serving in the military, he went back into uniform in 1945, pitching briefly for the Chicago White Sox. Four years later, he died unexpectedly at the age of forty-six. He lived the last six years of his life in Beaumont, Texas, where he operated a pool hall called the Service Amusement Club.

BOB HASTY, *THE STARTING PITCHER* and winner of Game Seven of the 1931 Dixie Series, returned to the Barons in 1932. In July, the Barons sold him to the Atlanta Crackers, along with his Game Seven catcher, Bill Eisemann. A year later on a June afternoon in Atlanta, Hasty went to his locker and discovered his uniform gone. That's how Atlanta broke the news that he was no longer with the team. He finished the season with Jersey City and retired from organized baseball.

Hasty continued playing on company ball teams, such as Atlanta Gas Light, until the start of World War II, when he moved to South Carolina to supervise the operation of a large farm. After the war, he returned to Atlanta for a managerial position at Foremost Dairies and played on the company baseball team. In 1951, he joined Lockheed Corporation, where he designed wiring for airplanes. He retired from his job in 1964.

Bob was a devoted supporter of the Braves when the team moved from Milwaukee to Atlanta in 1966. He and his wife, Wilma, attended spring training every year as members of the team's 700 Club, missing only the spring of 1972 when Bob had surgery on his hip. The surgery was a consequence of throwing thousands and thousands of baseballs over a lifetime. Three weeks after the operation, on Memorial Day weekend, Bob died from an embolism related to the surgery. His wife, Wilma, received a note of condolence from future home run king Henry Aaron.

EUGENE (BULL) CONNOR *WAS ELECTED* to the Alabama House of Representatives in 1934 but continued broadcasting Birmingham Barons games through 1937. From 1937 to 1963, he served six terms on Birmingham's city commission. As police commissioner, he achieved notoriety during the city's darkest hours, stubbornly defending segregation during the early sixties. Connor ran twice for governor, finishing sixth in a field of fifteen candidates in 1950 and fifth of seven in 1962. In late 1966, he was felled by a stroke and confined to a wheelchair for the final seven years of his life. In February 1973, he suffered another stroke and lingered twelve days in a Birmingham hospital before passing away. He was seventy-five.

William Nunnelley, in his book *Bull Connor,* wrote that "Bull Connor fit the mold of the stereotypical Southern politician of the first half of the twentieth century. He was loud, quick with the quip, racist, and theatrical. . . . He enjoyed a three-decade love affair with the white voters of Birmingham, who viewed him as a colorful, protective, 'dollars and cents' honest man of the people. He graduated from the school of hard knocks to become a success, first in local radio and then in local politics; blue-collar Birmingham, attracted by his rough-hewn charisma, applauded each step along the way."

BILLY BANCROFT, WHO PRODUCED THE winning base hit in Game One of the 1931 Dixie Series, played for the Barons through the 1933 season, moving on to Oklahoma City for 1934 and '35. This modest, humble man stood a shade over five-foot-six. His son, William Bancroft, Jr., said that when Billy played, because of his stature, "a lot of people would see him in person and not recognize he was the same guy everyone was talking about."

As far back as his student days at Howard College, Billy Bancroft intended to coach. Football season back then did not begin until baseball ended, allowing Billy to serve as an assistant football coach at Howard during the years he played professional baseball. In 1934, while still a baseball player for Oklahoma City, Bancroft was named head football coach at Howard. He remained in the position for six years. In his second season, 1935, Howard tied defending Rose Bowl champion Alabama, 6–6, in what stands as one of the biggest upsets ever in the state of Alabama. The game was broadcast over the radio by Melvin Allen Israel, a University of Alabama law student who later made a name for himself as baseball announcer Mel Allen. One of the players on the Alabama team in that game was an end named Paul (Bear) Bryant.

After four years away from baseball, Bancroft returned to the game in 1939 and '40 as manager and part-time player for Selma and Gadsden of the Class B Southeastern League. When America entered the World War in 1941, Bancroft was thirty-seven years old and took a job setting up the USO chapter in Birmingham. He couldn't stand seeing all the young men going off to war, said his grandson, Steven Bancroft, so he attempted to enlist in several sections of the military but was turned down each time—too old. Instead, he joined the American Red Cross and served as a program director in England and Scotland. After the war, Bancroft coached football and baseball at Anniston High School from 1946 to 1958. His football coaching record was 75–23–6. He coached the 1958 state champion baseball team and two baseball state runners-up.

"Bear Bryant asked him to come down and coach with him one time," said Billy's son, Chuck, "but Daddy said, 'Bear, you know we can't coach on the same team. We'd both want to be the head coach.'"

Billy Bancroft retired from coaching after 1958, returning to his alma mater, Woodlawn High, as boys' advisor until his retirement in 1970. He and his wife, Sammie, remained in Birmingham until his death in 1993 at the age of eighty-nine.

Deep down, Billy Bancroft was a country boy. Throughout his life, he enjoyed fishing and hunting, gigging frogs, and treeing possums. He loved being around good bird dogs and coon dogs. Steven Bancroft has fond memories of his grandfather, the old coach. "He always had a childlike excitement about fishing and hunting," Steven said. "Lucky for me, I was able to go fishing with him many times as a child. For me, that was when *the coach* would emerge and he would pass along tidbits of wisdom. I'll always remember two things he said: 'It's not how you start but how you finish that's important,' and 'Wherever you go and whatever you do, try to make the world a better place.'"

Billy Bancroft was inducted into the Alabama Sports Hall of Fame in 1974. At his induction he said, "You know, I've had a lot of firsts. I played on the first football team at Woodlawn High School. I was on the first freshman team at Howard, played in the first football game at Legion Field, and I'm the first minor-leaguer to make this major league Hall of Fame."

"I've had a good life," he once said, "and I don't think I would change a thing."

While Bancroft was living in Anniston, Dizzy Dean occasionally passed through town doing radio work. Billy's wife, Sammie, recalled that "every once in a while Diz would say, 'I still can't believe that little Alabama squirt got that hit off me.'"

DIZZY DEAN WAS HARD AT work in New Orleans only two days after the 1931 Dixie Series ended. He pitched seven innings in a semi-pro game for the Gulotta Grocers, striking out seven batters without allowing a run. The next season Dizzy was in the major leagues, pitching for the St. Louis Cardinals. He won eighteen games that year and struck out more batters than any other pitcher in the league. Two years later in 1934, he and brother Paul pitched the Cardinals to the world championship, Dizzy winning thirty games. No National League pitcher has won as many games since. The next year he won twenty-eight games and the year after, twenty-four.

Playing in the 1937 All-Star Game, Diz broke his toe when he was hit on the left foot by a batted ball. Two weeks later, he pitched a complete game for the Cardinals, but his catcher, Mickey Owen, said, "He wasn't the same that afternoon. His fastball had nothing on it, nothing at all." To compensate for his injury, Diz began favoring his foot, which altered his pitching motion and ultimately injured his arm.

A year after dueling Ray Caldwell in the Dixie Series, Dizzy Dean was a star pitcher for the St. Louis Cardinals. He won 18 games and led the National League in strikeouts in 1932. Two years later he won 30 games and, aided by brother Paul, pitched the Cardinals to the world championship.

"I was unable to pivot my left foot because my toe hurt so much," he said, "and with the result I was pitching entirely with my arm and puttin' all the pressure on it, and I felt soreness in the flipper right away. I shouldn't a been out there."

By the following spring, Diz had lost his fastball, and the Cardinals traded him to the Chicago Cubs. To compensate for his arm injury, he threw sweeping sidearm curves and other slow pitches. "Is that all he's got?" opposing players would ask. Indeed, all Diz had was a slow ball, control of his pitches, and a lot of heart. After his injury in the All-Star Game, Diz won only seventeen games the rest of his career. From the ages of twenty-two to twenty-seven, he was the best pitcher in baseball. At twenty-eight he was just another pitcher; at thirty-one he was out of the game. Though he pitched only six full seasons in the majors, Diz won 150 games and was voted into the Baseball Hall of Fame.

Branch Rickey, who broke baseball's color line by signing Jackie Robinson, once said of Dizzy Dean: "The greatest pitchers I have ever seen were Christy Mathewson and Jerome Dean." Rickey liked to address a man by his given name, and he especially liked referring to Dizzy as "Jerome."

Kirby Higbe, a pitcher for the Birmingham Barons in 1938 and later a major-leaguer, was, like Dean, a Southern boy. Higbe, from Columbia, South Carolina, was Dean's teammate on the Chicago Cubs. Four decades later he would say of his hero: "For all of us Southern boys, Dean was the Southern pitcher. He was up there representing us. That's how we looked at it. We all wanted to be Dizzy. One of the greatest guys that ever lived."

Writer Donald Honig once said that Dean's attraction for Higbe and other Southern boys went deeper than their pride in his pitching skill. "One cannot discount a satisfying sociological element," Honig said. "The shrewd and witty Dean had come muddy-shoed to the big city and with calculating cornpone charm put a reverse spin on the accepted concept of sophistication. If the big-city folk were laughing congenially with him, Dizzy was laughing even harder back at them. Higbe would echo his hero's tactical credo: 'I never tried to out-smart nobody. It was easier to out-dummy them.'"

Said sportswriter Zipp Newman: "It is doubtful whether Dizzy Dean ever pitched a game in the majors without hundreds of Birmingham fans studying the box score of the game. He was part of the conversation in every barbershop. For years he was the most discussed ball player in Birmingham. Dean has come to the end of the broad highway. And 'Gus Fan' is sad. We would liked for Dean to have gone on and on."

Little boys growing up in the 1950s and '60s didn't know—or much care—about Dizzy Dean's pitching career. To those little boys, Dizzy Dean meant one thing—baseball's Game of the Week. After Diz's pitching career ended in the early forties, he became a radio broadcaster for the St. Louis Cardinals. In 1953, he was hired by the Falstaff Brewing Corporation to broadcast major league games on network television. He was the voice of the Game of the Week until 1965, teaming the last six years with Pee Wee Reese. At the end, he was earning $100,000 a year just being himself—an old country boy wearing a Western string tie and a big Stetson hat. NBC replaced Diz with Curt Gowdy in 1966. Diz was dismayed, "but I'll be alright," he said. "I'm like that river there, you know. I'll just keep on rollin' and movin' along."

In later years, Diz's weight rose to 265 pounds, eighty-five pounds above his playing weight. In 1974, at a celebrity golf tournament in South Lake Tahoe, California, he experienced severe chest pains. He was hospitalized for three days

Ray Caldwell battled body and soul to remain in the game, but Father Time finally won. In 1933, at the age of 45, he pitched two games for the Charlotte Hornets and one game for the Atlanta Crackers. He pitched the final month of the season for Keokuk, Iowa, in a Class B league. Then he settled in the Allegheny foothills near Jamestown, New York, to live out his life.

and was preparing to return to his home in Mississippi when he had a major heart attack. He died two days later at the age of sixty-four.

THE YEAR AFTER THE *1931* Dixie Series, **Ray Caldwell** returned to Birmingham for his twenty-third season of professional baseball. In his second pitching start, he twisted his right knee trying to avoid an inside pitch while batting. In his next start, May 10, 1932, he lasted only three innings, allowing five runs. Ray believed that by sitting out a few games the knee would get better. Days turned into weeks, and still he did not pitch. On June 1, he had knee surgery. One surgeon remarked that Ray was "the most remarkable preserved athlete for his age I have ever seen." By July, Caldwell vowed to pitch again, but one of his doctors conceded that his condition was more serious than expected. He did not pitch again that year.

The Southern Association had been experimenting with a new baseball in 1932 in an effort to lower batting averages and reduce the number of home runs. The stitching on the ball was raised, making it easier for pitchers to throw curve balls. It was a change that would have benefited Caldwell. While Caldwell was out with his injury, Harley Boss, first baseman for the Chattanooga Lookouts, said, "When the Barons had Caldwell, they had a pitcher who could go out and put the opposing batters in a slump. You couldn't whale away with your bat and hit Caldwell. He just kept you fooled, making you hit at bad balls you swore you wouldn't strike at. And this less-lively ball will be a dangerous thing in the hands of the old pitching master."

The next season, 1933, Ray returned to the Barons. Age had hit him hard and fast, and his knee was no better. The Washington Senators, New York Yankees, St. Louis Cardinals, and Cleveland Indians came through Birmingham to play spring exhibition games against the Barons. On March 27, 1933, Ray pitched three innings against the Senators, giving up five runs. Six days later, he faced the Cardinals and pitcher Dizzy Dean. Dean, now a major league star, pitched a shutout against the Barons. Caldwell gave up nine hits and three runs in five innings. It was the last time he would pitch at Rickwood Field.

By now, Ray suspected he could no longer play championship-caliber baseball. He had worked hard to get in shape for the 1933 season, but because of his injured knee, he couldn't move fast enough to field ground balls. His last chance to pitch came on April 15 against the New Orleans Pelicans in New Orleans. In the fourth inning, the Pelicans pounded his offerings to all corners of the field, and he left the game having allowed seven runs. Four days later he retired, a week shy of his forty-fifth birthday. Ray's plan was to play exhibition games with a group of major league old-timers touring the country. But this was 1933: Times were hard, and fewer people were attending baseball games. The old-timers' tour failed, and Father Time had Ray in its clutches.

For twenty-four years, as man and boy, Ray Caldwell had played baseball — it was all he knew. He had battled body and soul to remain in the game and, now, Father Time had won. After the old-timers' tour failed in 1933, he caught on with the Charlotte Hornets, a Class B team owned by his old manager, Johnny Dobbs. After two games, he was released. He drifted back to the Southern Association, signing with the Atlanta Crackers. He made one start, won the game, and was released two weeks later.

"I don't know what I am going to do, but I still think I can win games in the Southern League," he declared. He returned to Birmingham hoping for a tryout, but nothing came of it. He caught on with Keokuk, Iowa, for the final month of the '33 season as player-manager. Keokuk was a last-place team in another Class B league. Ray Caldwell had reached the end of the line.

Ray settled in the Allegheny foothills near Jamestown, New York, twenty-five miles from his hometown of Corydon, Pennsylvania. He worked as a railroad telegraph operator, a bartender, even as a greeter at a Las Vegas casino. In the late 1950s, approaching his seventieth year, Ray's eyesight began to fail; he needed cataract surgery on both eyes. He had little money, but friends came

Ray Caldwell (right) was 66 years old in this picture in 1954. He is shown with Cleveland Indians pitcher Bob Feller, who was nearing the end of his Hall of Fame career. Caldwell also pitched for the Indians at the end of his major league career. A few years after this picture was taken, Caldwell's eyesight began to fail, and friends came to his aid to pay for cataract surgery on his eyes.

to his aid — the Lions Club raised money; an eye specialist donated his services; his old team, the Cleveland Indians, funded the surgeries.

"I never knew people could be like this," Ray admitted. "It makes you feel like you pitched a no-hitter."

After his eye surgery in 1961, Ray Caldwell lived a quiet life for six years. The Kinzua Dam was constructed on the Allegheny River in 1965, and the slowly rising waters consumed the community of Corydon. Two years later, Ray Caldwell, the man they called "Slim," was dead of cancer.

RAY CALDWELL LEARNED TO PLAY baseball in a pasture lot in Corydon. From there, it was a long jump to Broadway in New York. Said Ray, "I just sort of scratched around from the time I was born in Corydon, Pennsylvania, and it wasn't easy in those days."

During his playing days, Ray won 293 games—134 in the majors, 159 in the minors. Miller Huggins, the New York Yankees manager, once said, "Caldwell was one of the best pitchers that ever lived, but he was one of those characters that keep a manager in a constant worry. If he had possessed a sense of responsibility and balance, Ray Caldwell would have gone down in history as one of the greatest of all pitchers."

Fred Lieb wrote in *The Sporting News* of Ray Caldwell: "He was one of the playboys of his time. Caldwell loved baseball, but he loved the high lights better."

Ray Caldwell, at age seventy-three, said, "you know, stories have been printed saying I was a drinker. That's not true. I was sore about them. In fact, I was thinking about suing the papers. . . . I was always ready to pitch."

When Ray Caldwell died, the newspapers spoke only of his years on big league diamonds, of the might-haves and could've-beens. They didn't know, or perhaps they'd forgotten—maybe it didn't matter—that he'd beaten Dizzy Dean in a baseball game at Rickwood Field. But Ray Caldwell, his career almost done, would not forget. Neither would Dizzy Dean, just beginning his career. Nor Rick Woodward on his birthday. Nor Billy Bancroft on the biggest day of his life. Nor the soda hawkers, nor Henry Vance, nor Walter, nor Charles Stewart. For those souls, it was a day long remembered—a day that was like the World Series, in a city where hard times stayed the longest, when Birmingham needed a game but got much more. For on that September day, Ray Caldwell chiseled his name on a tablet of stone that will last as long as the game endures.

)(

RICKWOOD FIELD

THE DEPRESSION YEARS OF THE thirties and the war years of the forties were dark ones for the Birmingham Baseball Association, both in team performance and attendance. The *late* forties, however, were as glorious as the earlier years were lean. With skillful promotion and better ball clubs, the Barons averaged nearly four-hundred-thousand customers a year in the four seasons from 1948 to 1951. Rickwood was the most popular ball park in all of minor league baseball.

Society changed in the 1950s. Television and air conditioning kept families at home. People engaged in other leisure activities: boating, bowling, driving their cars, going to movies, spending weekends at the river. Interest in minor league baseball across the country began a long, slow decline. The crowds stopped coming. The 1970s were the darkest ever for Birmingham baseball and for the minor leagues generally. Attendance was so dreadful in Birmingham—twenty-one thousand for the entire season of 1973, for instance—that Rickwood went dark for five years—no team. Baseball returned in 1981, but Rickwood Field was in decay. The baseball-watching population had left the west side of town. The tidy homes of steelworkers that once surrounded Rickwood were now empty lots. Inside the ball park, steel was rusting and concrete was crumbling. There was faulty wiring, poor plumbing, inadequate parking, and security concerns.

In 1988, the Barons moved to suburban Hoover, leaving behind the ghosts of Mathewson, Ruth, Cobb, Paige, Hornsby, Caldwell, and Dean. The gates of Rickwood would be shuttered forever, we thought. But as a famous man once said, "The rumors of my death have been greatly exaggerated."

In his book *Good Wood*, Ben Cook wrote that by the early 1990s, Rickwood's roof was literally caving in. "The park was becoming more of a storage facility and school-bus terminal than the holiest of baseball shrines." Then, Cook said, "The Friends of Rickwood came to the rescue." The Friends, a group of baseball purists, restored and saved the park, and in 1996 the Barons came back to Rickwood for a "turn back the clock" game. On a humid afternoon in June, ten thousand returned to the shrine. Pre-game ceremonies honored the 1948 Negro American League champion Black Barons and the '48 Dixie Series champion White Barons. Once again, ball players in flannel uniforms hit from the same batter's box, threw from the same pitcher's mound, sat in the same dugouts as the ghosts once had. And the Barons beat the Memphis Chicks, 3-2.

They continue to play this Rickwood Classic every year. Rickwood also hosts up to two hundred events annually: high school and college games, tournaments, men's and youth travel ball, scout and instructional camps, and corporate events.

People have visited Rickwood from nearly every state in the union and from many foreign countries. Movies about Ty Cobb and Jackie Robinson have been filmed in the park.

David Brewer, executive director of Friends of Rickwood, says the significance of Rickwood is about more than baseball. "We know the park is rich with baseball history," he says, "but as a social historian, I see Rickwood Field as a core component of our community and of our nation's collective history and social fabric. The notion is that a ball park and a home team play a role in shaping community identity and a sense of pride. As the home of the Barons and the Black Barons, Rickwood Field filled that role for both the black and white communities."

Through the years, the grand old ball parks of America have fallen, one by one, until today Rickwood stands alone. It is the country's oldest ball park, older than Boston's Fenway Park. Rickwood Field is more than a century old. Yet this national treasure is open most every weekday for any fan to walk its grounds, to stalk its ghosts.

The grounds are silent now. The ball players have gone home. The peanut boy must rest. On your next visit to the 'Wood, remember the ball players who once romped this diamond. Reminisce about events of long ago, and you'll say, Rickwood, may you live another hundred years.

ACKNOWLEDGMENTS

To LEARN ABOUT THE BIRMINGHAM Barons and to gain a full flavor of the times, I searched the microfilm of two local newspapers for every day of the period covered by this book, 1910 to 1931. For information on the old West End Park—the Slag Pile—I reviewed newspapers as far back as 1901. Ninety percent of the material in the book is from newspaper accounts of the day. On occasion, the Birmingham Public Library borrowed microfilm for me from libraries across the country. This was particularly helpful in following the trail of Clarence (Pop Boy) Smith. Thank you, Dottie Turner of the Birmingham Public Library, for your diligence in obtaining out-of-state film.

One of the best baseball players in Birmingham history was Pie Traynor. I drew freely from the book *Pie Traynor: A Baseball Biography* by James Forr and David Proctor to tell the story of Traynor's formative years and his major league career.

I wrote the chapters on Burleigh Grimes' major league career without benefit of a biography on his life. To reconstruct Grimes' career, I relied on books of general baseball history and articles from the defunct *Baseball Magazine*. The book *Spitballers: The Last Legal Hurlers of the Wet One,* by Charles and Richard Faber, was especially helpful. The first full-length treatment of Grimes' life, *Burleigh Grimes: Baseball's Last Legal Spitballer,* was published by author Joe Niese after I had concluded my research.

A full-length biography of Ray Caldwell has never been written. However, author Steve Steinberg did ground-breaking research on Caldwell's life and career for an on-line biography he wrote for the Society for American Baseball Research. I relied on his biography for the details of Caldwell's major league career. Steinberg also furnished two photographs that heretofore have never been published. The Chautauqua, New York, Sports Hall of Fame provided newspaper articles on Caldwell's final years.

In writing of events of a century ago, one often does not possess the insight to fully develop the characters in a story. For information on Billy Bancroft and Eugene (Bull) Connor, I relied on two in-depth newspaper articles of the period. In the case of Bancroft, it meant borrowing extensive passages from an article on his high school and college careers. For Connor, it meant utilizing, at length, his own words in recounting his childhood and early adulthood. Thank you, *Birmingham News*.

Dr. Monique Seefried, chair of the Croix Rouge Farm Memorial Foundation, edited the segment on the Alabama 167th Infantry Regiment of World War One. The Foundation has memorialized the 167th and the U.S. 42nd (Rainbow) Division. Dr. Seefried was appointed by the Speaker of the U.S. House of Representatives to the World War One Centennial Commission.

Thank you to the families of the bygone ball players for photographs and personal recollections: Carlton Molesworth III, Steven Bancroft (Billy Bancroft), Susan Hughston and Melinda Ryberg (Clyde Milan), Dee Thompson (Bob Hasty), Marilyn Lenick (Pie Traynor), and Phillip Walker (Clarence Smith). In most cases, grandchildren were my link to the past. However, Johnny Dobbs' son, Nick, was alive and well in Chattanooga, Tennessee, at the age of ninety-five as the book went to press. Thanks to Charles and Ardeth Clark, curators of the Clear Lake, Wisconsin, Historical Museum, and to author Joe Niese for photographs of Burleigh Grimes.

The Indiana State Library in Indianapolis and the public libraries in the following cities furnished obituaries: Abilene, Texas; Clarksville, Texas; Beaumont, Texas; Nevada, Missouri; Noblesville, Indiana; Conshohocken, Pennsylvania; Ashland, Ohio; and Lake City, Florida. The National Baseball Hall of Fame in Cooperstown, New York, supplied information on ball players from its files.

Thank you, David Brewer and the Friends of Rickwood, for supplying photographs and leads during my four-and-a-half years of research on baseball in Birmingham. Thanks to Clarence Watkins, author of the book *Baseball in Birmingham*, for photographs, and to Chuck Stewart, a memorabilia collector, for photos and for the Dixie Series Game One ticket on the title page. Chuck, quite a storyteller himself, presents another side of Dixie Series, Game One, in his book *Angels at Rickwood*.

Coke Matthews, a long-time member of Friends of Rickwood, provided a never-before-published photograph of Rickwood Field before its remodeling in 1928. This picture was an invaluable component of the cover artwork.

Where photographs did not exist, artist Sonia Summers created illustrations from grainy newspaper photos. Of particular interest is her panorama of West End Park, the Slag Pile, home of the Barons from 1896 to 1910. A tip of the cap to Kerry Gossett of Springville, Alabama, for identifying and purchasing a team photograph of the Barons, circa 1910, at an estate auction in Ashville, Alabama. His photograph was vital to Sonia Summers in her illustration of West End Park.

The book contains one-hundred-year-old photographs that were in remarkably good condition. Photographs that did not meet our standards for publication were restored by a marvelous graphic artist, Beth Conklin. Beth also designed the front and back covers of the book.

Jerri Beck, proofreader and designer of the interior of the book, was extremely patient with the author in the final stages of production. Often, Jerri's love of language improved grammar and sentence structure within these pages.

Denise O'Rourke provided special photographs. Sarah Williams marketed the book. Thank you to my friends Anita Smith, Jim Barton, Jim Palmer, and David Reed for contributions large and small, for offering suggestions, for lending an ear.

I am grateful to my editors: Steve Millburg, for his wise counsel, for his remarkable ability to ferret out mistakes in grammar and fact, and for his conviction that this book was worthy of being published; Larry Wharton, a professor of creative writing, for convincing me to rewrite portions of the manuscript to improve narrative flow; and Liz Reed, for her ability to choose just the right word or phrase, while putting her final touches on the manuscript.

Finally, thank you to all who played the game, reported the game, and loved the game.

ILLUSTRATION CREDITS

194 Johnny Dobbs (Birmingham Barons)

195 Johnny Dobbs (National Baseball Hall of Fame Library, Cooperstown, New York)

198 Johnny Dobbs (Nick Dobbs)

203 Johnny Dobbs (Nick Dobbs)

206 Eddie Wells (Ernie Harwell Collection, Detroit Public Library)

209 Spirit of St. Louis (Birmingham, Alabama, Public Library Archives)

214 Rickwood Field (Memphis & Shelby County Room, Memphis Public Library)

215 Yam Yaryan (Clarence Watkins)

216 Stuffy Stewart (Clarence Watkins)

219 Jimmy Johnston (Ernie Harwell Collection, Detroit Public Library)

220 Jimmy Johnston (Carlton Molesworth III)

221 Elliot Bigelow (Chuck Stewart)

222 Elliot Bigelow (National Baseball Hall of Fame Library, Cooperstown, New York)

224 Eddie Wells (Clarence Watkins)

227 Art Weis (Ernie Harwell Collection, Detroit Public Library)

229 W. D. Smith, Rick Woodward (Birmingham Barons)

230 Bob Hasty (Dee Thompson)

233 Ray Caldwell (Birmingham Barons)

244 Dizzy Dean (National Baseball Hall of Fame Library, Cooperstown, New York)

255 Clyde Milan and Family (Susan Hughston)

257 Clyde Milan (Steve Bancroft)

258 Billy Bancroft, Shine Cortazzo (Steve Bancroft)

262 Ray Caldwell, Jimmy Walkup, Bob Hasty, Clay Touchstone (Steve Bancroft)

263 Art Weis (Birmingham Barons)

265 Ray Caldwell, Dizzy Dean (RG D 0005 Folder 7492, Houston Public Library, HMRC)

271 Billy Bancroft (Steve Bancroft)

286 Bull Connor (Sonia Summers)

304 Dixie Series Champions (Sonia Summers)

334 Dizzy Dean (National Baseball Hall of Fame Library, Cooperstown, New York)

336 Ray Caldwell (Chuck Stewart)

338 Bob Feller, Ray Caldwell (Steve Steinberg)

341 Rickwood Field (Denise O'Rourke)

NOTES

Abbreviations
Bham News: Birmingham News
Bham A-H: Birmingham Age-Herald
Bham P-H: Birmingham Post-Herald
Bham Post: Birmingham Post

Prologue

1 The story went like this: *Cleveland Plain Dealer,* August 25, 1919; *New York Times,* September 11, 1919

5 Italian art exhibit: The Italian art exhibit in September 1931 included a bronze replica of the fabled wolf that nursed twin brothers Romulus and Remus, who, according to legend, founded ancient Rome. The sculpture was a gift from Benito Mussolini and the Italian government and remains on display today at the Birmingham Public Library. See *Birmingham Age-Herald,* September 14/15, 1931.

6 third largest in the South: *Bham News,* November 6, 1931

6 the mightiest city: *Bham News* editorial, January 2, 1930

6 "Long before I reach Birmingham": *Bham A-H,* November 10, 1920

6 Hard-boiled ironworkers: *Bham News* editorial, May 9, 1924; *Bham A-H,* April 6, 1933

6 when at least one murder: For many years, life was cheap in Birmingham and Jefferson County. For example, according to newspaper accounts, the county experienced the following numbers of homicides: 159 in 1920, 181 in 1921, 192 in 1924, 172 in 1930. See *Birmingham News,* January 2, 1921; January 6, 1925; May 2, 1931; and *Birmingham Age-Herald,* January 1, 1922.

6 Two of the wildest: *Bham News,* October 30, 1927; *Bham A-H,* August 7, 1931. Names such as Buzzard Roost and Scratch Ankle denoted police walking beats. Buzzard Roost was the beat around the old Terminal train station, between First and Fifth avenues, from Twenty-first to Twenty-sixth streets. Before there was a Terminal Station, houses in that section were far apart. Buzzards roosted in trees between the houses. Scratch

Ankle, between First and Fifth avenues, from Fourteenth to Eighteenth streets, once had a lot of stockyards and a big ditch. All around where the patrolmen walked were thousands of fleas, so Scratch Ankle. See *Birmingham Age-Herald,* June 17, 1940. Buzzard Roost and Scratch Ankle were so dangerous that even the police stayed out except when they went in two and three together. Mayor George Ward once ordered The Dude saloon in Buzzard Roost closed, but no policeman would go in to close it. Ward had to do it himself. See *Birmingham News* magazine, April 20, 1941.

8   football in the South: College football games were played at Rickwood Field every year from 1910-1927. The largest crowd at Rickwood was 20,000 for the Alabama-Georgia game in 1924. See *Birmingham Age-Herald,* November 28, 1924. In 1927, Alabama and Georgia set a new record for the state of Alabama, drawing 24,000 to Legion Field. See *Birmingham News,* November 29, 1927. Three years later, a Thanksgiving Day game between Alabama and Georgia at Legion Field drew another record: 28,000. See *Birmingham News,* November 28, 1930.

8   linked by baseball: Wallop, Douglass, *Baseball: An Informal History,* p. 94

8   discovered by professional scouts: Dozens, if not hundreds, of players from Birmingham city and industrial league teams of the 1910s, '20s, and '30s signed professional baseball contracts. Those who later played in the major leagues include, among others, Frank Welch, Del Pratt, Virgil (Spud) Davis, Pop Boy Smith, Whitey Glazner, Fred Sington, Sam Byrd, Ben Chapman, Joe Sewell, Luke Sewell, Riggs Stephenson, Ivy Paul Andrews, Dixie Walker, Harry Walker, Clay Bryant, Dixie Parsons, Bobby Bragan, Wilson (Dee) Miles, Virgil Trucks, Luman Harris, Gus Niarhos, Dan Bankhead, and Artie Wilson. See *Birmingham News,* February 19/23, 1941, and May 24, 1942.

9   "Baseball is indisputably": *Bham News,* August 10, 1910

9   "I can hear the sparrows": *Bham News,* April 19, 1923

9   "From April to September": Marshall, Benny, *All Time Greatest Alabama Sports Stories,* pp. 2-3

10 merchants rewarded ball players: *Bham A-H,* April 22, 1904

10 Western Union messenger boy: The primary duties of Western Union messenger boys were to deliver telegrams and messages of birth, death, weddings, and business deals. In reality, they were summoned to do almost anything—take a pet dog out for fresh air, carry flowers to a sweetheart, fill in for an absent office clerk, even deliver liquor for a bootlegger. See *Birmingham News,* July 23, 1926.

10 re-created games called "matinees": The first baseball matinees in Birmingham were held in 1903 when "Commodore" Orcutt called games from the stage of O'Brien's Opera House. In 1905, matinees "hot from the wire" were held at the Jefferson Theater and the Apollo Billiard Hall. See *Birmingham Age-Herald,* May 1, 1903, and *Birmingham News,* May 3, 1905. In 1911, the Jefferson Theater announced that "management has secured an electric board, and every play will be illustrated by electricity." See *Birmingham Age-Herald,* April 20, 1911. The *Age-Herald,* June 29, 1919, stated: "Commodore is a telegraph operator, reads the click of the wires from the jump, and can put more pep into a fight, baseball, or racetrack matinee than any living man."

10 a siren was placed: For a brief period prior to 1920, a siren was placed atop the Saks department store. In 1922, a siren was placed atop the First National Bank building. In 1929, the siren was moved to the Odum Clothing Company. The sounding of the siren began one hour before game time and continued at

10-minute intervals. See *Birmingham Age-Herald,* April 26, June 3, 1922; May 11, 1925; April 25, 1926; April 24, 1929. A powerful searchlight atop the *Age-Herald* building flashed the results of the 1924 presidential election. A vertical beam straight up into the sky meant that incumbent Calvin Coolidge had won. If challenger John Davis had been the winner, there would have been a horizontal beam, east to west. Detailed presidential returns in 1924 were supplied at three high school auditoriums and at the *Age-Herald* building. See *Birmingham Age-Herald,* November 4, 1924.

11 met at the Morris Hotel: *Bham News,* October 22, 1900; February 1, 1925

11 baseball's most stable: Obojski, Robert, *Bush League: A History of Minor League Baseball,* pp. 217-218; Wright, Marshall, *The Southern Association in Baseball, 1885-1961,* pp. 77-78

12 played in the daytime: The first night game in the Southern Association was played between Birmingham and Little Rock at Little Rock, Arkansas, July 21, 1930. Both teams apparently had trouble with the floodlights early in the game, as several fielding errors were made. At bat, players had no problems; Birmingham's Shine Cortazzo hit the first pitch of the game for a single, and both teams kept on hitting. Little Rock won, 9-8. The first night game at Rickwood Field occurred on May 21, 1936, the Barons defeating Chattanooga, 6-5. The game drew 13,749, the fourth-largest crowd to that point at Rickwood. The first Sunday game at Rickwood was played on July 31, 1932, also against Chattanooga, drawing 9,000. See *Birmingham News,* July 22, 1930; May 22, 1936. Regarding the first night game at Rickwood, *The Birmingham Age-Herald* said in an editorial: "It was a sight to behold! For sheer beauty the scene was breathtaking. The green of the superb outfield, the near-maroon of the skinned infield were entrancing in the soft glow of these powerful yet somehow soft manmade suns."

12 One spring day: *Bham A-H,* May 28, 1922

12 spraying the ball: White, Edward, *Creating the National Pastime: Baseball Transforms Itself, 1903-1953,* p. 14

13 The Reach Company: Honig, Donald, *Baseball America,* p. 136

14 enlisted a boy: *Bham A-H,* May 11, 1917

14 first public address system: The public address system in 1928 was a short-lived experiment, apparently lasting only one game. It would be more than seven years before a P.A. was used again in May 1936, with Eugene (Bull) Connor at the mike. See *Birmingham Age-Herald,* August 25, 1928; *Birmingham News,* September 2/5, 1928; *Birmingham News,* May 16, 1936. For a picture of Henry Vance behind the mike, see *Birmingham News,* September 5, 1928.

14 strolling the streets: *Bham News,* August 31, 1922

14 Floyd Gardner: In 1923, there were two scoreboards along the outfield fence—a major league scoreboard in right centerfield and a Southern League scoreboard in centerfield. See *Birmingham Age-Herald,* August 21, 1923.

15 "spectacular double play": *Bham News,* July 31, 1931

15 Henry Vance claimed: *Bham A-H,* April 5, 1921

17 dreaded boll weevil: *Bham A-H,* August 18/19, 1910; October 17, 1913

17 boys were shooting craps: *Bham News,* June 24, 1912

17 Judge Hugo Black: *Bham A-H,* September 9, 1912. In 1910, Hugo Black was a struggling young attorney living in a boardinghouse, four men to a room, when a city commissioner, Judge A. O. Lane, asked him to serve as judge on the Police Court. Black held the position for one-and-a-half years. "I didn't want the job," Black said, "but Judge Lane urged me to take it, and I did…I tried to resign at the end of a year, but Judge Lane asked me to stay on longer…I stayed for another six months, then returned to my law practice." See *Birmingham News* magazine, January 31, 1937, and *Birmingham News,* August 12, 1937.

17 calling another man a liar: *Bham News,* August 10, 1912
17 cursing in his native tongue: *Bham News,* June 6, 1912
17 frequent sight around town: *Bham News,* March 26, 1927
17 twelve automobiles were registered: *Bham A-H,* August 5, 1927
17 horse, frightened by: *Bham A-H,* August 28, 1912
17 One man in 1910: *Bham A-H,* April 4, 1910
17 A mule entered: *Bham News,* December 5, 1924
17 A monkey belonging: *Bham News,* July 4, 1924
18 paved with concrete: *Bham News,* June 28, 1911; February 26, 1913; *Bham A-H,* July 16, 1912. Birmingham's first street was paved with Belgian blocks in 1887 in the area of 19th, 20th, and 21st streets and Morris, 1st, and 2nd avenues. The Belgian blocks remained in place until 1911 and 1912, when they were replaced with wooden blocks on a concrete base. The wooden blocks on 20th Street were replaced with asphalt in 1928. See *Birmingham News,* April 8, August 27, 1928.
18 Paving with asphalt: *Bham A-H,* February 15, 1911
18 blowing clouds of dust: *Bham A-H,* June 21/22, 1923
18 Chattanooga to Birmingham: *Bham A-H,* September 5, 1910
19 streets were lined with: *Bham News,* December 22, 1932
19 Phil Givhan, riding his horse: *Bham A-H,* October 6, 1921

Chapter 1

24 "Boys get recommended": For Molesworth's stance on signing amateur players, see *Birmingham News,* April 2, 1915, and *Birmingham Age-Herald,* March 13, 1921.
25 "fans rode me hard": In his first year with Birmingham in 1909, Roy Ellam made numerous errors and fans jeered him, but he was determined to make good. He eventually became a fan favorite and the finest shortstop to play for the Barons until Pie Traynor arrived in 1921. See *Birmingham Age-Herald,* May 19, 1911, and May 7, 1912, for his difficulties with fans.
27 You could hear him: *Bham A-H,* March 15, 1911
27 placid, slow-thinking chap: *Bham A-H,* March 6, 1911
27 clenched his teeth: *Bham A-H,* April 23, 1908
30 job as a newsboy: *Bham A-H,* September 3, 1910
30 foller Moley's rule: *Bham News,* June 3, 1910
31 "You'll be in the box tomorrow": Molesworth could see that Clarence Smith had a fine arm and asked him to pitch against the Barons in batting practice. See *Birmingham News,* July 16, 1912.
32 full of baseball brains: *Bham A-H,* March 18, 1912
32 Marcan got his nickname: *Bham A-H,* July 24, 1912
33 didn't have much of a windup: For a brief description of Clarence Smith's windup, see *Birmingham News,* April 3, 1912, and Dolly Dalrymple's column in *Birmingham Age-Herald,* July 23, 1912.
34 no one could hit him: Molesworth was disgusted that his players were unable to hit Clarence Smith during batting practice. He later signed Clarence for the 1911 season. See *Birmingham Age-Herald,* July 28, 1912.

Chapter 2

35 the leading topic: *Bham News,* August 15, 1910
35 torn by adverse fortune: *Bham News,* April 9, 1910

36   thousands of people rode streetcars: *Bham News,* August 15, 1910

36   messenger boys dashed: Ibid

36   at the Virginia Theatre: *Bham News,* August 15, 1910. For many years in the early 1900s, Commodore Orcutt called baseball, prize fight, and horse racing matinees in venues around Birmingham. A cotton broker by trade, Orcutt came to Birmingham from Pittsburgh in 1892. In 1903, he called Barons games from the stage of O'Brien's Opera House. See *Birmingham Age-Herald,* May 1, 1903. According to *The Birmingham News,* June 30, 1921, in the final days before calling a prize fight, Orcutt slept with a damp towel around his throat. He died in 1927 at the age of 61. See *Birmingham News* and *Birmingham Age-Herald,* June 14, 1927.

36   lettered over mirrors: *Bham News,* August 15, 1910

36   "playing magnificent ball": *Bham A-H,* August 14, 1910

37   "what shall we call the new field?": *Bham A-H,* July 19, 1910

37   nearly two hundred proposals: *Bham A-H,* July 21, 1910

37   next to Alice Furnace: Alice Furnace, located on the western edge of Birmingham, was the city's first pig iron furnace. Named for the eldest daughter of Henry DeBardeleben, one of the furnace's founders, Alice Furnace went into blast in November 1880, ushering in the great iron boom of the 1880s in Alabama. See White, Marjorie, *The Birmingham District: An Industrial History and Guide,* pp. 46-47.

38   Home to the Barons: According to *The Birmingham Age-Herald,* August 18, 1910, West End Park was dedicated April 18, 1896, with a game between the University of Alabama and Howard College. Prior to the formation of the Southern Association in 1901, the park had been used as a coliseum for bicycle racing for the previous two years. See *Birmingham News,* April 12, 1901.

38   capacity was expanded: *Bham A-H,* March 21, 1903

39   iron-making process: A single furnace could produce as much as 400 tons of slag a day. Piles of slag were scattered around Birmingham, creating an eyesore for a progressive city. One unsightly pile blocked the thoroughfare at Second Avenue and Thirtieth Street. The largest pile, located in Ensley, measured 1500 feet long, 1500 feet wide, and in some places 100 feet deep. The slag piles did have significance: the larger the piles, the more iron being produced. A pile of slag 30 to 40 feet high and half a block long signified that thousands and thousands of tons of iron had been produced. See *Birmingham News,* December 21, 1913.

39   "shack of a grandstand": *Bham A-H,* September 18, 1910

39   "Every fan should go": *Bham A-H,* August 13, 1910

40   situated on low ground: *Bham News,* February 1, 1925

40   a narrow alleyway: *Bham News,* March 15, 1925; July 31, 1932

40   a booth in the alley: *Bham News,* March 15, 1907

40   board seats without backs: Ibid

40   drinking Celery-Cola: *Bham News,* April 29, 1936. Celery-Cola, manufactured in Birmingham from 1899-1910, was the first soft drink ever sold at a Birmingham baseball game. The Pure Food and Drug Administration prosecuted Celery-Cola Company for unhealthy amounts of cocaine and caffeine in its drink. The decision against the company and subsequent publicity forced the company to close in 1910. See *Birmingham News,* April 29, 1936; "Celery-Cola and James C. Mayfield," Southernbottles.com.

40   Carriages were parked: *Bham News,* June 25, 1901

40   boys rented chairs: *Bham A-H,* June 26, 1910

40   jump the railings: *Bham News,* July 31, 1932

41   one day in 1902: *Bham A-H,* August 8, 1902

41   second baseman Frank Delahanty: *Bham News,* June 19, 1902; March 5, 1936. Delahanty, one of six ballplaying brothers, made life difficult for every baseball organization he played for. His troubles continued after he retired from the game. As Bill Lamb writes in his SABR baseball biography of Delahanty, "When he hung up his glove in 1918, life looked rosy for Frank Delahanty. Over the next decade, he threw it all away. By 1930 Delahanty was disgraced, divorced, and likely disbarred, an unemployed ex-con living in a Cleveland flophouse. But over the ensuing 35 years, Frank quietly rehabilitated his life." Read Lamb's interesting account of the life of Frank Delahanty at Sabr.org/bioproject.

41   an uncertain enterprise: *Bham News,* April 11, 1926

41   sat on board benches: Ibid

41   an enthusiastic rightfielder: *Bham News,* May 16, 1902

42   violent rainstorm erupted: *Bham News,* May 22, 1902

42   no attention was paid: *Bham News,* March 15, 1925

42   One day in 1898: Ibid

42   industrialist A. H. Woodward offered: *Bham News,* Woodward memoirs, February 11, 1934

42   As a young boy: *Bham A-H,* February 26, 1922

43   "change in ownership": *Bham News,* January 29, 1910

43   anxious for a photograph: *Bham News,* February 15, 1910

44   Woodward patterned: *Bham News,* April 15, 1923; March 22, 1935

44   two streetcar lines: *Bham News,* March 21, 1910

44   new grandstand accommodated: *Bham A-H,* March 6, 1910

44   Joseph, a wealthy capitalist: *Bham News,* Woodward memoirs, February 18, 1934

44   "It happened this way": *Bham News,* April 15, 1923

45   Hugh Roberts observed: *Bham A-H,* April 14, 1910

Chapter 3

46   Birmingham was deserted: *Bham A-H,* August 19, 1910

47   An ardent Catholic: *Bham News,* June 3/11, 1910

47   defeated the great Christy: Murphy, Cait, *Crazy '08,* p. 244

48   southern and eastern Europe: Seymour, Harold, *Baseball: The Golden Age,* pp. 453-454

48   Harry was a slate picker: Heiselman, John, "Harry Coveleski," *SABR Baseball Biography Project,* Sabr.org/bioproject

48   Sitting on a pine board: Kashatus, William, *Diamonds in the Coalfields,* p. 9

48   What is remarkable: Ibid, pp. 9-10

49   four of the Coveleski brothers: Murphy, *Crazy '08,* p. 240

49   Pitching for the Bunker Hills: Heiselman, "Harry Coveleski," Sabr.org/bioproject

49   first game at Rickwood Field: *Bham A-H,* August 19, 1910

51   Blach's department store: *Bham A-H,* September 14, 1910

51   "this is a great old town": *Bham A-H,* May 23, 1911

52   his arm went bad: Heiselman, "Harry Coveleski," Sabr.org/bioproject

Chapter 4

54   a thoughtful student: *Bham A-H,* July 28, 1912

54   "I think the kid can win": Ibid

55   leather-lunged vendors yelping: A tourist from the North thought it unusual to see vendors selling toys along sidewalks in Birmingham: "When did they place a midway on your prominent streets? I expected to see a sideshow every minute as I walked along Third Avenue around Nineteenth Street and over to Second Avenue. 'Get a funny ball, a monster toy balloon, see the monkey dance, see the monkey dance.' Why do your commissioners allow such things to go on in your city?" See *Birmingham Age-Herald,* December 22, 1920.

56   buzzing and popping of fireworks: Strange as it seems, in Southern cities during the first half of the twentieth century, it was Christmas, not July 4, that was celebrated with fireworks. See, for instance, a *Birmingham News* editorial, July 6, 1935.

56   "backbone of winter": *Bham News,* February 2, 1911

56   goose honked high: an expression from the period that means conditions are favorable

57   "Rowdy Elliott in Hot Springs": Hot Springs, Arkansas, a city of 14,000, was a popular health resort known for dozens of naturally heated springs that bubbled out of the ground. Ball players went to Hot Springs every February and March to hike the hills, drink the thermal waters, soak in mineral baths, and "boil out" the kinks and stiffness of the long winter. See Lackey, Mike, *Spitballing: The Baseball Days of Long Bob Ewing,* p. 210.

58   "Ninety dollars a month": *The Birmingham Age-Herald,* July 28, 1912, stated that Clarence Smith's contract in 1911 called for a salary of $75 a month. *The Atlanta Constitution,* June 27, 1912, quotes Carlton Molesworth as saying he paid Clarence $90 a month.

58   "I want to tell you a story": The story of Birmingham Manager Harry Vaughn attempting to sign Ty Cobb is based on accounts in *The Birmingham Age-Herald,* March 22, 1911, and February 26, 1922.

58   "fifty dollars a month": In 1927, Dr. L. L. Scarbrough, director of the Anniston ball club when Ty Cobb played there, was in possession of Cobb's contract, calling for a salary of $50 a month, according to a story in *The Birmingham News,* January 2, 1927. The newspaper story includes a photograph of the contract. For more on the contract, see *Birmingham Age-Herald,* July 12, 1910.

60   two hundred thousand: In 1911, Greater Birmingham was defined as the business district and a surrounding area of approximately five miles. An estimated 212,000 people lived in Greater Birmingham in 1910 and 235,000 in 1912, according to *The Birmingham Age-Herald,* September 22, 1912.

60   humming with industry: *Bham A-H* editorials, September 12/16, 1912

60   a city of broad streets: *Bham News,* June 9/13, 1912; *Bham A-H* editorials, July 31, August 26/27, 1912

61   march of progress: *Bham A-H,* February 9, 1913

61   wooded slopes, elegant homes: *Bham A-H,* August 2, September 13, 1912

61   fine restaurants: *Bham A-H,* September 11, 1912

61   horse-drawn vehicle: *Bham News,* July 27, September 14, 1912

61   a horse, frightened: *Bham News,* March 26, 1912; *Bham A-H,* August 28, September 28, 1912

62   "gotta da hot peanut": *Bham News,* June 21, 1912

62   Lum Mow stood: *Bham News,* June 11, 1921; *Bham Post,* June 11, 1921

62   the classiest bootblack: *Bham News,* April 10, 1912

63   stables of J. Fies: *Bham A-H,* April 2, June 11, 1920

64   "They ship it by rail": Newspapers were the primary source of news in the 1910s, '20s, and '30s and were shipped across the country. "If you want a copy of *The Birmingham News* in Cleveland or Toledo, you practically have to stand in line to get it," a man

said. "It is almost the same in Detroit. The Birmingham papers arrive in the afternoon, and if you are not right there on the spot when they come in, you don't get a copy....The dealer told me...that the papers sold out rapidly and that all of the 24 he gets daily are gone in a hurry." See *Birmingham News,* September 5, 1920.

Chapter 5

65   latest dope on the team: spring training reports, *Bham News* and *Bham A-H,* February 6 through March 8, 1911

67   Molesworth cautioned Clarence: *Bham A-H,* July 28, 1912

69   Cobb stood a few inches taller: Stanton, Tom, *Ty and the Babe: Baseball's Fiercest Rivals,* p. 4

69   ready to choke up: The description of Cobb's batting stance is from a series of stories on Cobb by H. G. Salsinger in *The Birmingham Age-Herald,* November-December 1924.

69   Clarence wasn't ready: *Bham News,* April 10, 1911; *Bham A-H,* July 28, 1912

70   Clarence won his first game: from game accounts in 1911, *Bham News, Bham A-H*

71   twenty-two and losing sixteen: *Bham A-H,* September 14, 1911

71   On the last day: *Bham A-H,* July 28, 1912

72   Boyd helped Clarence: Ibid

72   'Young Smith has shown': *Bham A-H,* April 5, 1912

73   "Some of those people": *Bham A-H,* December 13, 1924

75   The great iron heart: *Bham News,* April 15, 1929

75   Woodward dispatched Manager Molesworth: *Bham A-H,* April 23, 1912. In 1911, Rafael Almeida and Armando Marsans became the first Cubans to reach the major leagues since 1873.

76   "Because we have known": Ibid

76   a startling prediction: *Bham A-H,* May 12, 1912

76   Molesworth called Clarence: *Bham A-H,* July 24, 1912

76   Chicago White Sox purchased: *Bham A-H,* September 11, 1912; *Bham News,* September 18, 1912

76   sixteen wins and eight losses: Published statistics list Clarence Smith's 1912 pitching record as 15-8. However, a game-by-game analysis by the author revealed his record to be 16-8.

Chapter 6

78   arrival of a freight train: *Bham News,* August 27, 1912

79   "When I was a youngster": Molesworth's dramatized conversation with Clarence Smith was constructed from newspaper accounts. See *Birmingham News,* August 15, 1915, and March 6, 1921, and *Birmingham Age-Herald,* April 13, 1922.

81   fabulous sum of $10,000: *Bham A-H,* August 19, 1912

81   Marcan was standing: In presenting the dialogue of the meeting called by Lil Marcan, the author elaborates on a story from *The Birmingham Age-Herald,* September 5, 1912.

82   leader of the quartet: The leader of the Barons quartet, Bill Foxen, said, "There is but one Baron who objects to the quartet, and he is none other than Manager Molesworth. Although it is not the modest thing to boast, the manager has confessed that he has had trouble in getting the players to bed while the Baron

Harmony Tour is giving a performance." See *Birmingham Age-Herald,* August 1, 1912.

83   roarin'est rooters in town: *Bham A-H,* June 21, 1911

84   biggest man in Cuba: *Bham News,* February 9/19, 1913; *Bham A-H,* February 9, 1913

85   offered him to the Atlanta: *Atlanta Constitution,* July 3/4, 1913

85   all the comforts: Seymour, *Baseball,* p. 131

86   Walsh told him to try: *Los Angeles Times,* March 11/14, 1914

86   in the "booze cage": *San Francisco Examiner, Los Angeles Times,* March 31, 1914

86   Venice was a beach resort: *Venice Daily Vanguard,* May 16/22, June 18, 1914

86   until the eighth game: *Los Angeles Times,* April 9/22, 1914

86   calling him "U.S. Smith": *Los Angeles Times,* June 28, 1914

86   Venice fell behind, 8-0: *Los Angeles Times, San Francisco Examiner,* June 28, 1914

87   his teammate, Babe Borton: *Los Angeles Times,* September 5, 1914

88   Clarence and Walter Johnson pitched: *Cleveland Plain Dealer,* September 22, 1916

88   Clarence pitched the first five: *Cleveland Plain Dealer,* September 26, 1916

89   he pitched six innings: *Salt Lake Tribune,* July 8/13, 1918

89   ended its season: *Salt Lake Tribune,* July 14, 1918

89   sick in bed: *Fort Worth Record,* April 22, 1919

89   Clarence had tuberculosis: *Fort Worth Star-Telegram,* April 27, 1919

89   leading cause of death: *Bham A-H,* December 8/10, 1920

90   On May 12, 1919: *Fort Worth Star-Telegram,* May 9, 1919

90   a check for $200: *Fort Worth Star-Telegram,* May 8, 1919

90   stopped in Birmingham: *Bham A-H,* May 18, 1919

90   pleaded for aid: *Bham A-H,* May 19, 1919

90   *Age-Herald* received a letter: *Bham A-H,* June 28, 1919

90   walked through the stands: *Bham A-H,* July 6, 1919

90   received a thank-you letter: *Bham A-H,* July 11, 1919

91   Clarence remained at the sanatorium: *Bham A-H,* September 1, 1919

91   second in the league: *Amarillo Daily News,* July 23, 1922

91   Clovis, New Mexico, Cubs: *Abilene Daily Reporter,* February 17, 1924

91   Saturday, the sixteenth of February: *Bham A-H,* February 17, 1924

91   after life's fitful fever: Shakespeare, William, *Macbeth:* Act 3, Scene 2

Chapter 7

98   twenty to fifty dollars an acre: *Clear Lake Star,* August 1912

98   heated by wood fires: *Clear Lake Centennial, 1875-1975,* p. 12

99   groves of white pine: Ibid, p. 13

99   children of Clear Lake: Ibid, p. 10

99   came to school barefoot: Ibid, p. 11

99   father gave him fifteen dollars: Honig, Donald, *A Donald Honig Reader,* p. 570

101   Logging days began: *Clear Lake Centennial,* p. 11

101   His team of horses: *Clear Lake Star,* February 5, 1914; *Bham A-H,* March 15, 1914

101   to Birmingham for $400: *Bham News,* August 7, 1916

101   "Grimes has a world of stuff": *Bham News,* May 6, 1914

102   foreign trade declined: Speare, Charles, "American Business Transformed by the War," *The American Review of Reviews,* October 1915

102   In over thirty years: "A Million Men Out of Work," *The Literary Digest,* December 26, 1914, p. 1264

102   Europe would turn: *Bham News,* December 1, 1914; *Bham A-H* editorial, June 8, 1916

102   fifteen players and $3,200: *Bham A-H,* November 12, 1914

103 played Class A: Triple A, a new classification, was created in 1946, with Birmingham becoming a Double A team.

104 "ax fell in the Baron camp": *Bham A-H,* March 12, 1922

Chapter 8

105 earnest, sober man: *Bham A-H,* August 17, 1911

106 "We could win the pennant": *Bham News,* April 14, 1929

107 stopping them with his foot: *Bham News,* July 30, 1961

107 wasn't a natural hitter: *Bham News,* April 5, 1925; April 14, 1929

107 ruined that right arm: *Bham News,* August 15, 1915

109 Roy Ellam, blond-haired: *Bham A-H,* May 7, 1912; *Bham News,* March 5, June 20, 1915

109 Tod Sloan, an outfielder: *Bham News,* June 13, 1915

109 Cecil Coombs, a utility infielder: *Bham A-H,* March 14, 1915

109 Charlie (Red) Stewart, an outfielder: *Bham News,* January 19, 1915

109 he had won twenty-two games: *Bham A-H,* July 5, 1914

110 Seven rookie ball players: *Bham News,* February 27/28, 1915

110 hit three bases-loaded home runs: *Bham A-H,* June 6, 1914

110 McDuffie pitched for: *Bham News,* February 27/28, 1915

110 He looks rather hefty: *Bham News,* February 15, 1915

110 What's this?: *Bham News,* March 2, 1915

110 a splendid little town: *Bham News,* February 19, 1915

112 diamond has been carved: *Bham News,* February 19/28, 1915

112 The past winter has been: *Bham News,* January 14, 1915

112 The moment Bertie Grimes: *Bham A-H, Bham News,* April 19, 1915

112 his fifth man: *Bham News,* February 2, 1915

112 full of song and life: *Bham News,* February 14, 1914

112 twirled a two-hit contest: *Bham A-H,* March 11, 1915

112 inconsistent Sunday laws: *Bham News,* February 19, 1915

113 Rise and shine!: *Bham News,* March 1, 1915; *Bham A-H,* March 24, 1915

113 "As for your nightlife": *Bham A-H,* March 12, 1915

114 sliding pit will be: *Bham News,* March 3, 1915

114 Twenty pounds overweight: *Bham News,* February 28, March 1, 1915

114 a good deal of steam: *Bham News,* March 1, 1915

114 a perpetual smile: *Bham News,* March 5, 1915

114 Arthur pastimed: *Bham News,* March 8, 1915

114 Several millionaires are spending: *Bham News,* March 3, 1915

115 The Tampa newspapers: *Bham News,* March 6, 1915

115 cars bear pennants: *Bham News,* March 4, 1915

115 Get wise to this!: *Bham News,* March 1, 1915

115 a fruit packinghouse: *Bham News,* March 4, 1915

115 Woodward is yachting: *Bham News,* March 5, 1915

115 have sore limbs: *Bham News,* March 6, 1915

115 playing billiards: *Bham News,* March 9, 1915

115 ladies' man of the outfit: *Bham News,* March 6, 1915

115 carry some grapefruit: *Bham News,* February 28, 1915

116 "Shotgun" Jack Wallace, reported: *Bham News,* March 8/9, 1915

116 makes friends easily: *Bham News,* March 8, 1915

116 some real cutups: *Bham News,* March 26, 1915

116 its citizens own automobiles: *Bham A-H,* April 1, 1915

116   motored to Winter Park: *Bham News,* March 8/10, 1915
116   Florida rattlesnakes have been: *Bham News,* March 9, 1915
116   "I wouldn't sign up with Moley": *Bham A-H,* March 11, 1915
117   the head of pitcher Fields: *Bham News,* March 8, 1915
117   Barons will storm Daytona: Ibid
117   the best-looking man: *Bham A-H,* March 13/21, 1915
118   Grimes pitched four innings: *Bham News,* March 11, 1915
118   The boys were just about: *Bham News,* March 5, 1915
118   wonderful advertising opportunity: *Bham A-H,* March 19, 1915
119   seven-passenger touring cars: *Bham News,* March 14, 1915
119   swell bunch of fellows: *Bham News,* March 17, 1915
119   trip back to Orlando: *Bham A-H,* March 19, 1915; *Bham News,* March 20, 1915
119   five players have been released: *Bham News,* March 14, 1915
119   snares of a big city: *Bham News,* March 21, 1915
119   Board of Trade: *Bham News,* March 17, 1915; *Bham A-H,* March 19, 1915
120   Omar Hardgrove, the old: *Bham A-H,* March 19, 1915
120   Moley likes Cantley: *Bham News,* March 22, 1915
120   George Hale, the first-string: *Bham News,* March 25, 1915
120   in favor of Grimes: *Bham News,* April 19, 1915
121   a Mr. McIntyre: *Bham A-H,* March 26, 1915
121   Playing in mackinaws: *Bham News,* March 23, 1915
122   a beautiful country estate: *Tampa Tribune,* March 3, 1915
122   Rick has as much speed: *Bham News,* March 29, 1915
122   Havana Reds: *Bham News,* March 25, 1915
122   carelessness with men: *Bham News,* March 28, 1915
122   Today there was sadness: *Bham News,* March 30, 1915
122   In taking the team to Orlando: *Bham News,* March 28, 1915
123   at a delightful banquet: *Bham A-H,* March 27, 1915
123   Rochester, the hotel waiter: *Bham News,* March 30/31, 1915

Chapter 9

124   Inquiries from the Barons: *Bham A-H, Bham News,* March 29, 1915
124   the girls of Birmingham: *Bham A-H,* April 1, 1915. For many years, the Birmingham
      Baseball Association was headquartered at the Birmingham Arms and Cycle Co., a
      sporting goods store. Prior to 1912, the Arms was located at 1916 Second Avenue
      North. Sometime after 1912 the store moved to 1919 Third Avenue North. About the
      time the Barons returned from Orlando in 1915, the ball club moved its headquarters
      from the Arms building to the 17th floor of the Jefferson County Bank building.
      See *Birmingham News,* March 30, 1915. By 1922, the club had returned to the
      Birmingham Arms, now at 2017 Third Avenue North. Henry Vance, in his Coal Bin
      column in *The Birmingham News,* April 8, 1932, said that Bob Tyson, secretary of
      the Birmingham Baseball Association in the early 1910s, operated a cigar store in a
      ramshackle building on the northeast corner of Fourth Avenue and Twentieth Street.
      Tyson's cigar store, according to Vance, was the official hangout of the ball players
      in 1913. Later the players moved their hangout to the Birmingham Arms. By 1932,
      Vance said the players did not have an official gathering place downtown, though
      occasionally one would see a group of them at Gray's Sporting Goods.
124   Barons Night at the Jefferson: *Bham A-H,* March 30, 1915
125   their hard-luck stories: *Bham News,* April 6, 1915
126   Cantley will be one of his pitchers: *Bham News,* April 7/11, 1915

126 Lamar Jeffers, president: *Bham News,* April 11, 1915. On May 10, App McDuffie won his first game for Anniston, defeating Talladega, 2-1, striking out nine. He won his next game, May 14, 2-1. He lost his third game, May 17, 2-0. He was released from the Anniston club on June 5. See *Anniston Star.* As far as the author can determine, McDuffie never pitched another professional game. Beginning in 1915, newspaper stories mentioned McDuffie playing for amateur teams in the Birmingham area, specifically Brookside in the Miners League in 1915 and Ensley in the TCI League in 1916. See *Birmingham News,* July 4, 1915, and June 3, 1916. Apparently, he pitched for Central Park, a City League team, as late as 1925. See *Birmingham Age-Herald,* August 26, 1925. According to the 1925 Birmingham City Directory, Roger A. (App) McDuffie was a bricklayer living at 4216 Avenue S.

126 down to eighteen players: *Bham News,* April 11, 1915

127 opponents have mustered: *Evansville Press,* August 11, 1915

127 Barons recalled John Cantley: *Evansville Journal,* August 15/20/24, 1915

127 Dolly Stark, the Nashville shortstop: *Bham A-H,* August 31, 1915

127 Barons are in no mood: *Bham News,* September 7, 1915

127 John took ill: *Evansville Courier, Evansville Journal, Evansville Press,* September 6, 1915

128 simple service at his roominghouse: *Evansville Journal,* September 7, 1915

128 "Grimes has a great future": *Bham News,* August 27, 1915

128 stayed in Birmingham: *Bham A-H,* February 13, 1916; *Bham News,* February 20, 1916

128 lowered team salary limits: *Bham News,* January 30, 1916

129 the following month, four hundred: *Bham A-H,* July 1/28, 1916

129 free vaccinations at City Hall: *Bham A-H,* July 6, August 11, 1916

129 contaminated ice cream: *Bham A-H,* July 8, July 21, 1916

129 crisis was over: Though typhoid was not a major threat after 1916, contagious diseases continued to flourish in the 1920s and '30s. In Birmingham in 1925, there were approximately 400 deaths from pneumonia and nearly 2,000 cases of smallpox (six deaths). Tuberculosis, measles, whooping cough, influenza, and diphtheria claimed many lives during the period. See *Birmingham News,* July 22, 1940; December 27/31, 1925; *Birmingham Age-Herald,* July 8, 1925.

130 Elberfeld said of Burleigh: *Bham A-H,* August 6, 1916

130 "can't make more money": *Bham News,* August 7, 1916

130 Birmingham received eight players: *Bham A-H,* March 24, April 10, 1917. Among the eight players were Carmen Hill, Wheeler (Doc) Johnston, Howard Douglas, Pat Duncan, and Al Ellis. The Barons later sold Hill, Duncan, Ellis, and Johnston to major league clubs.

130 walked off the field: *Bham A-H,* September 9, 1916

131 returned to Birmingham to work: After working at TCI following the 1915 and '16 seasons, Burleigh Grimes again returned to Birmingham after the 1917 season to manage the Birmingham Bowling Alleys, according to *The Birmingham News,* January 18, 1918.

131 "I'm going to be a regular": *Bham News,* February 28, 1917

Chapter 10

132 "one of the few times": Faber, Charles F. and Richard B., *Spitballers: The Last Legal Hurlers of the Wet One,* p. 39

132 covered with resin: Honig, *A Donald Honig Reader,* p. 568

133 break like hell: Ibid, p. 569

133 you get a reputation: Ibid

133 "the spitball is like a revolver": Ward, John, "Burleigh Grimes, Star of Baseball's Great Pitching Staff," *Baseball Magazine,* October 1920

133 "How much I used it": Eisenbath, Mike, *The Cardinals Encyclopedia,* p. 195

134 a more determined pitcher: "Burleigh, the Belligerent," *Baseball Magazine,* January 1931

134 Burleigh threw at Frankie Frisch: Scheinin, Richard, *Field of Screams: The Dark Underside of America's National Pastime,* pp. 171-172

135 "When I was a teenager": Gelman, Steve, *The Greatest Dodgers of Them All*

135 Saturday night hop: Lieb, Fred, *The Pittsburgh Pirates,* p. 179

135 headline in the morning paper: *Bham A-H,* April 7, 1917

Chapter 11

136 twenty-one minor leagues: Wright, *The Southern Association in Baseball,* p. 190

137 one of nine minor leagues: O'Neal, Bill, *The Southern League: Baseball in Dixie, 1885-1994,* p. 37

137 things weren't the same: *Bham News,* June 28, 1918

137 audiences of two thousand spectators: *Salt Lake Tribune,* July 31, 1918

137 Twelve thousand boys: *Bham A-H,* August 20, 1918

137 on June 10 issued a resolution: *Bham News,* June 11, 1918

138 only a corporal's guard: *Bham News,* June 28, 1918

138 called the Alabamians "les tigres": Cooke, James, *The Rainbow Division in the Great War, 1917-1919,* p. 80

138 every major Allied offensive: 167th (Alabama) Infantry Regiment, Croixrougefarm.org

138 Germans attempted to take Paris: Frazier, Nimrod, *Send the Alabamians: World War I Fighters in the Rainbow Division,* pp. 3, 100, 104, 106

138 "He was a fine man": *Bham A-H,* July 28, August 12, 1918; Frazier, *Send the Alabamians,* p. 203

139 the most savage combat: "Doughboy Center: The story of the American Expeditionary Forces," WorldWarI.com

139 During the battle: *Bham A-H,* August 12, September 1, 1918; *Bham News,* September 18/23, 1918; *Bham News,* May 24, 1932

139 Mortimer Jordan's letters home: *Bham A-H,* August 18/20, 1918, and the Birmingham Public Library. Mortimer Jordan is memorialized by a monument in front of the VA Medical Center in Birmingham, and a public school is named for him.

142 a new illness was spreading: *Bham A-H,* September 12, 1918; *Bham News,* October 31, 1918; Tompkins, Vincent, editor, *American Decades: 1910-1919,* p. 388

142 Absolute quarantine: *Bham A-H,* September 12, 1918; *Bham News,* October 20, 1918

142 bodies of two dead babies: *Bham A-H,* October 13, 1918

142 "We urge people to remain": *Bham A-H,* October 16, 1918

142 233 people died: *Bham News,* December 13, 1918; January 15, 1919

142 Spanish flu killed twenty-one million: Tompkins, *American Decades,* p. 388

142 shortly before two o'clock: *Bham A-H,* November 11, 1918

142 news was delivered: *Bham News,* November 11, 1918

142 thousands of people joined: *Bham A-H,* November 12, 1918

143 Alabama troops sailed: *Bham News,* May 10, 1919

143 a minute of silence: *Bham A-H,* May 11, 1919

143 He was a local boy: *Bham A-H,* August 15, 1920

143 going nowhere in professional ball: *Bham News,* April 9, 1918. The TCI League

was named for the big steel works of the Tennessee Coal, Iron, and Railroad Company in Ensley and Fairfield, Alabama. The TCI semi-pro league and the Birmingham City League were important parts of life in Birmingham in the early 1900s. Numerous future major-leaguers played in the two leagues. For instance, Joe Sewell and Riggs Stephenson played for Westfield in the City League in 1919. Sewell also played for Red Mountain (1917) and Bessemer Rolling Mills (1918) of the TCI League.

144 "We were playing the Red Sox": *Bham News, Bham A-H,* April 10, 1918
145 "All they have to do": *Bham A-H,* May 18, 1918
145 soldiers, mainly from North Carolina: Johnson, Clarence, *The History of the 321st Infantry,* pp. 83, 133
145 arriving in France in August: Marshall, Jackson, "World War I: Wildcat Division," NCpedia.org
145 On the night of November 10: Ibid
145 they were in the act: Johnson, *History of the 321st Infantry,* p. 44
145 Over the next fifteen days: Ibid, pp. 70-71
146 train bearing Whitey Glazner: *Bham A-H,* May 30, 1919
146 "I thought I was a goner": *Bham News,* June 28, 1919
146 grueling, midsummer contest: *Bham News, Bham A-H,* July 16, 1919
147 Whitey went to a chiropractor: *Bham A-H,* July 17, 1919
147 he and Dazzy Vance dueled: *Bham A-H,* September 16, 1920
147 Black ball players did not have: *The Birmingham News,* April 14, 1929, noted that a black industrial league had been in existence for four years.
148 highest level of amateur baseball: Fullerton, Christopher, *Every Other Sunday: The Story of the Birmingham Black Barons,* p. 22
148 three strong black teams played: *Bham A-H,* August 8, 1919
148 the pinnacle of black baseball: Rogosin, Donn, *Invisible Men: Life in Baseball's Negro Leagues,* p. 9
148 John Peters, the white Barons catcher: *Bham News,* September 12, 1919
148 "The park has been taxed": *Bham A-H,* September 14, 1919
148 Near the entrance of Rickwood: *Bham News,* September 1/18, 1919
149 Also in the league were: Plott, William, *The Negro Southern League,* pp. 9-10. The Negro Southern League operated sporadically: 1920-23, 1926-27, 1929, 1931-36, 1945-51. See *The Negro Southern League,* p. 8.
149 first wave of black players: Klima, John, *Willie's Boys: The 1948 Birmingham Black Barons,* p. 13
149 world was recovering its balance: *Bham A-H,* January 6, 1920
150 richest nation in the world: Goldberg, Ronald, *America in the Twenties,* p. 64
150 season of 1919, financially: *Bham A-H,* September 4, 1919
150 "The baseball bug": *Bham A-H,* March 17, 1920

Chapter 12

151 Corydon was a farming town: "History of Corydon," Corydontwp.com
151 had to use his wits: *Bham News,* March 30, 1930; *Jamestown* [New York] *Post-Journal,* July 3, 1945
152 "I didn't know anything": *Bham P-H,* August 3, 1950
152 his first big league game: Ray Caldwell's debut in the major leagues was in late September 1910. Six months later he made his first appearance at Rickwood Field as a relief pitcher for the New York Highlanders in an exhibition game against the Barons, March 29, 1911.

152   "Ray had arm trouble": Steinberg, Steve, "Ray Caldwell," *SABR Baseball Biography Project,* Sabr.org/bioproject
153   Ray's 'Broadway training': Ibid
154   the Senators approached: Ibid
156   a patient for alcohol treatment: Ibid
156   *The Washington Post* wrote: Faber, *Spitballers,* p. 104
156   "This fellow Caldwell": Steinberg, "Ray Caldwell," Sabr.org/bioproject
156   He returned the ring: Faber, *Spitballers,* p. 105
156   the Yankees assigned: Steinberg, "Ray Caldwell," Sabr.org/bioproject
157   one stretch of forty-five innings: Lewis, Franklin, *The Cleveland Indians,* p. 105; *Bham News,* March 30, 1930
157   "Put Ray Caldwell on a winning team": Steinberg, "Ray Caldwell," Sabr.org/bioproject
157   Speaker had a reputation: Lewis, *The Cleveland Indians,* p. 105
160   "I started to pitch": *Bham News,* March 30, 1930
160   a man saw Ray drinking: Lewis, *The Cleveland Indians,* p. 106

Chapter 13

165   demand was brisk: *Bham A-H* editorial, January 8, 1920
165   it *looked* prosperous: *Bham A-H,* March 31, October 10, 1920
165   populated by 238,000: *Bham News,* December 5, 1920; *Bham A-H* editorial, July 22, 1924
165   thousand each month: *Bham A-H* editorial, April 23, 1924
165   "here before our eyes": *Bham News,* November 3, 1924
166   Enormous tonnages of steel: *Bham A-H,* February 24/25, March 8/27, 1923
166   ships made of Birmingham steel: *Bham A-H,* December 3, 1921
166   sixty-six thousand tons: *Bham A-H,* June 3, 1923
166   one of the few cities: *Bham A-H,* April 24/30, 1924
166   biggest business ever: *Bham A-H,* January 7, 1920
166   Jewelry stores sold smoking pipes: *Bham A-H,* November 12, 1920
166   a full head of steam: *Bham A-H,* January 7/9, February 14, October 1, 1923
166   a high tide of prosperity: *Bham News,* April 15, 1923
167   newsboys were on the street: *Bham A-H,* August 3, 1923
167   a snowfall of six inches: *Bham News,* March 14, 1924
168   "It's no secret": Kahn, Roger, *The Head Game: Baseball Seen from the Pitcher's Mound,* p. 143
168   Charles Ebbets responded: Gelman, *The Greatest Dodgers of Them All*
169   "I didn't want to leave": Honig, *A Donald Honig Reader,* p. 579
169   started and completed 260 games: Baseball-Reference.com
169   "call me an old pitcher": Lane, F. C., "The Ace of National League Hurlers," *Baseball Magazine,* October 1929
169   "rifle weighs ten or eleven pounds": "Burleigh, the Belligerent," *Baseball Magazine,* January 1931
169   "We all had to work": Lane, "The Ace of National League Hurlers," *Baseball Magazine,* October 1929
170   "If I get a lucky break": Ibid
170   "If he turns me down": Faber, *Spitballers,* p. 46
170   He badgered Manager Mack: "A Fighting Pitcher Discusses His Trade," *Baseball Magazine,* November 1931
171   an inflamed appendix: Faber, *Spitballers,* p. 47
171   The final putout: *Bham News,* October 11, 1931

172   lemons were thrown: Monteville, Leigh, *The Big Bam: The Life and Times of Babe Ruth,* p. 310

172   "I've still got the big strike left": Poling, Jerry, *A Summer Up North: Henry Aaron and the Legend of Eau Claire Baseball,* p. 76; Honig, *A Donald Honig Reader,* p. 525

Chapter 14

173   the latest craze: Allen, Frederick, *Only Yesterday: An Informal History of the 1920s,* p. 190

174   their hair cropped close: Ibid, p. 106

174   rolled below the knee: Ibid, p. 89

174   During the twenties, hemlines: *American Heritage History of the 20s & 30s,* p. 101

174   One Saturday afternoon: *Bham News, Bham A-H,* May 10, 1925

175   "powdering and rouging": *Bham News,* December 15, 1924

175   "a man would hardly think of smoking": *Bham News,* letters to editor, July 8/24, 1920

177   On a rainy day in March: Allen, *Only Yesterday,* p. 316

177   After the second game: *Bham A-H,* July 6, 1922. Through the years, *Birmingham News* sports editor Zipp Newman often wrote that Carlton Molesworth had been ordered by Birmingham management to bench shortstop Jesse Burkett, who had made numerous errors early in the 1922 season. When Burkett bobbled another chance during the road trip to Atlanta and Mobile in late June, Woodward phoned Molesworth in Mobile and asked for his resignation. See, for example, *Birmingham News,* July 30, 1961.

177   withdrawal was a bombshell: *Bham A-H,* July 4, 1922. Molesworth became the Barons manager in May 1908 and resigned in July 1922. His career record was 1,051-914. In his 13 full seasons, he had two losing seasons.

178   Two dozen of his players: Following is a list of Molesworth's players who went straight from Birmingham to the major leagues. These are players who had no significant time in the majors prior to playing for Molesworth and who had major league careers lasting more than a handful of games: Art Phelan, Jimmy Johnston, Clarence Smith, Pete Knisely, Walt Tragresser, Burleigh Grimes, Danny Clark, George Hale, Emil Meusel, Billy Southworth, Carmen Hill, Elmer Ponder, James (Kid) Caton, Pat Duncan, Whitey Glazner, John Peters, John Morrison, Clyde Barnhart, John Gooch, Earl Whitehill, Stuffy Stewart, Pie Traynor, and Floyd Wheeler. In addition, Rowdy Elliott and John (Flip) Neun played additional seasons in the minors after Birmingham before going to the majors. Another player, Cy Slapnicka, became an executive with the Cleveland Indians.

178   a headline bore the words: *Bham News,* May 18, 1924

180   "big as Tennessee hams": *Bham News,* April 19, 1921

180   Tornado-like winds: *Bham News,* April 16/17, 1921

180   killed nearly one hundred: *Bham News,* April 17/18, 1921

180   a "thunder squall": *Bham A-H,* April 20, 1921

181   groundskeeper at Rickwood: *Bham News,* April 17, 1921. Frank Smith, assistant to the groundskeeper, had been with the Barons forever, it seemed. According to Zipp Newman of *The Birmingham News,* Smith was born into slavery in 1846, which would have made him 75 years old at the time of the storm. See *Birmingham News,* January 16, 1930.

181   more than a hundred: *Bham News,* April 18, 1921
181-182   "The newcomer, Traynor": *Bham A-H,* April 17, 1921
182   Two days later Traynor: *Bham A-H,* April 19, 1921
182   "He cost the Pirates $10,000": *Bham News,* April 19, 1921
182   "all the stray dimes": *Bham A-H,* March 14, 1922
182   "priest who organized baseball games": Forr, James and Proctor, David, *Pie Traynor: A Baseball Biography,* p. 14
182   left school after the eighth grade: Ibid., p. 15
182   tried to enlist in the army: Ibid., p. 22
183   "When I was eight": *Bham News,* May 18, 1924
183   first man in uniform: *Bham A-H,* August 26, 1921
184   "I shall never be satisfied": *Bham News,* May 18, 1924
184   Dobbs made a prediction: *Bham News,* May 21, 1921
184   Never has a greener: *Bham News,* June 19, 1921
184   never would he forget Traynor: *Bham News,* May 24, 1923
184   they cheered him wildly: *Bham News,* August 28, 1921
185   position did not come naturally: Forr and Proctor, *Pie Traynor,* p. 53
185   Manager George Gibson left: *Bham A-H,* December 20, 1921
185   batter hit a fly ball: *Bham A-H,* August 31, 1922
186   In 1923, Wagner said: *Bham A-H,* December 22, 1923
186   a dreadful place: Forr and Proctor, *Pie Traynor,* p. 52
186   Traynor and two teammates: Ibid, pp. 61-62, 98
187   "He will go down in history": Ibid, p. 87
187   "We had taped it": Ibid, p. 108
187   with a torn ligament: Ibid, p. 117
187   "We're so lucky": Ibid, p. 125
187   he was psychologically unsuited: Ibid, pp. 132-133
188   Beneath his affable persona: Ibid, p. 90
188   "I always worried a lot": Ibid, p. 140
188   too kind and softhearted: Ibid, p. 147
188   grew deeply pessimistic: Ibid, pp. 179-180
188   Traynor received a telegram: Ibid, pp. 151-153
189   he mixed and mingled: Ibid, p. 193
189   remain graceful and athletic: Ibid, p. 219
190   Traynor smoked cigarettes: Ibid, pp. 217-218, 220
190   In April 1971, Traynor: Ibid, pp. 221-223
191   What is Pie Traynor's legacy?: Ibid, p. 227
191   Rabbi Solomon Freehof conducted: Ibid, p. 224
192   Pie Traynor was steadfast: Ibid, pp. 8-9
192   Rick Woodward, owner: *Bham News,* August 28, 1921

Chapter 15

193   Birmingham's population was growing faster: *Bham A-H* editorial, July 22, 1924
193   Dobbs To Pilot Barons In '25: *Bham News,* September 30, 1924
194   his mother would caution: *Bham News,* March 13, 1931
195   No set of players: *Bham News,* September 21, 1924
195   "time was when Rickwood": *Bham A-H,* June 25, 1924
196   players with long, worthy records: Baseball-Reference.com
196   complete charge of the club: *Bham News,* September 30, 1924
196   "I have always wanted": *Bham News,* February 10, 1925

196 "If the fans will just stick": *Bham News,* April 17, 1925

196 dozens of towns: *Bham News,* April 12, 1925

196 "Now has baseball assumed": *Bham A-H,* April 15, 1910

197 There would be days: *Bham News,* April 13, 1925

197 Johnny Dobbs stood: *Bham News,* April 17, 1925

197 He liked to kid himself: *Bham News,* September 15, 1929; March 13, 1931

197 Johnny loved hunting and horses: *Bham News,* April 11, 1926

197 John Nicklin heard tell: *Bham News,* July 14, 1929

198 an instinctive "fly chaser": *Chattanooga Times,* September 10, 1934

198 Glancing over the Cincinnati paper: *Bham News,* April 11, 1926. The word "charley horse" apparently originated from the name given to the family horse, which was usually lame or broken down in the legs. Those family horses were called old Charley horses, so when the leg muscles of a ball player got tied up, the injury was referred to as a "charley horse." See *Birmingham Age-Herald,* John McGraw memoir, January 15, 1923.

199 believed in leading, not driving: *Bham News,* September 15, 1929; *Chattanooga Times,* September 11, 1934

199 sunny, amiable disposition: *Bham A-H,* September 5, 1927

199 one of the best-dressed: *Bham News,* March 6, 1927

199 lusty chatterbox: *Bham News,* April 10, 1927

199 "Dobbs never says anything": *Bham News,* May 20, 1925

200 became a familiar sight: *Bham News,* May 20, 1925; April 14, 1929

200 fans imitated his hand-clapping: *Bham News,* September 4, 1927

200 Not so with the females: *Bham News,* August 12, 1912; *Bham A-H,* May 26, 1925

200 "Women are the best supporters": *Bham News,* August 8, 1929

200 a tide of prosperity: *Bham News,* January 2, 1925

200 Shrewd observers said: Ibid

201 Never before had there been: *Bham A-H,* August 5, 1925

201 Remarks such as these: *Bham News,* November 30, 1927

201 enforcing a "move on": *Bham A-H,* February 9, 1922

201 "Where have these husky young men": *Bham News,* January 28, 1925. The "race track," or "chicken run," was the downtown block between Second and Third avenues and Nineteenth and Twentieth streets, where men loitered, often making insulting comments to women who passed by. Women rarely testified in court against the offenders. Men also drove their automobiles around the "race track" block, hoping women would hop in, and often they did. For more on the race track, see editorials in *The Birmingham Age-Herald,* April 1, 1922, and *The Birmingham News,* February 6, 1923.

201 one hundred Ku Klux Klansmen: *Bham A-H,* February 22, 1925

201 snapping, fighting ball club: Sportswriter Zipp Newman recalled that the 1925 Barons had color and temperament: "They were no sooner out of a game than back in. They were no sooner out in front than they were trailing. There was no doping out what the players would do. One had to stick around until the final out....(The club) had gate appeal. It drew 182,500 at Rickwood, a record for a seventh-place club." See *Birmingham News,* July 14, 1938.

201-202 Ernest (Tex) Jeanes: One of the most colorful and popular players of the 1925 Barons was Jeanes, a genial, happy-go-lucky Texan. He often caught and made pets of green snakes, believing they brought him base hits. He would caress his green snake before going to bat. If he got a hit, he would caress the snake again before returning to the field. Sometimes he would get careless and leave snakes in the club lockers and his roommates' beds. See *Birmingham News*, February 24, 1937.

202 Foster (Babe) Ganzel: Foster Pirie (Babe) Ganzel played all or parts of four seasons with the Barons, 1924-1927. A graduate of Tufts College, he was a civil engineer for a construction company during the off-season and lived in a cottage near Boston within sight of the Atlantic Ocean, according to *The Birmingham Age-Herald*, September 1, 1927. Ganzel was on the field playing centerfield for the Washington Senators the day Babe Ruth hit his 60th home run, September 30, 1927.

202 always ready to pitch: *Bham News*, July 18, 1926

202 "Hottest weather I ever saw": *Bham News*, September 6/7/9/10, 1925

202 Birmingham turned out in large numbers: *Bham News*, October 31, 1925; *Bham A-H*, August 22, 1926. The first motion picture filmed in Birmingham was *Coming Through* in December 1924, starring Thomas Meighan, Lila Lee, and Wallace Beery. The movie was adapted from the novel *Bed Rock*, written by Birmingham's Jack Bethea. Scenes were filmed on Shades Mountain and in Birmingham-area coal mines. *Coming Through* played at The Strand theater in mid-February 1925 and again in April at The Rialto.

202 Total attendance at Rickwood: *Bham News*, April 10, 1927

202 sold to the Washington Senators: *Bham News*, July 18, 1926

203 WBRC, fifty watts: *Bham A-H*, October 17, 1926. WBRC began broadcasting on Fifth Avenue North in 1925. The front part of the building contained a radio shop. Curtained off in the rear were the studio and broadcast facilities. See *Birmingham News*, Coal Bin column, September 10, 1935.

203 located on the twenty-third floor: *Bham A-H*, October 10, 1926. The *Age-Herald* building, located at the corner of Second Avenue North and Twenty-first Street, was called the Comer building in the 1930s. Today it is known as the City Federal building.

203 "This is station WBRC": *Bham A-H*, October 24, 1926

203 Wearing earphones, he received: *Bham A-H*, September 26/29, October 3, 1926. To practice for his big event—the World Series, Dud Connolly called the blow-by-blow broadcast of two boxing matches over WBRC Radio in 1926: the light heavyweight fight between Jack Delaney and Paul Berlenbach on July 16 and the Jack Dempsey-Gene Tunney heavyweight fight, September 23. The author believes these two prize fights were the first live sporting events to be broadcast on radio in Birmingham.

203 Connolly's play by play: *Bham A-H*, October 3, 1926

203 streets were alive again: *Bham A-H*, October 4, 1926

203 former Baron Billy Southworth: The words "greatest" and "most popular" have become so commonplace in sports that they cease to have any meaning. In researching this book, the author discovered newspaper writers applying those words so frequently to Billy Southworth that he believes them to be true in this case. Undoubtedly, Southworth was the finest defensive rightfielder of his generation to play for Birmingham. He played for the Barons in 1917-1918 and had a lengthy major league career. Zipp Newman in *The Birmingham News*, April 15, 1937, said Southworth "captured the bleacher gods with his daring fielding and rifle throws." He was as popular a player as Stuffy Stewart. Writer Henry Vance said that of all the former Barons he encountered during visits to major league parks, Southworth was "one of the few who seemed really glad to see me. Not only that, but as a member of the Boston Braves he invited me down to the bench to sit with the team while they were playing the Giants at the Polo Grounds." See *Birmingham Age-Herald*, November 22, 1928.

Chapter 16

204 Dobbs had traded two players: *Bham News*, April 3, 1927

204 Over his previous six seasons: Baseball-Reference.com; Wright, *The Southern Association in Baseball*

204 several days of stormy weather: Kessner, Thomas, *The Flight of the Century: Charles Lindbergh and the Rise of American Aviation*, p. 81

204 light rain was falling: Ibid, p. 82

204 At midnight, Charles Lindbergh: Ibid, p. 87

205 buckled his seat belt: Ibid, p. 85

205 open ocean for sixteen hours: Ibid, p. 93

205 For nearly twenty hours: *Bham News*, May 22, 1927

205 without sleep for nearly sixty: Kessner, *Flight of the Century*, p. 106

205 announcers read cablegrams: *Bham Post*, May 21, 1927

205 spotted the Eiffel Tower: *Bham Post*, May 23, 1927

205 eager to salute him: *Bham News*, May 22, 1927

205 lifted him above their heads: Kessner, *Flight of the Century*, p. 103

205 Moments before the winning runs: The first game of the doubleheader concluded at approximately 4:00. Lindbergh landed at Le Bourget at 3:22 p.m., Birmingham time.

206 slept for ten hours: Bryson, Bill, *One Summer: America, 1927*, p. 98

206 seated on a stool: *Bham News*, July 4, 1927

207 Barons had a working agreement: Minor league clubs had working agreements with clubs of higher classification for two reasons: the minor club wanted (1) help in the form of players and (2) a team to which it could sell its promising players. Sometimes the higher classification club not only sent players but agreed to pay part of the salaries. In turn, the club rendering the help received an option to buy players it deemed major league prospects. The system enabled many minor league clubs to thrive while retaining local ownership. See *Birmingham News*, January 27, 1937.

207 Senators obtained a pitcher: *Bham News*, July 22, 1927

207 class of the league: *Bham News*, December 25, 1927

207 "If we can't beat": *Bham News*, August 21, 1927

207 Fifty-one thousand fans: *Bham News*, August 28, 1927

207 one hundred thousand customers: *Bham News*, September 7, 1927

207 every possible instrument: *Bham News*, September 10, 1927

207 fans attended baseball matinees: *Bham A-H*, August 29, September 5, 1927; *Bham News*, September 5, 1927

208 a ruptured appendix all but cost: *Bham News*, November 4/9/12, 1927; January 10, 1928; *Bham A-H*, November 2/11, 1927

208 299,150 full-price home admissions: *Bham News*, November 29, 1927. *Birmingham News* sports editor Zipp Newman speculated that Birmingham's attendance in 1927 would have been 400,000 if night games and Sunday baseball had been permitted in Birmingham. See *Birmingham News*, August 18, 1935.

208 If reduced-price tickets sold: Official attendance included only full-price tickets sold. If the number of reduced-price tickets sold to ladies on Tuesdays and Fridays had been included in official attendance, the total attendance in 1927 would have been approximately 350,000. The author bases this projection on the fact that the following season (1928), 52,000 women entered the park on Ladies' Day tickets. See *Birmingham News*, October 9, 1928. One can safely assume that at least 50,000 women in 1927 attended games at reduced prices.

209 looking for Lindy: For details of Lindbergh's visit to Birmingham, see *Birmingham News,* October 5/6/7, 1927, and *Birmingham Age-Herald,* October 6/7, 1927.

209 *New York Evening World:* Bryson, *One Summer,* p. 99

210 thirty million people: Berg, A. Scott, *Lindbergh,* p. 170

210 Ruth cracked a single: *Bham A-H,* October 6, 1927

Chapter 17

212 Dan Heaton wrote a letter: *Bham News,* September 20, 1927

212 a remodeled Rickwood: *Bham News,* January 25, February 8, March 6, December 18/20, 1927; February 5/19, 1928; April 8/11, 1928; *Bham A-H,* March 6, 1927; March 2, May 4, 1928. Prior to 1927, whites sat in concrete bleachers along the first and third base lines. Blacks sat in wooden bleachers further down the leftfield line. In 1927, blacks were assigned to wooden bleachers along the rightfield line; whites sat in wooden bleachers down the leftfield line. Also in 1927, the leftfield concrete bleachers were converted into a wing of the grandstand. See *Birmingham News,* January 25, February 8, March 6, 1927; *Birmingham Age-Herald,* March 6, 1927. In 1928, the grandstand was extended down the rightfield side, and blacks were assigned to the bleachers behind the rightfield wall. See *Birmingham News,* December 18, 1927.

    The streets paved during spring 1928 were Eleventh and Twelfth streets and Second Avenue. See *Birmingham News,* April 11, 1928.

    With the construction of the concrete wall in 1928, centerfield and leftfield were enlarged. In previous years, the ball park's outfield had been surrounded by a tall, wooden fence. In front of the wooden fence was a "low wire fence" that extended from leftfield to centerfield. The purpose of the low fence was to reduce the outfield expanse. A flag pole in centerfield was located behind the low fence. When the concrete wall was constructed, the low wire fence came down and the distances to left- and centerfields were increased. See *Birmingham News,* December 20, 1927.

    Leftfield and centerfield were full of undulating hills, bunkers, and ruts, according to *The Birmingham Age-Herald,* June 22, 1928: "There is no way of telling just what a ball is going to do when it hits that area on a roll. Many balls have slipped between fielders' legs and bounced over their shoulders."

213 vast spaces of the outfield: The dimensions of 334 to right, 470 to center, and 405 to left are from a 1932 Barons game program.

213 Stuffy Stewart had played on teams: *Bham A-H,* March 6, 1928

213 ten thousand grandstand and box seats: *Bham News,* April 9, September 19, 1928

213 Dobbs was at his desk: *Bham News,* April 7, 1928

213 Dobbs had spent lavishly: *Bham News,* April 4, 1928

214 no nearer a decision: *Bham News,* April 7, 1928

214 pruned his roster to eighteen: *Bham News,* April 10, 1928

214 After his appendix operation: *Bham News,* September 26, 1928

214 prepare his obituary: *Bham News,* March 31, 1929

215 A sore arm kept him: *Bham News,* April 10, 1928

215 led the Southern Association in stolen bases: *Bham News,* April 11, 1926; Wright, *The Southern Association in Baseball*

215 a bright, happy character: *Bham A-H,* September 15, 1920

215 He'd been called "Stuffy": newspaper clipping, Baseball Hall of Fame, dated September 15, 1929

216 made a big impression: *Bham News,* July 28, 1925

216 Stewart promised the Birmingham owners: *Bham News,* June 17, 1923

217 Opponents feared seeing him: Ibid

217   to unsettle a team: *Bham A-H,* May 26, 1922; June 27, 1928; *Bham News,* July 3, 1929

217   "I owe what credit": *Bham News,* March 29, 1921

217   hitting .323 and waging: *Bham News,* December 12, 1921

217   asked to return to Birmingham: *Bham News,* June 17, 1923

217   he batted .300: Wright, *The Southern Association in Baseball*

217   worked out a deal: *Bham News,* June 17, 1923

217   yearned for was to be in the action: *Bham A-H,* April 20, 1922

217   hitting .306 and stealing forty bases: Wright, *The Southern Association in Baseball*

217   his piping voice was back: *Bham A-H,* June 1, 1923

217   as popular a manager: *Bham News,* October 11, 1923

217   third in attendance: *Bham News,* October 19, 1923

218   Interest in Birmingham baseball: *Bham News,* April 20, 1924

218   Ty Cobb, player-manager: *Bham News,* August 7, 1924

218   blue eyes, a florid face: *Bham News,* September 25, 1928

218   he could outrun anyone: *Bham A-H,* September 13, 1928

218   Johnston's aging legs: *Bham News,* April 12, 1934

218   stole second, third, and home: *Bham News, Bham A-H,* September 9, 1928

218   inside-the-park home run: *Bham A-H,* June 4, 1930

219   team's most popular player: *Bham News,* September 12, 1928

219   Pat Monahan, said: *Bham News,* July 31, 1928

219   "This is the best ball club": *Bham A-H,* June 25, 1928

220   The bountiful offense led: *Bham News,* December 23, 1928; Wright, *The Southern Association in Baseball*

221   a good throwing arm: *Bham A-H,* March 21, 1929; *Bham News,* March 26, 1929

221   His career batting average: Nowlin, Bill, "Elliot Bigelow," *SABR Baseball Biography Project,* Sabr.org/bioproject

221   He had a good fastball: Ibid

221-222   pitched in a cold, drizzling rain: *Bham A-H,* March 18, 1931

222   with a powerful snap: *Bham News,* July 22, 1928

222   top of the centerfield scoreboard: *Bham News,* April 17, 1928

223   better than any other hitter's: *Bham News,* July 22, September 15, 1928

223   fourteen-year-old daughter: *Chattanooga Times,* July 5, 1928

223   If Johnny Dobbs had a favorite book: *Bham News,* May 30, 1928

224   a mark that would stand: Wright, *The Southern Association in Baseball*

Chapter 18

225   Woodward's balance wheel: *Bham Post,* March 12/15, 1931; *Bham News,* January 27, June 30, 1929. According to *The Birmingham News,* March 6, 1932, W. D. Smith acquired his stock in the Barons from former Barons Manager Harry (Dad) Vaughn in 1907 in exchange for groceries. Vaughn owned three shares of stock and was in need of cash, having recently lost his job as manager.

226   more good young players: *Bham News,* February 14, 1929

226   like a ballet dancer: *Bham News,* March 31, 1929

226   hail-fellow-well-met: *Bham News,* March 2, 1930

226   he led the Texas League: Baseball-Reference.com

226   could field and throw: *Bham News,* April 1/24, 1929

227   had the perfect hitter's swing: *Bham News,* April 25, 1929

227   finest defensive outfielders: *Bham News,* April 25, 1931

227 powerful, tattooed arms: *Bham News,* April 3, 1943

227 struggling at the bat: *Bham News,* June 7/9, 1929

227 Sturdy hit forty-nine: *Bham News,* April 2, 1929

227 best-fielding first baseman: *Bham A-H,* May 9, 1929

227 a bearer of good fortune: *Bham News,* March 9, 1934

228 241 games in seventeen professional seasons: Baseball-Reference.com; *Reach Baseball Guide,* 1926

228 size 13DD feet: correspondence with Bob Hasty's daughter, Elva Hasty Thompson, November 2014

228 didn't know how to wind up: *Bham News,* July 2, 1919

228 impressed with his size and his fastball: *Bham A-H,* August 11, 1928

228 According to the Hasty family: correspondence with Elva Hasty Thompson and Hasty's granddaughter, Dee Thompson, August 2016

228 quiet and unassuming: *Bham News,* April 17, 1929

228 fellow Georgian Ty Cobb: Elva Hasty Thompson, November 2014

230 Morgan Blake, sports editor: *Bham News,* June 5, 1929

230 pitching staff was shot: *Bham News,* July 21, 1929

231 called the "sinking champions": *Bham News,* July 22, 1929

231 he had sought a doctor: *Bham News,* August 6, 1928

231 Caldwell had taken a job: *Arkansas Gazette,* June 17, 1929

232 "every player on the club": *Bham News,* August 29, 1929

232 Caldwell entered the game: *Bham News,* September 4, 1929

232 "These be stirring days": *Bham News,* September 5, 1929

232 three players contended for the league: *Bham News,* September 8, 1929

232 playing like champions: *Bham News,* September 4, 1929

233 "You have accomplished": *Bham News,* September 13, 1929

234 within the last sixty days: *Bham News,* September 14, 1929

234 T. G. Holt, writing in *The News: Bham News,* September 15, 1929

234 fans voted shortstop Ernie Smith: *Bham News,* September 13, 1929

234 driving in ninety-two runs: *Bham News,* March 2, 1930

234 Ludolph led the league: *Bham News,* December 1, 1929

234 "One day I was in a drugstore": *Bham News,* March 30, 1930

234 Frank Gibson, the Texan: *Bham News,* September 13, 1929

235 "How does Johnny Dobbs do it?": *Bham News,* May 13, 1929

235 Morgan Blake of *The Atlanta Journal: Bham News,* June 5, 1929

235 a breathtaking correction occurred: *Bham A-H,* September 6/7, 1929; *Bham News,* September 6, 1929

235 In Game One, the two teams: *Bham News, Bham A-H,* September 26, 1929; *Bham News,* September 29, 1929

235 fly balls were risky for Clabaugh: Miles, Sam, "Moose Set Pro HR Mark in 1926 As Tyler Trojan," Etfinalscore.com, July 11, 2012

236 stock market was in despair: *Bham News,* September 25, 1929

236 Game Two at Rickwood: *Bham News, Bham A-H,* September 27, 1929

236 stock market regained its poise: *Bham News,* September 26/27, 1929

236 "I'm glad the two games": *Bham News,* September 29, 1929

236 hundreds of people in Birmingham: *Bham News,* April 16, 1930. The first radio broadcast of a Barons baseball game occurred on Tuesday, August 6, 1929, the Barons playing at Chattanooga. Henry Vance broadcast the game from telegraph reports. See *Birmingham News,* August 7, 1929. Vance continued broadcasting all road games for the remainder of the season over WAPI. Home games were not broadcast for fear it would hurt live attendance at the ball park.

236   trailing 4–2 in Game Three: *Bham News,* September 29, 1929
237   In Game Four the Barons: *Bham News,* September 30, 1929
237   heroes of Game Five: *Bham News, Bham A-H,* October 1, 1929
237   "I am now pitching for a manager": *Bham News,* September 27, 1929
237   market traders continued liquidating: *Bham News,* September 30, 1929
237   reached into their pockets: *Bham News,* October 2, 1929
237   Bedlam and chaos: *Bham News, Bham A-H,* October 3, 1929
237   enormous losses were registered: *Bham A-H,* October 4/5, 1929
238   a violent storm of selling: *Bham News,* October 19/21, 1929; *Bham A-H,* October 22, 1929
238   Wall Street was alive with workers: *Bham A-H,* October 25, 1929
238   In the final hour of trading: *Bham A-H,* October 29, 1929
238   ten to seventy dollars a share: *Bham News,* October 29, 1929
238   a report from Atlanta: *Bham A-H,* October 30, 1929
238   Dobbs was at his farm: *Bham News,* October 30, 1929
238   he publicly confirmed: *Bham News, Atlanta Constitution,* November 3, 1929

Chapter 19

241   only thing he owned: Smith, Robert, *Baseball,* pp. 294-297
241   "always a little stubborn": *Bham News,* October 5, 1934
242   didn't like his middle name: Gregory, Robert, *Diz: The Story of Dizzy Dean and Baseball During the Great Depression,* pp. 162-163
242   Nobody ever taught Diz: Smith, Red, "And All Dizzy's Yesterdays," *The Best American Sports Writing of the Century,* Halberstam, David, editor, p. 163
242   Tall and lanky: Honig, Donald, *Baseball America,* p. 184
242   Dizzy "acted up": *Bham News,* April 1, 1933
242   Talking to a reporter over breakfast: *Bham News,* September 10, 1931
242   stepping from the train in Birmingham: *Bham News,* September 16, 1931
243   "I'm just an ol' country boy": *Bham Post,* September 16, 1931
244   not an advertising sign: Rickwood Field did not have advertising signs inside the stadium until 1936, with the exception of a Chero-Cola sign in right centerfield. The first newspaper mention of the Chero-Cola sign discovered by the author occurred in 1923. According to *The Birmingham News,* January 23, 1936, when batters came to the plate, a curtain dropped over the sign, giving the batters a green background. Henry Vance, in his Coal Bin column, September 24, 1941, said: "As long as Rick Woodward was operating the Birmingham Baseball Association, he would not allow commercial signs within the enclosure. Later, when the thing went out of his hands, advertising signs became the rule rather than the exception."
245   "iron ore that went into building": Hornady, John, *The Book of Birmingham,* pp. 102-103
246   a bet of $7,000 to $5,000: *Houston Chronicle,* September 17, 1931
246   "if you combined all the cows": *Bham News,* March 25, 1925
248   stood five-foot-eight: Nunnelley, William, *Bull Connor,* p. 11
249   Edward (Crip) Whitley: *Bham News,* September 16, 1931
249   "water on the knee": Caldwell missed a start in early August with an ailing knee. Manager Clyde Milan feared the injury would cause him to miss the rest of the season, so he ordered Caldwell to stay away from the park for a few days and take treatment at TCI Hospital. See *Birmingham News,* August 12/16, 1931.
250   "I'll tell you a story": *Bham A-H,* July 22, 1931
251   "Jimmy Morgan's radio store": *Bham News,* October 5, 1930

Chapter 20

252 "hide my blushes of shame": *Bham News,* September 16, 1931

253 bacon, eggs, and biscuits: Marshall, *All Time Greatest Alabama Sports Stories,* p. 4

253 became hunting companions: Simon, Tom, "Clyde Milan," *SABR Baseball Biography Project,* Sabr.org/bioproject

253 Milan had introduced Johnson: Thomas, Henry, *Walter Johnson: Baseball's Big Train,* pp. 114-115

254 When the boy was eighteen: *Bham News,* March 18, 1932

254 playing for Blossom's rival: Thomas, *Walter Johnson,* p. 30

255 "He was too good a fellow": Ibid, p. 181

255 Walter's wife, Hazel: Ibid, p. 316

255 "Were you anxious": *Bham News,* November 26, 1929

256 He had a ruddy face: *Bham News,* April 13, 1930

256 "Milan never scolds": *Bham News,* February 20, 1930

256 "Ball players are temperamental": *Bham News,* April 13, 1930

256 best shape in three years: *Bham A-H,* March 6, 1930

256 In a game in New Orleans: *Bham News, Bham A-H,* April 28, 1930

256 "Hard times are upon us": *Bham News,* July 4, 1930

256 President Herbert Hoover, speaking: *Bham News,* May 2, 1930

257 Milan's crew staggered helplessly: *Bham News,* May 25, 1930

257 Employment conditions in 1930: *Bham News,* July 8, 1930

257 had become a grandfather: *Bham News,* July 30, 1930

258 "Look at those legs go!": *Bham A-H,* March 11, 1930

259 Bancroft had been marked: *Bham News,* April 2, June 2/3, July 13, 1930; *Bham A-H,* July 30, 1930

259 One of the most beloved: *Bham News,* February 1, 1931

Chapter 21

260 "We have heard much": *Bham News,* September 15, 1931

260 a winner of 289 games: Baseball-Reference.com

260 roommates on the road: *Bham News,* April 17, 1929; August 3, 1938

260 use all his resources: *Bham News,* July 3, 1931

260 timid country boy: *Bham News,* August 7, 1932

261 won 259 games: Baseball-Reference.com

261 He liked to fill a drinking straw: Sullivan, Neil, *The Minors: The Struggles and the Triumph of Baseball's Poor Relation from 1876 to the Present,* p. 161

261 One April afternoon in 1928: *Fort Worth Star-Telegram,* March 8, 1961

261 He was powerfully built: *Bham News,* May 20, 1930

261 perfected a crossfire delivery: *Bham A-H,* July 1, 1933. Many pitchers in the first half of the 20th century threw with a "crossfire delivery;" Ray Caldwell sometimes did. When a righthander threw crossfire, he placed his right foot on the right side of the pitching rubber, stepped toward third base as he delivered the pitch, and threw across his body from a three-quarter angle or sidearm. The pitch was especially effective from a righthanded pitcher to a righthanded batter, the pitch seeming to come from third base.

261 finished his career with 272 victories: Baseball-Reference.com

261 "Name a ball player in the league": *Bham News,* June 19, 1931

262 Thousands watched from vantage: *Houston Post-Dispatch,* September 18, 1931

262 tracks of the Atlanta, Birmingham, and Atlantic: *Bham A-H,* July 15, 1925

263 edged up to Ray Caldwell: *Bham News,* September 17, 1931

263   cross section of plug-cut: *Bham News*, May 18, 1919

263-264   games with four new balls: *Bham Post*, March 15, 1931

267   "Ray cuts the corners": *Bham A-H*, September 11, 1931

269   To his mother he was William: This segment on Billy Bancroft contains excerpts from a story in *The Birmingham News* by James Saxon Childers, August 30, 1931.

269   Weighing 120 pounds: *Bham News*, November 10, 1922

269   By his senior year: *Bham News*, October 1, 1923

273   a girl everyone called "Sammie": According to Claudie Hoover's grandson, Steven Bancroft, Claudie and a friend attended an out-of-town gathering as teenagers where few people knew them. The two girls decided to assign themselves temporary names. Her friend suggested that Claudie take the name "Sammie," and the "temporary" name stayed with her the rest of her life.

273   for a thousand dollars: Marshall, *All Time Greatest Alabama Sports Stories*, p. 4

273   "there are only three minutes to play": *Birmingham Post*, September 17, 1931

274   "He threw a curveball": Marshall, *All Time Greatest Alabama Sports Stories*, p. 8

276   "The very crafty Caldwell": *Houston Post-Dispatch*, September 17, 1931

276   "Ray Caldwell was slow in getting": *Bham News*, September 17, 1931

276   "Long before game time Rickwood's": *Bham A-H*, September 17, 1931

277   "No pitcher could have shown a greater": *Bham News*, September 17, 1931

277   "Bancroft furnished the knockout": Ibid

277   "With the game in his big right": Ibid

278   "When you stop to consider": *Bham A-H*, September 17, 1931

278   "Uncle Ray Caldwell, granddaddy": Ibid

279   "Congratulations, Dizzy Dean" *Bham News*, September 17, 1931

279   "I'd say twenty-five thousand": *Houston Post-Dispatch*, September 18, 1931

280   "That Dean is really great": *Bham Post*, September 17, 1931

280   "I got the breaks, and": *Bham News*, September 17, 1931

280   "greatest game I ever pitched": *Houston Chronicle*, September 17, 1931

280   "my fastball vanished": *Bham A-H*, September 18, 1931

280   A good-natured crowd gathered: *Bham News*, September 17, 1931

Chapter 22

282   stormed the Rice Hotel: *Bham News*, September 19, 1931

282   appear in nine hundred career games: Baseball-Reference.com

283   "Say, who is this Touchstone": *Bham News*, March 15, 1933

284   a nut from a buckeye tree: *Bham News*, March 30, 1934

284   one-quarter of the work force: "The Great Depression," *World Book Encyclopedia*, 2013, p. 340

285   "Leave it to the great Dizzy": *Bham News*, September 25, 1931

285   "I'm going to pump 'em in": Ibid

286   This is Bull Connor behind the mike: The remainder of this chapter presents Game Seven as Bull Connor might have broadcast it.

286   Birmingham Athletic Club: The Birmingham Athletic Club occupied a ten-story building on Third Avenue and Twenty-third Street built in 1925, though the club had existed since 1888. The top six floors of the building served as bachelor quarters for members. The club also housed a gymnasium (seating 2,300), swimming pool, handball courts, bowling alleys, rifle and pistol ranges, billiard parlor, barbershop, and library. The club hosted wrestling and boxing matches, indoor swim meets, and indoor baseball games. In the early 1900s,

members played football, basketball, and baseball against amateur and collegiate teams. See *Birmingham News,* August 16, 1925, Social, p. 14. For a history of the club, see *The News,* October 22, 1918, p. 6.

286   "tell me about yourself": The remarks from Bull Connor presented in this segment appeared in *The Birmingham News,* October 18, 1931.

287   born in 1897 in Selma: Nunnelley, *Bull Connor,* p. 9

287   Beara Levens, the daughter: Ibid

287   Eugene did not complete high school: Ibid, p. 10

289   "got a job working on the telepic": The Telepic, or Telepix, machine came into general use in 1925. Newspapers used the Telepix to send and receive photographs by telegraph. Before Telepix, photographic plates were sent by mail, airplane, or train from town to town or across the continent. To transmit an ordinary photograph by Telepix required 60 to 75 minutes. A full-page ad in *The Birmingham News,* March 15, 1925, shows Bull Connor operating the Telepix and explains its operation. For more on Telepix, see *Birmingham News,* March 4/5/6, 1925.

289   "Eugene Connor will conduct baseball matinees": *Bham News,* May 9, 1926

289   moved the operation to: *Bham News,* April 21, 1929

289   a dozen venues in the city: *Bham News,* May 20, 1927

Chapter 23

293   "radio is being run into the ground": *Bham News,* March 19, 1930

293   two hundred licensed stations: Rudel, Anthony, *Hello, Everybody: The Dawn of American Radio,* p. 47

294   range was around two thousand miles: *Bham News,* January 11/18, 1923

294   "WSY, broadcasting services from the Heart": *Bham News,* February 18, 1923. Alabama Power Company gave radio station WSY and its equipment to Auburn University in 1925 and closed the station's operation in Birmingham. The station in Auburn was renamed WAPI. WAPI moved to Birmingham and began broadcasting from the 14th floor of the new Protective Life building on New Year's Eve, 1928. See *Birmingham News,* January 6, 1925.

294   heard programs from Chicago: *Bham A-H,* July 11, August 23, 1922

294   two cages of canaries singing: *Bham A-H,* September 20, 1922

294   "Our little town sits up": *Bham A-H,* August 25, 1922

295   "there's twenty thousand men in town": *Bham Post,* August 14, 1931

295   "Will Rogers says ten men": *Bham News,* August 16, 1931

296   Iron ore was smelted: White, *The Birmingham District,* p. 7

296   one by one the furnaces: Leighton, George, "Birmingham, Alabama: The City of Perpetual Promise," *Harper's Magazine,* August 1937, p. 238

296   Layoffs started in 1927: Bennett, James, *Historic Birmingham and Jefferson County,* p. 117

296   hardest hit city in the nation: Hamilton, Virginia Van der Veer, *Alabama: A History,* p. 137

296   The Red Cross Family Service: *Bham News,* "100 Years: 1888-1988," March 13, 1988

297   food conservation campaign: See *Birmingham News* and *Birmingham Age-Herald,* August through September 1931, for numerous stories on the food conservation campaign.

300   "The other morning a woman": *Bham News,* May 29, 1931

303   "We were licked": *Bham News,* September 26, 1931

304   "It has never been my lot": Ibid

305 Someone had brought a coffin: *Bham News,* September 28, 1931
305 "I wanted to show my appreciation": *Bham News,* September 27, 1931

Epilogue
311 "in the interest of baseball": *Bham News,* July 3, 1922
311 at the team's headquarters: *Bham A-H,* July 4, 1922. According to the 1923 Birmingham City Directory, baseball headquarters were located at the Birmingham Arms and Cycle Co., 2017 Third Avenue North.
312 Association took a gamble: *Bham News* editorial, May 29, 1922; *Bham News,* April 14, 1929
312 owner Rick Woodward said: *Bham A-H,* July 4, 1922
312 The Phillies had a young prospect: *Bham News,* March 14, 1926
313 He quit school: correspondence with grandson Carlton Molesworth III, January 2015
313 "Woodward calls me a 'pot hunter'": *Bham News,* July 30, 1961
313 his modern farm: *Bham News,* February 22, 1914; March 6, 1921
313 Molesworth made his first visit: *Bham News,* September 1, 1928
313 "he didn't do much except be retired": Carlton Molesworth III, January 2015
314 those up for consideration: Lamb, Bill, "Carlton Molesworth," *SABR Baseball Biography Project,* Sabr.org/bioproject
314 Over the next nine years: Baseball-Reference.com; *Sporting News,* February 22, 1934
314 trouble with Manager Carlton Molesworth: *San Francisco Examiner,* November 26, 1912
315 "Elliott is not a scholar": *Bham A-H,* March 14, 1912
315 "a little highbrow conduct": *Bham News,* September 21, 1912
315 "Maybe if Rowdy Elliott": *Bham News,* January 15, 1921
315 "for misconduct and insubordination": *Bham News,* August 30, 1922
315 "a hustler and a fighter": *San Francisco Examiner,* November 26, 1912
315 picked up by police: Baseball Hall of Fame clipping file
315 Donations from friends: *Sporting News,* February 22, 1934
315 played the 1923 and '24: Baseball-Reference.com
315 Fleharty settled in Nevada, Missouri: *Nevada* [Missouri] *Daily Mail,* March 23/25, 1956
316 "had the longest little fingernail": *Bham News,* Woodward memoirs, February 25, 1934
316 finished his career with Bloomington: *Indianapolis Star,* February 19, 1920; *Indiana Daily Times,* February 19, 1920; *Noblesville* [Indiana] *Daily Ledger,* February 20, 1920; 1920 U.S. Census; Boyd's World War I Draft Registration Card; Ancestry.com
316 Ellam had major league trials: Baseball-Reference.com
316 he prepared to inspect: *Conshohocken* [Pennsylvania] *Recorder,* October 29, 1948
317 May 25, 1931: *Bham News, Bham A-H,* May 26, 1931
317 sent a petition to Martin: *Bham News,* May 27/31, 1931
317 Nick Dobbs, Johnny's son: correspondence with Nick Dobbs, January 2015
317 League President Martin considered: *Bham A-H,* May 29, 1931
317 Everyone around the league: *Bham News,* June 4, 1931
318 Dobbs' style met with disfavor: *Atlanta Constitution,* January 17, 1932
318 "I've heard the rumors": *Bham News,* November 26, 1931
318 admitted he did not want to return: *Atlanta Constitution,* January 13, 1932

318   after making these remarks: *Atlanta Constitution,* January 21, 1932

319   Dobbs remained at his Ringgold: *Chattanooga Times,* September 10, 1934

319   Wilbert Robinson died suddenly: *Charlotte News,* September 10, 1934

319   "There has never been a greater personality": *Bham News,* September 10, 1934

319   tryout with the Chicago White Sox: *Bham News,* May 14, 1939

320   was slow of hoof: *Bham News,* February 1, 1931

320   ideal build for a catcher: *Bham P-H,* November 17, 1964; *Bham News,* November 22, 1964

320   strongest man in the league: *Bham News,* April 7, 1926

320   forty to fifty homers a year: *Bham News,* August 18, 1960

320   successful salesman at Sears: *Bham News,* November 16, 1964; *Bham P-H,* November 17, 1964

320   better than average fastball: *Sporting News,* May 26, 1986

320   married a Birmingham girl: *Bham News,* October 18, 1929; *Montgomery Advertiser,* May 3, 1986

321   Wells recalled playing with: Baseball Hall of Fame clipping file

321   Stewart's asset was his foot speed: *Lake City* [Florida] *Reporter,* circa 1979

321   Stewart worked a series of jobs: *Lake City Reporter,* circa 1980

321   died at the Veterans Administration Hospital: *Lake City Reporter,* December 31, 1980

322   Johnston farmed until 1941: *Chattanooga Times,* February 15, 1967

322   Johnston was a teammate of Casey: *Chattanooga Times,* February 17, 1967

322   Bigelow was adrift in baseball: *Bham A-H,* July 8, 1931

322   Zipp Newman recalled: *Bham News,* August 11, 1933

323   "I started out hitting everything": *Bham News,* April 28, 1932

323   he complained of a headache: *Bham News,* August 11, 1933; *Tampa Tribune,* August 13, 1933

323   he was making $25,000: Faber, *Spitballers,* p. 50

324   "I spent nine years in Brooklyn": Lane, "The Ace of National League Hurlers," *Baseball Magazine,* October 1929

325   "I can remember some of the clubhouses": Connor, Anthony, *Voices from Cooperstown: Baseball's Hall of Famers Tell It Like It Was,* p. 299

325   thirty-six of his teammates were named: Niese, Joe, *Burleigh Grimes: Baseball's Last Legal Spitballer,* p. 5

325   economy slumped nearly every month: "The Great Depression," *World Book Encyclopedia,* 2013, p. 340

326   losses were dire: *Bham News,* August 25, 1933

326   one million fans had attended: *Bham News,* September 17, 1937

326   many clubs feared they wouldn't survive: *Bham A-H,* August 10, 1933

326   nine thousand banks failed: "The Great Depression," *World Book Encyclopedia,* p. 340

326   few had money to buy: *Bham A-H,* August 31, 1933

326   "We are on our way": Sherrow, Victoria, *Hardship and Hope: America and the Great Depression,* p. 86

326   Christmas shopping season: *Bham News,* December 24, 1933

326   back in their old jobs: *Bham News,* January 1, 1934

326   industrial production dropped by a third: *Bham News,* June 10, 2011

326   Woodward asked sportswriter Zipp: *Bham News,* August 14, 1960

327   ups and downs of the Barons: *Bham News,* March 10, 1928

327   Zipp Newman often said: *Bham News,* February 7, 1938; June 29, 1947; November 24, 1950

327   Woodward recalled his first year as owner: *Bham News,* Woodward memoirs, February 11, 1934

327 Woodward Iron Company suffered: In October 1936, Woodward Iron Company, which had suffered financially during the Depression, filed a petition for reorganization and a successful plan of reorganization, dated December 1, 1936. The petition was confirmed by the court on April 29, 1937, and implemented with the participation of investment banker Mervyn H. Sterne and other business leaders, providing for recovery over time by the creditors, bondholders, and stockholders of the company. (See page 25, Plan of Reorganization. Page 3 lists names of bondholders, noteholders, preferred stockholders, and common stockholder committees. Mervyn Sterne was a member of both the bondholder and noteholder committees. Historians of the Birmingham business community will recognize names of other committee members as being heads of substantial enterprises.) Unlike some bankruptcies, where equityholders are wiped out and only creditors and senior debtholders recover funds, the Woodward Iron Company plan provided for the preferred and common stockholders to receive comparable equity shares in the reorganized company. The reorganization plan may be viewed at the website of the Hoole Special Collections of the University of Alabama. A history of the court approval of the bankruptcy reorganization plan and its confirmation can be found, for example, in the court opinion in a tax case, Woodward Iron Co. v. United States, 59 F.Supp. 54 (N.D. Ala. 1945).

327-328 created sizable indebtedness: *Bham A-H,* February 8, 1938; *Bham P-H,* April 12, 1967

328 sale of the ball club: *Bham News,* February 7, 1938. In 1942, Carlton Molesworth confided to sportswriter Zipp Newman that he would like to have returned as Barons manager when Ed Norton purchased the team from Rick Woodward. See *Birmingham News,* August 9, 1942.

328 *The Birmingham News* declared: *Bham News,* February 8, 1938

328 Some thought Woodward sold: *Bham News,* February 11, 1938

328 Fandom took the change: *Bham A-H,* February 9, 1938

328 "Well," said Norton: *Bham A-H,* February 8, 1938

329 "Our losing streak was due": *Bham News,* June 7, 1935

329 one of the most active members: Red River County Library, Clarksville, Texas; *Sporting News,* March 11, 1953

329 Clyde Milan regretted: *Bham News,* March 5, 1953

329 Weis dislocated a vertebra: *Bham News,* June 7, 1933

329 a favorite of small boys: *Bham News,* July 11, 1933; *Bham A-H,* September 14, 1937

330 "Anytime I could get a ball": unidentified newspaper, circa 1992, Baseball Hall of Fame clipping file

330 led the league in best humor: *Fort Worth Star-Telegram,* March 8, 1961; undated newspaper clipping, *The Daily Oklahoman; Sullivan, The Minors,* p. 161

331 he died unexpectedly: *Beaumont Journal,* April 29, 1949

331 Hasty went to his locker: *Bham News,* June 27, 1933

331 Hasty continued playing: correspondence with granddaughter Dee Thompson, January 2015

331 Connor ran twice for governor: Nunnelley, *Bull Connor,* pp. 169, 174, 180-181

332 son, William Bancroft, Jr., said: *Bham News,* December 7, 1993

332 football coaching record: Ibid

332 "Bear Bryant asked him": Ibid

333 "I've had a lot of firsts": *Bham News,* February 16, 1974

333 "I've had a good life": *Bham P-H,* February 14, 1974

333 Dizzy Dean occasionally passed through: *Bham News,* December 7, 1993

333 semi-pro game for the Gulotta Grocers: *Bham A-H,* September 28, 1931

333 "He wasn't the same": Gregory, *Diz,* p. 336

335 "The greatest pitchers I have ever": Holland, Gerald, "Mr. Rickey and the Game," *The Best American Sports Writing of the Century,* Halberstam, David, editor, p. 233

335 "For all of us Southern boys, Dean": Honig, Donald, *The Fifth Season: Tales of My Life in Baseball,* p. 196

335 Said sportswriter Zipp Newman: *Bham News,* May 15, 1941

335 "I'll just keep on rollin' and movin' along": Gregory, *Diz,* p. 390

336 he twisted his right knee: *Bham News,* June 2, 1932

336 "the most remarkable preserved athlete": *Bham News,* June 22, 1932

336 "When the Barons had Caldwell": *Bham News,* June 3, 1932

337 "I don't know what I am": *Bham News,* August 1, 1933

337 Ray's eyesight began to fail: *Jamestown* [New York] *Post-Journal,* October 4, 1962

338 "Slim," was dead of cancer: Steinberg, "Ray Caldwell," *SABR Baseball Biography Project,* Sabr.org/bioproject

338 "I just sort of scratched around": *Jamestown Post-Journal,* August 19, 1967

339 "Caldwell was one of the best pitchers": Steinberg, "Ray Caldwell," *SABR Baseball Biography Project,* Sabr.org/bioproject

339 "one of the playboys of his time": Ibid

339 "stories have been printed saying": *Cleveland Plain Dealer,* May 27, 1961

339 newspapers spoke only of his years: Marshall, *All Time Greatest Alabama Sports Stories,* p. 8

340 Rickwood was the most popular: Cook, Ben, *Good Wood: A Fan's History of Rickwood Field,* p. 60

340 roof was literally caving in: Cook, *Good Wood,* p. 119

341 significance of Rickwood: Cook, *Good Wood,* p. 123

BIBLIOGRAPHY

Books

Allen, Frederick Lewis, *Only Yesterday: An Informal History of the 1920s,* Harper & Row, Publishers, New York, 1957

American Heritage History of the 20s & 30s, American Heritage Publishing Company, Inc., New York, 1970

Bennett, James R., *Historic Birmingham and Jefferson County,* Historical Publishing Network, San Antonio, Texas, 2008

Berg, A. Scott, *Lindbergh,* G.P. Putnam's Sons, New York, 1998

Bryson, Bill, *One Summer: America, 1927,* Doubleday, New York, 2013

Connor, Anthony J., *Voices from Cooperstown: Baseball's Hall of Famers Tell It Like It Was,* Galahad Books, New York, 1998

Cook, Ben, *Good Wood: A Fan's History of Rickwood Field,* R. Boozer Press, Birmingham, 2005

Cooke, James, J., *The Rainbow Division in the Great War, 1917-1919,* Praeger Publishers, Westport, Connecticut, 1994

Eisenbath, Mike, *The Cardinals Encyclopedia,* Temple University Press, Philadelphia, 1999

Faber, Charles F. and Richard B., *Spitballers: The Last Legal Hurlers of the Wet One,* McFarland & Company, Inc., Jefferson, North Carolina, 2006

Forr, James and Proctor, David, *Pie Traynor: A Baseball Biography,* McFarland & Company, Inc., Jefferson, North Carolina, 2010

Frazier, Nimrod T., *Send the Alabamians: World War I Fighters in the Rainbow Division,* University of Alabama Press, Tuscaloosa, 2014

Fullerton, Christopher, *Every Other Sunday: The Story of the Birmingham Black Barons,* R. Boozer Press, Birmingham, 1999

Gelman, Steve, *The Greatest Dodgers of Them All,* Putnam, New York, 1968

Goldberg, Ronald Allen, *America in the Twenties,* Syracuse University Press, Syracuse, New York, 2003

Gregory, Robert, *Diz: The Story of Dizzy Dean and Baseball during the Great Depression,* Viking (Penguin Group), New York, 1992

Halberstam, David, editor, *The Best American Sports Writing of the Century,* Houghton Mifflin, New York, 1999

Hamilton, Virginia Van der Veer, *Alabama: A History,* W.W. Norton & Company, Inc., New York, 1977

Honig, Donald, *Baseball America: The Heroes of the Game and the Times of Their Glory,* MacMillan Publishing Company, New York, 1985

_____, *A Donald Honig Reader,* Simon & Schuster, New York, 1988

_____, *The Fifth Season: Tales of My Life in Baseball,* Ivan R. Dee, Chicago, 2009

Hornady, John, *The Book of Birmingham,* Dodd, Mead & Company, New York, 1921

Johnson, Clarence Walton, *The History of the 321ˢᵗ Infantry: Wildcats,* R. L. Bryan Company, Columbia, South Carolina, 1919

Kahn, Roger, *The Head Game: Baseball Seen from the Pitcher's Mound,* Harcourt, New York, 2000

Kessner, Thomas, *The Flight of the Century: Charles Lindbergh and the Rise of American Aviation,* Oxford University Press, New York, 2010

Klima, John, *Willie's Boys: The 1948 Birmingham Black Barons, the Last Negro World Series, and the Making of a Baseball Legend,* John Wiley & Sons, Inc., Hoboken, New Jersey, 2009

Lackey, Mike, *Spitballing: The Baseball Days of Long Bob Ewing,* Orange Frazer Press, Wilmington, Ohio, 2013

Lewis, Franklin, *The Cleveland Indians,* Kent State University Press, Kent, Ohio, 2006

Lieb, Fred, *The Pittsburgh Pirates,* Southern Illinois University Press, Carbondale, 2003

Marshall, Benny, *All Time Greatest Alabama Sports Stories,* University of Alabama Press, Tuscaloosa, 2003

Monteville, Leigh, *The Big Bam: The Life and Times of Babe Ruth,* Doubleday, New York, 2006

Murphy, Cait, *Crazy '08: How a Cast of Cranks, Rogues, Boneheads, and Magnates Created the Greatest Year in Baseball History,* HarperCollins Publishers, Inc., New York, 2007

Niese, Joe, *Burleigh Grimes: Baseball's Last Legal Spitballer,* McFarland & Company, Inc., Jefferson, North Carolina, 2013

Nunnelley, William A., *Bull Connor,* University of Alabama Press, Tuscaloosa, 1991

Obojski, Robert, *Bush League: A History of Minor League Baseball,* MacMillan Publishing Company, Inc., New York, 1975

O'Neal, Bill, *The Southern League: Baseball in Dixie, 1885-1994,* Eakin Press, Austin, Texas, 1994

Plott, William J., *The Negro Southern League,* McFarland & Company, Inc., Jefferson, North Carolina, 2015

Poling, Jerry, *A Summer Up North: Henry Aaron and the Legend of Eau Claire Baseball,* University of Wisconsin Press, Madison, 2002

Rogosin, Donn, *Invisible Men: Life in Baseball's Negro Leagues,* Atheneum, New York, 1983

Rudel, Anthony, *Hello, Everybody: The Dawn of American Radio,* Harcourt, Inc., New York, 2008

Scheinin, Richard, *Field of Screams: The Dark Underside of America's National Pastime,* W.W. Norton & Company, New York, 1994

Seymour, Harold, *Baseball: The Golden Age,* Oxford University Press, New York, 1971

Sherrow, Victoria, *Hardship and Hope: America and the Great Depression,* Twenty-First Century Books, New York, 1997

Smith, Robert, *Baseball,* Simon and Schuster, New York, 1947

Stanton, Tom, *Ty and the Babe: Baseball's Fiercest Rivals,* St. Martin's Press, New York, 2007

Sullivan, Neil J., *The Minors: The Struggles and the Triumph of Baseball's Poor Relation from 1876 to the Present,* St. Martin's Press, New York, 1990

Thomas, Henry W., *Walter Johnson: Baseball's Big Train,* Phenom Press, Washington, D.C., 1995

Tompkins, Vincent, editor, *American Decades: 1910-1919,* Gale Research, Detroit, 1996

Wallop, Douglass, *Baseball: An Informal History,* Bantam Books, New York, 1970

White, Edward, *Creating the National Pastime: Baseball Transforms Itself, 1903-1953,* Princeton University Press, Princeton, New Jersey, 1996

White, Marjorie, editor, *The Birmingham District: An Industrial History and Guide,* Birmingham Historical Society, 1981

Wright, Marshall, *The Southern Association in Baseball, 1885-1961,* McFarland & Company, Inc., Jefferson, North Carolina, 2002

Newspapers

Abilene Daily Reporter
Amarillo Daily News
Anniston Star
Arkansas Gazette
Atlanta Constitution
Beaumont [Texas] Journal
Birmingham Age-Herald
Birmingham News
Birmingham Post
Birmingham Post-Herald
Charlotte News
Chattanooga Times
Clear Lake Star
Cleveland Plain Dealer
Conshohocken [Pennsylvania] Recorder
Daily Oklahoman
Evansville Courier
Evansville Journal
Evansville Press
Fort Worth Record
Fort Worth Star-Telegram
Houston Chronicle
Houston Post-Dispatch
Indiana Daily Times
Indianapolis Star
Jamestown [New York] Post-Journal
Lake City [Florida] Reporter
Los Angeles Times
Montgomery Advertiser
Nevada [Missouri] Daily Mail
New York Times
Noblesville [Indiana] Daily Ledger
Salt Lake Tribune
San Francisco Examiner
Sporting News
Tampa Tribune
Venice [California] Daily Vanguard

Magazines

American Review of Reviews
Baseball Magazine
Harper's Magazine
Literary Digest

Websites

Baseball-Reference.com
Corydontwp.com
Croixrougefarm.org
Etfinalscore.com
NCpedia.org
Sabr.org/bioproject (SABR Baseball Biography
    Project)
Southernbottles.com
WorldWar1.com

Interviews, Correspondence

Steven Bancroft
Nick Dobbs
Carlton Molesworth III
Dee Thompson
Elva Hasty Thompson

Other

Clear Lake Centennial, 1875-1975
Reach Baseball Guide
World Book Encyclopedia
Baseball Hall of Fame clipping file

INDEX

David Reed

ABOUT THE AUTHOR

Art Black lives and writes in Birmingham, Alabama. In the late 1960s and early '70s, he kept a scorecard at Rickwood on many summer nights, unaware of the park's ghosts — until now. This is his first book.